D1058184

MERCHANTS OF DEBT

Merchants of Debt

KKR and the
Mortgaging of
American Business

GEORGE ANDERS

BasicBooks
A Division of HarperCollins*Publishers*

Copyright © 1992 by George Anders. Published by BasicBooks, A Division
of HarperCollins Publishers, Inc.

All rights reserved. Printed in the United States of America. No part of this
book may be reproduced in any manner whatsoever without written permission except in the case of brief quotations embodied in critical articles and
reviews. For information address BasicBooks, 10 East 53rd Street, New
York, NY 10022-5299.

Designed by Ellen Levine

Photo insert designed by Helene Berinsky

Library of Congress Cataloging-in-Publication Data
Anders, George, 1957–
    Merchants of debt : KKR and the mortgaging of American business /
George Anders.
       p. cm.
    Includes bibliographical references and index.
    ISBN 0–465–04522–7
    1. Consolidation and merger of corporations—United States—
Finance.   2. Leveraged buyouts—United States.   3. Kohlberg Kravis
Roberts & Co.—History.   I. Title.
HG4028.M4A56   1992
332.1'78—dc20   91–58601
                                                        CIP

92 93 94 95 CC/HC 9 8 7 6 5 4 3 2 1

For Betsy

Contents

Preface

In 1989, partway through the adventures that ultimately led to this book, I got an unusual phone call from my sister. During a business trip to Baltimore, Nanci told me, she had met an executive at Maryland Cup Co. who was looking for new managers to hire. The job sounded interesting, but my sister had one big concern. Maryland Cup had just undergone a leveraged buyout. Was it a good idea, she wanted to know, to work for an LBO company?

Good question. From 1982 onward, I had written repeatedly about buyouts for *The Wall Street Journal,* chronicling the growth and turbulence of this new kind of high-debt takeover. What had begun as a casual interest had turned by 1989 into a specialty that bordered on obsession. I had studied the financing of buyouts, and knew which major companies had been acquired this way; I followed the arguments, pro and con, concerning the effect of buyouts on America's economy. Now, however, background financial data didn't matter; neutral journalistic analysis wouldn't suffice. Either Nanci should take the job, or she shouldn't.

After about a day of hard thinking, I offered my sister the following advice: "Find out if you'll be in the small circle of top managers that gets stock ownership in a buyout company. If so, sign up right away. It'll be exciting work and may make a lot of money for you, but most of all you'll feel in charge of your own destiny at a very exciting time in a company's life. And if you can't get part-ownership, don't touch the job. You're liable to be overworked and underpaid. Even worse, you could be fired or transferred at any moment in the name of efficiency."

Those phone calls have stayed with me ever since, even though our family's direct encounter with the leveraged buyout business ended almost as quickly as it began. (Maryland Cup's job offer wasn't that attractive after all.) As I learned more about the buyout business, the scope of this book began to widen. What I really wanted to write about were the convictions and passions of people swept up in an age of high-debt finance—and how hard-working, well-meaning people kept clashing as they pursued drastically different visions of how American business ought to operate. The purely financial aspects of buyouts, familiar ground from my *Journal* reporting, were still important, but just a small part of a bigger story. As I traveled to banks and bottle factories, to courthouses and corporate boardrooms, I collected stories from many people who were affected for better or worse by KKR's work.

These accounts aren't meant to deride or flatter Henry Kravis, George Roberts, and Jerry Kohlberg, but simply to depict them as they are. All three are complex people, with traits—such as Roberts's mischievous sense of humor, or Kravis's vulnerability at the peak of his career—that I never expected to find when I started this project.

Once the nature of my project became known, a mixed blessing arrived: a wide range of partisans eager to share their insights and prejudices. The economic and moral issues raised by the leverage movement are so profound that it's little wonder that, in the past two years, a Nobel Prize has been awarded to a pro-buyout economist and a Pulitzer Prize to an anti-buyout journalist. Debating the merits of buyouts with articulate advocates of both camps has produced plenty of irritation and sparks, but also a lot of light. More than once, I found it helpful to come back to the simple standard of, "Would I want my sister to work there?"

Away from the fray, many friends and colleagues have helped make this a better book. Editors at *The Wall Street Journal* aided me in countless ways over the past ten years. Dick Rustin taught me to approach Wall Street's work in general with skepticism but also with an abiding sense of fair play. John Prestbo and Alfred Malabre nudged me from 1986 through 1988 to look more closely at the buyout business. More recently, markets editor Dan Hertzberg has encouraged me to cover KKR for the *Journal,* even as I was completing this book. Dan's judgment, wit, and news sense have immensely aided both my newspaper work and this book. The *Journal*'s executive editor, Norm Pearlstine, deserves special praise. He encouraged me to begin this book, gave me time off to research it thoroughly, and kept doors open during a much longer development period than we ever expected.

Many *Journal* colleagues contributed in other ways as well. Bernie Wysocki and Roger Lowenstein were tireless readers of drafts good and bad, encouraging me to make the most of my material at many crucial stages. John Hinge provided vital research help. Ron Suskind, Kevin Helliker, Jim White, Connie Mitchell, Bryan Burrough, John Helyar, Michael Siconolfi, Laurie Cohen, and a host of other reporters generously shared information and insights.

My editor at Basic Books, Steve Fraser, graced this project with one smart suggestion after another. He knew when to pull me away from a tangent, when to help me tell an anecdote better, and how to keep a complex story as straightforward as possible. Most of all, Steve repeatedly pushed me to use KKR's adventures to tell a much broader story. Everyone else on the Basic Books team—including Martin Kessler, Lois Shapiro, Amit Shah, Michael Cain, Helena Schwarz, and Gary Murphy—brought first-rate professionalism to their part of this project. David Brecher helped bring this book to its right home; his determination and good humor were contagious.

A host of outside readers and advisers made valuable suggestions as this manuscript developed. They include Jack Corcoran, David Golub, David Salzman, Michael Schrage, Bill Comfort, Peter Truell, John Quigley, and my parents: Joan and Edward Anders.

Most of all, Elizabeth Corcoran nurtured this project in ways that it would take an entirely separate book to enumerate. She was the first reader of countless drafts, the mischievous "Moneypenny" who faxed me documents in the midst of research trips, and an inspiration to behold as she achieved her own career successes while unfailingly making time for the book's endless demands on our home life. Without her, this book would not have been possible.

Introduction

Ernie Pyle, the great World War II correspondent and champion of the common man, sketched some of his most spirited civilian portraits in the summer of 1941, when he visited the Toledo, Ohio, glass-making plants of Owens-Illinois Co. There, Swedish and Czech immigrants stood a few feet from an open furnace and plied a trade that to Pyle was nothing short of amazing. "Right before your eyes you see a miracle," Pyle wrote. "A wheelbarrow load of sand, lime and ash . . . heated to 2,600 degrees, gets fluid, about like molasses. And then, when you let it cool, instead of turning back to dirt again, as it should, it comes out clear and clean and brittle, like glass. It is glass!"

Some forty-five years later, the Owens-Illinois glass company once again became a source of public wonder. This time, the entire company was thrust into a furnace of debt at the height of the 1980s stock-market boom, as part of a curious new takeover known as a leveraged buyout. What emerged a few years later were profits of $10 million for the company's chairman, fees of $60 million for the few men who arranged the takeover, and a gaunt, scaled-back company. Some 47,000 employees found themselves working harder than ever to increase profits and preserve their jobs. For the few owners lucky enough to control the process, buyouts transformed common stock and bank loans into vast piles of cash in a manner as wondrous as anything Pyle had beheld.

Something was jarringly different about this financial alchemy, though. Progress no longer was measured by America's ability to build better goods in its factories. The winners of these new transformations weren't craftsmen, U.S. consumers, or even entrepreneurs with a product to sell. Instead, the United States in the 1980s found itself in the midst of a legendary period of unchecked profiteering—on a par with the Robber Baron era of the 1880s or the frenzied stock-market speculation of the 1920s. The fastest fortunes were created by financiers who seized control of America's showcase companies in takeover battles. Wall Street's own prosperity became all absorbing, as stock-market averages tripled from 1980 to 1989, and a ten-year bull market added more than $2 trillion to Americans' paper wealth. Giant public corporations turned into acquirers' private fiefdoms, to be run or dismantled in whatever way would make the new owners even richer.

It was an era when debt ran wild. The U.S. financial system—and to a large extent the entire economy—over the past ten years became propelled by daredevil use of credit that allowed a select group of people to grow rich. Participants seldom worried whether the new wealth aided society or was being widely dispersed. The important thing was to join in the getting. Growing rich no longer required an apology; it was a point of pride.

Vaulting far ahead of any other competitor in this age of casino capitalism was the firm that bought Owens-Illinois and more than thirty other companies: Kohlberg Kravis Roberts & Co. Tiny, secretive, and incredibly powerful, KKR carried out the largest takeovers of all time. It commandeered the biggest investment profits. And it built the widest retinue of lawyers, takeover advisers, consultants, and industrial managers willing to do its bidding. Almost unknown outside Wall Street circles until the late 1980s, KKR became such a potent economic force that when the giant accounting firm of Deloitte & Touche tallied its biggest clients in 1989, KKR ranked number one. General Motors Corporation was second.

This is the story of KKR and its two dominant partners: cousins Henry Kravis and George Roberts. But it also is a look at the maneuverings and personalities of an entire era. Gung-ho young bankers stopped financing highways or factories; instead they lent billions to pay for KKR's acquisitions. Legions of Wall Street's most renowned advisers became takeover minstrels, touring the United States to clear the way for KKR's next takeover. Nervous corporate chief executives worried about losing their jobs in hostile takeovers; when crisis struck, these CEOs embraced either the ebullient Kravis or the coolly analytical Roberts as their rescuer.

Across the United States, hundreds of thousands of rank-and-file workers and midlevel managers found their lives changed, too, when KKR took control of their companies.

Although a few threads of this story began before World War I, most of the adventure is a tale of our times. Kohlberg Kravis Roberts & Co. opened for business in the final months of the Gerald Ford administration, on 1 May 1976, with just $120,000 of its partners' capital and some tawdry metal furniture left over from the offices' previous tenant. Rapidly, KKR grew into a takeover machine with an appetite unlike anything American business had ever seen. In the course of the 1980s, the firm completed nearly $60 billion in acquisitions, buying companies as diverse as Safeway Stores, Duracell, Motel 6, Stop & Shop, Avis, Tropicana, and Playtex. In late 1988, Kravis and Roberts prevailed in a rough-and-tumble takeover battle that let them claim the biggest prize of all: RJR Nabisco Inc., maker of Oreo cookies, Ritz crackers, and Winston, Salem, and Camel cigarettes. They paid $26.4 billion, carrying out the largest takeover in history.

The two cousins bought companies with such rapidity and élan that at one point, when KKR was contemplating four multibillion-dollar buyouts at once, the Federal Reserve Board's head of banking supervision, William Taylor, paid a rare private visit to KKR's Manhattan offices. Did the world banking system contain enough ready cash, Taylor asked, to finance the firm's acquisition desires? The answer: Yes, but it was getting tight.

Even more audacious than the size of KKR's appetite was the way that it bought these companies. Nearly every cent used for its acquisitions was borrowed—either from banks, from buyers of risky new securities known as junk bonds, or from pension funds that became part-owners of companies being acquired. The KKR partners drew upon only trivial amounts of their own money in gaining control over businesses that employed nearly 400,000 people, enough to fill two congressional districts. Ordinary language no longer sufficed; a special vocabulary had to be created to describe KKR's work, beginning with a new term for its acquisitions: leveraged buyouts. In this new world, pushing a company deeply into debt wasn't dreadful; it was desirable.

For a brief time, this daring attitude toward debt became contagious. Long-overlooked tax breaks associated with heavy borrowings began to be exploited throughout American industry. During the longest economic upturn of the post–World War II period, from 1982 to 1990, U.S. companies by the thousands piled on debts that, in an earlier era, would have been regarded as enough to wreck their balance sheets. Big corporations were "learning to love leverage," a leading finance magazine declared in 1986. The stunning successes of KKR prompted first dozens, then as many as 400 imitators to spring up. Business schools began teaching buyout case studies, showing a generation of students how to buy companies with borrowed money. With a personal computer to carry out financial analysis, and the complicity of a few bankers willing to lend money, even a freshly minted MBA could take control of a sizable corporation.

How did an acquired company's new owners make money in spite of the heavy debt involved? Tax savings played a big role, thanks to the deductibility of interest expense. Efficiency steps and cost-cutting helped jack up profit margins, at least for a few years. And a long-running bull market made almost any business appear more valuable with the passage of time.

Because buyouts were orchestrated by small groups, they reversed a nearly fifty-year-long trend toward economic egalitarianism in the United States. Suddenly power and riches were shunted into the hands of a tiny elite. A few impresarios at the center of a buyout could control a giant company's money-making capacity, by drawing upon borrowed money and borrowed management talent. Risk and responsibilities were left in lesser people's hands.

The author William Greider once observed that in the U.S. system of democratic capitalism, "there is a natural tension between those two words: 'democracy' and 'capitalism.' " Much of American business history is shaped by this unending tug of war. The most durable business structures—such as the public corporation with many thousands of small shareholders, or the community bank dedicated to financing local growth—reflect a workable union of profits and populism. Buyouts, however, have proven to be an entirely different story. They simultaneously amounted to one of the finest capitalist ideas of the century, and one of the most profoundly undemocratic ventures that the United States had ever seen.

The aristocratic nature of KKR's world hit first-time visitors the moment they stepped into the buyout firm's lavishly decorated offices. The ambience—marble floors, oil paintings, fresh-cut flowers, and soft voices—made the firm seem more like an exclusive Swiss hotel than a bustling clearinghouse of finance. The New York office, run by Kravis, never housed more than fourteen partners and associates. The San Francisco office, run by Roberts, was even smaller; it employed just six. First names prevailed; everyone knew who Henry and George were. A smattering of secretaries, receptionists, accountants, and cooks boosted KKR's total payroll to about fifty. The coffee shop around the corner from KKR's midtown Manhattan offices employed more people than the buyout firm ever did.

As they each built up fortunes of more than $500 million, Kravis and Roberts shrewdly invited their allies to share small pieces of KKR's good fortune. Anyone who could help KKR achieve its ends was courted with an air of elegance, friendship, and intimacy. This coalition-building, as much as any financial maneuvering, was at the heart of the buyout firm's success and its appeal in the business world. Time and again, Kravis and Roberts made it very attractive for other people to work within their system. Only once—in the shunting aside of their mentor and former partner Jerome S. Kohlberg, Jr., when he lost his effectiveness—did Kravis and Roberts engage in a power struggle that produced an embittered loser. The rest of the time the two cousins shared the wealth, excitement, and bragging rights of the takeover business with such grace and politeness that people in positions of power regularly invited them to come back and do it again. Critics assailed the KKR partners as plunderers—but to make that argument was to miss the essential nature of the buyout firm's success. Kravis and Roberts built their power not by competition and confrontation, but with trust.

Like suitors going courting, Kravis and Roberts worked their way into the lives of dozens of chief executive officers of industrial companies. Time after time, the KKR men presented a tempting offer. The CEO could cash out his company's existing shareholders by agreeing to sell the company to a new group that would be headed by KKR, but would include a lot of room for existing management. The new ownership group would take on a lot of debt, but aim to pay it off quickly. If this buyout worked out as planned, the KKR men hinted, the new owners could earn five times their money over the next five years. Presented with such a choice in the frenzied takeover climate of the 1980s, managers and corporate directors again and again said yes. At times it seemed as if no company were safe from takeover. To top management, a leveraged buyout was the most palatable way to ride out the merger-and-acquisition craze.

On Wall Street, Kravis and Roberts recruited the allies they needed with the shrewdness of big-city patronage bosses. They hired advisers for almost every task and used KKR's checkbook—or the threat of its withdrawal—to win obedience. Each year in the late 1980s, KKR controlled the disbursement of $200 million or more in advisory fees. Ambitious takeover advisers at firms such as Merrill Lynch, First Boston, and Salomon Brothers saved their best efforts for KKR, the premier paymaster on Wall Street. Partners at one of America's top law firms, Wachtell, Lipton, Rosen & Katz, practically made their careers by "defending" giant companies against takeovers and then agreeing to sell those companies to KKR. Scattering fees around "was important to do," Kravis once explained: "We were hoping that we would be the first name on everybody's list. If they had an idea, they would come talk to us first. This was a cheap way of doing it."

Lenders were courted with a different sort of panache, though by the mid-1980s a nationwide euphoria about debt made the buyout firm's work much easier. KKR had the great fortune to be seeking loans in a period when the federal government ran $150 billion deficits each year and MasterCard routinely boosted consumers' credit limits unasked. Eager to see the best in every borrower, bankers proclaimed KKR to be the ideal corporate client. Criticism about making "nonproductive" loans was swept aside. The buyout firm paid its bills unfailingly, and it always borrowed more.

Taking this natural interest one step further, the KKR partner most involved with the banks, George Roberts, coaxed loans with a slyness reminiscent of Tom Sawyer trying to get a fence painted. Better dressed and better paid than his bankers, Roberts seldom outright asked to borrow money for KKR's deals. Instead, he turned the traditional borrower/creditor relationship inside out, making it seem like a privilege to lend to his buyout firm. Star-struck bankers gladly yielded to his terms, pushing billions of dollars into KKR's hands.

And when bank money wasn't enough, KKR turned to the rogue financial firm of the 1980s, Drexel Burnham Lambert Inc., and its junk-bond chief, Michael Milken. It was an odd pairing: The prim KKR men wouldn't even install slot machines in the lobbies of the Las Vegas Motel 6 for fear of associating with the wrong sorts of people; the Drexel junk-bond brigade was known for its licentious parties, its strong-arm market tactics, and its brushes with the law. Yet the KKR executives brushed aside their usual scruples and from 1984 to 1989 borrowed more money through Drexel than any other client of the junk-bond firm. "It was one of the most symbiotic relationships of all time," a top Drexel deal-maker later said. "They blessed us and we blessed them."

By their own admission, the KKR executives knew little about day-to-day management of the companies they pursued or acquired. Remarkably, they portrayed that as a virtue, rather than a shortcoming. "We're financial people, not operating people," Kravis repeatedly told chief executives. "We don't know how to run a company. We'd only mess it up if we tried. We're counting on you." At such times, Kravis seemed refreshingly self-effacing. But his modesty concealed the buyout firm's colonial-style grip on the businesses it owned. In KKR's world, a helper could be found to perform almost every task, from shining the partners' shoes to running RJR Nabisco.

The elitism of KKR's system registered with full force at the companies the buyout firm acquired. Top executives at Safeway, Duracell, RJR Nabisco, and all the other acquired companies were allowed to buy large amounts of their companies' stock, and then told that either big riches or a near-total loss of their money awaited them depending on how skillfully they increased operating profit and reduced debt. "Grab a man by his W-2 and his heart and mind will follow," a KKR associate once quipped. Sure enough, senior executives would storm through their companies the first year or two after the buyout, taking once-unthinkable steps to increase the enterprise's economic value. Virtually any retrenchment—including shutting down factories, firing workers, or selling off subsidiaries en masse—was hailed as good if it made more money for a company's new owners.

Far outside this lucky ownership circle, production workers and low-level managers watched in dismay as the buyout scythe cut through their lives. At Safeway, the loss-making Dallas division was quickly closed, and 8,600 workers were thrown out of work. At Owens-Illinois, a crusade to improve productivity grew so fervid that one low-level manager took on five different full-time jobs simultaneously. And at a machine-tool company that KKR owned, hourly workers went for six years without a pay raise. The efficiency of acquired companies became legendary, but so did stories of human anguish.

Uninvolved in the sweaty details of making a company work, the KKR executives monitored financial reports, helped set broad business strategies—and prepared to cash out. Over several years' time, most companies' balance sheets recovered briskly from the initial debt shock of a buyout. Once borrowings had been reduced sufficiently, the big profit potential of a buyout had largely played out. And at that point, KKR executives sold each company, no matter how dull or glamorous, to new owners. "Never fall in love with anything except your wife and kids," Roberts once remarked. The KKR men prided themselves on a rigid financial discipline, according to which they sought annual profits for their fellow investors of 40 percent or better. Holding on to a company too long could only hurt those returns. And so, as quickly as the KKR men had roared into a company's life, they roared off.

Until 1989, giant new deals always beckoned. Buyouts swept across American industry so fast that a Harvard scholar predicted "the eclipse of the public corporation." But in every capitalist boom, the most frenzied period comes just before the crash. The Robber Barons' predations succumbed first to the Panic of 1893, and then to the trust-busting efforts begun with the Sherman Act of 1890. The stock-market speculation of the 1920s ended in an even more dramatic crash, followed by the accusatory Pecora hearings of the early 1930s and sweeping securities legislation. The Age of Leverage in late 1989 and early 1990 came to a cataclysmic halt as well. Some of the reasons were embedded in the debt cycle itself—even-riskier deals assembled by fee-hungry deal-makers, and increasing defaults, bankruptcies, and financial losses. More fundamentally, however, public indignation at the profiteering of the past decade led to an angry populist leveling—in which tax laws were changed, criminal financiers were sent to jail, and a national revulsion toward high debt and its consequences set in.

If history were simple, Kohlberg Kravis Roberts & Co. would have disappeared along with the Age of Leverage, wiped out in a financial downfall of its own making. In the spring of 1990, in fact, KKR did come much closer to ruin than almost anyone outside a few closed-doors meetings ever realized. The biggest acquisition of all time, the RJR Nabisco takeover, teetered close to the brink for three months, mired in deep financial troubles relating to its junk-bond debt. The story of that financial crisis—and the desperate rescue that KKR engineered—has been one of Wall Street's most closely kept secrets. It emerges here for the first time.

For the time being, the deal-making powers of Henry Kravis and George Roberts are greatly circumscribed by what the two men call "politics" and almost everyone else calls the public interest. Many of their old lenders are incapacitated by rampant corporate defaults. But the companies that KKR controls are venturing back into the public arena: listing their shares on the New York Stock Exchange, expanding their operations, and hiring workers once again. As the high-debt era disintegrates into rubble, Kravis and Roberts have accomplished the hardest thing of all: to survive and be ready to fight again.

Very savvy—and very lucky—the cousins have mastered much more than finance in their pursuit of riches. Kravis and Roberts have also relied on two of the most enduring American characteristics of all: a handshake and a smile.

1
Courting CEOs

In the autumn of 1973, most people in Greensboro, North Carolina, had no idea of the troubles that gripped one of their leading businessmen, 46-year-old Bill Jones. On the surface, everything about his life looked fine. He was president of a profitable brick company that was expanding every year. He was increasingly being referred to as a community leader—joining the board of trustees at Greensboro College and leading a Boy Scout fund-raising drive. His marriage to the daughter of the brick company's former chairman was thriving. And in a part of the United States where storytelling is a prized art, Jones knew how to spin tales that would make his friends laugh, sputter, or shake their heads in disbelief.

But that fall, Bill Jones was in agony. The company that he ran, Boren Clay Products Co., was being torn apart by feuding among its elderly owners. No matter what decision Jones made, at least one of the families that controlled Boren's stock hated it. If he expanded into new sales territory, it was too fast, too slow, or the wrong region. If he promoted a promising manager, it was a foolish choice. Leading the attack was Jones's father-in-law, Orton Boren, the former chairman, with a viciousness that Jones had never seen before. At the end of one quarrel, Boren threatened to cut both his daughter and his son-in-law out of his will. Another time, he threatened to sell the company to outsiders who knew how to run a brick company better.

And then came the breaking point: the day Orton Boren drove up to the brick company, got out of his car, and began waving a pistol in the vicinity of Jones's office for no apparent reason. Before Boren's 600 employees, Jones tried to act as if nothing had happened. To his wife he confided: "I've enjoyed about all of this I can stand."

One after another, potential buyers of Boren Clay began arriving in Greensboro. They met with Orton Boren, who demanded a high price for his stock, and with Jones, who explained the company's operations to them. Most of the potential acquirers came from large corporations. But a Los Angeles merger broker suggested that Jones also meet with a thirty-year-old from a small Wall Street firm who might be able to arrange a different sort of acquisition.

It was Henry Kravis. Just starting his Wall Street career at the time, Kravis arrived in Greensboro with no reputation, good or bad, to speak of. He was simply an energetic, curly-haired young man, about five-foot-seven and athletically built. A trace of an Oklahoma accent lingered in his voice; his face projected a middle-American freshness. As it happened, Kravis made a living traveling from town to town like this, looking for small acquisitions that his employer, Bear, Stearns & Co., could arrange for a hefty fee. Greensboro was one of many, many stops in an itinerary that also brought Kravis to Providence, Rhode Island, Chicago, Pittsburgh, and a host of other cities. At each stop, Kravis greeted chief executives in distress with a warm smile, a confident manner, and a willingness to talk about whatever was on their minds.

To Bill Jones, watching Kravis in action was both charming and a little amusing. The Oklahoman turned New Yorker was so full of pep that he couldn't sit still. Kravis jumped up, sat down, got up again, and paced around Jones's office as he talked. "Here's our plan," Kravis said, as he rested in his chair for a moment. If Boren Clay's finances looked solid, Kravis said, there was a way that Jones and some executives at Bear, Stearns could buy control of the brick company from the feuding family shareholders, without having to make more than a modest down payment. The rest of the purchase price would need to be borrowed. But Kravis said he could raise loans from banks and insurance companies.

Whenever Jones had a question, Kravis had a surprisingly poised answer. At one point, Jones guardedly asked what role Kravis envisioned for Orton Boren. The company wasn't big enough for both Jones and the old man, he explained. "I understand," Kravis calmly replied. "This isn't the first time I've come into a situation like this." Orton Boren wouldn't be part of the new group, he said. Instead, with a small down payment of perhaps $1 million, Kravis, Jones, and their allies could win control of the company. Management of the business would be left almost entirely in Jones's hands; Kravis explained that he and his colleagues didn't know much about the brick business and weren't inclined to meddle. It would take a lot of hard work by Jones and his managers to pay off the new debt. But if they could do it, their original investment would surge in value.

A little later, Kravis was brought around to meet Orton Boren—who instantly despised the visitor from Wall Street. Boren took one look at Kravis and began calling him "boy." He asked him his religion, and when he found out, began calling him "Jewboy." Still, Boren didn't care who owned the brick company, as long as they paid him a lot of money for his stock. Regarding Kravis by then as a serious potential buyer, Jones and Boren took their guest on a tour of the company's brickmaking kilns. Wet clay lined the floors, and Kravis—attired in shiny Gucci shoes—had to step delicately to avoid wrecking his footwear. A moment later, a worse indignity awaited him. Walking by one of the red-hot kilns, Boren turned to Kravis as a blast of hot air reached out to both men, and quipped: "Those are just like the ones the Germans used." Kravis shuddered and walked quickly ahead.

Yet Kravis hid his anger so well that, years later, an onlooker didn't think the remark had even troubled him. "Henry took it without flinching," the witness said. "He was there to do business." When Orton Boren demanded $310 a share for his stock in the company—a total of more than $4 million—Kravis said he could come up with the money.

Moving steadily closer to buying the brick company, Kravis scheduled more visits with Jones, the man he needed to court. (He talked to Orton Boren as little as possible.) Their friendship blossomed. They barbecued steaks together in Jones's backyard. They discovered that Jones's best friend had gone to Lehigh University at the same time as Kravis's father. On their third or fourth visit, they introduced their wives to each other, and sent the women on a happy day of antique shopping along North Carolina's back roads. "Henry was such an attractive young guy," Jones recalled many years later. "He was in complete control of himself. His ambition came out gradually. He was so unpretentious."

Six months later, Kravis and his colleagues at Bear, Stearns put together all the pieces of the acquisition he had talked about with Jones. The new investor group paid $18 million for Boren Clay, borrowing all but $1 million of the price. Orton Boren got his $4 million. As the sale of the company became official in July 1974, the patriarch's rage subsided. Orton Boren was hospitalized after a minor heart attack; when he was released, he said he wanted to retire to his farm, spend his winnings, and forget about the brick company and his foolish son-in-law. Kravis and Jones were left to wax optimistic about the future. Kravis picked up a

$325,000 fee for Bear, Stearns for arranging the buyout. Jones got to run the company unimpeded—and worry about how to pay off $17 million of debt.

As Kravis finished up his work in Greensboro and prepared to start his next deal, he left Jones with the impression that big profits for both of them lay ahead. If this acquisition worked out, Kravis said—and he was confident that it would—perhaps Boren Clay could even sell stock to the public at a premium price someday. "Nothing would make me happier than for you to be the rich man at the end of this," Kravis told his new friend.

And Bill Jones believed him.

In the past twenty years, hundreds of chief executives like Bill Jones have confronted moments when they suddenly become very susceptible to a Wall Street deal-maker like Henry Kravis. Ordinarily a CEO's life is rich with power, perks, and security. Yet abruptly a crisis can spring up, threatening to throw a company's leader out of his job and eradicate every trace of his impact on the company. The upheaval may grow out of a feud among family shareholders, the threat of a hostile takeover by a corporate raider, or dissension in the boardroom. Whatever the source, the prospect of being ousted becomes outright sickening to a CEO. It means an abrupt stripping away of titles, salary, and friends. It means public humiliation for men who have known virtually uninterrupted success all their lives.

Such crises have been the breeding grounds for nearly all of Kohlberg Kravis Roberts & Co.'s deals. The anxiety that a small-company executive like Bill Jones felt in 1973 is remarkably similar to the fears that gripped countless executives at much larger companies in the 1980s. Each time, the KKR partners have offered a way to soothe the chief executive's anxieties: taking control of a company through a leveraged buyout. Playing the classic role of well-intentioned visitors from Wall Street, Henry Kravis, George Roberts, or Jerry Kohlberg would arrive at an embattled CEO's office ready to talk about their solution. Big amounts of money would need to be borrowed so that a friendly new group could buy control of the company. Carrying out such an acquisition would allow the KKR men to work their way into financial control of the company. Even so, the buyout specialists said, they would treat the company's top executives with deference after the acquisition was completed. The CEO could count on wide autonomy to run the business as he saw fit—as well as the chance to get rich as a part-owner of the company once the buyout proceeded.

Barely mentioned during these courtships were the hidden risks that a buyout entailed. The debt that KKR planned to pile onto a company's books would turn managers' priorities inside out for the next few years. Executives would need to work harder than ever to wring cash from their company's operations, often shrinking their business, cutting expenses, and passing up growth in the name of frugality. In many cases, top managers' own careers survived the process and even thrived. But this combination of increased debt and greater ownership embraced the needs of only a few senior executives. It seldom made allowances for a company's rank-and-file employees, its suppliers, its creditors, or the towns in which it operated. There was no guarantee of well-being for the many, many people indirectly tied to a company's well-being. Potential for harm abounded.

All the same, Henry Kravis, George Roberts, and Jerry Kohlberg proved so engaging and personable that even if a chief executive suspected he was being seduced, even if he believed that the only reason the Wall Street men came to see him was to get rich from insinuating their way into his predicament—even if a CEO knew he should be wary, he nonetheless welcomed the financial men into his corporation and told himself years later that he was glad he had done so.

If one had to pick the securities firm in the early 1960s that was most insensitive to the delicate psychology of buyouts, it would be Bear, Stearns & Co. Many of its partners were loud-mouthed, witty in a coarse way—and openly eager to get rich. They took their cue from the firm's number-one partner, Salim "Cy" Lewis, a huge bull of a man who didn't bother with a fancy corner office, preferring instead to sit in the middle of the firm's big stock-trading area and scrabble every day for quick stock-trading profits. Bear, Stearns's windows were grimy; its floors were covered in bare linoleum. Partners didn't care. They had few outside customers to impress. They preferred to hoard the firm's profits themselves instead of wasting money on decor. Naked pursuit of riches was encouraged so much that partner Sigmund Wahrsager once began a job interview by leaning forward and boldly asking a candidate: "How do you feel about money?"

The odd man out was Jerome S. Kohlberg, Jr., a bald man in his late thirties with a law degree from Columbia University and the face of a friendly, caring uncle. Kohlberg had joined Bear, Stearns in 1955 when the start of his law career had petered out; he had gravitated into the firm's modest corporate finance department. There, Kohlberg called on top executives of midsize companies, offering to help them issue stock, sell bonds, or negotiate acquisitions. In contrast to the rough-and-tumble traders' world, this required a gentleman's air in proposing deals to clients and winning their trust. At more prestigious firms, corporate finance meant catering to the AT&Ts or General Motors of the world. At Bear, Stearns, Kohlberg did the best he could with a client roster led by Saxon Paper, which took his advice regularly and provided periodic fees of $50,000 to $200,000.

Never totally at home at Bear, Stearns, Kohlberg nonetheless subtly maneuvered himself into a position of moderate power. He became co-head of the corporate finance department (along with Wahrsager) in 1962, and gradually wangled his way into the sixth-largest partnership share at Bear, Stearns, ahead of most of the loud-mouthed stock traders. Fussy and bumbling at times, Kohlberg inched ahead by displaying a clenched-teeth tenacity rather than an effortless grace. Each morning, Kohlberg was one of the first to arrive at Bear, Stearns. He also kept a notepad and pencil beside his bed on business trips so that if he woke up at three A.M. with a good deal-making idea, he could write it down promptly and not lose it by daybreak. Colleagues sometimes found his deliberate pace exasperating. "With him, you had to document everything," former Bear, Stearns partner Gil Mathews recalled. "He was slow to catch on. He couldn't see things quickly."

Yet for all his flaws, Jerry Kohlberg possessed a gift that put him miles ahead of the average Wall Street deal-maker: he radiated integrity. "We're all on the same side of the table," Kohlberg repeatedly assured clients. His awkwardness and shyness actually became an asset; it helped assure executives that he wasn't a slick Wall Street hustler. And whenever Kohlberg summed up his work, he submerged his own ego and presented himself simply as a man out to do good. "I liked the long-term thinking," Kohlberg later said when asked what attracted him to corporate finance. "I liked working with management and bringing more than just financial legerdemain."

Uncomfortable speaking alone before a group, Kohlberg formed the first of several crucial alliances in the mid-1960s, frequently bringing a colleague, Walter Luftman, with him on sales calls. A jovial, round-faced lawyer who had joined Bear, Stearns a few years earlier, Luftman was technically junior to Kohlberg. But executives who saw the Luftman-Kohlberg team in action remember Luftman as the more engaging personality. Luftman was the one who got executives excited about doing a deal with Bear, Stearns, and then haggled about the fine points, recalled former Bear, Stearns associate Steven Hirsch.

One of the first executives that Kohlberg and Luftman wooed was H. J. Stern, the seventy-one-year-old president of a small gold-refining company in Mount Vernon, New York. Ready to retire in late 1964, Stern said he preferred to cash out his ownership of the company rather than hand the business over to any of his three sons. "A company isn't like an oil well, where all you have to do is hold a pan out and collect the oil," Stern told Luftman at one point. "It's like a violin. And I'm not sure my sons have what it takes to play the violin."

The two Bear, Stearns interlopers promised to ease H. J. Stern's worries—which turned out to be surprisingly difficult to do. Stern had worked at the company for fifty-five years, and he didn't want a large corporation to buy him out. Stern told his sons that big acquirers had ruined some of his friends' businesses. He also wanted all his cash right away, rather than gradually selling stock and having his fortune dependent on the ups and downs of the equity market. Stern had nearly issued stock in 1962, only to have his plans wrecked by a market plunge. This time, he wanted his fortune securely set aside for his wife, three sons, and thirteen grandchildren.

Luftman and Kohlberg seemed stuck. The two easiest ways to sell Stern's business—to a corporate buyer or in a public stock offering— were blocked off. Slowly, awkwardly, they spent the spring of 1965 devising a third way. The business, then known as Stern Metals, would be sold for $9.5 million to a small investor group led by Bear, Stearns and the Stern family. Together they would put up just $1.5 million; they would borrow the remaining $8 million of the purchase price from banks and insurance companies. H. J. Stern would get his $8 million without totally surrendering control of the company. "You can have your cake and eat it, too," Kohlberg said.

In the process, Kohlberg and Luftman maneuvered a quick $400,000 paper profit for Bear, Stearns, buying some of Stern Metals' stock at the bargain price of $2.50 a share in July 1965 while arranging to take the company public at $11.75 a share just three months later. That markup was so big that regulators in South Carolina and Wisconsin barred the sale of Stern Metals stock within their states, citing "unreasonable" and "unfair" profits for the deal's promoters. But that controversy wasn't mentioned much in front of the Sterns. Instead, the Bear, Stearns men and the Stern family congratulated one another on what fine gentlemen they were. When they met for an August 1965 dinner to celebrate completion of the deal, H. J. Stern rose to give a toast. Quoting from the Declaration of Independence, the crusty old executive declared: "We mutually pledge to each other our lives, our fortunes, and our sacred honor." It was just what Kohlberg loved to hear.

Over time, Kohlberg and his friends refined the story of those early efforts until they cast Kohlberg as the Abner Doubleday of the buyout business, the man who had started everything with the Stern Metals acquisition. "Some people say I fathered the leveraged buyout," Kohlberg righteously declared at a 1989 New York state hearing into takeover practices. Inconvenient facts—such as Walter Luftman's crucial role in the early deals, or the many small buyouts that other financiers had arranged prior to the Stern Metals deal—were simply left out.

In fact, no single person can take credit for inventing leveraged buyouts. The rudiments of the leveraged buyout business—the practice of going deep into debt to buy a company—had been well established for ages. The history of U.S. buyouts includes the 1961 acquisition of Anderson-Prichard Oil by its own management with 80 percent borrowed funds, the 1954 purchase of Hubbard Co. by financier Charles Dyson with even greater leverage, and an unending series of deals ever further backward in time. No one working on the Stern Metals transaction appears to have regarded themselves as inventing much of anything, Kohlberg included. Kohlberg's own secretary in the 1960s, June Lawyer, said she never heard her boss specifically refer to buyouts as a specialty. "They were just financings," she later recalled. Regular use of the term *leveraged buyout* by the future partners of KKR (or anyone else) began only in the mid-1970s.

With his constant refinement of the Stern Metals myth, however, Kohlberg invented something of great power in its own right. He created a story to tell nervous chief executives. In the years to come, there would be immense appeal to the notion of a financial maneuver that put a lot of cash in the hands of existing shareholders, yet allowed management to stay in charge. The practitioner who claimed to have been doing this the longest, with the best results, would gain a huge competitive edge over everyone else. Such a legend could become self-expanding, in fact, to the point where all sorts of doors would open for the lucky "inventor."

In the first few years after the Stern transaction, Kohlberg and his colleagues dabbled at what later would be called buyouts—but it was hard work. Wahrsager carried out one such leveraged acquisition in 1966; Luftman another in 1967. Kohlberg added two of his own in 1966 and

1968. "We talked to chairmen and chief financial officers [about buyouts] until we were blue in the face," Kohlberg later recalled. But most of their attempts failed; of every twenty contacts initiated, perhaps one produced an actual transaction.

All the big action in Wall Street in the 1960s involved the stock market. Small companies wanted to go public with their first stock offerings. Bigger companies wanted a New York Stock Exchange listing. The top takeover artists of the time, such as Charles Bluhdorn at Gulf & Western and Harold Geneen at ITT, paid for their acquisitions with stock. The Dow Jones industrial average had leapt from about 600 in 1960 to 995 in 1966 and seemed poised to go higher. There weren't any lenders that specialized in financing buyouts; there wasn't any speculative mania for debt or any body of financial theory that legitimized such deals. To specialize strictly in debt-based acquisitions of private companies would have been to invite ridicule and to miss out on a great stock-market boom. As a result, about 80 percent of the Bear, Stearns men's time was spent on typical corporate finance work—bringing companies public, underwriting bond issues, and arranging small mergers.

In 1967, Bear, Stearns became the scene of nasty clashes between Luftman and Kohlberg. Luftman didn't make partner at Bear, Stearns that year, and blamed Kohlberg for not sponsoring him actively enough. A tussle developed over who really deserved credit for Bear, Stearns's modest deal-making success to date. That degenerated into a spat over which man should oversee two little buyout companies: Stern Metals (which was later renamed Sterndent) and Bally Case & Cooler. Kohlberg won one; Luftman won the other. A well-meaning Wall Street lawyer who knew both men called Luftman and told him: "You and Jerry are engaged in a no-win situation. I think it's a mistake. I would like to act as an intermediary and try to effect a rapprochement."

"I'm very grateful," Luftman dryly replied. "I've got a message for Jerry that you can communicate. You can tell him to go screw himself."

As Luftman faded out of the picture, Kohlberg found two new allies.* They were nearly twenty years younger than Kohlberg, and willing to learn Wall Street's ways from an experienced hand. They also were outgoing and even charismatic in a way that Kohlberg never was. "Even then, Jerry had a knack for finding people who would fill out his missing qualities," former Bear, Stearns partner Jim O'Neil later observed.

---

*Luftman quit Bear, Stearns in 1967, worked briefly for several small companies, became head of the Culinary Institute of America, and then retired to Florida, where he continued to pursue small buyouts on a part-time basis into the late 1980s.

The first to join Kohlberg's team was George Roberts, a slender, soft-spoken Texan in his early twenties. Roberts worked a series of summer and part-time jobs at Bear, Stearns from 1965 to 1968 while finishing college and law school. The son of a free-spending Houston oil broker who spent a year in jail for tax evasion, Roberts combined a quiet, resolute intensity with occasional flashes of wild optimism. In years to come, Roberts would be the premier strategist and financing specialist at KKR, most at home with the complexities of raising money for buyouts. In the mid-1960s, he was simply a student who had suddenly discovered what he wanted to do with his life. Enchanted by his first glimpses of the Wall Street takeover world, Roberts spent much of his senior year at Claremont Men's College in California banging out letters to Fortune 500 chief executives on a Hermes manual typewriter, suggesting takeover possibilities and asking to be paid a "finder's fee" if the executives acted on his idea. No company ever agreed, and his roommates teased him endlessly. But Roberts kept trying.

Gradually Roberts learned how to command a chief executive's attention, taking tips from Kohlberg and often asking the older man to come with him on sales calls. One of their early joint buyouts, the acquisition of the Cobblers Inc. shoe company, ended in disaster when the company's chief executive committed suicide several months after selling the company to the Bear, Stearns investor group. Another early Roberts buyout, the acquisition of a San Francisco broadcasting school that advertised on matchbook covers, ended in bankruptcy a few years later. But several of Roberts's early deals did work out, and he began bringing in remarkably big fees for Bear, Stearns.

For about a year in 1969–70, Roberts worked directly for Kohlberg at Bear, Stearns's headquarters—but he hated Manhattan. Before long, he asked Kohlberg if he could transfer to San Francisco, where his wife's family lived. That would be fine, Kohlberg said, if Roberts could find a replacement. The candidate: Roberts's bon vivant cousin, Henry Kravis, who had bounced around four Wall Street jobs already without much success.

From the moment he arrived at Bear, Stearns at age twenty-six in 1970, Kravis was the salesman. Gregarious and a master of small courtesies, he seemed to have spent his whole life making friends and trying to charm people. Many of those habits Kravis had picked up from his father, Ray Kravis, an Oklahoma petroleum engineer and consummate networker in the oil industry. Two New England prep schools, a college degree from Claremont, and an MBA from Columbia had left Henry Kravis well connected on his own, too. Eager to skip the drudgery involved with an investment banking apprenticeship, Kravis was much happier mingling with people than working through the calculations on a new financing.

At first, Kravis and Kohlberg didn't get along well. Kravis was too impetuous, Kohlberg too cautious and fussy. But after a little while, they created a new—and much better—version of the old Kohlberg-Luftman alliance. Impressionable and a good mimic, Kravis set about copying as much of Kohlberg's buyout patter as he could. When Kohlberg explained buyouts by telling CEOs "You can have your cake and eat it, too," Kravis picked up that phrase. Colleagues at Bear, Stearns sometimes snickered at the hokeyness of those early buyout speeches. Yet, every now and then, Kohlberg and his young associates found an agitated small-company CEO who welcomed them in. "Like all good salesmen, Henry really believed in the pitch," recalled Ron Shiftan, a onetime office mate of Kravis's. "He felt it was the right thing for you to do, and the right thing for your family."

In his early years at Bear, Stearns, Kravis was constantly on the go. "There was no such thing for Henry as ten minutes with nothing to do," Shiftan remembered. Stuck at Chicago's O'Hare Airport one day, waiting for a connecting flight, Shiftan settled into a waiting lounge and read the newspaper, expecting Kravis to join him. Kravis didn't. He found a pay phone, riffled through the yellow pages, and began cold-calling local business brokers, asking if they knew of any companies up for sale. (They didn't.)

Frequently, Kravis and Roberts arranged to do their prospecting together, meeting in an unfamiliar city, renting a car, and calling on executives in the belief that the next attempt would really work. A favorite drill was the "industrial-park tour," in which the two cousins pitched their buyout story to a company president with offices in a big industrial park. Kravis or Roberts would write down the names of all the nearby companies, and ask the first CEO for introductions to his neighbors. Each time, Kravis and Roberts were certain that a few more cold calls would generate another buyout. "I don't think we ever got a deal that way," Roberts later recalled. "But we sure tried."

While the cousins chased after deals, Kohlberg established himself as the "statesman" in the background who could soothe the anxieties of lenders and senior executives at crucial stages. "Jerry Kohlberg was a genteel, very caring person," recalled Richard Wakenight, the treasurer of a small company acquired by the Bear, Stearns trio in 1972. "You felt comfortable with him. His word was as good as gold."

As Kohlberg, Kravis, and Roberts kept poking around for more buyouts, the three men soon found themselves estranged from the rest of Bear, Stearns. The recession of 1973 to 1975, and the accompanying stock-market slump, took a toll on every Wall Street firm's profits. Top partners at Bear, Stearns wanted to husband their firm's capital, which had grown to $35 million. The safest course, they thought, was to concentrate on stock and bond trading, where investments could be liquidated in minutes if necessary. Good traders bragged that they "put money in the register"—made profits—every day. The buyout specialists couldn't say the same. Some buyouts, such as the Cobblers deal, were total losses. And even the financially successful deals involved locking up money for years in an illiquid investment before a cent of income emerged. "We were allergic to lockups," Bear, Stearns partner E. John Rosenwald recalled years later.

Kohlberg, meanwhile, was becoming a target of scorn at Bear, Stearns. Colleagues by the mid-1970s had begun to taunt him, regularly barging into his lunches with clients just so Kohlberg would have to interrupt his sales pitch and do a round of introductions. When Kohlberg turned fifty in 1975, a much younger Bear, Stearns executive, Glen Tobias, was brought in to be administrative head of the investment banking department. Tobias didn't quite become Kohlberg's boss, but he was at the very least his peer. Bear, Stearns's other partners prepared to cut back Kohlberg's share of the firm's profits—an assault on a Wall Street man's virility. "This is not for me," Kohlberg told a confidant at one stage. "I can't stand this. I want out."

In 1975, after much agonizing, Kohlberg prepared to quit and set up his own firm. He asked Roberts and Kravis if they wanted to join him. Yes, Roberts quickly said. The office politics of Bear, Stearns disgusted him. He admired Kohlberg, who had become a second father to him. "I wanted to work at a small firm with a few people that I respected," Roberts later said. Besides, for several years, Roberts had been telling lenders that arranging buyouts could be a full-fledged business in its own right, instead of just a minor adjunct to all the other "services" that a Wall Street deal man provided. This was his chance to prove it.

Kravis vacillated. Bear, Stearns's managing partner, Cy Lewis, tried to influence Kravis by telling Kravis's father that Kohlberg's breakaway firm was doomed. "No one has ever left Bear, Stearns and been a success,"

Lewis said at one point. Unsure what to do, Kravis spent a long dinner at Joe & Rose's steakhouse in New York talking out his options with Roberts. Finally Kravis decided to quit Bear, Stearns, too. Lewis didn't mind seeing Kohlberg go, but he called Kravis and Roberts "traitors."

Then war broke out. In a crafty move in December 1975, Kravis and Kohlberg secretly arranged to take personal control of the final buyout that they negotiated at Bear, Stearns. The charter of an obscure voting trust for the company, Incom International Inc., was changed at the last moment to delete references to Bear, Stearns and replace them with the names of Kravis and Kohlberg. When Bear, Stearns executives discovered the subterfuge, they were furious. The "traitors" were about to run off with a corporate client that Bear, Stearns would have liked to keep. When Kohlberg and Kravis prepared to take with them the files on nine existing buyouts, the outrage within Bear, Stearns boiled over. As former Bear, Stearns partner Jim O'Neil remembered it: "There was a feeling of: Let's get even."

One Friday morning in April 1976, the locks were changed on Kohlberg's office door, and it was sealed shut. Armed guards were summoned to stand at the entrance to Bear, Stearns's New York offices at 55 Water Street. Their mission: to keep Kohlberg and Kravis off the premises. Even the San Francisco office was told to freeze out George Roberts. When Kravis returned that afternoon to collect his files, he confronted a pistol-toting security guard who barked at him in a German accent: "You will not go in there!" Bear, Stearns impounded all the controversial files—as well as Kohlberg's bookcase and even his wooden Eames office chair, which had been a gift from Kohlberg's wife.

Kohlberg seethed. He had spent twenty-one years at Bear, Stearns, building up a reputation for probity and decency, while rising to become a senior partner. Now he had been thrown out in such lurid fashion that it seemed like something out of the pages of the *National Enquirer*. He demanded his chair back, saying that Bear, Stearns's actions were tantamount to theft. When Lewis insulted him, Kohlberg hired feisty takeover lawyer Joe Flom to respond with his customary harsh language and occasional obscenities. Kohlberg never talked publicly about the ouster, but friends say he was angry, hurt, and deeply embarrassed.

"Things were very bitter," recalled Jim O'Neil, Bear, Stearns's head of administration at the time. "Neither group would let go until they felt they won." For the next eleven years, in fact, as Kohlberg, Kravis, and Roberts sprinkled fees throughout Wall Street, they avoided ever doing a single piece of business with Bear, Stearns.

On 1 May 1976, the new firm of Kohlberg Kravis Roberts & Co. opened its doors for business. It wasn't much of an opening. In Manhattan, Kohlberg and Kravis sublet a drab midtown office that had just been evacuated by Tosco Corporation, an oil-shale company. For an extra $5,000, Tosco let the new tenants inherit all its furniture and fixtures: cheap metal desks, gray wall-to-wall carpeting, and some vinyl artwork that looked like it came from a Holiday Inn. In San Francisco, George Roberts rented a few empty rooms in the Embarcadero Center office complex. His brother-in-law, Bob MacDonnell, joined him as KKR's first "associate," or nonpartner employee. The firm's name had so little meaning in the business world that an early New York receptionist began answering the phone with "Radio station KKR!" or "Double-K-R Ranch!" Kohlberg and Kravis lacked the nerve to stop her.

KKR's first year in business was "in some ways the best of times and in some ways the most harrowing," Kohlberg later recalled. The firm's three founding partners were as close as they ever would be, playing tennis with one another, sharing Christmas dinners at Kohlberg's Larchmont, New York, home, and swapping countless cross-country phone calls of encouragement. But as a for-profit business, KKR got off to a slow start. Kravis and Kohlberg spent several months in 1976 pursuing a buyout of Booth Newspapers, only to be decisively outbid by the Newhouse publishing group. Other marketing calls didn't pan out at all. Companies weren't in crisis; the chief executives didn't want to hear about buyouts. Without the Bear, Stearns name behind them, the KKR partners lacked any immediate status in a stranger's office.

Some prospecting calls failed so horribly that they became legends in later years. Bob MacDonnell ended up outside Sioux Falls, South Dakota, one winter, hoping to persuade a maker of grain-handling equipment to sell his company for about $3 million. Talks began in the company's office but soon moved into the executive's pickup truck. Just as MacDonnell reached the crescendo of his appeal to the executive's fears and hopes, the man said: "Do you want to plink?"

"Plink?" MacDonnell replied, in total bewilderment.

Plinking, it turned out, was a South Dakota form of target shooting. The executive pulled out a .32 revolver and two Campbell's soup cans, opened his truck door, walked outside, and put the cans on a ledge about fifty feet away. "Let's see how many of these you can hit!" the grain-equipment maker excitedly said. For the next thirty minutes, MacDonnell and the executive took turns blasting at soup cans in blustery, fifteen-below-zero weather.

"Come back and we'll talk again," the executive told MacDonnell at the end of the shoot-up. MacDonnell did so, only to discover that the executive had no intention of selling at a reasonable price. All that MacDonnell could do was return empty-handed to San Francisco.

Kohlberg, the most financially secure of the three partners, had the patience to wait out the dry spells. On slow afternoons, he would leave work early and walk up Fifth Avenue to one of New York's quietest museums, the Frick Collection, to look at paintings. Roberts and Kravis, meanwhile, raced around the country and strained to keep up a façade of success. They flew first-class and stayed at pricey hotels on prospecting trips; it was desperately important that KKR project an air of wealth and success. But before long, KKR's original $120,000 in capital began to dwindle. When $4,300 mysteriously disappeared from the San Francisco office, the firm's resources grew even more stretched. "All the money's going out," Roberts nervously confided to a friend a few months after opening up his own shop. "Nothing's coming in."

Then came the break the KKR partners needed: a chance to soothe the personal turmoil of Ray O'Keefe, another small-company manufacturing executive. Born and raised in rural Missouri, O'Keefe had reluctantly moved to Los Angeles in the early 1970s to take charge of a dilapidated conglomerate called A. J. Industries Inc. By 1976, O'Keefe wondered why he had bothered. The company was embroiled in four different suits involving money purportedly owed to a previous chairman; some customers who had bought badly developed vacation-home land from A. J. were preparing to sue the company; and a small-time corporate raider was threatening a takeover. The stock of A. J. Industries was performing so poorly that the New York Stock Exchange threatened to delist the company.

Driving home one afternoon from a board meeting at the resort town of Arrowhead Lake, California, O'Keefe got so depressed he nearly decided to quit and head home to the Ozarks. Still, he felt sure he could get A. J. back on track if he just had time and the right allies. He phoned Joe Flom, the renowned New York corporate lawyer, to ask him for advice. Flom, who seldom took clients as puny as A. J. Industries, suggested O'Keefe see Kohlberg instead. In a face-to-face meeting in New York a few weeks later, Kohlberg told O'Keefe there wasn't anything he could do right away, but suggested that O'Keefe invite Roberts to join A. J.'s board. Simultaneously, Roberts found an entry point at A. J. as well, cultivating one of the company's existing directors, Los Angeles merger broker Harry Roman.

Granted a board seat at A. J. in April 1976, Roberts exploited it for all he could. Throughout the summer of 1976, he and O'Keefe dined together in Los Angeles, either before or after board meetings. O'Keefe was the talker, blustery and expansive. He wanted to sell off the pieces of A. J. that weren't doing well, such as the raw-land holdings, and expand the two parts that he knew best: making brake drums for trucks and refueling tanks for jet aircraft. "Dendritic growth," O'Keefe called his strategy—pointing to a small green tie pin of his that showed a tree's roots, or dendrites. Other people found O'Keefe rambling, but Roberts never complained. "Make a list of the most important things you want to tell me," Roberts told O'Keefe, gently nudging the older man to keep his thoughts organized. Throughout their dinners together, Roberts listened thoughtfully, occasionally asking a penetrating but sympathetic question. O'Keefe liked it. "He absorbed my ideas," O'Keefe later said.

After a few sessions, Roberts presented KKR's solution to O'Keefe's troubles: a buyout of A. J. Industries. That would sweep away the specter of a corporate raider, Roberts said. It would let O'Keefe replace his board of directors with an entirely new group of sympathetic KKR partners. The lawsuits could be dealt with over time. When Roberts asked to present his idea at the 31 August 1976 board meeting of A. J. Industries, O'Keefe agreed. Some other directors were wary at first, but Kohlberg came to Los Angeles for the next A. J. board meeting and assuaged their worries. When Roberts said he was prepared to push ahead with a buyout if a bare majority of directors agreed, Kohlberg interjected: "It would be far better for everyone if it can be a unanimous decision." The afternoon of 30 September 1976, KKR prevailed, winning authorization to buy A. J. for $26 million.

Until late that fall, O'Keefe thought KKR was arranging the buyout simply because its partners thought A. J. was a good investment. But at a dinner with Roberts and a bank lender to the company, O'Keefe learned otherwise. Ticking off various aspects of the deal, banker David Street mentioned that the buyout would include a $275,000 fee for KKR's work in arranging the deal. "What?" O'Keefe asked. Turning to Roberts, he snapped: "I'll be damned if I'm going to pay you a fee!" Frantically, Roberts tried to calm O'Keefe down. Such fees were standard, Roberts insisted. He just hadn't had a chance to mention them yet. By the end of the evening, O'Keefe's outrage had faded. The fee would be paid. The first in a long line of executives had learned that, for all of KKR's good manners, the buyout firm was hardly an eleemosynary institution.

In 1977, Roberts, Kohlberg, or Kravis found three more executives willing to negotiate buyouts. The U.S. economy was growing, but anxieties about inflation kept stock prices bogged down at levels barely higher than those of the mid-1960s. Companies could be taken private cheaply in buyouts. Small-size loans were readily available; lenders that had financed the KKR partners' deals at Bear, Stearns unhesitatingly switched their alliances to the new buyout firm.

Whatever early jitters the KKR partners had felt about failing as independent deal-makers soon gave way to self-confidence on Kohlberg's part and even a little smugness on the part of his younger partners. In July 1978, Kohlberg told *Forbes* magazine that his firm was enjoying "the greatest environment ever for management buyouts. . . . With very low stock prices, companies are increasingly disenchanted with being public. So, many [companies] are instead going the buyout route."

Roberts, meanwhile, raced up and down the West Coast, looking for small companies to acquire. Just a few months after completing the A. J. Industries buyout, Roberts negotiated the $22 million purchase of a similar little Portland, Oregon, conglomerate, U.S. Natural Resources. His banker friend, David Street, had introduced Roberts to the company after Street learned that its elderly controlling shareholders wanted to sell. As the buyout took shape, Street half-jokingly asked for a finder's fee, only to be snubbed by the proud young deal-maker. "Street, that's no big deal," Roberts snapped. "We would have heard about it anyway."

In North Carolina, Bill Jones watched the rise of the KKR executives with bittersweet feelings. When Boren Clay had embarked on a buyout in 1974, the buyout men had seemed as down-to-earth as Jones's neighbors. Barely thirty at the time, Kravis had driven a dented Mercedes and enjoyed a steak or a drink on Jones's patio. When Jones had teased Kravis about how much his stylish clothes must cost, Kravis earnestly told him: "Bill, I never bought a $500 suit in my life."

Then, year after year, all three KKR men—especially Kravis—floated into grander circles. The dented Mercedes disappeared, to be replaced by a Rolls-Royce with a driver. Kravis's clothes got costlier. And the homey visits with Jones became ever rarer. The first few years after the buyout, Kravis flew down from New York every June to play in the annual Boren Clay golf tournament. He gladly mingled with masons, contractors, and other customers of the brick company. But each year, Kravis's stay grew briefer. One time, Kravis bolted off the eighteenth green late Sunday afternoon, still wearing his golf shoes, and asked to be driven to the airport right away. A fresh deal beckoned in a new city. The next year,

Kravis didn't come at all. Still, Bill Jones remained very fond of his fast-climbing Wall Street friend. From the late 1970s onward, Jones periodically got phone calls from anxious chief executives of bigger companies, in much the same straits that he, Jones, had been in 1973. Their companies were in crisis. Their jobs were in jeopardy. They had just met Kravis, heard his pitch, and anxiously wondered what the KKR partners would be like to work with. "They're great guys," Jones always replied.

Ultimately, Boren Clay fared far worse with its big new debts than Jones had expected, or Kravis had predicted. Twice the brick company was forced into humbling negotiations with creditors to get more financial breathing room. In the recession of 1980, Boren closed three of its sixteen brick plants. In 1986 the brick company was sold to a Canadian buyer, allowing Jones to retire at age sixty. When he cashed out, Bill Jones collected $590,000 for stock that had cost him $125,000 some 12 years earlier. It was a pretty good showing, but hardly enough to qualify him as the "rich man" from the deal.

That honor went entirely to the KKR men.

2
The Growing Allure of Debt

A s KKR rose to power in the late 1970s, the generation of executives who came of age in the Great Depression was beginning to retire. With them disappeared firsthand knowledge about widespread defaults, bankruptcies, and hard times. That loss of fear may have been one of the most important factors in the buyout movement's rapid proliferation in the 1980s. For most of the postwar era, American business had been tinged by memories of a time when millions of people couldn't pay their bills. The intense—even excessive—conservatism of American corporate finance all through the 1950s, 1960s, and early 1970s reflected a "never again" attitude among top executives. As long as such CEOs ran American companies, debt-based buyouts would never gain more than a tiny toehold.

Gerald Saltarelli typified the Depression-era survivor. Chairman of a Fort Lauderdale, Florida, conglomerate, Houdaille Industries Inc., Saltarelli had been eighteen years old when the great crash of 1929 occurred. Living in New York City's Little Italy neighborhood at the time, Saltarelli watched his older brother's construction business collapse. Then he was out of work himself for a while. And when Saltarelli did find a job in the early 1930s, it was one that made him shudder decades later. For less than $20 a week, Saltarelli entered the homes of people who had defaulted on their mortgages, to clean out the premises so that lenders could take possession of the houses. Ignoring the signs of families in distress, Saltarelli carted out sofas, carpets, chairs, and anything else of value. "It made an indelible impression on me," Saltarelli said decades later. "I saw with my own eyes what debt did. I saw people lose their homes."

From the time he took charge of Houdaille in 1962, Saltarelli's financially conservative values prevailed at the company, a Fortune 500 maker of machine tools, pumps, and car bumpers. "Debt was anathema to me," Saltarelli later explained. "I felt that whatever you did, you should do it with as little debt as possible." Nearly all of Houdaille's growth was financed through the stock market; the company relied on debt for less than 15 percent of total capital. Everything about Houdaille's balance sheet was meant to be rock-solid. In mid-1978, the company had cash reserves of $40 million, more than enough to pay off its $22 million of debt. Saltarelli was surrounded by cautious blue-chip lawyers and Wall Street advisers. No one would have expected the sixty-seven-year-old chairman and his advisers to let Houdaille suddenly plunge deeper into debt than any company its size had ever dared.

Starting in the summer of 1978, though, Saltarelli's values began to be uprooted. A takeover bid higher than anything that shareholders had expected came forward. Advisers who once might have shared Saltarelli's concerns found new "duties" and "obligations" that caused them to condone—even welcome—a high-debt takeover of the company. Saltarelli's top subordinates saw ways that a new set of owners might benefit them. Finally, the lawyers and regulators who could have restrained this corporate conquest declared after a few months that, while they might be wary, they were powerless to stop it.

The source of all this debt and the upheaval that came with it? Kravis, Kohlberg, and a single junior colleague in New York. Drawing upon a remarkable financial, legal, and accounting coalition, the KKR men slipped past every barrier that Houdaille and the Wall Street establishment of the time could erect. The KKR men did so while using their own capital for less than $\frac{1}{300}$ of the total purchase price. They borrowed the rest.

More than any other KKR acquisition, the taking of Houdaille in 1978 marked the transformation of buyouts from obscure deals into front-page news. Virtually every takeover-related issue of the next decade was encapsulated in KKR's ten-month struggle to buy the Fort Lauderdale company. Heavy use of debt, a generally overlooked hallmark of KKR's previous small-scale buyouts, suddenly became an exciting, alluring, dangerous force that could reshape big companies' destinies.

The acquisition of Houdaille also coincided with much broader political and economic changes that would greatly aid high-debt financiers. The austere Carter administration was drawing to an end; the laissez-faire Reagan era was about to begin. Swamping a company with debt stopped being seen as crazy. A "credit culture" sprang up, in which borrowing heavily became a way of life. Consumer debt more than tripled in the 1980s, rising to $3.7 trillion. Corporate debt grew even faster, climbing to $2.1 trillion. The U.S. government became an especially profligate borrower, expanding the national debt more than threefold, to $2.87 trillion.

For the KKR executives and their closest allies, this emerging enthusiasm for high debt provided a delicious route to riches and power. KKR could use millions or even billions of dollars of other people's money to buy a company. Very little of the purchase price had to come from the KKR partners' own pockets. Kravis, Roberts, and Kohlberg simply linked other people's money with other people's management, becoming impresarios in the center of these schemes. As merchants of debt, the KKR men could control a giant company's stock and claim a fat share of eventual profits, at hardly any cost to themselves. All they needed was the audacity to propose and carry out these combinations of borrowed money and borrowed management.

As far back as 1909, the incentives for an eventual tilt toward heavy corporate debt had been put in place. In that year, Congress enacted a "tariff" that really amounted to the first corporate income tax. Legislators fatefully decided to make interest payments tax-deductible for corporations, while providing no such benefits for dividends on common stock. As a result, companies that financed themselves largely with debt could shield themselves from taxes; those that financed themselves with common stock could not. "It seems to me . . . that it will be within the powers of corporations to convert in a large measure their stock into bonds, and . . . in so doing, they will escape the payment of this tax," Senator Augustus O. Bacon of Georgia prophetically declared during Senate debate in July 1909.

Senator Bacon was right—but he was seventy years ahead of his time. Early corporate tax rates were minuscule, as low as 1 percent of profits. Companies didn't bother reshuffling balance sheets just to avoid such small levies. Besides, heavy debt was only for farmers, immigrants, and the disaffected left. The idea of plunging a respectable business into hock seemed repugnant and terrifying. For several generations, executives' attitudes were shaped by a litany of antidebt arguments—ranging from evocations of eighteenth-century debtors' prisons and the upheaval of the Depression, to the moralistic tenets of traditional East Coast financial theory, which looked askance at too much borrowing. Businessmen saw little to be gained, and entire careers to be lost, if they flirted with excessive debt at their companies.

In theory, the tax benefits of high-debt finance grew steadily greater for companies after World War II, as corporate tax rates climbed. But most business leaders and finance scholars hesitated to let debt amount to more than 20 percent of total capital. In the 1962 edition of his classic finance textbook, *Securities Analysis*, Columbia University professor Benjamin Graham warned against the "hazards" of a high-debt, "speculative capital structure, with consequent instability and even possible insolvency." Executives of the 1960s and 1970s believed that their interest bills shouldn't be any larger than one-sixth of operating profits. Any heavier reliance on debt was seen as risky. And with most big American companies in the hands of men like Gerry Saltarelli—who had learned firsthand about the horrors of unmanageable debt during the Great Depression— few executives cared to tempt fate by borrowing heavily just to cut their company's tax bill.

In the late 1970s and early 1980s, however, a scattering of iconoclasts, most of them academics on the political right, took a fresh look at debt. Forty years of steady post-Depression economic growth made these scholars think that the perils of debt-induced bankruptcy were greatly overstated. Meanwhile, big tax savings beckoned. Before long, a remarkable political inversion started to take hold. At the University of Rochester, free-market economist Michael Jensen in 1976 put forth the idea that managers of public corporations squandered the companies' assets on perquisites and wasteful projects because they didn't own much of the companies. This problem could be solved, Jensen argued, if managers of big companies owned a large part of the company's stock and financed the rest of the company with debt. That might involve borrowing vast sums, Jensen conceded, but he wasn't sure that was all bad. Unwittingly foretelling the management-led buyouts that would sweep through the United States in the next fifteen years, Jensen asked in a research paper: "Why don't we observe large corporations individually owned, with a tiny fraction of the capital supplied by the entrepreneur in return for 100 percent of the equity, and the rest simply borrowed?"

Simultaneously, the appeal of debt was being reassessed for consumers and the U.S. government itself. At the University of Southern California, supply-side economist Arthur Laffer began spelling out theories under which the government should cut taxes and willingly accept big deficits for a year or two, on the belief that a stronger economy would expand the tax base so much that the government would soon recoup the lost revenue. Big borrowings shouldn't be feared, the maverick economists argued. They should be welcomed.

The partners of Kohlberg Kravis Roberts & Co. found themselves in the right place at the right time. They didn't participate in the first stirrings of the ideological debate about debt. They didn't draft a master plan that envisioned a rapid-fire series of giant acquisitions in the 1980s. They simply bought some midsize industrial companies, using borrowed money to pay their way. But as traditional opposition to high-debt finance collapsed, immense opportunities beckoned. Someone had to fill the void. The first available candidate was KKR.

By the time Jerry Kohlberg and Henry Kravis began pursuing Houdaille, the KKR partners had worked with debt for about a dozen years. In their fifteen previous small-scale buyouts, the KKR partners had borrowed 70 to 95 percent of the purchase price. Through early missteps, such as the buyout of the Cobblers shoe company, the KKR partners knew something about when big debts were suitable and when they weren't. A handful of other high-debt financiers had begun to circulate in the late 1970s, but few of them inspired much trust among banks, insurance companies, or other lenders. Some came across as greedy; others seemed like somewhat seedy gamblers who were destined to go bust.

The three KKR partners, especially Jerry Kohlberg, stood out because they brought an air of respectability to high-debt maneuverings. Behind closed doors at KKR's New York offices, secretaries saw Kravis, Kohlberg, and their colleagues wink at one another in gleeful acknowledgment of their deals' audacity. But in public, the KKR partners projected nothing but rectitude and caution. "You have to structure the thing so a company can stand a bad year or two," Kohlberg told a newspaper interviewer in the late 1970s. He spent as much time explaining why certain companies (ones with erratic earnings or high capital-spending needs, such as high-technology and real estate companies) were inappropriate for a buyout as he did talking about the buyouts that KKR had completed.

Careful of the image he projected, Kohlberg regularly talked about the satisfaction he felt "in watching a company's progress." Kravis and Roberts, meanwhile, struck lenders as diligent young men when it came to making financial projections and defending the analyses that underpinned their takeover schemes. All three men stayed patient and cordial as they tried to sell their buyout ideas to executives, corporate advisers, and potential lenders. Gradually, word got around on Wall Street that most of

KKR's daredevil acquisitions—in financial terms at least—were working out successfully. Before long, the little buyout firm began making remarkable headway with the lawyers and Wall Street advisers who surrounded big companies in crisis.

Houdaille was the first really big, Fortune 500 company to be stalked by leveraged buyout specialists. Founded in 1925 by French immigrant Maurice Houdaille, the company by the late 1970s had grown into a good-size conglomerate that made steel bumpers for Chrysler and American Motors cars, quarried gravel in Florida and New Jersey, produced pumps, and operated a small Texas steel company. Houdaille (pronounced "hou-DYE") employed 7,700 people and racked up yearly sales of $400 million. Its star divisions were those that made machine tools: the master machines that make other machines. Except for a few brief factory tours, however, Kravis and Kohlberg ignored Houdaille's industrial might. The lure of Houdaille lay in its balance sheet, its earnings power—and its vulnerability.

A routine newspaper article first put Kohlberg on the company's trail. On 7 July 1978, *New York Times* columnist Robert Metz noticed a minor flurry of trading in Houdaille's stock and asked in his column: "Is Houdaille . . . a takeover candidate?" It was a smart question. Although Metz didn't say so, an unwelcome suitor, the Jacobs family of Buffalo, had secretly bought 2 to 3 percent of Houdaille's stock and begun stalking the company. Saltarelli was "very worried," recalled his investment banker, Goldman, Sachs & Co. partner Peter Sachs. The company chairman asked Sachs how to ward off this new shareholder—perhaps unaware of where such an innocent request for help would lead. One of Goldman, Sachs's top specialties was to put companies up for sale, with top management's consent, and collect multimillion-dollar investment banking fees at the end of the deal. In the next few months, Sachs might look at a lot of options—but by the very nature of his Wall Street job, he wanted to tug Saltarelli and Houdaille's other directors into authorizing a friendly sale of the company. That might soothe Saltarelli; it would enrich Goldman, Sachs.

An avid reader of the business press, Jerry Kohlberg pounced on the opportunity presented by what sounded like an executive in distress. Rather than contact Saltarelli directly—and risk offending him—Kohlberg decided to work more delicately through Sachs, a fellow investment banker. Would it be possible for Sachs to set up a get-acquainted meeting with Saltarelli in Florida? Kohlberg asked.

The courtship started badly. Sachs relayed Kohlberg's request, but Saltarelli balked. Kohlberg persisted. After about a month, Sachs urged Saltarelli at least to see the KKR men briefly. Other suitors for Houdaille were scarce, Sachs said, while KKR had "a very high reputation in our business." So Jerry Kohlberg and Henry Kravis flew from New York to Houdaille's Fort Lauderdale headquarters in August 1978. Accompanying them was Don Herdrich, a stocky, thirty-three-year-old Chicago banker who had just joined KKR as the firm's fifth deal-making employee.

Sitting around a big conference table at Houdaille's headquarters, Kohlberg laid out his firm's standard opening pitch. KKR had teamed up with managements to acquire a number of companies. KKR always kept the existing management. In fact, executives in previous acquisitions had enjoyed great autonomy to run their businesses as they saw fit. Kohlberg "was very quiet and unassuming," Saltarelli recalled. "It was a very soft sell. It was precisely the right way to deal with me."

Kravis spoke next, going into the specifics of KKR's acquisition plan. The Florida executives shuddered at first. Most of KKR's purchase capital would be borrowed—and the debt would be dumped onto Houdaille's books. "This was a company with almost no debt," adviser Peter Sachs later said. "Now they were talking about taking the capital table and turning it on its head. That was a bizarre concept to Mr. Saltarelli. He found it an unnatural act."

Kravis was undeterred. He handed over KKR's estimates of what Houdaille's finances would look like after a buyout, and confidently told the Houdaille executives: "You take these numbers, and you do whatever you want with them. You massage them, and you figure out in your own mind how they look. But please, don't jump to conclusions about them. I'm sure, knowing how you've run your company in the past, that this is going to scare you. Okay. You're telling me initially that it's not going to work. I'm telling you: I think it will work."

On his own, Saltarelli might have resisted forever. But three people whom he trusted began to gnaw away at his opposition. The first were two younger Houdaille executives: executive vice president Phil O'Reilly and treasurer Don Boyce. They were fifty-two and thirty-nine years old, respectively, too young to share Saltarelli's Depression-era dread of debt. Boyce and Kravis hit it off quickly and began talking regularly; before long, Boyce joined in championing KKR's high-debt proposals. O'Reilly found himself at ease with Kravis and Kohlberg, too. It wasn't the exact words they used, O'Reilly said; it was "their candor and their sincerity." Besides, KKR provided a path to power and riches for O'Reilly and

Boyce. If the sixty-seven-year-old Saltarelli retired soon—which was likely—O'Reilly and Boyce would take command of Houdaille. Early in the negotiations, Kohlberg invited O'Reilly to his vacation home in the Virgin Islands, with the simple hope of improving personal chemistry. When O'Reilly stepped off the plane, he clutched drafts of employment contracts for himself and Boyce, designed to win job security and big pay raises. O'Reilly got his way; Kravis and Kohlberg agreed to boost the top men's salaries more than 50 percent, to $200,000 a year for O'Reilly and $100,000 for Boyce.

The final nudge came from Peter Sachs—Saltarelli's trusted Wall Street adviser. Sachs had represented himself as being sensitive to Saltarelli's desires. To an extent, he was. But Goldman, Sachs also stood to collect a fee of $3 million or more if Houdaille were sold. And Sachs soon seized on the exact line of reasoning that would force a sale of Houdaille, if Saltarelli knew what was best. It now was clear that Houdaille wasn't seriously menaced by its unwelcome stockholders, the Jacobs family. Yet Sachs explained that Saltarelli, as Houdaille chairman, had an obligation to shareholders to get the best price possible for the stock. The auctioning of Houdaille had begun, and the process couldn't be stopped. KKR appeared willing to acquire Houdaille's stock at a big premium above the market price of about $25 a share. No other bidder had emerged, even though Sachs had talked with thirty candidates. Houdaille's stock was surging on takeover rumors. If Houdaille's directors rebuffed KKR and the stock price crashed, Sachs insinuated, Saltarelli would have a hard time answering to shareholders. He might even be sued.

"I felt it was my duty, probably, to go along," Saltarelli later said. "I was a reluctant accepter of that proposition."

In mid-October 1978, Gerry Saltarelli made the toughest decision of his career. He agreed to let Houdaille travel down a strange new course that almost certainly meant ramming huge borrowings onto the company's books. Sachs's arguments were irrefutable. Saltarelli decided that he would retire as chairman a few months later. His age was a factor; in addition, he couldn't stomach the idea of trying to run Houdaille awash with debt. He also stood to collect $5.2 million from the sale of his own Houdaille stock to the acquirers—a tidy windfall on which to base his retirement. KKR could pursue its takeover designs without his interference, Saltarelli said. In fact, Kohlberg and his KKR colleagues could see Houdaille's most sensitive internal data: its business forecasts and internal profit breakdowns. The KKR men always liked to see such data; it made it far easier to line up loans to buy a company. Such data could ruin

Houdaille if it fell into the hands of a competitor. But Saltarelli had come to trust Kohlberg enough that in late October 1978, he signed a four-page agreement to show KKR everything.

While Kohlberg put Saltarelli at ease, Herdrich and Kravis embarked on the numbers-crunching necessary if KKR was to make a well-thought-out bid for Houdaille. This was a crucial exercise in any buyout, requiring a caustic new look at a company's finances, followed by a lot of precise forecasting. When the KKR men were done, they would create a gaunt new version of Houdaille, without dividends, meaningful per-share earnings, or significant book value. But by new yardsticks—chiefly the company's ability to service its debts—Houdaille would still be viable.

First Kravis and Herdrich sized up Houdaille's true earning power. The company's post-tax profits were running at a $28.5 million yearly rate. After a buyout, however, Houdaille would also have the use of $22.3 million a year that ordinarily was paid to Uncle Sam. With big debts ahead, and the tax deductibility of interest, Houdaille's tax bill would drop to nearly zero. That meant KKR could count on pretax profit of $50.8 million a year, far beyond what public shareholders saw. What's more, the confidential data that Kohlberg had obtained showed a bright outlook for Houdaille. Pretax profit was expected to rise to $60 million in 1979 and climb 5 to 10 percent thereafter. Punching numbers into a primitive Bowmar Brain calculator, Herdrich calculated Houdaille's likely earnings as far out as 1988. It was a sunny outlook, without a glimmer of recession, with profits rising year after year.

Next, Kravis, Kohlberg, and Herdrich looked hard at how high a price they needed to pay for Houdaille. Too low a bid and they would simply invite a higher offer from another suitor, they figured. Swallowing hard, Kravis and Kohlberg decided to aim high and see if they could win Houdaille without touching off a bidding contest. They told Sachs and Saltarelli they would offer $40 a share for all the company's stock, or a total price of $355 million. It was nearly four times more than KKR had ever bid for any company.

Then Kravis and Herdrich began the tough calculations about how to finance the acquisition. At this preliminary stage, debt was as malleable as soft clay. The KKR men could pile on extra debt, take some away, or reshape the debt profile by changing maturity dates, interest-rate assumptions, or any other loan terms. Once the buyout was completed, though, the company's debt would be as rigidly set as if it had been fired in a kiln. If interest payments ever proved unmanageable, the company's only recourse would be to plead for creditors' indulgence, or else default and face bankruptcy proceedings.

Getting the debt level right was so crucial that the KKR executives ran a special set of worst-case calculations. Houdaille, and to a lesser extent KKR, would have to live for years with the debt levels that Kravis and Herdrich patched in. Always a worrier, Kohlberg peppered Kravis and Herdrich with questions. What would happen if interest rates shot up? If the U.S. economy entered a recession? A few days later, the answer emerged: Houdaille still could just barely service its debts. Such questioning sessions were a crucial part of KKR's success over the years; they prevented the buyout firm—for all its ambition—from embarking on overly risky deals that could lead to financial disaster down the road. Kohlberg asked the questions then, secretary Peggy Coiro recalled, as a way of teaching his younger partners. In later years, Kravis and Roberts would assume their old mentor's role, posing similar questions to younger men working for them.

For Houdaille, KKR wanted to borrow a shade more than $300 million, about 85 percent of the purchase price. The final $50 million would be financed partly by selling preferred stock to banks, and partly by having Houdaille management, the KKR partners, and some loyal passive investors put up a mere $25 million of risk capital that would let them own the company. Through a series of limited partnerships, KKR would control Houdaille after the buyout and have sizable claims on any eventual rise in the value of the Florida company. Kohlberg, Kravis, and the rest of the KKR men would invest only $1 million of their own.

Working six days a week, Kravis and Herdrich partitioned Houdaille's new debt into four classes—a maneuver that created a smorgasbord of ways lenders could help finance the buyout. For safety-minded lenders, such as banks, there would be senior debt. It would have the strongest claim on Houdaille's assets, the assurance of being repaid first, and the lowest interest rate. For lenders, such as insurance companies, that were willing to take bigger risks in the hope of earning more, Houdaille would sell three categories of subordinated debt. These loans might take as long as twenty years to be repaid, and would have a weaker claim on Houdaille's assets. But they also would carry higher interest rates and potentially profitable "kickers"—part-ownership of Houdaille after the buyout. Such debt partitions were standard but arcane at the time; the explosive growth of the subordinated-debt market, under the new name of "junk bonds," was still a few years away.

Within a few weeks of getting Houdaille's confidential data, Herdrich produced a seventy-seven-page Houdaille acquisition plan that he and Kravis wanted to show to America's biggest banks and insurance companies. This was their buyout manifesto, filled with financial data meant to coax forth the loans they needed. It was a ragged document, banged out on manual typewriters and splattered with so many revisions that many pages were covered with Wite-Out and Scotch tape. Herdrich sent the unwieldy mess to a photocopying service, which tried to produce duplicate copies that looked a bit more professional. But KKR's Houdaille memo still had the frantically improvised look of a high school senior's first big term paper. Could this memo coax more than $300 million in loans for KKR? Herdrich didn't think so. "This is all very nice, Henry," he told Kravis at one point. "But where are we going to get the money?"

"Don't worry," Kravis replied. "We'll find it."

An early ally popped up at Chicago's biggest bank, Continental Illinois. A twenty-seven-year-old Continental loan officer, Michael Tokarz, had learned about KKR's hopes to buy Houdaille by reading *The Wall Street Journal* as he rode a 5:04 A.M. commuter train into work. "This sounded terrific," Tokarz later recalled. Continental had told him to make loans to Florida companies, a territory that had been fruitless for the bank for years. Although Tokarz didn't know anyone at either Houdaille or KKR, helping finance this acquisition looked like his big chance. Arriving in Continental's downtown Chicago offices around six A.M., Tokarz dragged two phones to his desk, called Houdaille on one line and KKR on the other, and waited for an answer. No one answered at either office; it was long before opening hours. Tokarz nearly hung up, but then summoned up his courage to wait. Eventually someone would have to answer—and that way, Tokarz could be the first banker to pitch his services. After about fifty minutes, Henry Kravis arrived at KKR's offices. "You don't know me, but I read in the newspaper . . . ," Tokarz said, as he fumbled through an introduction, worried that other bankers might have beaten him in a race to make the loan. They hadn't. Kravis gladly accepted Tokarz's offer of a $30 million loan from Continental.

Simultaneously, the KKR men targeted a likely big source of the riskier loans needed for the buyout: Prudential Insurance Co. For years, Jerry Kohlberg had cultivated senior lending officials at the Pru, America's largest insurer. "Jerry was a hands-off, elder statesman figure," recalled Milan Resanovich, a Prudential loan officer in the 1970s. Kohlberg "brought contacts and integrity to the business. He was constantly talking about integrity." For the Houdaille deal, Kravis and Kohlberg made a very effective double team. Kravis pitched the details of the Houdaille buyout to loan officers like Resanovich. Kohlberg won the confidence of the older, senior managers at the Pru. In the fall of 1978, Prudential tentatively agreed to lend $107 million.

With KKR's first two major lenders seemingly on board, Kravis embarked on a giant game of divide-and-conquer. Calling on banks and insurance companies in the fall of 1978, Kravis coaxed each one to join a big lending syndicate that was forming. In his presentations, Kravis radiated a belief that KKR's Houdaille memo had the ring of greatness to it. If things went as planned, Houdaille's giant new debts could be paid down at least $10 million a year. Houdaille's net income would plunge at first, because of the extra interest expense involved with the big debt. But taxes would shrink to almost nothing. By 1983, he projected, Houdaille would have clawed its way back to record profitability and greatly reduced debt.

In KKR's eyes, the numbers told the whole story; there wasn't any room to wonder what it would be like to work at a company with so much debt. Houdaille was simply "an extremely attractive investment opportunity," according to KKR's memo. Endless columns of financial projections didn't have an extra category for the sweat, fears, and hopes of Houdaille's 7,700 employees. There wasn't any mention of rising Japanese competition in the machine-tool industry, or the costly retooling needed to stay a step ahead of emerging rivals such as Yamazaki Machinery. The deal-makers focused entirely on their own "financial engineering."

Once the first few signs of interest emerged from major lenders, Kravis drew in others by whipping up as much of a stampede as he could. People were signing up quickly to lend to Houdaille, Kravis asserted. The entire lending team would be assembled by Christmas 1978, and the "opportunity" to help finance the Houdaille buyout mightn't last long. To junior loan officers, Kravis was a Teddy Roosevelt of finance, winning people over by his energy, good cheer, and unshakable conviction that greatness was on its way.

All the same, Kravis's ebullience—and sometimes outright bluff—were pitted against the inertia of the biggest U.S. banks and insurers. Low-level loan officers at such institutions as Allstate Insurance, Bankers Trust, and Manufacturers Hanover tentatively agreed to help bankroll KKR. The 10 to 12 percent interest rates that KKR offered looked attractive. The financial projections by Kravis and Herdrich looked plausible; Houdaille almost certainly could survive the debt. But as negotiations proceeded, and senior executives picked over KKR's proposal, fights broke out.

At Prudential, the proposed Houdaille loan was so big that it needed approval not just from the regular loan committees, but also from the insurer's board of directors. Prudential's loan officers thought this was a formality; no one could remember directors rejecting a loan that the staff had already approved. But no one had seen a loan like Houdaille before. At a protracted board meeting, one of Prudential's outside directors, a former governor of New Jersey, railed against the Houdaille buyout for hours. "He thought it was the craziest thing he had ever seen," Prudential loan specialist John Childs later recalled. Directors refused to approve the Houdaille loan at first, sending it back to the lending staff for "further review." That was perilously close to rejection. To get the loan approved, Prudential's loan officers—and KKR—waited for a board meeting at which their number-one opponent was absent, and then pushed the Houdaille loan through as quickly as they could.

Old-guard forces nearly prevailed at Continental Illinois, too. At one point, a senior Continental executive pressed Kravis for better terms and snapped: "This is a potential deal-breaker, Henry. If you aren't going to agree on this, we're out of the deal."

"You're absolutely right about one thing," Kravis shot back in a booming voice. "This is a deal-breaker. And if you don't agree to our way of doing it, you're out of the deal."

The idea of KKR "firing" a potential lender was absurd. But the Continental executive was so stunned by Kravis's retort that he quickly gave ground. Don Herdrich, the Chicago banker turned KKR associate, cherished that moment. Tiny, upstart KKR, a two-and-a-half-year-old firm with only five professional employees, had begun to order big banks around. Kravis's bubbly, flamboyant ways might occasionally irritate Herdrich—but in a negotiating session, there was no one Herdrich would rather see in action than brash, well-dressed, and supremely confident Henry Kravis.

KKR's great debt-raising effort still had to endure one more crisis, though, at which the entire buyout nearly fell apart. In a closed-doors meeting on 3 March 1979, at KKR's offices, loan officers from Prudential and the commercial banks burst into a shouting match about whose loans would be paid off first if Houdaille got in trouble. Word leaked out that major lenders were clashing, and that KKR might lose the backing it needed for its buyout. Houdaille's stock fell $3 a share before the New York Stock Exchange halted trading. When a reporter phoned Kravis for comment, he sounded flustered. Stock traders had "pretty good information [about] some points of dispute," Kravis conceded. By five P.M. that day, tempers still raged, and a Bankers Trust executive proposed that everyone go home, cool off, and try again the next day. Only Kravis refused. "If we don't resolve this tonight," Kravis told about twenty of his main prospective lenders, "this deal is history. Finished. Forget about it. We're going to stay here tonight until it gets done." Over the next two hours, the bankers and the Prudential men finally reached a compromise, with Kravis and Herdrich goading them on. When Houdaille stock reopened for trading, it soared $5 a share. The financing battle was over.

All that remained was to win over the lawyers—and the U.S. government.

On any big corporate acquisition, a coterie of lawyers springs into place to fuss about each stage of the transaction. The lawyers see themselves as guardians of a system that is supposed to prevent illegal, shady, or ill-thought-out deals from happening. To such corporate lawyers, precedent is all-important. If a proposed takeover resembles dozens of other previous acquisitions in form, it will be easy to enact. If a proposed takeover is unlike any other, it is viewed with deep suspicion. Every piece of legal verbiage and protocol becomes a subject of debate. With the Houdaille deal—which was an attempt to fly in the face of fifty years of corporate acquisition practice—KKR faced some of the deepest distrust that the legal establishment could muster. Houdaille's attorneys regarded KKR as an unwelcome upstart that should be challenged whenever possible, and swatted down if found wanting. For KKR to seize control of Houdaille, the tiny buyout firm had to change the legal community's entire way of thinking about what was allowable in an acquisition, and what wasn't.

The fussiest lawyer was Saltarelli's New York friend, Rodney Dayan of Cadwalader, Wickersham & Taft. Dayan, a Princeton and Oxford graduate in his early forties, epitomized the East Coast establishment, from his love of tennis and rowing to his nervous habit of fidgeting with his hands while he talked. He had already saved Saltarelli from going ahead with one ill-fated deal—an early 1970s brewery acquisition—and he was determined to make sure that the KKR buyout didn't turn out to be an even bigger problem.

"We made them [KKR] prove themselves as they went along," Dayan later recalled. At the start of buyout negotiations, he imposed a timetable on Kravis and Herdrich. He allotted the KKR men so many days to line up their financing, so many days to prepare their materials for Houdaille shareholders, and so on. Only when each stage had been completed would Dayan allow KKR to advance to the next step. A careful legal researcher, Dayan saw pitfalls in almost every action that KKR proposed. In rhetorical flourishes before the Houdaille board, or in private conversations with Saltarelli, Dayan kept asking questions that showed just how dubious he was of this small buyout firm's prospects. "Who are these people?" Dayan recalled asking. "What have they done? Can they get the deal done?" When Saltarelli asked Dayan early on for advice, Dayan replied: "You don't want to spend six months on the deal and come away with egg on your face when it can't get done."

In the person of Rod Dayan, Henry Kravis for the first time jousted with America's financial old guard over the right to control a Fortune 500 company. Before long, Dayan and Kravis found their first major battleground. It involved a shrewd accounting technique that delighted Kravis, and made Dayan very nervous.

On any tough accounting issue from the mid-1970s onward, Kravis turned to Tom Hudson, a Southern gentleman in his mid-fifties who ran the Greensboro, North Carolina, office of Deloitte, Haskins & Sells. Hudson had shown Kravis some ingenious, though perfectly legitimate accounting procedures in 1974, when the two of them worked on the Boren Clay buyout. First-time visitors to Hudson's Greensboro office thought of him as a grandfatherly, storytelling sort, which he was to some extent. But Kravis had come to realize that Tom Hudson was one extraordinary accountant. If there was a legal way to shrink a company's tax bill, Tom Hudson knew about it, was ready to try it, and was willing to battle anyone dumb enough not to use it. In the case of Houdaille, Kravis was itching to unleash Hudson's talents.

Kravis and Herdrich had always figured they could cut Houdaille's tax bill in half, simply by piling more debt on its books. But after a while, Kravis began to wonder if it might be possible to shrink Houdaille's tax bill to nearly zero, for years to come, by radically boosting the value of all the assets on Houdaille's books, and then taking much bigger depreciation allowances against these newly more valuable assets. This maneuver, known as step-up depreciation, was legal if done properly. But it would be nervy work at a company as large and well-established as Houdaille.

Hudson's initial report delighted Kravis. Most of Houdaille's factories, equipment, and inventories were carried at drastically low valuations on its books, Hudson said. They had been bought in the 1950s and 1960s, before a long run of inflation. With a stroke of his pencil, Hudson thought he could boost the value of Houdaille's assets by $100 million or so. That would let the company claim an extra $15 million a year in depreciation allowances—which would shield Houdaille from taxes.

Houdaille provided "unusual opportunities," even "unique opportunities," for Deloitte to work its tax magic, Hudson declared.

When Dayan learned what Kravis and Hudson were planning to do, he sputtered in protest. In meeting after meeting, he grilled Kravis with disdainful questions. Shouldn't KKR disclose this depreciation maneuver to Houdaille's selling shareholders? Did it bring into question whether KKR was paying a fair price for Houdaille? "He didn't like the transaction at all," Hudson recalled. "We would go over the details ad nauseum. He was one of the last hold-outs."

Dayan later said he was just carrying out his responsibility to Houdaille's directors and shareholders. But people in the KKR camp sensed disdain in Dayan's remarks. They began to worry that Saltarelli, who trusted Dayan's advice, would turn outright hostile to the buyout. Dayan "had Saltarelli all tied up in his underwear" about the suitability of KKR's depreciation plans, recalled another attorney working on the transaction. Finally, Peter Sachs himself had to plead with Dayan to calm down.

KKR embarked on fresh adventures by creating several shell companies that would carry out different stages of the Houdaille acquisition. Determined to project a top-notch air, Kravis and Kohlberg spent about $200,000 to hire top-flight lawyers from Skadden, Arps, Slate, Meagher & Flom. Those lawyers concocted Houdaille Associates, HH Holdings Inc., and HH Acquisition Corporation—three phantom companies that were devoid of any purpose except to arrange KKR's borrowings in the right order and to help Hudson carry out his tax maneuvers. Nonetheless, these shell companies needed to hold board meetings and correspond with one another.

What followed was out of *Alice in Wonderland,* or perhaps Robert De Niro's desperado role in *Taxi Driver.* On 5 March 1978, Henry Kravis convened a board meeting of HH Holdings at KKR's offices. As the only director of the company, Kravis was furiously busy. He proposed eighteen resolutions—covering everything from the official corporate seal to the company's role in the Houdaille buyout. He wrote down each resolution, and approved them all, by a unanimous 1–0 vote. A few days later, Kravis did the same thing for HH Acquisition.

Later that spring, Kravis conducted business with himself in an even more bizarre fashion. KKR's lawyers discovered a minor drafting error in an agreement between Houdaille Associates and HH Holdings. The only remedy was for Henry Kravis, the general partner of Houdaille Associates, to write a letter to himself as president of HH Holdings, asking for permission to change the relevant clause. "Accepted and agreed to,"

Kravis wrote back, in perhaps the only peaceful moment in all the negotiations.

Eventually, Dayan's resistance wore down. As much as KKR's acquisition unsettled him, his mandate was only to make sure that the buyout was legal, properly documented, attractive to shareholders, and designed so that Houdaille's directors wouldn't face any legal risks. KKR eventually passed all of those tests. Besides, KKR's financing of the acquisition was being expanded by about $6 million to include fees for everyone. Goldman, Sachs would collect $3.4 million; various lawyers, led by Cadwalader's team, would collect $1.6 million; and KKR would collect $1 million.* As the acquisition reached its final stages, all parties retreated to a rationale that would be heard over and over in the giant takeover battles to come. They were doing what was best for shareholders. Their big fees reflected that. As long as the acquisition was structured legally and produced a big payout for shareholders, this line of reasoning went, the acquisition was good.

By late March 1979, only one party still could block KKR's acquisition of Houdaille: the U.S. government. Any purchase of a publicly traded company, especially a big one, must be reviewed by the chief stock-market regulator, the Securities and Exchange Commission. And if Rodney Dayan had been dubious about KKR's plans, the SEC was outright incredulous. V. J. Lavernoich, a branch chief at the SEC in Washington, began bombarding Houdaille's Cadwalader lawyers with directives. Houdaille needed to tell shareholders much more about the reasons for the acquisition, he ordered. It needed to disclose its 1979 projections and make clear how speculative they were. Soon afterward, the SEC ordered KKR to construct a detailed mural showing exactly how HH Holdings and all the other shell companies functioned. That would be stapled into the midst of the dry financial language of the prospectus, as a centerfold of sorts. A few days later, KKR's lawyers produced an absurdly intricate diagram. Boxes, arrows, and dotted lines careened around the page in Rube Goldberg complexity. Herdrich found the chart uproariously funny. He ordered a three-foot-wide jumbo edition of the chart for his office and coined a new name for it

---

*KKR's belated proposal that it, too, collect a fee was met with disbelief and indignation on the part of Houdaille's top management. Kohlberg started by proposing that KKR collect $3 million, its highest fee ever. Saltarelli was furious. "I kept saying: Goddamn it, you're the buyers," Saltarelli later recalled. "Why should you get a fee?" Kohlberg, according to Saltarelli, repeatedly replied: "No, I'm the investment banker." After an hour of dickering—which some observers thought might cause the whole buyout to collapse—Kohlberg agreed to scale down KKR's fee to $1 million. Those negotiations, Saltarelli later recalled, were "the toughest hour I've had in my life."

each week. "This is the control room of the Three Mile Island nuclear plant," he told visitors at one point.

Niggling as the SEC's review seemed at the time, the government actually did nothing to change the buyout itself. The SEC's emphasis was entirely on increased financial disclosure, on the belief once expressed by Louis Brandeis that "sunshine is the best disinfectant." The SEC wanted the final prospectus to serve shareholders' interest, which it did. There wasn't any mechanism for the government to intercede on behalf of any other parties affected by the buyout.

Having survived all challenges, Houdaille in April 1979 mailed out its offering document to shareholders, awaiting the inevitable yes votes that would make shareholders wealthy. Just two and a half years after being tossed out of Bear, Stearns, the partners of Kohlberg Kravis Roberts & Co. had bought their first Fortune 500 company, borrowing huge sums to do so.

Houdaille itself faltered in the years following KKR's buyout. The earnings projections that Kravis and Herdrich had sketched out so confidently proved way off track. Houdaille's car-bumper business was uncompetitive and had to be closed. The company's machine-tool operations, instead of boosting operating profit 10 percent per year, were hammered by Yamazaki and other rising Japanese rivals. Houdaille's overall earnings from 1980 to 1984 were barely half what KKR had forecast. Only the big debt bills, quarter after quarter, amounted to exactly what KKR had predicted. To make ends meet, Houdaille sold off many smaller divisions and diversified with the acquisition of a sealant and packaging manufacturer. Kohlberg had warned early on that it would be tough for Houdaille's managers to operate with big debts—and he had been right.

On Wall Street, though, Houdaille's travails didn't matter. Financially speaking, the KKR buyout "worked." It had produced big capital gains for Houdaille's old shareholders when they sold their stock at $40 a share. It subsequently produced a lot of interest income for banks and insurance companies that had lent money to finance KKR's acquisition. Whatever its operating troubles, Houdaille never missed an interest payment. The buyout had even produced plump fees for lawyers, investment bankers, and other advisers. No one on Wall Street worried too much if the company was being vitiated by recession and debt. Instead, people in the financial community set out to do more buyouts.

From 1978 to 1982, a host of other buyout boutiques were formed, or stepped up their pursuit of acquisitions big enough to make a difference. Much like KKR, most of these firms consisted of a few ex–Wall Street deal-makers who quit large organizations, rented small offices, and named a tiny firm after themselves. Among these boutiques were Clayton & Dubilier; Forstmann Little & Co.; Adler & Shaykin; and Gibbons Green van Amerongen. Traveling a few steps behind KKR, all of these firms would soon gain the means with which to buy Fortune 500 companies, too.

Attracting the most attention for a few years was William E. Simon, the former Salomon Brothers partner and Treasury secretary, who founded Wesray Capital Corporation. In 1981, Simon's group bought a greeting-card company, Gibson Greetings, from RCA Corporation for $80 million, putting up just $1 million in equity capital and borrowing the rest of the purchase price. Within three years, Wesray sold stock in Gibson Greetings to the public at 290 times the price it had paid, producing a $290 million windfall for Simon and his fellow investors. That headline-making gain—coupled with KKR's relentless rise—turned heads on Wall Street.

In 1981, the first year that anyone bothered to keep track, some 99 buyouts were completed. That tally grew to 164 in 1982 and 230 in 1983. The dollar volume of buyouts climbed steadily, too. From $3.1 billion in 1981, total buyouts rose to $3.5 billion in 1982 and $4.5 billion in 1983. Overall, buyouts in the early 1980s accounted for just 5 to 10 percent of all U.S. takeovers. But this new type of acquisition was clearly on the rise.

As these high-debt acquisitions became more common, the circle of advisers that surrounded target companies became more amenable to KKR's way of doing business. After all, KKR's buyouts generated sizable fees for everyone. In 1981 Goldman, Sachs solicited KKR's help when a potential raider began acquiring stock in Marley Co., a maker of cooling towers. KKR made an initial buyout bid, increased it, and won control of Marley for $329 million. Goldman, Sachs pocketed a $300,000 fee.

Business leaders' attitudes toward debt did an about-face, switching to a radical new tolerance of big borrowings. Taking on more debt could cut taxes and boost a company's stock price, chief financial officers argued in a mid-1980s survey by *Institutional Investor* magazine, headlined "Learning to Love Leverage." The chief financial officer of Philip Morris said he wanted to make sure that the tobacco and food company wasn't "under-leveraged." If it were, he said, "I wouldn't be doing my job." The chief financial officer of Colt Industries added: "Lenders and shareholders are accustomed to a lot more leverage today. It's not a dirty word."

The Houdaille buyout itself, which had evoked scoffs of disbelief in the

Prudential boardroom in 1978, became the subject of a Harvard Business School case study in 1982. The Harvard presentation was flat and matter-of-fact; it didn't try to assess the cleverness or folly of the buyout technique. But by being written up as a Harvard case study—in any form—KKR's maneuverings in Houdaille acquired a new degree of legitimacy. In fact, in a 1982 fund-raising memo, KKR told corporate executives that its kind of buyout "is now an accepted and respectable alternative to merging with a large company." The choice of words was significant; Jerry Kohlberg and his two younger partners were tacitly acknowledging that until a few years earlier, high-debt buyouts hadn't been respectable.

On its own, KKR in the early 1980s accounted for at most five to seven buyouts a year. In the tough recession year of 1982, in fact, KKR didn't complete any buyouts. But KKR's market impact was far greater than the mere number of its deals. The Houdaille prospectus, for example, "became a best-seller in Wall Street and accounting circles," a leading investment banker recalled. Other deal-makers studied the deal and looked for ways to emulate it.

What's more, the KKR partners kept pursuing bigger buyouts than any of their competitors—giving their firm the most clout in dollar terms. In 1981, KKR accounted for 40 percent of all buyouts completed in dollar terms. All three KKR partners at the time seemed to believe that their firm should use its extra expertise and close relations with lenders to concentrate on the largest buyout that seemed feasible at the time. "That's where the opportunities are," Kohlberg told a friend from his undergraduate alma mater, Swarthmore College, in the early 1980s.

Again and again, the KKR partners found that the calculus of Houdaille could be applied in acquiring other manufacturing companies. First the KKR men would estimate a company's true earnings power—profit before interest and taxes—which invariably was much larger than the company's reported net income. Then they estimated how much money could be borrowed against that earnings stream. A big debt bill would help shelter operating profit from taxes; so would any depreciation maneuvers that Tom Hudson and his colleagues at Deloitte could devise. Usually, the KKR men preferred stagnant or slow-growing companies that made mundane products such as lawn-mower engines, plumbing fixtures, or paper cups. Such companies didn't require a lot of money for capital spending, thus allowing most cash flow to be channeled into debt service. They also had predictable earnings and little risk of technological obsolescence. "The more boring, the better," Kravis once remarked.

The drama for KKR wasn't in a company's operations; the drama was in the financing and pursuit of a deal. Each new financial structure glistened with a sterile beauty, far removed from the real-world implications of imposing so much debt on a company. Senior debt, subordinated debt, and other types of loans were tied together with an intricacy and cleverness much like that of a mathematician solving simultaneous equations or an engineer designing bridges.

For Roberts especially—the brightest, most private member of the initial KKR team—this financial engineering was the best part of the buyout business. Friends said they thought Roberts's idea of the perfect weekend was to sit by the side of his swimming pool in California, reading annual reports and looking for new companies that could be plunged into a high-debt world. On one occasion, flying across the Atlantic to watch Kohlberg's youngest son, Andy, play tennis at Wimbledon, Roberts asked the British Airways flight attendant for some stationery and began sketching out a capital structure for a new acquisition. While other passengers watched a movie or snoozed, Roberts took high-debt finance a little further than it had ever gone before. Once he got to London, Roberts called on the Kohlberg family and proudly, shyly showed Jerry Kohlberg the financing master plan he had just created. "George was very good at that," Kohlberg later observed.

With just a few deputies to help them on the numbers, the three KKR partners realized, they could stalk almost any company. Adding one or two aides, or "associates," a year, KKR increased its roster of deal-makers and internal accountants to all of eleven people in 1984, and to twenty people from 1987 onward. Nearly all the recruits were young men who joined KKR after working closely with the buyout firm at the law firms, banks, or securities houses that serviced KKR. But there was room for one older associate, too: Deloitte's Tom Hudson, who joined KKR in 1984 after he reached Deloitte's retirement age of sixty. What little hiring that KKR did was carried out almost entirely by Kravis and Roberts; Kohlberg argued for keeping KKR's payroll as small as possible. Even Kravis—an exuberant spotter of talent who periodically proposed expanding KKR a bit—got the message. Each time he did make a job offer, he solemnly assured the candidate: "You're the last guy we're going to hire."

There were two reasons why a firm so tiny could wield such clout. One involved human networks; the other, computer technology.

The leanness of KKR's own staff belied the huge amount of work that Kohlberg, Kravis, and Roberts contracted out to various allies. Again and again in the 1980s, the KKR men turned to Deloitte for accounting work, at times using as many as 200 accountants on a single project. At the end of the decade, in fact, Deloitte executives discovered that the buyout firm and the companies it owned were generating $80 million a year in billings, making KKR the accounting firm's largest worldwide client.

A similar story unfolded at two major law firms. In Los Angeles, Roberts retained Latham & Watkins to advise him on the buyouts he pursued. In New York, Kravis and Kohlberg turned repeatedly to Simpson Thacher & Bartlett for similar legal work. These alliances became cozy relationships for KKR, allowing the buyout firm to draw on dozens of lawyers any time it needed to. Latham & Watkins partner John McLoughlin became a regular investor in KKR's buyouts and set up trust funds for Roberts's children. Simpson Thacher partner Dick Beattie was offered a chance to become a KKR partner (he turned it down), a chance to invest in KKR deals (he accepted), and a business opportunity for his wife as well, catering the celebratory dinners at the end of KKR's acquisitions. When *Forbes* magazine in 1989 listed the 100 best-paid lawyers in America, McLoughlin ranked number 28 and Beattie was number 43. Each was earning more than $1 million a year.

As much as these human allies helped magnify KKR's clout, a breakthrough in computer technology provided the decisive advantage. In the 1970s, KKR couldn't rapidly stalk several companies at once, because its financial blueprints required weeks of calculations by hand. Then microchips came to Wall Street. In 1980, Herdrich stopped at a midtown Manhattan electronics store outside Grand Central Station to buy a toy "home computer" for one of his children. Eager to see if he could ring up a second purchase as well, the salesman asked Herdrich what line of work he was in. Finance, Herdrich replied. Quickly the salesman demonstrated a VisiCalc financial-analysis package, which would automatically make five-year financial projections using whatever annual growth rate a user cared to inject. If a 9-percent growth rate seemed too optimistic, within seconds VisiCalc could recalculate all the projections at, say, a 5-percent rate. Herdrich was enthralled. "I said: 'We've got to have these for work,' " Herdrich recalled. Herdrich's son got an Osborne home computer; KKR got its first Apple II.

All of a sudden, giant companies' finances could be picked apart in an afternoon. By 1982, KKR upgraded its office computers to IBM PCs. A few years later, the buyout firm acquired sophisticated *Lotus 1-2-3* and *Symphony* software that let its associates map out financial spreadsheets in a jiffy. Such numbers-crunching capacity was hardly unique to KKR. *The*

Wall Street Journal began running advertisements for $99 "LBO software packages" that let even a neophyte race through the types of calculations that had once taken Herdrich and Kravis weeks to carry out. In the decade after the Houdaille deal, the personal computer accomplished for Wall Street's buyout boutiques what the advent of gunpowder did for Mongol warriors. With the right financial plan, a small buyout firm could wield considerable power. And if the buyout firm's partners knew how to charm and cajole money from a wide range of allies—as Roberts, Kravis, and Kohlberg did—then their power became even more vast.

3
In Pursuit of Profits

Throughout KKR's early years, Jerry Kohlberg and George Roberts kept visiting the Pacific Northwest as they prospected for business. Kohlberg's fondness for the region dated back to the early 1950s, when, fresh out of law school, he had spent a year in Portland, Oregon, clerking for a renowned liberal judge, Gus Solomon. For the next thirty-five years, Kohlberg returned repeatedly to Oregon to visit Solomon, whom he regarded first as a mentor and then as a very dear friend. On many of the visits, Kohlberg took time to cultivate local bankers, lawyers, and politicians. "I have a number of business investments and a lot of wonderful friends here," Kohlberg declared in 1989, in one of his many interviews with the Portland *Oregonian*. "I love Portland."

Roberts was attracted to Oregon and Washington State purely because it was untrammeled acquisition territory. In 1975, he tried to negotiate the buyout of a Portland brewery, Blitz-Weinhard, only to lose out at the last moment when the company's management decided it could finance its own buyout without his help. Disappointed at his loss, Roberts nonetheless kept coming back to the Pacific Northwest in pursuit of fresh deals. In 1977 he carried out the buyout of U.S. Natural Resources, a small Portland, Oregon, conglomerate. In 1979, Roberts and Kohlberg tried—and failed—to buy a maker of fork-lift trucks in Oregon; the two men successfully negotiated a small timber acquisition in Washington State a few months later.

Starting in early 1980, Kohlberg began pursuing the Oregon company that he wanted to acquire most of all. It was Fred Meyer Inc., a supermarket and department-store chain with almost $1 billion a year in sales. For 56 years, the company had been run by its feisty founder, Fred G. Meyer. He had died, however, in 1978 at the age of ninety-two. Since that time, the Fred Meyer company had been vulnerable to a takeover. Some 23 percent of the company's stock was held by the dead founder's estate. Meyer had hoped his estate would never have to sell his stock, but within two years of his death, disputes had broken out among the estate's four trustees about whether their legal obligation to maximize the trust's value might require them to sell the stock and diversify.

The two-year conquest of the Fred Meyer company proved to be a memorable deal for KKR for two reasons. First, it became the high-water mark in Kohlberg's career—the deal in which he most effectively combined persistence, self-effacement, and a professed desire to help others. When KKR finally bought Fred Meyer in December 1981 for $425 million, Kohlberg had accomplished the impossible. He had seized control of a major business after countless rebuffs, made a lot of money for himself, and yet been hailed at the end of the deal as a savior of the company.

Just as important, the Fred Meyer deal brought a crucial financial ally into KKR's fold: the Oregon state pension fund. Some 40 percent of the money that KKR needed for the Fred Meyer buyout was provided by the Oregon fund, nearly 100 times the amount of money that Kohlberg, Kravis, and Roberts themselves invested in the deal. Yet the state pension plan obligingly took a backseat to the KKR deal-makers, letting them take control of Fred Meyer's board and claim a big slice of Oregon's own profits from part-ownership of the company. Oregon's investment in Fred Meyer ultimately proved to be quite a good money-maker for the state. The terms that KKR negotiated with Oregon, however, also allowed Kohlberg, Kravis, and Roberts to make spectacular profits for themselves.

Over the next five years, pension funds in nearly a dozen other states followed Oregon's example and agreed to help bankroll KKR's deals. Civil servants who watched over the retirement savings of teachers, fire fighters, toll collectors, and other state employees put billions of dollars at KKR's disposal. Associating with the buyout firm provided these civil servants with an unbeatable mix of profits and thrills. Even after the KKR executives collected hefty management fees, the state pension funds' investments earned 40 to 50 percent a year for much of the 1980s—triple the returns from ordinary stocks during a mighty bull market. The chief reason for those gains: KKR's rampant use of debt. For just a modest down payment, the pension funds and other investors led by KKR acquired control of one big company after another. As the debt was paid off and the economy did well, the value of the owners' stakes soared—in much the same way that a homeowner with a big mortgage can do very well in a time of rising property prices.

Investing pension money with KKR also provided civil servants with a ticket into a glamorous new world. They didn't need to be mere spectators in Wall Street's biggest, most exciting takeover battles. By allying themselves with KKR, the Walter Mitty types who ran big state pension funds could feel that they were players, too. Roberts, Kravis, and Kohlberg very shrewdly cultivated this "fan club," playing tennis with their pension fund backers, sending them confidential briefing books, and inviting them to private two-day conferences at elegant hotels. At those sessions, modestly paid civil servants got the chance to rub shoulders with KKR's founders, and to address them as "Jerry" and "Henry" and "George."

Drawn closest to KKR was Roger Meier, the long-time chairman of the Oregon Investment Council. In conversations about the buyout firm, Meier sometimes would say "we," then pause, correct himself, and say: "I mean, KKR." In 1983, Meier joined the board of a KKR-controlled company, Norris Industries, based in Los Angeles. Several times a year, right before or after board meetings, Roberts and Meier played doubles tennis matches at the plush Beverly Hills Hotel, pairing up with the hotel pro, former Wimbledon champion Alex Olmedo. "It was delightful," Meier later recalled. "Here was a little yokel from Portland, Oregon, operating with really some pretty fantastic high fliers. I was pretty impressed."

Investing with KKR, Meier once said, was "almost like giving George a blank check."

Yet managing other people's money brought heavy obligations upon the KKR executives, which they took quite seriously. Making money for their passive pension fund investors was how the KKR men proved their virtue, and satisfied some very human desires to be liked and respected. By the early 1980s, the KKR executives had become multimillionaires themselves, earning money far faster than they could spend it. By choosing to see themselves as "fiduciaries" for the pension savings of 500,000 or more state employees across the United States, the KKR executives created a justification—even an obligation—to earn money even faster.

From the moment that Kohlberg Kravis Roberts & Co. was founded in 1976, its executives knew they wanted passive co-owners to help finance their acquisitions. This was partly out of habit; the early Bear, Stearns deals had been arranged that way. In addition, a lack of cash forced the KKR partners to look outside. The buyout firm's startup capital consisted of just $100,000 from Kohlberg and $10,000 each from Kravis and Roberts—hardly enough to do more than pay the rent and hire a secretary or two. In the spring of 1976, therefore, all three men set out to raise a $10 million buyout fund from banks, insurance companies, and other institutional investors. Their first effort flopped. Only one candidate, Pittsburgh venture capitalist Henry Hillman, agreed to sign on. Everyone else regarded the fledgling buyout firm as too unproven and risky.

Undaunted, Kravis and Roberts began a second search in the summer of 1976. This time they focused on rich people, looking for five to ten outsiders willing to make money available in a new pool called KKR Partners. These investors were asked to chip in $50,000 a year to meet the buyout firm's expenses. In return, these investors would become limited partners in the investment activities of KKR, stepping in as passive co-owners of any companies that the general partners of KKR—Kravis, Roberts, and Kohlberg—decided to buy in the future.

When KKR Partners formally took shape, it felt like family to the KKR executives—and in part, it was. The first investors included Kravis's father and one of Kohlberg's wealthy Scheuer cousins, as well as Hillman, First Chicago Corporation's venture capital group, and four other individual backers. Investing family money carried with it heavy responsibilities not to make mistakes. Henry Kravis remembers an upbeat message from his father, Ray, who told him: "I'm one hundred percent behind you. I left a big company and started my own business when I was your age." But Ray Kravis's version of the story suggests that a sterner family dynamic was at work, too. Every father-to-son loan within the Kravis family had been paid back up to that point. "That's the way it should be," Ray Kravis later said. "I don't care how much money you make. It shows your character. If you owe something, you want to pay it back."

Quickly, KKR's buying appetite exceeded the resources of its first seven backers. When one early backer, Chicago drug company executive William Graham, got his fourth request for cash within a year, he called up Kravis in late 1977 and told him: "Henry, you're going to bankrupt me." Graham was joking; he was glad that KKR brought him deals in which to invest. But Graham also was trying to tell Kravis: "If you plan to make so many acquisitions, find investors with deeper pockets." The message registered.

In 1978 Kravis, Roberts, and Kohlberg began a second attempt to recruit institutional investors. This time the KKR men succeeded in raising a $30 million fund that could be spent on whatever acquisitions they selected over the next twelve years. Such "blind pool" arrangements were standard in venture capital and oil-and-gas investing, as institutional investors entrusted pools of cash to specialist managers and let the experts decide how the money should be invested. Blind pools for buyouts were a new idea, but KKR's track record had grown sufficiently that insurers such as Allstate and Teachers Insurance agreed to support the project. Venture capital subsidiaries of major banks, including Citicorp, Continental Illinois, and Security Pacific, also joined in. From that point onward, institutional backers would be the major outside investors with KKR.*

One of those 1978 investors, John Hines of Continental Illinois, later recalled that when Kravis and Kohlberg called on him, the two dealmakers spent hours talking not just about how they did business, but about their personal values, too. The soft-sell approach worked. When Hines was deciding whether to bankroll KKR, he was impressed by Kravis's and Kohlberg's explanations of their criteria for picking buyout candidates, and their projections of potential profits and risks—but more important, Hines liked what he saw of their character. "They were big thinkers," Hines recalled. "Extremely precise. Logically oriented. They weren't just financiers. There are a lot of jerk financiers in the world. What they sold, and don't ever kid yourself, was themselves."

As much as the $30 million buyout fund enhanced KKR's scope, it became more than half-depleted after the Houdaille acquisition was completed in May 1979. To replenish their funds, the KKR executives once again called on banks and insurance companies in 1980, raising a $75 million fund. That provided KKR with the ownership capital for a half dozen more buyouts, chiefly of midsize manufacturing companies. Among them were Rotor Tool, PT Components (a maker of car transmissions), and Lily-Tulip (a maker of paper cups.)

Then came the pursuit of a more ambitious buyout: the Fred Meyer

---

*KKR Partners has continued to operate on a small scale ever since, however, as has a second such entity, KKR Partners II. These two partnerships have become little-known conduits for friends and business allies of Kravis and Roberts who want to invest $50,000 to $250,000 with the buyout firm, rather than the much larger sums that institutional investors put up.

company in Oregon. Kohlberg at the outset was an unwelcome intruder, unable to win even a face-to-face meeting with the company's chief executive, Oran Robertson. "We had made money and had nothing but rising quarterly earnings," Robertson later recalled. "So why in the hell should we sell the company?" On one occasion when Kohlberg showed up at the company's offices, Robertson ordered him to leave.

Over and over, though, Kohlberg portrayed himself as a selfless public servant, seeking to further everyone else's well-being. His first sign of headway came with the trustees of Fred G. Meyer's estate, two of whom were at odds with the others. "There is a great deal of clashing of interests here," Kohlberg told trustees in a December 1980 meeting in Portland. "I would like to feel that I could restore a healing influence. Our interest in the Fred Meyer company can be good for you and good for the management and for Portland," Kohlberg added.

Each time Kohlberg came to Portland in 1981, he repeated that message of peace to trustees, to advisers to the company, and to chief executive Robertson. One by one, Kohlberg won them over—especially after an unexpected French suitor, Carrefours S.A., made a hostile bid for the Fred Meyer company in June 1981. At that point, directors and management had to choose between KKR and an unfriendly bidder. Suddenly KKR's offer, with its implicit promise to keep top management in place, looked very good.

On 25 August 1981, Kohlberg finally won what he wanted: an acquisition agreement with the retailer's directors and top management, allowing KKR to snap up the Fred Meyer company for $425 million. For KKR, that meant riches and power galore. The buyout firm collected a $4 million investment banking fee, its biggest to date. All three KKR partners were vaulted onto the retailer's board of directors, with Kohlberg gaining the title of vice chairman. And the KKR executives, who invested less than $2 million of their own money in the acquisition, became entitled to a hefty slice of future profits from the ownership of Fred Meyer.

Yet Kohlberg never bragged publicly about what a good deal he had arranged for himself. Years later, one of the trustees of the Meyer estate, Gerry Pratt, smiled at his recollection of how unselfish Kohlberg had seemed while wooing him. "Jerry when he wants to has this warm, personal, intimate side," Pratt commented. "He's anxious that people recognize the benefits of the deal to all parties. He wants to bring in everyone that has a part. He has this soft voice that makes people listen carefully. It implies an intimacy." At their first breakfast meetings in 1980, the usually jaded Pratt was won over right away. Asked why, Pratt replied: "Jerry did it with his idealism."

While Kohlberg soothed the trustees and management at Fred Meyer, Roberts took care of the money. KKR needed to borrow more than $300 million for this buyout, and line up another $100 million from passive investors who, alongside the KKR executives, would share in the owner-ship of the company after the buyout. Interest rates in mid-1981 had climbed to 15 percent or more—the highest levels since the 1940s. Arranging loans of any kind, let alone for a proposition as risky as a leveraged buyout, was extremely difficult. Nonetheless, Roberts devised an ingenious capital structure in which Fred Meyer's real-estate holdings were broken off into a separate company, which could borrow mortgage money on better terms than the retailer itself could command. Pitching this borrowing plan to KKR's traditional financial backers on the East Coast, Roberts coaxed forth half the money that KKR needed from three major banks and Metropolitan Life Insurance Co.

The biggest lender for the Fred Meyer buyout proved to be in Oregon itself, just an hour's drive south of Fred Meyer's Portland headquarters. It was the Oregon public employees' pension system, based in the state capital, Salem. Roberts approached the Oregon pension plan with a potent set of choices. It could make mortgage loans at 18-percent interest for $100 million; it could invest another $50 million in various partner-ships that would pay off well if Fred Meyer thrived after the buyout; and Oregon could become a part-owner of the retailer, keeping the company's ownership in the state and preventing the upheaval that might occur if a French buyer took over. After several months of internal debate, pension system executives provided the full $178 million that Roberts wanted for the Fred Meyer buyout—the biggest single investment that the Oregon pension plan had ever made in any company.

In the process, Roberts made a friend for life in Roger Meier, the top official overseeing the pension plan. Meier's background was in retailing; his forebears had founded the Meier & Frank department store in Port-land. Meier's own retailing career had come to an end after the St. Louis–based May Co. acquired Meier & Frank in 1966. Well connected politically in Oregon, Meier in 1970 had landed an unpaid part-time job as chairman of the Oregon Investment Council, where he scouted for top-flight investment managers to handle the state's pension money. "It was the kind of thing that absolutely thrilled me, working with money managers," Meier later said. "With the state of Oregon behind me, I could attract the biggest people in the world."

Roberts, in particular, became one of Meier's favorites. Meier liked the way Roberts dressed: elegantly. He found Roberts's height appealing: both men were a bit shorter than average. And Meier especially liked the way Roberts presented a financial investment. "He was exceptionally quick with numbers," Meier recalled. "He could listen. He wouldn't talk. Then he would ask a very incisive question." Quickly, Meier embraced Roberts as a friend and a savvy financier.

As word of the Oregon pension system's plans to bankroll KKR's buyout became public, Meier drew plenty of flak for investing so much of the state's pension money—8 percent of all assets—in such an offbeat transaction. Members of Oregon's business elite, who bumped into Meier at Portland's Arlington Club, berated him about the $178 million of state money that he was putting at risk, saying: "Roger, how could you do that?" In a private memo to the state treasurer, deputy treasurer Fred Hanson in the summer of 1981 called the investment "too risky." Hanson also wrote: "I am convinced this type of deal would never be contemplated . . . if it did not involve people Roger knows personally."

But Meier didn't budge an inch. As he and full-time investment staff members in the Oregon pension system studied the Fred Meyer buyout in detail, they grew convinced that KKR's financing plan was sound. What's more, Meier believed that by financing the buyout, the Oregon pension system was helping a hometown company stand tall against an unwelcome French raider. A few years later, Meier's investment judgment was vindicated. The Fred Meyer company was able to go public again at an attractive price, and Oregon's investment had more than doubled in value.

Just a few months after the Fred Meyer buyout was completed, Roberts came back to Oregon with another investment proposition for Meier and his state pension fund. KKR was about to raise another blind pool for its buyout investing. This time, though, Roberts and his KKR colleagues planned to widen their list of backers significantly beyond insurance companies and venture capital departments. They wanted state pension funds to help bankroll a blind pool that could be as big as $300 million.

For pension funds, the new buyout fund looked lusciously appealing. Changes in many states' laws in 1980 and 1981 had allowed public-employee pension funds to broaden greatly their investment mix beyond bonds and safe, dividend-paying stocks. State investment managers, convinced that a diversified portfolio could provide high returns while reducing the risks involved in any single investment, began looking for new areas in which to put their money. Once again, KKR showed up at exactly the right time. In an offering memorandum circulated among pension funds in early 1982, KKR disclosed that it had begun selling the companies acquired in buyouts a few years earlier. In several cases, the value of the original investors' stock in the buyout companies had soared in value by eleven to twenty times. The KKR men didn't make any promises that this sort of spectacular payoff would continue. In muted, conservative language, however, the buyout firm dangled the possibility that more such whopping payoffs might lie ahead.

Oregon was the first state to answer KKR's new call for cash. In early 1982, the Oregon Investment Council approved a request by Roberts that the state pledge $25 million to KKR's new buyout fund.

A few weeks later, Roberts took his fund-raising appeal to Washington State. The state's investment chief, John Hitchman, had heard from his colleagues in Oregon that KKR had a good story to tell, so he set up a private meeting with Roberts. "I just instantly liked him on a personal basis," Hitchman later recalled, "as well as having an enormous regard for his professional abilities." Soon after Roberts won his $25 million commitment from Oregon, he appeared in Seattle seeking an encore. "We've drummed people out of that boardroom," Hitchman later recalled. "But George was a tour de force. He spoke extremely well. He never left any sentences unfinished or changed his train of thought halfway through. There was no sense of anxiety to his voice. His knowledge of the nitty-gritty was just incredible." Most of all, Hitchman recalled, Roberts "created a calm over everyone." At the end of the meeting, board members voted to give KKR $10 million. Then they pressed their business cards upon Roberts like star-struck fans, asking him to call them anytime—even if it was just to chat about the economy.

While Roberts covered the western United States in 1982, Kravis handled the East. He pitched buyout investing to Michigan's pension chief, William Amerman, and got him to pledge money. Kravis also signed on one of America's most prestigious institutional investors, the endowment fund of Harvard University. And he began what would be a series of long-shot marketing trips to Europe and the Mideast over the next few years, seeking buyout fund investors wherever they might be. Except for a few small English additions, Kravis struck out abroad. At one stage, he thought Kuwait was about to invest with KKR—a development that would have contributed to an even more meteoric ascent by the buyout firm—but after a series of meetings with Kuwaitis as senior as the crown prince, Kravis had to settle for a "not now" that meant "no."

Kohlberg took a backseat in KKR's fund-raising efforts from 1982 onward. He had put up the bulk of KKR's capital in 1976, but he didn't have nearly the appetite for cold-calling on new investors that Roberts had, nor the tolerance for endless travel that Kravis had. Still, Kohlberg added a few investors, including Metropolitan Life Insurance, some Canadian banks, and the endowment of his alma mater, Swarthmore College. Kohlberg also helped clinch investments by several big U.S. banks after Kravis or Roberts had done most of the prospecting. "Jerry was the gray-haired guy who came in and gave everyone confidence," recalled John Canning, the buyout investing chief at a major Chicago bank, First Chicago Corporation.

Few investors at the time noticed the extent to which KKR's executives assured themselves of making millions—no matter how their buyout investments fared—because of the fee schedule imposed in the 1982 fund. In percentage terms, that schedule largely paralleled the rates that KKR had set in its earlier 1978 and 1980 funds. In absolute dollar amounts, however, KKR had enacted a fee schedule so daring, and so important as a source of future revenue for the buyout firm itself, that it merits a moment's study.

In essence, the KKR executives had assured themselves of three types of money-management fees, and a sizable cut of any profits that pension funds made on KKR investments. First the KKR executives charged their passive investors an annual management fee of $1\frac{1}{2}$ percent of funds committed, for the privilege of having KKR handle their cash and look for deals. For the 1982 fund, that amounted to $4.5 million a year, before KKR completed any work. Kravis, Roberts, and Kohlberg had a second source of fees: the typical 1 percent of each acquisition's price that they collected for themselves. On the $435 million Fred Meyer deal, that had amounted to $4 million. And once the KKR executives acquired a company, they collected either a "monitoring fee" of as much as $500,000 a year, or annual directors' fees of $25,000 or more each.

In a still larger source of wealth, the KKR executives laid claim to 20 percent of any investment gains ultimately achieved from buyouts by their passive investors. Such 20 percent "carried interests," as they were known, were standard fees for venture capital and oil-and-gas investment pools. Those funds typically were $50 million or less, however, and the sponsors of those funds seldom built giant fortunes from their 20 percent winnings. The KKR executives, with their ever-growing buyout funds, were in line to become enormously wealthy by handling other people's money instead of risking their own. Of the $316 million that KKR raised in its 1982 buyout fund, just $5 million came from Kravis, Roberts, and Kohlberg themselves. From this point onward, the KKR partners' own direct investments in the buyouts that they arranged became increasingly minuscule. On some of KKR's later buyouts, the firm's partners would contribute as little as one one-thousandth of the total purchase price themselves, yet lay claim to fees and slices of other people's profits that topped $200 million.

As comfortable as KKR's own arrangements were, the buyout firm's reputation was nearly broken by the deep recession of 1982. Much of the heavy-industry manufacturing sector of the U.S. economy experienced its toughest times since the Great Depression of the 1930s. Companies with conservative balance sheets, such as Ford Motor, were forced to eliminate their dividends as losses mounted. Companies with big debt loads—such as the ones that KKR had bought—faced even tougher times. Fred Meyer's financial performance stayed fairly close to its projected results, but other businesses, such as Lily-Tulip and PT Components, skidded into serious financial difficulties. At one point, bank lenders to both those companies nearly foreclosed, a step that would have pushed KKR out of its cherished position as the controlling owner of these companies.

Just barely, the KKR-controlled companies managed to avoid disaster. At both Lily-Tulip and PT Components, the KKR executives were forced to replace the companies' chief executives, dropping longtime managers in favor of new outsiders who could cut costs and stop the businesses from hemorrhaging further. Years later, Kravis said one of his proudest accomplishments was to have survived the 1982 recession without losing any money for his limited partner investors. Wooing chief executives was a nice prelude to KKR's buyouts—but the top priority was to make money and protect the passive investors' cash, even if it meant firing a chief executive or two.

As the economy picked up in 1983, the KKR executives ended a year of cautious economy watching and began carrying out new buyouts again. In 1983 and early 1984, the firm carried out six more buyouts with the money from its 1982 buyout fund, acquiring businesses that ranged from Golden West Broadcasting in Los Angeles to soft-drink bottler Wometco Enterprises in Florida. Inevitably, though, the $316 million "Big Fund" of 1982 proved too puny once again. "We were always running out of money," recalled Paul Raether, a onetime Wall Street investment banker who joined KKR as an associate in 1981. Larger and larger companies were coming into buying range, prompting Roberts and Kravis to talk every year or two about going out to raise the ultimate Big Fund. A $980 million fund followed in 1984, and then a $1.8 billion fund in 1986.

Other buyout specialists began hunting for pension backers, too. A few, such as Forstmann Little, built up circles of investors that were nearly as formidable as KKR's, but most others couldn't keep pace. "We were always a year or two behind KKR," recalled one competitor, Leonard Green of the buyout firm Gibbons Green van Amerongen & Co. In delicate ways, the KKR men kicked away any rivals creeping up on them. Ignore our competitors, the KKR men would tell pension chiefs in Oregon, Washington, and other important states. Stick with us. The two most loyal KKR backers, Oregon's Meier and Washington's Hitchman, decided to do just that. "We just said no to everyone else," Hitchman later said. In the profitable but high-risk buyout business, Hitchman decided, "It comes down to what horse you ride. And we had every confidence in the [KKR] guys."

At times, KKR could build on its own success. In the mid-1980s, Kravis met New York State controller Edward Regan for breakfast in Manhattan to try to interest him in bankrolling KKR's buyout funds. "He was very nervous because he didn't understand leveraged buyouts," Kravis recalled. "He didn't want to be the only guy." But Kravis assured Regan that he would have good company. When Regan said he wanted to ask around about KKR, Kravis ticked off the participation of Michigan, Oregon, and Washington, and concluded: "Fine. Call some of these other states if you want." Before long, Regan signed on with KKR, too.

For every yes, though, the KKR executives heard quite a few nos from pension chiefs who were troubled by the very nature of the buyout business. "I cannot condone activities that divert so much time and energy from investments that create new jobs and opportunities," New York City comptroller Harrison Goldin told a magazine interviewer in the midst of one buyout flurry. His city's $25 billion in pension funds would have been a prime investor prospect for KKR, but Goldin dismissed buyouts as a financial activity that simply served to "reshuffle chairs." In his eye, pension fund managers should "invest in the American economy" rather than support financial profiteering.

Corporate pension fund chiefs generally stayed away from KKR's buyout funds for similar reasons. Companies such as AT&T, General Motors, and the like had vast, multibillion-dollar pension plans for their workers, with funds spread across stocks, bonds, venture capital, and other investments. Their pension managers were charged with investing the money "prudently" and achieving the best returns possible. Repeatedly, the KKR executives tried to recruit big corporate pension funds to invest with them. With a few exceptions, such as the pension funds of Coca-Cola, Hughes Aircraft, and Avon, they failed. Corporate pension chiefs looked at the investment profit record that KKR was showing and said it was very good. But, they explained, buyout investing didn't fit their investment strategy. It was an oblique brush-off that reflected concern in the corporate world that—as Goldin had put it—buyouts were a money-making technique that didn't help the economy.

For the cadre of loyal KKR backers, however, the notion that buyout investing could be fabulously profitable without directly producing anything was actually seen as a virtue, not a shortcoming. As the U.S. economy reached the later stages of industrialization, Washington state pension chief John Hitchman once argued, there simply weren't that many opportunities for new companies or industries to emerge. "All the squares on the Monopoly board have been taken," he remarked. That put added pressure on Hitchman, whose job was to find the best investments possible for his state's $10 billion pension fund. His duty, as he saw it, was to increase retirement savings and lessen the pension system's tax burden on the state. If Roberts, Kravis, and Kohlberg had figured out a way to achieve eye-popping profits without rapid industrial growth, that was all the more impressive in Hitchman's eyes.

"If you had to name, on the fingers of one hand, the people who have had the greatest influence on U.S. capitalism in the second half of the twentieth century," Hitchman asserted in a 1989 interview, "those three guys are there."

As KKR commanded ever bigger pools of money from its pension fund backers, the fees that personally accrued to Kravis, Roberts, and Kohlberg reached stunning levels. The 1½ percent annual management fee, which amounted to $4.5 million a year for the 1982 fund, swelled to $27 million for the 1986 fund. The buyout firm's yearly influx of takeover fees approached $100 million in the peak years of the 1980s takeover boom. Meanwhile, thanks to the ready cash provided by various lenders and limited partner investors, the KKR executives needed to ante up hardly any of their own cash to control a company.

"It's very Machiavellian," one competing investment banker remarked, his voice filled with awe and horror. "It's as if KKR set up its limited partnerships according to the guiding principle of: 'How do we make tons of money with almost no risk to ourselves?'"

Most of KKR's investors didn't make fees an issue. They were soothed both by the buyout firm's profit record and by the gracious ways of the

KKR executives. At least one or two times a year, KKR sold one of its buyout companies at a big gain or took it public at a substantial premium to the price that its buyout fund investors had paid. In the years that KKR owned them, most of its buyout companies had paid down their debt quickly, while jacking up operating profits. A relentless bull market had made almost any company more valuable with the passage of time. When KKR chose to sell one of the companies it had acquired, the passive investors generally collected profits on their money of 40 to 50 percent a year, even after KKR's fees.

Just as important, Kravis, Roberts, and their colleagues charmed almost all their limited partners, big and small, with unfailing courtesies. "George Roberts will return a phone call as quickly as anyone," Chicago bank investor John Canning once remarked. "Even if he's in Europe, I'll get a call as soon as he gets his messages. Henry doesn't get back quite as quickly, but he will take all the time in the world on a call. He'll never rush; he'll talk about whatever you want to talk about." That counted for a lot in Canning's eyes. For many people on Wall Street, rudeness was a way to show power. For the KKR executives, politeness was a way to gain power.

When officials of the Montana state pension fund said at the peak of KKR's money-raising prowess that they might want to invest a few million dollars in buyouts, KKR rolled out a top-flight team, sending Roberts and two junior colleagues to Whitefish, Montana, for a briefing. "There's no doubt our [money] is a drop in the bucket," Montana investment chief James Penner later observed. "But they spent an hour and a half taking our questions." When the Montana officials wanted an update from KKR about its biggest investments later on, KKR flew out another of its partners, just before a snowstorm. "We couldn't ask for better treatment," Penner said.

One of the main ways that KKR soothed its limited partners was at a mutual cheerleading session known as the annual investors' conference. Generally held at the Portman Hotel in San Francisco, the Helmsley Palace in New York, or an equally plush hotel in Los Angeles, these sessions formally were a review, for the passive investors' benefit, of KKR's buyout holdings. A purely financial ethos dominated the meetings, as top managers of each buyout company delivered forty-five-minute speeches about the health and progress of KKR's portfolio. Speaker after speaker ran through details about operating profit, debt reduction, and the rising per-share value of a buyout company's equity. Attendees loved it. "They held wonderful investment meetings," recalled Continental Illinois's Hines. "Of all the groups I dealt with, theirs were the most informative. If you walked away and didn't get a feel for your investments, you had to be pretty stupid."

Friendly and approachable, the KKR executives won the hearts of their guests every spring. A young banker from Chase Manhattan was thrilled when Roberts walked up to him during a coffee break and softly asked: "Do you mind if I sit down and join you?" Kohlberg got his chance to be seen as the father figure of the firm—a role that he cherished. Taking the podium at the end of each spring gathering, he would sum up the conference, thank everyone for coming, and offer some broad thoughts about where the buyout business might be headed in the year to come.

As the best-known partner of KKR, Kravis basked the most in the admiration of this audience. At one banquet, Ray O'Keefe, the chairman of A. J. Industries, grew sleepy around dessert time and was tempted to head to his hotel room for a night's sleep. Stay a moment, his neighbor told him with a wink. "Watch Henry work the tables." Sure enough, Kravis rose from his seat and began wheeling from one investor to another, shaking hands with everyone he could. "Hey, good to see you!" Kravis enthused. "How's everything?" Pausing a few moments with each guest, Kravis looked them in the eye and immersed himself in their every concern. "When he does that," O'Keefe mused, "Henry makes you feel that you're the only person in the room that he's interested in."

Never on Wall Street had good manners paid off so resoundingly. When KKR's investment banking fees were added to its management fees, KKR executives by the late 1980s were clearing as much as $130 million a year in fees, even after deducting their own personal investments in acquired companies. Yet most of KKR's limited partner investors didn't want to change a thing.

One of the few limited partners who squawked about fees was Yale University endowment fund manager David Swenson—and he ran into an icy refusal by KKR to moderate its ways. Yale had invested about $15 million with the buyout firm in 1982 and 1984, and was considering investing more in 1986. The more Swenson looked at KKR's fee structure, however, the more upset he got. The fee arrangements were "insulting" and "outrageous" to limited partners, Swenson later said. "We don't want to be regarded as mullets, simply providing the money." At the very least, Swenson argued, KKR ought to split its investment banking fees with its limited partners. Otherwise, he said, Yale wouldn't invest any more money with the buyout firm.

Swenson got nowhere. Keeping all deal fees within KKR had been standard since day one, KKR associate Perry Golkin later explained. "That's not negotiable," Golkin said. The message to Swenson, who ultimately dropped out of the KKR funds, was: "If you're not interested, you don't have to invest."

KKR's crucial backers in Oregon and Washington weren't about to indulge in such carping. Asked about KKR's fees, James George, the day-to-day head of Oregon's pension investing, told an inquirer in 1989: "Our response is: Who cares? Let's look at the bottom line." KKR kept making money for Oregon, and that was what mattered most. Meier was even more lavish in his praise for KKR, at one point writing a tribute to the buyout firm that appeared in local newspapers under the headline: LET'S BUILD OREGON.

Meier's gee-whiz attitude toward KKR later made some Oregonians wonder if their pension chief had grown too close to the buyout firm.* Oregon, which had started with a $25 million pledge to KKR in 1982, committed $100 million to the 1984 fund and $200 million to the 1986 fund—jacking up its contribution eightfold in just four years. An even bigger commitment would follow in 1987.

In fact, Oregon's pension investments with KKR consistently proved to be financial winners. At the end of 1990, the $1.05 billion that Oregon had entrusted to the buyout firm over the prior decade had grown to $2.25 billion in cash and securities. Had Meier made bad investment decisions in return for personal favors, as happened with several other major investors who went into the junk-bond market, Oregon would have had a first-rate financial scandal on its hands; but as long as KKR's buyouts thrived, Meier's friendship with Roberts passed muster. In a warm tribute to Meier after he retired from the Oregon Investment Council in 1986, the *Oregonian* declared: "No one has a stronger claim to the title of: Taxpayer's Best Friend."

To be sure, values for almost anything—stocks, bonds, condo apartments, entire corporations—were rising briskly in the mid-1980s bull market. The big profits associated with buyout investing largely reflected the fact that anyone who bought with borrowed money got a bigger bang

---

*The most diligent prober was Portland *Oregonian* reporter Jim Long. He noted in 1989 that Meier, soon after retiring from the Oregon Investment Council in 1986, had personally bought stock in a KKR-controlled company, U.S. Natural Resources, at what appeared to be a bargain price. Attorneys for Meier said no improper favors were involved; Roberts added in an affidavit that Meier had paid the prevailing price at the time and was welcome to buy stock simply as "an astute professional investor." That explanation sufficed; in mid-1991, both the Oregon attorney general and an Oregon ethics panel cleared Meier of any charges of wrongdoing.

for their buck. As a mischievous exercise, Goldman, Sachs partner Leon Cooperman at one point devised on paper a crude variation on the principle of the leveraged buyout, involving taking out big loans to buy stocks.* For a few years, Cooperman pointed out, his method would have yielded annual profits of 74 percent, an even better showing than the returns that KKR's passive investors were collecting. In that context, Cooperman slyly suggested, KKR's profit record of about 60 percent a year didn't look so remarkable at all. Still, year after year, KKR was making money for its investors—as promised.

The way that KKR had arranged its fees, a huge potential existed for abuse of the limited partners' trust. The firm's executives wagered so little of their own money on any new buyout that, in most cases, KKR's fee income from a new buyout would greatly exceed what the firm's executives could possibly lose from their own investments if a buyout company went bankrupt. That created the danger that fee hunger, ego, miscalculation, or laziness could cause the buyout firm to squander its limited partners' money on outright foolish acquisitions, just to bring in new fees.

More than outsiders realized, though, the presence of the limited partners governed KKR's ambition. Of all the business relationships that Kravis and Roberts developed in their careers, the ones they were most proud of involved KKR's cheering section, the loyal boosters who shared the buyout firm's belief that the best way to run a company was the way that maximized shareholders' profits. This wasn't just a distant grouping of check-writers whom KKR could ignore if a deal or two went sour: they were Kravis's father and Roberts's lawyer and Kohlberg's cousin. They included new friends like Roger Meier, John Canning, and John Hitchman, who had made very clear to the KKR partners how much trust they had placed in the buyout firm. If KKR could nurture its reputation a little more with each deal, it could look forward to continued access to other people's cash, in one Big Fund after another. But it would take only a few acquisitions that turned into financial wipeouts, Kravis once remarked, "and we're out of business."

More than twenty times in the 1980s, the KKR executives came close to announcing a buyout bid, then backed away because they thought the acquisition might be too pricey. At times, the KKR executives were too timid, passing up buyouts, such as that of Borg-Warner Corporation, that

---

*Cooperman's method: Buy a cross section of the stock market, paying nine-tenths of the purchase price with borrowed money at a 15 percent interest rate. Then wait a few years, see how much the stock price has climbed, and tally up the profits on the one-tenth "equity" portion of the purchase price.

proved richly profitable for other buyers. At least as often, however, KKR's team shunned acquisitions of companies—such as Federated Department Stores, Southland Corporation, and Westpoint-Pepperell— that ultimately couldn't pay the buyout debts taken on by other buyers. A few years later, those companies ended up in bankruptcy proceedings.

Superstitious at times, Kravis declared entire industries off-limits if an early buyout in that field had gone sour. Trucking-company deals were taboo after one of his first deals at Bear, Stearns, the 1973 purchase of Eagle Motor Lines, proved to be a loser. Even more repugnant were shoe-company deals; everyone at KKR was scarred by stories about the tragedy of Cobblers and the suicide of its chief executive in 1972. When Raether at one stage proposed to look into a buyout of the Converse sneaker company, Kravis snapped: "You've got better things to do." Raether responded that he could visit Converse's headquarters in a quick day trip and wouldn't miss anything. Unswayed, Kravis sternly told him: "I don't care what you're working on. You've got better things to do."

Unaware of the intense psychological ties that linked KKR to its passive investors, a Wall Street investment banker, Dean Kehler, once made what he thought was a clever suggestion. "Why don't you get rid of the limited partners?" Kehler asked Raether and another KKR executive, Ted Ammon. "You can do smaller buyouts without a fund." That way, the KKR executives would put up all the equity themselves—and keep every nickel of profits. That technique was becoming popular for a lot of buyouts by the mid-1980s, including ones as large as the acquisition of Trans World Airlines by financier Carl Icahn. By relying so much on pension-fund backers, Kehler argued, KKR was repeatedly letting most of the profits from its deals slip through its fingers.

When Kravis and Roberts heard about Kehler's idea, though, it died. Roberts dismissed it for business reasons, arguing that the billions of dollars piled up in each buyout fund gave KKR an invincible edge in pursuing giant takeovers. He didn't want to jeopardize KKR's number-one position by operating on the smaller financial resources of its executives alone.

Kravis was even more opposed. "Our partners helped us when we were just getting started," he said at one point. "They were there when we needed them." Ready cash from KKR's passive investors had allowed him to get very rich at almost no risk to himself. The constant praise and support of KKR's limited partner investors met his needs for reassurance. This was much too good an arrangement to forfeit.

4
How to Talk to Banks

Armed with their nucleus of pension money, the KKR partners from the early 1980s onward sought giant loans with which to finance their buyouts. The first stop, invariably, was at the banks, for whom Kravis and Roberts quickly became dream clients. Their buyout firm appeared supremely creditworthy, yet constantly needed new loans. If KKR hadn't existed, America's largest banks would have been forced to invent it.

Everywhere else they looked in the early 1980s, bank lending officers saw trouble. For generations, their mission had been to finance worldwide industrial expansion, making the loans that built railroads, factories, fifty-story headquarters buildings, power plants, and pet rocks. But after the twin recessions of 1980 and 1982, the largest U.S. corporations stopped coming to banks for money. Financial deregulation made it cheaper for Ford or IBM to bypass banks and raise money by selling ninety-day commercial paper to money-market funds. Smaller U.S. manufacturers operated so far below capacity after the 1982 recession that they wouldn't need to build factories for a long time. And Third World lending—which had been a favorite of banks in the late 1970s—turned into a morass. First Mexico in August 1982, then Brazil and Argentina a few months later, declared that they were incapable of making timely payments on their debts.

Buyout lending didn't directly contribute one whit to economic growth, but it began to look very attractive to bankers anyway. Interest rates on buyout loans were a little higher than usual—and that meant extra profits for banks. Buyout firms such as KKR passed credit checks with high marks; they repaid their loans on time. Best of all, a new KKR deal needed to be financed every few months. Bankers scrambled to enter this wonderful new business, and then to build up their lending capacity. In 1981, bank loans to finance leveraged buyouts totaled at most $1.5 billion. Six years later, that figure had soared more than twentyfold, to $34.1 billion. Those loans were spread among hundreds of buyouts, but nearly 20 percent of them were originated by the premier buyout firm, KKR.

Starting in 1984, a banking evangelist for KKR came forth. It was the Los Angeles office of Bankers Trust Co., run by a street-smart veteran lender from New York, Ron Badie. First by chance and then by design, Badie and two of his top lieutenants, George Hartmann and Morgan St. John, grew close to KKR's San Francisco office. As executives at Bankers Trust's headquarters in New York began to see the profit potential of buyout lending, they encouraged Badie to regard KKR as the bank's most important corporate client, and attend to the firm's needs and desires as best he could. From 1982 to 1989, Bankers Trust lent more than $2 billion to KKR itself. Even more important, Bankers Trust corralled dozens of other banks into becoming giant lending syndicates that channeled tens of billions of dollars to KKR in record time. The reward for Bankers Trust: bragging rights, fat interest income, and the chance to earn fees as large as $20 million for organizing giant loans to KKR. As one Bankers Trust lender put it: "If anyone else is prepared to pay us as well as KKR, we're willing to have that kind of a relationship with them, too."

Just as the banks empowered KKR, so too did George Roberts and other KKR executives transform the banks. Better than anyone else in the 1980s era of easy credit, Roberts understood how to extract billions of dollars in a few weeks or even days from normally cautious bankers. KKR's assault on lending tradition began with the language that its executives used when dealing with banks. Most people feel intimidated when seeking a loan—whether to buy a car or a corporation. Bankers like to view potential borrowers with suspicion, asking for detailed financial disclosures and dallying a bit before deciding whether a borrower is sufficiently creditworthy. But Roberts never asked to borrow money. He always asked if his bankers could *raise* a loan for him. The slight difference in wording proved crucial. Suddenly Roberts controlled the situation. The bankers, even if they represented a giant institution a thousand times KKR's size, were the ones put to the test. "You can say that's smart salesmanship," observed John McLoughlin, the Latham & Watkins lawyer who worked on nearly all of KKR's big acquisitions. "But it's awfully hard to do it right."

To keep the upper hand with the banks, Roberts and Kravis worked very hard to be known as men of wealth and taste. They relocated offices several times in the early 1980s until KKR ended up with some of the choicest real estate in America: the forty-fifth floor of 101 California Street in San Francisco and the forty-second floor of 9 West Fifty-seventh Street in Manhattan. Both offices featured breathtaking views of their respective cities. Inside, Kravis and Roberts packed oil paintings, oriental carpets, and other trappings of success into every room. When Kohlberg wanted to decorate a hallway with a pleasant but ordinary aerial photo of some family property in Haiti, Kravis snapped: That won't do. KKR needed a more patrician look. Kravis got what he wanted, impressing not just bankers, but also British royalty. At one point Britain's Princess Margaret made a special stop at his office during one of her U.S. tours just to behold one of his paintings. It was an English masterpiece that hung behind Kravis's desk: a horse portrait by John Herring known as *Streatlam Stud.*

Commercial bankers grew mesmerized by the two younger KKR partners. With their custom-tailored suits, their elegant offices, and their confident but gentle ways, Kravis and Roberts seemed like two of the most creditworthy men in America. Bankers Trust's Ron Badie ate hamburgers for lunch at Carl's Jr. restaurants; Kravis and Roberts never did. They each hired a personal chef around 1985 and installed full kitchens and dining rooms at KKR. From the mid-1980s onward, lunch at KKR was served on Wedgwood china that full-time waitresses brought in and took away. Operating top-notch private dining rooms within KKR's small offices might have cost $200,000 a year, but the benefits in prestige were incalculable.

As KKR grew grander and more ambitious, Kravis and Roberts began to pull far ahead of Kohlberg, whose cautious, fussy ways were grossly unsuited to the task of luring billions from bankers. The nature of the buyout business was changing dramatically in the mid-1980s, and Kohlberg's original specialty—heart-to-heart negotiations involving small companies—was becoming obsolete. One of the clearest signs of change involved the new rituals of arranging loans. From 1984 onward, this became the preserve of Roberts, Kravis, and KKR's younger associates.

Getting started with the banks in the late 1970s had been so hard, so full of what seemed like unjustified obstacles, that Roberts and Kravis sometimes acted as if they deserved lucky breaks later on. KKR's first close bank relationship in the late 1970s was with First National Bank of Chicago. The bank's San Francisco office manager, David Street, financed three KKR buyouts in a row and dropped hints that he wanted to do more. But then Street was abruptly promoted to a different part of the bank, left San Francisco, and was replaced by a new banker who viewed KKR's high-debt forays with distaste.

For a few years, Kravis and Kohlberg built up close ties with another Chicago bank, Continental Illinois Corporation. The bank's frisky young Florida lending specialist, Mike Tokarz, had been the first banker to volunteer loans for the Houdaille buyout. After the KKR partners brought a few more buyout proposals to Continental's attention, a more senior Continental executive, Michael Murray, took charge of what was termed "the KKR relationship." Murray, a stocky, bespectacled man with a wicked laugh, chided the KKR partners at times about their own lavish living, but he became a loyal booster of KKR's financial methods—to the point where his wife stitched two special "LBO pillows" for the sofa in Murray's office. On one of the beige pillows, in neat needlepoint letters, appeared the slogan CASH. On the other, CASH FLOW.

From 1981 to 1984, Murray and Continental regularly provided $50 million to $100 million in loans for each new KKR buyout. Typically a half-dozen other banks in New York, Chicago, and Los Angeles rounded out the list of KKR lenders. But in June 1984, everything changed. Continental's energy lending department had squandered more than $1 billion in foolish Oklahoma energy loans. Nearly every cent of that money was lost—and with it, Continental's financial health. In a matter of days, Continental's stock price plunged more than 70 percent; depositors began pulling money out, and federal regulators were forced to take control of the Chicago bank.

One evening in June 1984, Murray glumly called Kravis at home to cancel two buyout loan commitments. Even though Continental had promised to help KKR pursue two new acquisitions, Murray explained, he had to break his word. Continental's spare cash had evaporated. "Henry was very good about not kicking us in the teeth," Murray later said. But both men were clearly frustrated at the collapse of a money-making alliance. Every bit as irate was Mike Tokarz, who by this time had been put in charge of Continental's Philadelphia and New York offices. A rambunctious deal-maker when he got the chance, Tokarz was told by his bosses to sit idle for months, perhaps years. When KKR executive Paul Raether asked Tokarz in mid-1985 if he wanted to leave Continental and pursue buyouts at KKR instead, Tokarz jumped at the chance. "That's what I'm good at," he told Raether.

Fortunately for KKR, a lending juggernaut formed at Bankers Trust even as Continental collapsed. Bankers Trust had entered buyout lending gingerly at first, when Los Angeles lending officer George Hartmann in 1978 arranged a $9.5 million loan to help finance KKR's acquisition of Sargent Industries Inc. Subsequently, a series of transfers and reassignments in Bankers Trust's Los Angeles office had meant that no one there paid much attention to KKR for several years. In early 1983, however, one of Bankers Trust's top executives, Ralph MacDonald, asked Badie to leave a management job in New York and take charge of the Los Angeles office. Badie's number-one priority, MacDonald said, was to assess Bankers Trust's opportunities in buyout lending. After a few months, Badie phoned MacDonald with an upbeat reply. "If we do it right," Badie said, "this could be a very, very good business."

In February 1984, the first of many big chances arrived on Badie's doorstep. Roberts phoned from San Francisco and coyly told Badie that something big was brewing—big enough that they should talk about it face-to-face as soon as possible. Arriving at Badie's Los Angeles offices the next day, Roberts started out testy. Bankers Trust was bungling the paperwork on a small existing loan, Roberts complained. Could it be straightened out? Yes, Badie said, wondering what Roberts really wanted to discuss. Before long, the moment came. "Let's take a walk down the hall," Roberts said, touching Badie on the shoulder. As they walked along the empty corridor, Roberts turned to Badie and asked him point-blank: "Do you think you can raise $8 billion?"

Badie burst out laughing. That was an impossibly huge number. In an entire year, Bankers Trust didn't lend that much money to its top ten corporate clients combined. It was more money than the stock market value of Bankers Trust and its two biggest competitors put together. "You're kidding," Badie said. "You must be joking." And then Badie realized that Roberts was utterly serious.

KKR wanted to buy Gulf Corporation, one of the world's largest oil companies, Roberts explained. The company was vulnerable and up for sale. Some top Gulf managers had approached KKR, asking for help in putting together a leveraged buyout. Gulf was a tremendously rich energy company, with immense oil and gas reserves. It wasn't particularly well managed, but perhaps KKR could fix that. Badie noticed the insouciant tone in Roberts's remarks, but it didn't bother him. Making a giant loan for the history books was every banker's fantasy. Now, the deal of the year was right before him. And once fee negotiations started, Badie figured, Bankers Trust could charge KKR a lot for putting together the buyout loan.

Within days, Bankers Trust harnessed much of its worldwide might to Roberts's desires. Badie flew to New York and joined a team of senior bank managers to pore over Gulf's financial data. The first task: to assess Gulf's earnings power and oil reserves, and its financial outlook if it took on giant loans. Then the bankers needed to create a "downside case" that would depict Gulf's fate in a recession, an Arab oil embargo, a price war, or some crazy amalgam of all disaster scenarios at once. Only if KKR's buyout looked rigorously sound would Bankers Trust start rounding up other banks to join in the loan.

For the first two days, Roberts's plea for money appeared doomed. Gulf was too huge to analyze quickly; the company had 497 subsidiaries stretched around the globe. Bankers Trust's top energy specialist, William Pelly, reacted with horror at first when the $8 billion loan idea was broached. At nine P.M. the second evening, Bankers Trust's central computer system crashed, causing all analysis to stop. Desks began to pile up with pizza crusts, as the bankers subsisted on fast food while waiting for the computers to be fixed.

After the computers came back to life, Badie and Pelly kept crunching numbers until both felt confident enough about the loan's merits to take the proposal to the ultimate judge: chief credit officer Joe Manganello. A small, balding man with deep-sunken eyes, Manganello had risen to great power in Bankers Trust by saying no to loans that he felt were suspect. A tattered wooden sign on his desk proclaimed Manganello to be CAPO DEL MAESTRI PUNTATORI—which he loosely translated as the "chief sniffer of the cheese." For what seemed like ages one evening, Manganello silently reviewed Badie's proposal, then tossed the papers down and delivered his verdict.

"I like it," Manganello said. "I like it a lot."

Excitedly, Badie called KKR's San Francisco office and asked George Roberts to come to New York. It was time to talk about how Bankers Trust could raise the $8 billion. As Roberts walked into Bankers Trust's headquarters, he greeted bleary-eyed and unshaven bankers who had just finished marathon sessions of trying to fathom Gulf. By contrast, Roberts looked surprisingly refreshed for someone who had just completed an overnight flight. He talked for a bit and then excused himself to go to his hotel. An hour later, Roberts returned, having retired his original yellow shirt for a snappier blue one with a white collar. Then Roberts began upbraiding the Bankers Trust men. Their proposed loan fees of 2 percent were much too high. Gulf was a world-class company. KKR had a superb track record. "You're trying to gouge us," Roberts declared. Manganello, a twenty-three-year veteran of Bankers Trust who thought he had seen everything, sputtered in disbelief. "You know what the trouble with you is?" he said, pointing at Roberts. "You're a two-shirt-a-day kind of guy. Around here, we're working so hard we're lucky if we can change our shirts every other day."

Everyone in the room, Roberts included, burst out laughing. Within a few minutes, he and Manganello reached a compromise concerning the loan fees. The thrill of working on the biggest oil-company acquisition in history spurred on both the small KKR team and the much larger Bankers Trust squad. The New York bank opted to lend just $250 million itself—but it agreed to yield its boardroom to Roberts and some KKR colleagues for a presentation to other banks that might lend $250 million apiece, too. If the loan could be raised, Bankers Trust executives figured, their fees for organizing it would total tens of millions of dollars, even after subtracting out the portions that would be shared with other lending banks. That promised to be among the biggest fee totals Bankers Trust had ever booked from a single commercial loan. It would prop up the 1984 profits for the entire bank.

Unfortunately for Roberts, his dream of buying Gulf lasted barely another week. In a daylong board meeting in Pittsburgh on Monday, 5 March 1984, the oil company's directors conducted an auction of the company and set out to pick a winning bidder. Late in the day, the board chose a bid of $13.4 billion in cash from Standard Oil of California, passing up a KKR offer that had a higher nominal value but was cluttered with new securities that might not appeal to investors. Bankers Trust, in its dash for cash, had rustled up $4 billion of loan offers from other banks, but those had to be withdrawn when it was clear that KKR wasn't authorized to buy Gulf.

For the next fifteen months, KKR retreated to midsize buyouts. A lot of team-building would be necessary between Bankers Trust and KKR before either side dared pursue a jumbo buyout again. Gradually, however, a camaraderie took hold that in its closeness and importance exceeded KKR's old ties to Continental. When KKR considered buying sugar producer Amstar Corporation, a twenty-eight-year-old Bankers Trust banker, Morgan St. John, spent days gleaning facts from Washington bureaucrats about the world sugar market. Bankers Trust didn't need all that information itself; but the research efforts aided KKR and helped build friendship between the bank and its client. A few months later, another of Badie's subordinates, Jamie Greene, caught hepatitis from tainted sandwiches in the midst of negotiating a loan for KKR's buyout of food wholesaler Malone & Hyde—then won points for completing the loan from his bedside.

As relations with KKR grew profitable and cozy, Badie began a crusade that would drastically expand the buyout lending business. Bankers Trust on its own seldom lent more than $50 million or $100 million to a single borrower. KKR's borrowing appetites, however, were clearly growing far larger. Rather than let the very biggest U.S. banks, such as Citibank, steal away KKR as a client, Badie argued, Bankers Trust should change its mission. It should lead multibank syndicates that would lend $1 billion or more for big buyouts. Bankers Trust itself would lend as much as $500 million, but would rapidly reduce its own loan exposure by "selling" pieces of that loan to regional or foreign banks that didn't deal with KKR directly. Bankers Trust in effect would become a powerful middleman in the buyout lending game. Badie's group would hook up lenders worldwide with KKR, charging fees all the way.

Badie's boss, Bankers Trust management committee member Ralph MacDonald, loved the proposal. In September 1985, in a two-day managerial retreat at Tarrytown, New York, Badie, MacDonald, and a handful of other bank executives agreed to take on this new middleman role. There was only one catch. Bankers Trust already had a department that peddled pieces of large loans to other banks, and those loan traders turned up their noses at trafficking in buyout loans. Too risky, they said. There wouldn't be any buyers for them. Fuming, Badie threatened in the autumn of 1985 to set up his own loan-trading department. But MacDonald had a better idea. Over dinner at Hunam, a rough-and-tumble Chinese restaurant in midtown Manhattan that MacDonald loved, he briefed the head of loan trading on the new strategy.

"We can't do it," the loan trader replied.

"You don't understand," MacDonald coolly replied. "As of tomorrow, Bankers Trust *is* trading LBO loans. And if you can't find buyers, we'll give the job to someone that can."

Within minutes, the recalcitrant trading chief gave in. "I guess we can give that a try," he sheepishly told MacDonald.

Bankers Trust was about to transform itself into a very well paid agent for KKR, rather than a fully independent bank.

The next move was KKR's. Annoyed but not humbled by their failure to buy Gulf, Kravis and Roberts in 1985 kept looking for giant companies to acquire. Lending markets were booming; so were the aspirations of the KKR partners. When Kravis took a photo-safari vacation in Kenya in August 1985, he quickly grew restless at being away from the Wall Street chase. Rising at dawn one morning, Kravis trudged several miles to the only general store in the midst of the Kenyan bush, found a hand-cranked phone, and called Roberts in San Francisco to ask for an update on the U.S. takeover scene.

"I've got news for you," Roberts told his cousin, over the transatlantic phone line. "Jim Dutt has quit."

"That's great!" Kravis replied.

KKR's biggest buyout campaign to date was about to get under way. Dutt was the autocratic chairman of Chicago-based Beatrice Cos., an $11 billion conglomerate that owned Avis, Tropicana, Playtex, Hunt-Wesson, Samsonite, and dozens of other well-known food and consumer products companies. Three times before, Kravis and Roberts had tried to buy some of those businesses, but had been thwarted each time. With Dutt gone, however—squeezed out in a boardroom power play—Beatrice was leaderless. The company's stock price was low; its operating companies robust. If KKR could quickly round up the $5 billion or more of loans that it would take to acquire Beatrice, an attempted buyout of the Chicago company had a very good chance of succeeding. Rather than court the caretaker management team that had hastily been brought in to replace Dutt, the KKR men could simply install their own new management team and count on their top-dollar offer to win the assent of Beatrice's directors.

Within two weeks of Beatrice's boardroom coup, Roberts arrived at Badie's offices in Los Angeles, ready to do business once more. First came the ritual scolding about minor loans being poorly handled. Then came the classic Roberts question: "Do you think you can raise $3 billion for us?" One of Badie's protégés, Morgan St. John, was terrified by the amount. But Badie wasn't. "Yes, I think we can," he said.

For the next four months, the Los Angeles office of Bankers Trust turned into a financial command post for KKR. An entire floor was locked off from regular bank traffic, to keep intruders from prying. A secret code name was coined for the Beatrice project: Andretti, after the race car driver Mario Andretti, whom Beatrice sponsored. Every few days, Roberts phoned Badie from San Francisco with questions or an update. After each call, Badie rounded up five or ten bankers for a quick briefing in his office. "He had these two couches," recalled Dexter Paine, a young Bankers Trust lender at the time. "You had to get in early to get a seat. If not, you'd steal a chair from the conference room. Ron would be all excited, putting up paper on the wall and going through the structure of the deal." St. John, the young Harvard graduate on Badie's team, was assigned to gather undercover intelligence. When KKR needed to assess quietly the value of Beatrice's Stiffel lamps subsidiary, St. John walked into a lamp store in west Los Angeles on a weekend, posing as a major buyer. "I spent hours talking to this guy about lamps," St. John recalled. "Were the imports any good? All kinds of questions. I led him to believe I was going to buy a lot of lamps." It wasn't quite James Bond material, but it was as much fun as commercial banking ever got.

Wrapped up in the takeover tactics that their bid for Beatrice would involve, Roberts and Kravis soon turned over the details of the bank financing to their newest associate, banker-turned-deal-maker Mike To-karz. Tokarz had quickly picked up KKR's sense of self-importance, though he projected it with a rawer edge than Kravis or Roberts did. When Bankers Trust's St. John visited KKR's New York offices at one point, he and Tokarz began to clash about a minor point in the loan terms. St. John turned to leave Tokarz's office and head for Kennedy airport, to return to California. Suddenly, Tokarz grabbed a huge stack of Beatrice loan documents and dropped them to the floor with such a crashing thud that KKR colleagues thought their building was being shaken in an earthquake. "No!" Tokarz fumed. "You're staying right here until we get this sorted out." St. John stayed; Tokarz prevailed, and the loan negotiations proceeded.

In mid-October 1985, the banking activity subsided for a time as KKR began a four-month tactical battle to win Beatrice. Negotiating the acquisition itself was a hugely complex task, with its own stories of tearful boardroom showdowns, battling egos, and an insider-trading scandal that eventually sent two people to jail and left others under a cloud for years. That saga, along with the stories of KKR's other big takeover battles of the 1980s, is the material of later chapters.

Badie's team had one shining moment on 17 October 1985, when Beatrice's Wall Street advisers asked how in the world KKR proposed to pay for a company as huge as Beatrice. A KKR adviser, investment banker Martin Siegel of Kidder, Peabody, whipped out two brief letters that promised the money. One was from the junk-bond underwriting firm of Drexel Burnham Lambert Inc., which said it was highly confident that it could raise $2 billion. The other letter was from Bankers Trust, which said it would pitch in $500 million itself and seek to raise a further $3 billion from a wide syndicate of banks. "We were very concerned about their financing package," recalled Salomon Brothers investment banker Ira Harris, who was advising Beatrice. "But they seemed to have enough things that fit together so that their bid made sense."

For the rest of the autumn of 1985, the KKR and Bankers Trust men fended off one financing crisis after another. Not since the Houdaille buyout had KKR tried so aggressively to push its high-debt takeover methods onto a doubtful and distrusting world. The Beatrice acquisition was too huge to be financed by a half dozen loyal banks that had lent to KKR over the years. It would require loans from banks in Pittsburgh, Los Angeles, Tokyo, and Frankfurt that had never even considered financing a buyout before. For Bankers Trust to raise the promised $3 billion this time, a lot of bankers around the world would have to start changing their most basic beliefs about why they lent money to businesses.

Methodical as always, the KKR executives and their Bankers Trust allies started by compiling a thick "bank book" about Beatrice. The document was packed with every fact a banker could want to know—and a pep talk every few pages. How strong was Beatrice's bottled-water unit? Why, it controlled 34 percent of the residential water-delivery market in Dallas and 70 percent in Houston. How good a company was Beatrice? Why, it had "excellent market position" and a "strong" new management team that KKR had selected. Unlike the ragged Houdaille memo of 1978, with its Wite-Out and Scotch tape, this was an immaculately typeset, inch-and-a-half-thick book. Badie's crew in Los Angeles shipped copies of the document to nearly a hundred major banks, pitching each one with as much excitement as the Bankers Trust men could muster.

Faraway bankers grimaced at first. Beatrice for decades had boasted one of America's most conservative balance sheets, with so little debt that its operating profit had covered its interest expense by as much as fifteen times. In 1984, Beatrice's management had taken on a lot more debt to pay for acquisitions, so that operating profit covered interest expense by only 2.5 times. Now KKR was proposing to swamp the company with even more debt. Projected operating earnings in 1986 would be only 1.3 times Beatrice's overall interest bill. Some bankers saw grounds to be nervous, even though KKR assured them that the bank loans would be repaid rapidly, thanks to an estimated $1.5 billion of asset sales.

But the KKR executives knew how to talk to banks. They decided to show bankers, up close, all the industrial might of Beatrice—and to coddle them at every step of the way. In mid-November 1985, Badie and

Tokarz invited other bankers to come to New York's Pierre Hotel and hear Beatrice's new CEO, Donald Kelly, describe his plans for the company. Breezy and confident, Kelly appealed to lenders with his style as much as with any numbers he cited. "Kelly was terrific," one foreign banker said. "You just knew he was going to win somehow." A chartered jet—paid for by the loans that KKR was raising—then flew bankers to Beatrice sites in Chicago and California. Worries about huge debts began to recede in some bankers' minds as they tasted sausages in Chicago, played with Samsonite garment bags at another Beatrice site, nibbled on tomato sauce in California, and got a dozen other largely inconsequential but reassuring signs of Beatrice's vitality.

By mid-November, KKR and Bankers Trust had raised about $2 billion. Three other banks, Citibank, Manufacturers Hanover, and Bank of Nova Scotia, each joined Bankers Trust in promising to lend $350 million apiece. But because of an increase in KKR's proposed purchase price, the bank loans needed now totaled $4.1 billion. And the remaining $2.1 billion would have to be raised from all corners of the world.

For Tokarz and Badie's crew, the search for the final lenders was excruciating. Unsure that U.S. banks would lend enough, Tokarz began wooing German, Italian, French, and even Japanese banks. For two weeks in early December, he arrived at KKR's offices at six A.M. to start phoning the European banks during their workday. Then he stayed until eleven P.M. or later in order to telephone Japanese banks during Tokyo office hours. At one point, fellow KKR associate Kevin Bousquette stopped by Tokarz's office and told him: "You're about to have the shortest career of anyone at KKR. You were hired to raise the bank money. And you haven't done it."

The eeriest moments would come late at night, when only a handful of people were scattered through the fifty-story New York office tower that housed KKR: security guards patrolling the hallways, cleaning women emptying out garbage cans, and one deal-maker in a suit and tie, talking to bankers halfway around the world. Tokarz's reedy Midwestern voice carried down KKR's empty hallways. To have any hope of winning further loans, Tokarz had to sound like the most self-assured man in America. Over crackling phone lines to Tokyo, Tokarz tried to explain the complex structure of the Beatrice acquisition. KKR's Deloitte accountants had devised a fresh piece of tax wizardry—the creation of "mirror subsidiaries"—that would let KKR break up Beatrice, if necessary, without having to pay capital gains taxes. "Mr. Tokarz," a Japanese voice would ring out at two A.M., "could you explain mirror subsidiaries?"

Tokarz, a gabby sort who never gave a short answer to any question, would lecture on the subject for nearly thirty minutes. Then a fresh Japanese voice would ring out—that of a different loan officer who had just walked into a conference room in Tokyo. "Mr. Tokarz. We do not understand mirror subsidiaries. Please explain them."

One night Tokarz napped on a chair in the office. The next morning over breakfast, Kravis debriefed him on the bank talks. With a smile, a joke, or an encouraging word, Kravis got his new associate ready for another day's pursuit of bank money.

Keeping up spirits was not always easy. Whenever Bankers Trust and Tokarz picked up a new bank, it seemed, an existing one would drop out. And each time Badie's team or Tokarz won one bank back, another lender would develop doubts.

On 18 December 1985, the mood at both Bankers Trust and KKR approached panic. The bank loans raised so far were more than $1 billion short of the $4.1 billion needed. If the rest of the money didn't arrive within the next 48 hours, KKR would miss the financing deadline set by Beatrice's directors. Failure to raise the money on time could jeopardize KKR's ability to complete the Beatrice buyout, as well as the firm's credibility on Wall Street. Sitting in a conference room at Bankers Trust's offices, Ron Badie and his crew started what they gamely referred to as "dialing for dollars." Like rookie stockbrokers, they phoned bank after bank, asking: Have you seen our Beatrice deal? Are you interested in lending? Can we settle any questions for you? Every fifth or tenth phone call paid off, sometimes at the price of a dose of humiliation for the Bankers Trust team.

The most worrisome holdout was Citibank—one of the first four banks that had pledged to lend money to KKR. One of Citicorp's leveraged lending specialists, Ron Kominski, insisted that KKR agree to sell major Beatrice divisions within nine months, to ensure that banks got much of their loans repaid rapidly. On his own, Tokarz couldn't budge Kominski, so he asked Kravis to help. Stepping up to a speaker phone, Kravis began with a sunny greeting, then let Kominski start his argument. Partway through, Kravis cut him off.

"Do you recognize that you are holding up the biggest LBO in history?" Kravis boomed, filling his voice with incredulity.

"Yes," Kominski sheepishly replied. Suddenly, Kominski recalled, the negotiating point didn't matter. It was one thing to dicker with Tokarz, but Kravis had an aura about him that made it churlish to argue.

Finally, hours before the Beatrice board's deadline, a swarm of holdout banks came on board. Bank of America promised to lend $250 million. An Italian bank was good for $50 million. Five Japanese banks lent a total of $250 million. The last straggler was Citibank, where the bank's lawyers announced that they had found "seven nonnegotiable sticking points." By midnight, Tokarz and another KKR executive, Paul Raether, had bargained Citibank down to two points. At three A.M., Tokarz and Kominski split the difference and caught a few hours sleep.

At nine A.M. on 20 December, as promised, Tokarz sent a messenger to Beatrice's New York law firm with fifty-three loan commitment letters, from banks around the world, that just barely covered the total amount KKR needed. Tokarz was bleary-eyed, and wore a rumpled shirt that he hadn't had time to change from the night before. The Citibank commitment letter was marred—in Tokarz's eyes—by a special clause that made it more stringent than all the other loan pledges. A stickler of an attorney might have questioned the Citibank letter and left KKR lacking the cash required for the acquisition. But Beatrice was being represented by Wachtell, Lipton, Rosen & Katz, a firm that was pragmatic in approach, and that specialized in arranging the sales of besieged companies. Wachtell lawyer Richard Katcher noticed the aberrant Citibank letter, did not consider the conditions material, and called Tokarz to tell him that the bank financing was officially complete. Exhausted, Tokarz fell asleep, glad to have the LBO bank loan assembled successfully.

It took four more months to complete the other stages of KKR's Beatrice acquisition. By the spring of 1986, it was time to celebrate.

Not only had KKR completed its first giant takeover, but Kravis and Roberts in the process were becoming Medici-style patrons of Wall Street's takeover community. Of the $6.2 billion that KKR had raised from all sources—banks, the junk-bond market, and KKR's own investment pools—a hefty $248 million was being disbursed as fees for investment bankers, lawyers, and other deal-doers. "Unheard of," *The Wall Street Journal* opined in a brief comment about the fees that year. Some fifty-three banks split $44 million. Lawyers got at least $20 million. Kidder, Peabody's Marty Siegel asked for a $10 million fee, his biggest ever, only to be told by KKR that his firm had done such good work that it deserved $12 million. Beatrice's new management team got $8.8 million. Even a minor adviser to KKR, investment banker Jeff Beck, collected $4.5 million.

In total, Kravis and Roberts were presiding over perhaps the greatest self-enrichment scheme that Wall Street had ever devised. During the first three months of 1986, the 100,000 Beatrice employees who rented cars at Avis, made suitcases at Samsonite, or carried out hundreds of other conventional tasks, had helped Beatrice produce $240 million of operating income. A scattering of deal-makers and lenders had earned just as much without soiling their hands in industrial labor at all, simply by figuring out how to buy Beatrice. The biggest winner in this fee derby was the tiny firm of KKR, which collected a $45 million fee.

On the evening of 18 April 1986, some 190 of KKR's allies in the Beatrice deal arrived at the New-York Historical Society, a sedate museum in the midst of Manhattan's residential Upper West Side. Such a lavish and boisterous party awaited the guests that some of them talked about it for years afterward. "It was extraordinary," recalled Dresdner Bank executive Nicholas Greene. "I wouldn't say it got out of hand, but it was just barely restrained."

As the guests walked in, they were met by nineteen tuxedoed waiters and ten wine stewards pouring champagne. In a rear corner, a rented pianist tapped out Gershwin tunes on a baby grand piano wheeled in for the evening. The society's immense fourth-floor exhibition hall had been converted into a dining area, without disturbing the walls packed with original Audubon watercolors of swallow-tailed kites, great gray owls, and other birds. Those historic artworks conveyed exactly the old-money elegance that KKR craved. Kravis beamed as the happy host at center table; Roberts and Kohlberg sat less conspicuously at side tables. The evening cost KKR at least $30,000, but that was a trifle.

After dinner, the high jinks began. Kravis and Beatrice's new chief executive, Don Kelly, took the podium next to a giant marble statue of a dying American Indian. Kelly surveyed all the bankers, smirked, and said: "Hey. This is the same group of dummies who lent me too much money before. And guess what? You've gone and done it again!"

The bankers howled. They loved being insulted by big-name clients. It was much better than being ignored.

Kravis and Kelly bantered for a while, exchanging hats, joke telephones, and giant cardboard cutouts. Then it was the bankers' turn. A top banker at Citibank got a ceramic pig for all of his squabbling about loan terms. A French banker got a Berlitz phrasebook. An Italian banker was told to collect a certificate for "understanding the least about the transaction." To everyone's surprise, the unashamed lender got up from his seat, accepted the award, and smiled.

It was a heady, exciting evening in an era that promised unlimited wealth and power for Wall Street. As the crowd filed out around midnight, Bankers Trust paid tribute to its number-one client by producing

190 red T-shirts. Each shirt carried a wicked variant on Jim Dutt's old advertising slogan, WE'RE BEATRICE. YOU'VE KNOWN US ALL ALONG. Stenciled on the front and back, in thick white letters, was a cheeky new slogan: WE'RE KKR. YOU'VE KNOWN US ALL ALONG. Some young bankers, stumbling along Central Park West in their new red T-shirts, didn't want the night to end. "We didn't go to bed at all," one Bankers Trust lender recalled. "We stayed out all night."

With the completion of the Beatrice buyout, a new financial frontier opened up. The small band of banks that had financed buyouts in the late 1970s now had swelled into an army of eager lenders round the world. Buyouts became acclaimed as the "leading edge" of lending. For the rest of the 1980s, a ready squadron of lending banks enabled corporate raiders, buyout specialists, and even a few outright crooks to acquire some of America's largest companies while putting up only small amounts of their own money. These acquirers could simply borrow the rest.

At the time, leveraged-takeover lending looked like a terrific money-making business for banks. Usually, banks' profit margins on loans to big companies are so thin that they are measured in basis points—one one-hundredth of a percentage point. The rates on buyout loans were deliciously plump—typically 150 basis points over the prime rate, and 225 points over the London interbank offered rate, which approximates the cost of funds to banks. The lead banks that underwrote these loans also collected up-front fees of 1 to 3 percent of a loan's total amount. Taken together, this interest and fee income for a few years made buyout lending one of the most lucrative specialties that banks had ever seen. Through buyout lending, Ron Badie's Los Angeles office of Bankers Trust pushed up its pretax profits to more than $80 million a year, from less than $20 million in the years before the big KKR deals began. Other bankers calculated that they could make more money by financing a onetime buyout of a Fortune 500 corporation than they could by supporting all the regular business activities of such a company for four years.

To Federal Reserve Board chairman Paul Volcker, this rush into buyout lending was profoundly troubling. Such loans might be profitable, he observed, but they were blatantly nonproductive. No new factories would be built; no oil fields discovered; no theoretical patents turned into exciting new devices. Buyout loans simply sloshed money between different parts of a company's financial structure. Twice during Volcker's 1979-to-1987 tenure, he issued strictures against "nonproductive loans," strictures that bankers soon found ways to sidestep. Even after he retired from the Fed, Volcker continued to seethe about what he saw as a perversion of banks' main lending mission. When Metropolitan Life Insurance Co. in late 1988 sued to try to stop a KKR buyout, Volcker had a one-word reaction: "Bravo!"

Volcker's grumblings didn't deter America's biggest banks one bit. Getting rich and making financial history was too exciting in its own right. "It was a constant charge," recalled Bankers Trust's Dexter Paine. "The deal you were working on was on the front page of *The Wall Street Journal.* It was an adrenaline high." Top bank executives fueled this enthusiasm, transferring their best young bankers into leveraged lending groups. "There's a natural migration toward what people perceive as a hot area," observed Bankers Trust executive Ralph MacDonald. "We permitted that migration to go forward."

Before long, practically all the top fifteen "money center" banks in the United States had created big leveraged lending groups. Conferences devoted to buyout lending sprang up. So did newsletters. Convinced they had found a great new business, bankers set out to propagate it as quickly as possible. Citibank recruited a refugee from Continental Illinois, Todd Slotkin, who built a vast buyout lending department that at its peak totaled 400 people. At Chase Manhattan Bank, Maria Beechey, a young Englishwoman who began her career making loans to Greek shipping tycoons, transferred into buyout lending in the mid-1980s. She was on the corporate fast track, being named a managing director after just a few years in the department. New banking publications such as *Corporate Finance* magazine began profiling these buyout lenders, giving them star quality of their own.

The most striking career ascent came at another big New York bank, Manufacturers Hanover Trust Co. There, bankers marveled at the rise of Mark Solow, a street-smart Long Island native who had made garment-business loans in the 1970s and joked that his suit and shoes together cost less than $50. Starting in 1982, though, Solow turned his attention to buyout loans and began bringing in six-figure fees for the bank. Promotions quickly followed. In December 1985, Solow took charge of Manny Hanny's buyout lending group and set his sights on the top. "We were kind of a second- or third-tier player," Solow recalled later. "We wanted to be a first-tier player." One of the first things Solow did in his new job was to visit Kravis and say: "I'd like to lead deals for KKR." Solow's bank never fully dislodged Bankers Trust's position as KKR's number-one bank, but soon won standing as a close number two.

When asked in 1989 and 1990 what they had accomplished by all this buyout lending, bankers did come up with a few economic justifications for their frenzied activity. Such loans put cash in the hands of shareholders dislodged by a buyout, bankers observed—and those shareholders had to reinvest their proceeds somewhere. Eventually productive investment would ensue. In a late-1980s annual report, Bankers Trust earnestly told its shareholders that piling debt on the books of American companies had "brought about the corporate efficiency which ultimately will help pay down that debt." As if trying to reassure themselves that they hadn't lost track of their banking mission, Bankers Trust's top executives went on to assert that "the leveraging of capital is a useful means to broadly desirable ends." Bankers Trust's chief credit officer, Joe Manganello, elaborated on that argument in a 1989 interview, adding that buyouts "created intrinsically more value by tightening a company up."

Manganello conceded, however, that when most big buyout loans were made in the mid-1980s, people "didn't ask about social questions much." Making money was what mattered.

A case in point was KKR's 1986 acquisition of Safeway Stores Inc. Once again, KKR was looking for more than $3 billion of bank loans. Early indications of banks' responses were mixed. On the plus side, Safeway was by far America's largest grocery chain. KKR executives were promoting what they believed was a sound financial plan: to raise $2 billion or more by selling off pieces of Safeway's business, giving them enough cash to repay much of the buyout debt quickly. Safeway's profit record wasn't as strong as Beatrice's, however, and this made the new buyout a riskier financial proposition. So Tokarz—once again the leader of KKR's bank negotiations—decided to try a small lure. Pitching the Safeway buyout to bankers in San Francisco in late July 1986, Tokarz offered a special $1 million "commitment fee" to any bank that pledged to lend $400 million within three days. If banks wanted to take longer, they could—but the $1 million fee was being offered only for the first lenders, a tactic known among some bankers as an "early-bird special."

Tokarz's grasp of bankers' psychology was perfect. The $400 million that KKR wanted was a remote sum that had little meaning to any of the bankers. That money would be electronically transferred from central funding sources to a KKR repository, without ever really registering in the bankers' lives. The $1 million fee, on the other hand, was as tangible as the metal chairs on which the bankers sat. At some banks, 5 to 10 percent of fee income went into a bonus pool for the individual bankers who had generated those fees. At year's end, those bankers could boost their paychecks by as much as $100,000 if they hurried to join the KKR loan. Such a fee brought bragging rights, too; bankers could tell colleagues that in a single week they had pulled in a $1 million fee for the bank. Within four days, more than $6 billion in bank-loan commitments for the Safeway buyout tumbled forth—twice as much as KKR needed.

Ordinary industrial lending had never been this good. Before long, banks' loans to big industrial companies atrophied. A survey by the Federal Reserve in 1987 found that at some big banks, lending for buyouts and other takeovers accounted for as much as 40 percent of overall corporate lending. The big fees and interest income of LBO lending simply looked irresistible. A veritable army of U.S. and foreign banks now marched behind the KKR banner being waved by Bankers Trust. Badie's team could call on other banks with a very seductive pitch that went something like this: "We're bringing you a chance to join in making a big loan to the premier buyout group in the world. You will be able to put your bank's dollars to work faster in this jumbo loan than in almost any other transaction that will cross your desk. The terms are potentially quite profitable for your bank. But a lot of banks will want to be in on this loan, and there may not be room for everyone. You had better hurry."

To ensure that banks' lending appetite stayed strong, the KKR partners crafted one more essential attribute: an immaculate track record. Nearly every banker's biggest dread is that he or she will make a big, stupid loan that will be a "career ender." Junior loan officers might be swept off their feet by the KKR story as told to them by Bankers Trust. Somewhere within each bank, however, a crusty, old-line credit officer would veto foolish loans before they were made. For all the grand appearances that KKR might create, Kravis and Roberts were realistic enough to know that if a few of their buyout companies couldn't pay their debts, bankers would rapidly judge KKR much more harshly—by the status of its worst-performing deals.

In fact, KKR's financial record was very good—but not perfect. At any one point, 85 to 95 percent of KKR's buyout companies hummed along financially, paying their interest on time. Tucked inside the KKR portfolio, however, were a few buyouts gone awry. The Cobblers shoe company, which Roberts and Kohlberg bought in 1971, had ended up in bankruptcy proceedings. So had Eaton-Leonard, a small machine-tool business that KKR bought in 1980. Boren Clay had needed to have its debts restructured on losing terms to lenders. In the biggest misstep, American Forest Products Co., which Kohlberg and Roberts had bought for $425 million in 1981, had fallen victim to a deep timber industry slump, and couldn't pay its debts on time. Behind closed doors in the mid-1980s, KKR partners clashed with American Forest's lenders about whether to cancel some of the company's debt. When KKR recited its track record, however, flaws like American Forest were simply stricken from the ledger. That timber acquisition was a special, "tax-advantaged" transaction, the KKR partners quaintly explained to anyone who asked. From 1986 onward, that acquisition ceased to be listed in KKR's semipublic summaries of its work for distribution within the financial community.

Impressionable bankers, with little inclination to pick over the buyout firm's history in great detail, began to feed a myth. KKR had an "unblemished" record, the story went. In one investment banker's image, KKR's record was "as perfect as [actress] Michelle Pfeiffer." The talk in banking circles in the mid-1980s was that KKR had never had a deal that got in financial trouble. That legend wasn't true. But Kravis and Roberts let it persist.

Convinced that they could never have too big an entourage of loyal lending banks, KKR executives periodically left their New York or San Francisco offices to recruit new banking allies firsthand. George Roberts, for example, repeatedly visited Portland, Oregon, in the mid-1980s to call on John Elorriaga, the chairman of U.S. National Bank of Oregon. "We're looking for a lead bank in the Northwest," Roberts said on his initial visit. "You're our first choice." It was an approach that was flattering and that also carried a veiled threat: If Elorriaga didn't sign on, one of his local rivals would get KKR's business. Elorriaga got the message. His bank gladly helped finance four KKR buyouts in a row. "We'd be missing the boat if we didn't do it with him," Elorriaga later said.

More often, remote banks were pulled in by Bankers Trust's energetic loan-syndication desk, without KKR having to lift a finger. Dozens of Japanese, German, French, and even Middle Eastern banks became regular participants in KKR buyout loans. "If you're a foreign bank trying to build up business in the United States," one Middle Eastern banker wryly explained, "you can follow whatever Citi and Bankers Trust do. Or you can squirm." Determined to sweep as many banks into its lending parties as possible, Bankers Trust moved its Los Angeles branch into bigger quarters and set up a twenty-person loan-trading desk to complement the trading operation in New York. Intense young traders in white shirts phoned around the globe all day, peddling $5 million chunks of loans for Beatrice, Safeway, and dozens of other buyout companies.

The entire banking infrastructure, which had stood in the way of KKR's designs in the mid-1970s, now was being customized to suit the desires of Roberts, Kravis, and other buyout specialists. At Manufacturers Hanover, Citibank, and other big banks, loan syndication and trading departments sprang up. Thousands of bankers at scores of banks were steered into jobs that could only make sense if KKR and other buyout firms kept borrowing in a big way.

For a few younger bankers, there was the added lure of switching sides and joining a buyout sponsor like KKR. To do so meant a chance to earn bonuses of $1 million or more, an amount easily four or five times what commercial banks paid even their most successful lenders. Over the years, KKR had hired Don Herdrich from First Chicago and Mike Tokarz of Continental Illinois. And in late 1986, Ron Badie got a memorable phone call from George Roberts.

"As you know," Roberts said, "we only hire people into our firm that we've worked with for a long time."

Badie perked up right away. "I was expecting an offer," he recalled.

"We would very much like to talk with Jamie Greene," Roberts continued. "You tell me if this creates a problem. If it does, we'll go to our next best choice, if there is one. But we think Jamie makes sense. We like Jamie. He would fit into our organization. He's worked on a lot of our transactions. I'd like your permission to talk to him."

For a moment, Badie was flummoxed. *You've got the wrong guy,* he thought. But then he recovered. Yes, it was all right if Roberts recruited Greene. Badie walked down the hall to brief his thirty-five-year-old subordinate. "Jamie," Badie said. "I'm going to make your day. George Roberts wants to talk to you about a job."

"Bull," Greene said.

"Seriously, Jamie, Roberts wants to talk to you."

"Ron, you're kidding. No. You are kidding. You're just having fun with me. Come on. Stop it. Stop it."

Then Greene realized that his boss was serious. He stopped sputtering and broke into a wide grin. A month later, Jamie Greene joined KKR.

By the late 1980s, bankers' priorities, month by month, were being bent ever further from the actual merits of the loans, and more toward the big fees involved. The most powerful banker in America, Citibank chairman John Reed, later said that his own bank's internal credit memos underwent a strange metamorphosis in the late 1980s. Traditionally, Citicorp memos had begun with detailed analyses of a company's prospects, and concluded with details of the bankers' fees. As the leveraged lending boom reached its peak, Reed observed, the fees began to appear at the *beginning* of the memos, with the actual business analysis tucked in the back.

The consummate stampede by eager lenders occurred one morning in February 1987, at the Park Lane Hotel in New York. Packed into the hotel's red-carpeted ballroom were about thirty major bankers, ready to hear about the virtues of Owens-Illinois Inc., America's largest glass container company. This would be KKR's latest conquest—a buyout that required more than $3 billion in new bank loans. Objectively, it was a riskier proposition than the Beatrice or Safeway deal. The company's interest-coverage ratios would be skimpier after the buyout, and its business was much more vulnerable to the economic cycle. But KKR was on a tremendous roll that winter, generating huge winnings for people lucky enough to help finance its buyouts. None of the bankers in the room felt like being skeptical. They wanted to make money.

To the astonishment of Owens-Illinois's top executives, bankers hardly listened to each fact-filled talk. Instead, as one witness would recall, "a catfight broke out" in the audience as bankers scrambled to collect an early-bird special being offered by KKR's Jamie Greene. The first seven bankers who agreed to lend $400 million had been promised the title of "agent bank," and an extra $1.25 million fee. As word got out that four of those slots had already been snapped up, gung-ho bankers bolted from their chairs partway through the Owens-Illinois talks, elbowed other bankers aside, and tried to claim slots five through seven. Agile bankers from Continental Illinois, Bank of America, and Chemical Bank got the prize. One of them, in fact, later won a "Carl Lewis Award" from his peers for racing so fast to KKR.

Hot behind the first seven bankers, another seven piled in with $400 million loan pledges in the next few days. Desperate to win special fees, these second-round bankers pleaded with Greene until he relented and dubbed them "agent banks" as well. All told, the Owens-Illinois buyout attracted more than $7 billion in loan pledges from the most powerful banks in the United States, Japan, Canada, and Europe. The Apollo space program hadn't consumed so much money in its busiest year. Greene was so awash with bank loans that he could ration each bank down to just 45 percent of its pledged amount, disregard nearly $4 billion of promised loans, and still finance the Owens-Illinois deal.

At that moment in 1987, KKR was the most sought-after bank borrower in the world.

5

The Enchanting World of Drexel

The eeriest part of the 1980s credit boom originated in Beverly Hills, California, in a white five-story building at the intersection of Wilshire Boulevard and Rodeo Drive. To tourists, that location marked a prime shopping district, known for its boutiques and jewelry stores. But to people in the financial markets, the white building at 9560 Wilshire Boulevard was the West Coast headquarters of Drexel Burnham Lambert Inc.—the office where Michael Milken worked. With a single visit to 9560 Wilshire, corporate raiders, buyout specialists, and fast-track entrepreneurs could pick up vast amounts of money to spend in pursuit of their business dreams. Banks alone in the mid-1980s were pushing attitudes toward business borrowing into uncharted territory. But Milken and his Drexel acolytes helped take the pro-debt cause much further than the banks alone ever would have dared.

Gaunt and charismatic, Milken built his career on "junk bonds," one of the great ready-credit schemes of all time. Drexel's junk bonds superficially resembled the standard corporate bonds that had been issued in America since the early 1800s. They paid interest twice a year, they matured in anywhere from three to twenty years, and they generally were sold in lots of $1 million or larger to big institutional buyers. But these bonds were unabashedly speculative from the moment they were issued. They carried remarkably high yields: 11 to 15 percent when ordinary bonds offered 8 to 10 percent. And they were designed to put extra capital in the hands of borrowers who had already taken out giant bank loans, thus greatly augmenting the power of buyout specialists such as KKR.

In his peak years, Milken towered over his clients in a manner that evoked comparisons to J. P. Morgan. He and a team of several hundred Drexel colleagues underwrote $20 billion or more of junk bonds annually, an amount equal to the entire U.S. national debt as recently as 1940. Drexel raised billions for new entrepreneurs such as broadcasting executive Ted Turner, as well as for corporate raiders such as Carl Icahn and T. Boone Pickens. Meanwhile, Milken created and stoked huge appetites among insurance companies and savings and loan associations, persuading their top executives largely to abandon their traditional forms of lending and gorge on Drexel's junk bonds instead. Alternately hailed as "brilliant" and "dangerous" throughout the 1980s, Milken and his operations evoked feelings of awe, fear, and ultimately, great bitterness.

Beginning with a very slow courtship, Henry Kravis and George Roberts became first intrigued, then dazzled by Milken's money-raising power. From 1984 to 1989, they called on Milken and his number-one lieutenant, Peter Ackerman, to help finance thirteen of KKR's boldest buyouts. Before long, KKR became Drexel's biggest borrowing client. Milken boasted about the relationships, and depicted the buyout firm as a great agent of change in a sweeping financial revolution. "It was one of the most symbiotic relationships of all time," a top Drexel official later said about working with KKR. "They blessed us, and we blessed them."

A strange mix of relentless work, a can-do spirit, and outlaw behavior contributed to Milken's success. He started work at four A.M. and routinely logged eighteen-hour days. He gave endless pep talks for his clients and his employees, making them feel part of an exciting new world. Yet Drexel's junk-bond world was tinged with corruption and illegal practices. Bond issuers were pressured to raise more money than they needed, then reinvest the proceeds in other Drexel deals. Money managers were given personal payoffs by Drexel in return for packing their portfolios with securities that Drexel might otherwise have trouble selling. And Milken, who positioned himself as a selfless champion of his clients, secretly collected a $550 million salary in 1987, the year that Drexel began aggressively pushing clients into deals they would later regret.

Kravis and Roberts—normally fastidious about whom they would do business with—chose to ignore all the signs of Drexel's seamier side. Whenever people pressed him about Drexel, Kravis had a stock reply: "They deliver. No one else can raise the amount of capital that they can." KKR hired Drexel to perform one of the toughest tasks in a buyout: raising the loans considered too risky for banks to make. The KKR partners had a burning desire to do big deals, and Drexel was the ally that made giant acquisitions possible. As long as billions of dollars of junk-bond money arrived on KKR's doorstep, the buyout firm's executives showed little interest in learning how Drexel had done it.

In their five-year association with Drexel, George Roberts and Henry Kravis got tremendous mileage from their pact with Milken's gamy world. Remarkably, KKR suffered very little for it.

The pairing of KKR's buyout ingenuity and Drexel's junk-bond sales-manship both began and ended because of a quarrel.

In almost any effort to finance a buyout, the hardest stage occurred in raising the risky loans at the bottom of the capital structure: subordinated debt. The senior loans from commercial banks ordinarily amounted to at most 60 percent of the total purchase price.* Meanwhile, KKR wanted to acquire control of a company on behalf of its limited partner investors with as small a down payment as lenders would allow—typically 5 to 20 percent of the total purchase price. That left a final 20 to 40 percent of the purchase price to be borrowed somehow. Those loans usually carried higher interest rates than bank loans. They also involved longer payback periods and greater risk to the lender.

In the 1970s, KKR relied on America's biggest insurer, Prudential Insurance Co., for subordinated loans that helped finance a series of small buyouts. But as KKR's acquisitions got bigger and more complex in the early 1980s, loan negotiations with the Pru grew protracted and warlike. The KKR partners clashed especially often with Ray Charles, a stocky ex-Navy man in his late fifties, who supervised much of the Pru's corporate lending. "It was like dealing with the Mafia," Kravis later complained. As Kravis saw it, hostile bureaucrats at the Pru kept trying to take advantage of his small, up-and-coming buyout firm.

To Ray Charles, the KKR partners were the rapacious ones. Charles simply wanted to protect the Pru in return for making undeniably risky loans to finance buyouts. Charles wasn't enchanted by any borrower—even fast-rising KKR. On one occasion, bumping into Kravis unexpectedly in Prudential's hallways, Charles looked at him, laughed, and said: "Who are you bilking today, Henry?" The Pru executives refused to lend money unless they got steep interest rates, tight restraints on a company's future spending plans, and a big ownership stake in the acquired company. That way, the insurers could share in the eventual profits of a

---

*Even in their most gung-ho days, when bankers competed frantically to be part of that 60 percent, the banks refused to widen their total share of the financing any further. The banks always wanted lesser creditors to take the biggest risks.

successful deal. It rankled Charles to see Kravis, Roberts, and Kohlberg building a small circle of passive KKR investors who would own most of a buyout company on terms that greatly benefited KKR. "My feeling was: There wasn't any place for people to buy purely equity in a company," Charles later said. "The equity should go to the subordinated lenders, to the finders of the deal, and to management."

Tempers erupted over one of KKR's best-known passive investors, Pittsburgh billionaire Henry Hillman. Even years later, Charles couldn't restrain himself on the subject. "People who put in subordinated debt deserve equity more than Henry Hillman," he snapped. "If you only buy equity, you've got a gravy train. Equity shouldn't go to Henry Hillman, who brings nothing to the deal."

The final confrontations with Prudential and like-minded East Coast insurers came on two 1981 buyouts: the purchase of Marley Co., a Shawnee Mission, Kansas, maker of cooling towers, and the acquisition of Norris Industries, a Los Angeles conglomerate. Rising U.S. interest rates and the onset of recession made it maddeningly tough for the KKR men to wrap up the loans required to complete each buyout. Ultimately, KKR paid insurance company lenders a stiff 15 percent interest rate for the subordinated loans in the Marley buyout and an even higher 19½ percent interest rate for subordinated loans in the Norris buyout. Prudential and other lenders ended up with a whopping 51.3 percent of Norris's post-buyout stock and an even greater 65 percent of Marley. KKR and its passive investors (including the unexpectedly controversial Hillman) got less than 40 percent of each company, two of their lowest stakes ever.

The insurance companies had won everything they wanted from KKR on the Norris and Marley deals—but in doing so, Prudential lost its star client. During one of their showdowns, Charles had bluntly told the KKR partners: There is nowhere else to raise money; you have to deal with us. Kravis and Roberts smoldered. They weren't about to concede anything, especially the idea that they and their passive investors were grabbing majority ownership of a company too easily. Instead, the KKR men began looking for ways to wriggle free of the Pru.

Some 2,500 miles away from Prudential's offices, Mike Milken and his Drexel colleagues had begun searching for new opportunities, too. As a new employee at Drexel in the early 1970s, Milken had begun to specialize in what were known as "fallen angels"—bonds issued by mainstream companies, such as Penn Central Corporation, that had subsequently sagged in price as these companies got into financial trouble. Milken routinely approached such companies' original lenders, many of whom despaired of ever getting their money back, and offered to take these shaky bonds off their hands—albeit at a steep discount from their face value. Shrewdly, Milken figured that the big yields and potential recovery prospects from a cross section of such junk bonds more than offset the risks of periodic defaults.

But the U.S. economy wasn't wrecking companies fast enough for Milken's needs. New fallen angels were being created at a rate of a mere $2 billion a year. Milken and Drexel needed a way to conjure up more junk bonds on the spot, instead of waiting for old-line industrial companies to stumble.

The solution jumped out at Milken and a Drexel colleague, Peter Ackerman, when they started looking at KKR's deals. With every buyout, KKR plunged companies into at least modest financial trouble—paying hefty 15- to 19-percent interest rates on its subordinated debt as a result. Most times, though, managers of these buyout companies guided their businesses back to financial health. To Milken and Ackerman, it didn't make sense for KKR to pay such stiff terms to raise subordinated loans from the Pru. Everyone would do much better if KKR could be wooed away from the insurance companies—and converted into a junk-bond issuer.

Ackerman pounced in late 1981, right after the financing terms of the Norris buyout were announced. Telephoning Roberts, whom he had never met, Ackerman began with a famous Drexel greeting: "We can help you."

Ackerman was a curious envoy for Milken to have picked. A slim, curly-haired man in his mid-thirties, he was a refugee from academia, with a Ph.D. in political science from Tufts University. He had arrived at Drexel by accident in the mid-1970s, after failing at a quixotic effort to improve Third World living standards by setting up a pan-African trading company that trucked cattle from Niger to Lagos. (The cattle died in a drought.) At Drexel, Ackerman approached finance with few preconceived ideas, and periodically tossed out a surprisingly creative approach—traits that endeared him to Milken. Diffident at first, Ackerman wore blue jeans and cardigans to the office, quoted Kierkegaard, and won the nickname "the absentminded professor." Before long, however, Ackerman mastered the Wall Street game. He swapped his shabby graduate-student clothes for elegant suits and white shirts. He packed the den of his Santa Monica, California, home with small Lucite mementos of all the deals on which he had worked. Most important, Ackerman picked up the salesman's gift of making whomever he talked to feel like the most important person in his life.

In those early 1982 phone calls, Ackerman had an intriguing pitch for Roberts. By selling junk bonds through Drexel, Ackerman argued, KKR could cut its borrowing costs and surrender less equity than by continuing to deal with the Pru. Unlike Ray Charles, Ackerman didn't scold Roberts about the supposed moral issues involved in making an already wealthy man like Henry Hillman even richer. Whatever else Drexel's executives did, they never subjected the KKR men to ethics lectures.

Roberts was wary of Drexel at first, regarding it as a financial light-weight with pretensions bigger than its skills. In New York, Drexel deal-maker Don Engel called on Jerry Kohlberg, but he too got nowhere. Milken's junk-bond division was in its infancy at the time. Few companies turned to Drexel for bond underwritings, and those that did were a shabby lot: casino operators and small-time conglomerators. "We were too small, too unproven, and too gamy" for KKR's tastes, a Drexel executive later said. Yet the more Ackerman and Roberts talked in 1982 and 1983, the more they began to like and respect each other. They were soulmates: shy, proud men who harbored secret ambitions to do deals so big and clever that their work would rock the business establishment.

Then, in 1983 and 1984, the battle for Gulf Corporation made the KKR executives look at Drexel in an entirely different light. KKR and Drexel were rivals in a way in the bidding—and both lost. But Drexel gained tremendous standing in that takeover fight, while Kravis and Roberts became aware of a painful gap in their financial repertoire.

Roberts, Kravis, and Raether suffered a humiliating defeat in the last-day auction at Gulf's Pittsburgh headquarters. Addressing the entire Gulf board of directors, they presented their biggest takeover bid ever, which they valued at $87.50 a share, or $15.4 billion. Nominally, theirs was the highest offer for the oil company, well ahead of a $13.4 billion, $80-a-share offer from Standard Oil of California. But in the madcap dash to put together a plausible bid, the KKR men hadn't figured out a good way to arrange the subordinated-debt segment of their offer. Lacking any alternative, Roberts and Raether had proposed to "finance" KKR's take-over bid in large part by pushing new bonds and preferred stock into the hands of Gulf shareholders in exchange for their stock, whether the shareholders wanted these speculative new securities or not.

The moment the KKR men left the boardroom, Salomon investment banker Jay Higgins thumbed through a Moody's bond manual until he reached the boilerplate description of "speculative" securities. With as much disdain as he could muster, Higgins read the definition to the assembled directors. The Gulf board should realize, Higgins said, that

KKR's speculative new securities wouldn't be worth anywhere near their purported value. In total, the KKR bid might be worth just $75 to $79 a share, he warned. "You could defend taking the KKR bid," Higgins added. "But you would have to do that—defend it."

After a brief debate, Gulf's directors voted to heed Higgins's warning. They snubbed KKR and opted for the safer choice: Standard Oil's $13.4 billion, all-cash bid.

Drexel, meanwhile, had done remarkably well by backing another long-shot bidder for Gulf, Oklahoma oilman T. Boone Pickens. He had been stalking Gulf since late 1983, and hadn't bothered entering the final bidding round. But Pickens's investment group cleared a profit of $760 million on the Gulf stock that it had bought in the runup to the eventual takeover. Gulf executives had tried at first to laugh off Pickens as just an unimportant gadfly. They had begun taking him much more seriously in February 1984—and had decided to put the company up for auction— after Milken in a matter of weeks raised a whopping $1.5 billion in subordinated-loan commitments for Pickens's takeover efforts. To say that Milken had an uncanny knack for raising money, Pickens later observed, "was the understatement of the year."

Beckoning for KKR's business immediately after the Gulf drama were Peter Ackerman, Mike Milken, and the rest of the Drexel crew. Their siren song: *We can help you.*

In August 1984, Kravis climbed aboard. He had nearly completed the money-raising for the $318 million purchase of Cole National Corporation, a Cleveland retailer, when one of the main lenders, Continental Bank, dropped out. Aware of the problem, Drexel deal-makers Leon Black and Peter Ackerman invited Kravis to come to Beverly Hills and consider arranging a $100 million junk-bond financing through Drexel instead. Kravis agreed. In early August 1984, Kravis, Raether, Cole National president Jeffrey Cole, and a newly hired KKR associate, former New York lawyer R. Theodore Ammon, arrived in Southern California. They joined Black, Ackerman, and a couple of other Drexel executives for dinner. They were told to report to Drexel's offices at nine A.M. the next day to see Milken.

That morning, Kravis encountered a mixture of tawdriness and raw power whose impression would stay with him for years to come. Drexel's offices on Wilshire Boulevard looked grand from the outside. Inside, however, Kravis, Cole, and their aides were herded into a dingy little fourth-floor conference room overlooking a rear parking lot. Tagging along with them was Milken, who suddenly stopped in the hallway, pointed to a visiting money manager from a small East Coast insurance company, and told him: "Come sit in this meeting. I've got something I want you to hear."

In the meeting room sat a handful of loyal Drexel clients, including the two most important ones, Tom Spiegel and Fred Carr. Spiegel ran one of the fastest-growing thrift institutions in the United States, Columbia Savings & Loan Association, which by reputation invested in nearly every junk-bond deal that Milken underwrote. Carr ran an equally go-go Los Angeles insurance company, First Executive Corporation, that was known to invest in *all* of Drexel's junk bond deals. Together, Spiegel and Carr made an odd, Mutt-and-Jeff couple. Spiegel was young and muscular; Carr was older, bald, and droopy-looking. But they had tremendous investment power—which Milken was both stoking and guiding.

As Jeff Cole got up to explain his company's finances, he expected this to be the first of many speeches to potential investors. From his experience, it took weeks to raise $100 million. He had packed a week's worth of clothes and thought of himself as a traveling salesman, much like Bob Hope in *The Road to Mandalay*. Partway through his talk to the tiny audience, Cole began to wonder if things were going badly. Carr began hectoring him with harsh questions about the merits of his stores. Drexel's caterers made no effort to impress anyone; they just dropped off a big bowl of pasta salad and left. Milken was nowhere to be seen; he had gone back to Drexel's trading desk for a few hours. Only Black and Ackerman remained.

Then Drexel's money-raising clout rang through. "I like this," Carr abruptly said. "I think I'm going to buy a lot of these bonds." Spiegel and the put-upon East Coast insurer sounded interested, too. Milken popped back into the meeting for a couple of minutes, huddled with Black and Ackerman, and turned to Kravis.

"Meeting's over," Milken said. "You've got your money."

Just like that, Drexel had raised the final $100 million that KKR needed for the Cole National buyout. Jeff Cole didn't need to unpack his six spare suits. Kravis could return home that night. Drexel itself was acting strictly as an intermediary, without itself lending any of the $100 million needed for the buyout; clients like Carr and Spiegel would put up all the money. But Milken had just shown Drexel to be an awesomely effective conduit for fast cash. "It was the damnedest thing I'd ever seen," Kravis remarked years later.

Kravis's awe at Drexel's power resonated throughout KKR for the rest of 1984. "We were used to arduous, arduous negotiations with insurance companies," KKR executive Ted Ammon later recalled. "This was so much faster." Until the Cole buyout, the KKR partners had sweated firsthand to raise subordinated debt for all their buyouts. That money-gathering role, after all, was part of what they regarded as their legitimate function as the impresarios making the buyouts happen. But now Drexel offered a much more seductive alternative. The KKR men didn't have to shuttle from the Pru to Met Life to Allstate anymore. They didn't have to joust with Ray Charles or his successors. Kravis and Roberts could hire Drexel to do their work for them. Drexel, in effect, became a turnkey contractor for KKR and other buyout firms, raising vast loans quickly through Milken's junk-bond network.

Milken's terms weren't cheap. On the $318 million Cole buyout, most of the bonds carried a 14½-percent interest rate, and KKR had to earmark about $3 million of the $100 million proceeds as a fee to Drexel. In addition, Milken demanded that 11-percent ownership in Cole be entrusted to Drexel, to be passed along to bondholders. But Drexel's cut still left KKR with the bulk of Cole's profit potential—especially compared with the terms that the Pru had charged. Particularly upbeat about Drexel were Kravis, Raether, and Ammon, the three KKR executives who had seen Milken's power firsthand in the dingy Drexel conference room. "If Drexel can raise $1.5 billion for Pickens on a hostile deal," Raether kept saying, "imagine what they could do on a friendly deal!"

Wariest of Drexel's power, at first, were Don Herdrich and George Roberts. (Jerry Kohlberg, out sick for much of 1984, didn't express strong opinions about Drexel one way or another, according to his colleagues' recollections.) After one meeting at Drexel's offices in late 1984 on the buyout of Pace Industries, Herdrich took Kravis aside and warned him that he was dealing with a fast crowd. "Look around," Herdrich said. "No one writes anything down. There are no pads in the meetings. That's because promises don't mean anything." For several days, Herdrich and midlevel Drexel executives had haggled about the exact interest rates of the bonds, what restrictions Pace would operate under after it borrowed the money, and other technical issues. Herdrich began to suspect that all his righteous negotiating was for naught. "When you get ready to do the underwriting," he told Kravis, "they're going to say: 'Guess what? Things have changed.'"

Kravis simply shrugged. "They're the only people who can do it," he told Herdrich. "No one else is in a position to provide that amount of capital."

Roberts was edgy at first about Drexel's reliability. In January 1985, a new KKR associate, former Latham & Watkins lawyer Saul Fox, was in the late stages of negotiating a buyout of Motel 6 Inc. for $832 million. Of the total purchase price, $132 million was supposed to come from Drexel, and the fund-raising wasn't going smoothly. Fox walked into Roberts's office to tell his boss: If we don't get the money, we aren't going to be able to close the deal on time. Roberts turned livid. "It was the angriest I've ever seen George get," Fox said years later. "He pointed at me and said: 'Didn't I tell you? I don't ever, ever want to have to depend on Drexel to get a deal done.' " Fox went home that night thinking he was about to get fired. Only when Drexel finally rustled up its share of the money could Fox breathe easier.

Ironically, Roberts soon afterward became one of Drexel's biggest champions within KKR. The reason: a crucial promise that Milken made in the midst of KKR's next big acquisition hunt, the $2.5 billion buyout of Storer Communications Inc.

The pursuit of Storer in mid-1985 marked a radical departure from KKR's usual business guidelines. Until that time, the buyout firm had focused on slow-growing manufacturing companies with surplus cash and little preexisting debt. Such businesses had seemed best able to cope with the big new debt loads that came with a KKR buyout. Storer broke all the rules: It didn't manufacture anything; instead it operated television stations in Atlanta, Cleveland, Detroit, and four other cities, and operated a fast-growing cable-TV network. Storer had no surplus cash, few physical assets, and plenty of debt even before KKR showed up. Kohlberg argued against the buyout, contending that it looked as risky as the ill-fated American Forest Products deal of 1981. But Kravis, Roberts, and their associates became convinced that Storer's cash flow was growing fast enough to let them rewrite the rule book. Greatly increased earnings in the next few years would let Storer handle a buyout's extra debt, they argued.

Storer had already become a takeover target in March 1985. The company had been pursued by other suitors, who had driven up its stock price to about $75 a share. A corporate-raiding group calling itself the Committee for Full Value of Storer had sought and won four seats on Storer's nine-member board and was pressing for liquidation of the company. Leading the committee was long-haired lawyer turned raider Gus Oliver, whose presence spooked Storer chairman Peter Storer. In a typical gesture of managements under siege in the 1980s, Peter Storer asked his investment bank advisers at Dillon, Read to see if another suitor could put together a higher-priced, more attractive bid for the company he ran. Some twenty-two parties were contacted; KKR emerged with the strongest bid.

A KKR team led by Kravis, Raether, and Ammon began bidding for Storer in April 1985 by offering $87.50 a share—with 14 percent of that amount consisting of low-grade preferred stock that would be pushed into the hands of Storer shareholders, whether they wanted it or not. In an echo of the battle for Gulf, Storer's investment bank advisers derided KKR's terms. Dillon, Read's George Weigers branded the KKR offer "inadequate" and began looking closely at a bid by a third suitor, Comcast Inc. All bidders were told to submit their best offer on 29 July. If KKR wanted to stay in the running, Weigers indicated, it had better improve its offer.

Kravis and Roberts seemed stuck. They had lined up every cent of bank loans that they could find. Drexel had already promised to issue about $1.2 billion in junk bonds. It had been crucial to top out KKR's bid with preferred stock—because Roberts, Raether, and Ammon had designed the preferred stock so that it wouldn't pay cash dividends for years, thereby lightening the immediate pressure on Storer's finances after the buyout. Weigers, however, had dug in his heels, insisting that this $255 million of preferred stock not be crammed down the throats of unwilling Storer shareholders. To mollify Weigers, KKR needed to find an immediate buyer for that $255 million of preferred stock—one who would give KKR cash that could instantly be passed on to Storer share-holders.

Only one man in America could rescue KKR: Mike Milken.

Just a few days before Weigers's deadline, Roberts flew to Los Angeles and called on Drexel's offices. Milken was tied up; Ackerman was free. Unwilling to suggest that he and his partners were on the verge of defeat, Roberts artfully understated KKR's problem. Dillon, Read was playing off the bidders against one another, Roberts complained. "If we're going to win this, Peter, we have to be decisive," Roberts told Ackerman. "The best way to do that is to monetize the preferred." In essence, that meant tying up a further $255 million of Drexel's cash in this high-wire deal, on the hopes that the preferred could then be remarketed to Drexel's clients.

Ackerman gulped. "Look," he told Roberts. "I have to speak to Mike. But if we're going to do this, you've got to be damn sure that you're right about the company."

"I'm right," Roberts stubbornly replied. "There's value there."

Within a day, Milken was briefed about KKR's predicament. His verdict was quick and decisive. "It sounds like we should do an all-cash deal," he told Ackerman and Roberts. Not only would Drexel sell $1.2 billion of junk bonds for KKR, Drexel would also take a vital extra step: it would agree to buy $255 million of the scorned preferred stock from KKR for remarketing to Drexel clients.

The afternoon of Friday, 29 July 1985, members of the KKR bidding team arrived at Storer's Miami headquarters, where they flaunted their newfound financial power. Kravis and Raether entered the Storer board-room and unveiled a new bid of $92.50 a share, or $2.5 billion. The objectionable preferred stock was gone from the offer. Instead, the KKR men said, Storer's shareholders would get $90 a share in cash, with just a small amount of low-grade securities to be shunted into the hands of Storer shareholders.

Weigers was flabbergasted. "You guys can't do this deal," he told Raether in disbelief. "How are you going to finance it?"

"I know how to finance it," Raether proudly replied.

"Well, tell me."

"No," Raether declared. "You tell me I can buy the company. And then I'm going to sit down with you and tell you how I'm going to fi-nance it."

Raether prevailed. The main other bidder, Comcast, couldn't come close to KKR's nearly all-cash bid. Weigers and Storer's other advisers had no choice but to declare KKR the winner. Waiting until a handshake agreement was reached, Kravis then left the Storer boardroom to catch a British Airways flight to London, so he could start an overseas vacation. Ammon and Raether stayed behind to sign the remaining documents. About an hour later, as Kravis began his transatlantic flight, the pilot of the plane summoned Kravis to the cockpit. A small private jet had just radioed the British Airways plane, in an attempt to contact passenger Kravis. It was Raether and Ammon, who had signed all the Storer merger documents, boarded a private KKR jet, and now were flying back to New York. "We did it!" Raether excitedly told Kravis over the crackling radio channels. Thanks to Drexel's help, KKR wasn't a loser; it was the new owner of the Storer broadcasting empire.

Over the next four months, Drexel marketed $1.45 billion of Storer junk bonds and preferred stock to its clients. Rather than summon bond buyers to Beverly Hills, Drexel organized a nationwide road show in which it brought Storer's management and an upbeat video presentation about the company to bond buyers in Boston, Chicago, and nearly a dozen other cities. KKR's Ted Ammon tagged along, but his presence was hardly needed. Drexel was building up immense marketing clout—

not just with West Coast clients like Fred Carr and Tom Spiegel, but with mainstream East Coast investors such as General Electric Co.

All autumn, Drexel did an astonishing job of getting potential investors excited about owning Storer's junk bonds. Wary minds could find dozens of reasons to shun the bonds, many of them spelled out in the cautious, lawyerly language of the bond prospectuses themselves. One section, labeled "Risk Factors," read like the warning label on a bottle of Drano. For three pages, it ticked off one reason after another why Storer might have trouble paying its debts. In the hands of the Drexel sales force, however, the Storer deal sounded like a sure winner. "This is a smart management team," the Drexel salesmen told clients. "There are great values here."

On their own, the KKR executives never could have whipped up such enthusiasm. They were too prickly, too proud of their own work to infuse bond buyers with the essential ingredient of any speculative boom—what economist John Galbraith once called "the conviction that ordinary people were meant to be rich." Drexel could do that.

For its work on Storer, Drexel collected underwriting and advisory fees totaling $55 million. Ackerman also demanded and won the right to allocate 32-percent ownership in Storer as Drexel saw fit in its marketing of the junk bonds and preferred stock. KKR executives were told that Drexel would ration this ownership (in the form of warrants convertible into Storer's post-buyout stock) among securities buyers. But KKR allowed Drexel surprisingly wide latitude in doling out these warrants. Ammon, who traveled with Drexel executives during the Storer road show, agreed he wouldn't ever mention the warrants to bond investors. Drexel could decide what tack to take.

Drexel's approach should have raised eyebrows right away. When the first few bond buyers asked whether equity was available with the Storer bonds, a young Drexel associate traveling with Ammon, Dean Kehler, said: "Yes, but I'm not the right person to talk with. Ask one of our salesmen in Beverly Hills." After a few days, though, Kehler took a more evasive approach. He didn't say yes anymore. He just said: "Ask Beverly Hills." But Ammon and the KKR partners didn't make a big issue of the Storer warrants at the time. Drexel had been hired as a turnkey subcontractor to raise subordinated debt. Whether Drexel was passing along full value to its clients or skimming the best part of the Storer deal for itself didn't seriously concern Ammon or the rest of the KKR crew.

Just as the giant Storer junk-bond deal was wrapping up, Roberts and Kravis brought an even more ambitious plan to Drexel's doorstep—the

Beatrice acquisition. As sketched out at KKR's New York offices, the buyout of the giant Chicago conglomerate would be financed with $4 billion of senior loans from banks; $2.5 billion of subordinated-debt junk bonds sold by Drexel; and $407 million of equity from KKR's limited partner investors. Taken together, KKR would borrow nearly all the money needed to carry out the deal.

This time Milken presented a weirder, more reclusive face to the KKR men. Drexel in late 1985 was near the peak of its power, underwriting a new junk-bond issue every week for clients that ranged from broadcasting entrepreneur Ted Turner to corporate raider Carl Icahn. Milken was both everywhere and nowhere, whirring from deal to deal so fast that people seldom commanded more than a few moments of his attention. On the rare occasions when the KKR men met Milken face-to-face, he rambled about world issues with a zany unpredictability. At one meeting, he lectured visitors about the risks of rampant tampering with food packages. At another session, Milken held forth about the potential for housing the world's surplus population on floating hotels. The oddest Milken performance came in early 1986, as the Beatrice bond offering neared its conclusion. Several KKR executives arrived in Beverly Hills to hammer out some remaining details. Milken sat down with them, but let them know right away that his mind was absorbed with much bigger things than a mere bond issue. "I've been thinking about human longevity," Milken began. The average human lifespan had increased greatly from the eighteenth century to the twentieth century, he observed. But if one looked at the people who lived the longest—three standard deviations from the mean—their typical lifespans had hardly increased at all over the past two centuries. Wasn't that curious? Milken asked. The KKR men just stared at him in befuddlement.

Aware of Milken's proclivity for strange, rambling discussions, his closest lieutenants at Drexel stepped in to handle most of the face-to-face negotiations with KKR. "We didn't want Mike to negotiate directly with clients," recalled Lorraine Spurge, a Drexel office manager. "He was too soft. We left the tough negotiating to Peter Ackerman and Leon Black." It was a potent tactic, which kept Milken both remote and all-powerful.

To sell the Beatrice bonds, Drexel once again organized a giant road show—bringing an upbeat story about the food company and its new bonds to the doorsteps of potential investors across the nation. Whizzing along at a rate of six cities a week, Beatrice's new top management, some Drexel advisers, and a lone KKR associate, Kevin Bousquette, began barnstorming the United States. Every detail was artfully organized by Drexel executives—from limousine schedules to the luncheon menus at elite clubs in each city's financial district. In a ploy often used by "advance men" on political campaigns, Drexel would book tiny banquet rooms in some cities, then whip up an overflow crowd of potential investors. The goal, Drexel officials cheerfully admitted a few years later, was to make the Beatrice bonds seem like such a hot ticket that junk-bond buyers would be lucky if Drexel *let them* acquire some. Sure enough, the forty-seat banquet room in the Chicago Club proved woefully small when more than one hundred potential bond buyers lined the walls. The investors dragged in metal chairs from other rooms and regarded it as a good omen when the food ran out before everyone could be served.

Drexel sold sizzle. It adorned the front covers of each bond prospectus with lavish color foldouts showing all of Beatrice's brands. Orville Redenbacher popcorn nestled alongside Tropicana orange juice, Hunt's tomato paste, and nearly sixty other consumer products. Boring financial data were relegated to the back.

Bond buyers loved it. Fred Carr at First Executive bought more than $100 million of Beatrice bonds. So did Tom Spiegel at Columbia Savings. And scores of smaller buyers joined in. "I thought: Golly, they have all these different household names," recalled San Diego money manager Jim Caywood. "If they run into trouble, they can always sell off the pieces." Caywood asked to buy $50 million worth of bonds; he got only $20 million. Other buyers snapped up Beatrice bonds on the belief that the big conglomerate would actually be run better under the buyout. In particular, bond buyers put their faith in incoming chief executive Don Kelly, a brash, beefy man with a wicked sense of humor. Kelly time and again delighted bond buyers with stories about how Beatrice's old management had frittered away $40 million a year by sponsoring Indy 500 race car driver Mario Andretti. "Can you believe it?" Kelly asked. "Race cars! That's gone. Finished. You won't be seeing Beatrice doing that anymore." Bond buyers loved it. "Getting rid of the old excesses had great visceral appeal," recalled Sheldon Stone, a Los Angeles portfolio manager. "The whole history of the high-yield market was antiestablishment. There was a derision of corporate bureaucracy." By bankrolling the Beatrice buyout, bond buyers felt, they would both make money and fix America.

As the stampede to own Beatrice bonds gathered speed, Drexel's salesmen in March 1986 embarked on their biggest sleight-of-hand maneuver of the decade. As much as possible, Drexel suppressed any mention of the Beatrice warrants that KKR had allotted to Drexel—supposedly for bondholders' benefit. In Drexel's custody were more than

1,000 warrant prospectuses—146-page financial documents meant to be shipped to potential bond buyers. But with few exceptions, those warrant documents never left Drexel's Beverly Hills offices. Instead, the only public trace of the warrants were a few oblique sentences on page 80 of the prospectuses for Beatrice's junk bonds. The information was "buried" amid arcane financial data, a Drexel executive later admitted. To have even a hope of getting warrants, clients had to scrutinize every word of the bond prospectus, then badger their Drexel salesman for a copy of the curiously scarce warrant prospectus. Caught up in the excitement of being part of a "hot" deal, few bond buyers did so.

The ultimate destiny of the Beatrice and Storer warrants would be overlooked by everyone outside Drexel for nearly a year.

Drexel's junk-bond prowess reflected an extraordinary mix of charismatic salesmanship and outlaw behavior. Both of those elements meshed together in a way that was thrilling to participants, and profoundly troubling to outsiders. Most Drexel clients, including KKR, chose to see only the "good" side of Drexel. Most outsiders saw only the "bad" side. To properly understand Drexel and its junk-bond world, however, it is necessary to see both the glorious and the corrupt aspects of the firm at once, and to realize how tightly they fit together.

A onetime cheerleader at Birmingham High School in Van Nuys, California, Milken promoted junk bonds and his clients with contagious optimism. "Money isn't the scarce resource," Milken told potential borrowers. "Human capital is." With example after example, he talked about how much America needed entrepreneurs, how important it was to defy conventional wisdom, and how dedicated he was to putting money in the hands of people bold enough to do great things.

Clients of all stripes—including Henry Kravis—loved this pitch. At one meeting in the mid-1980s, Kravis asked Milken: "Why are you able to sell all these bonds? Why is it that you've got this capability?"

"Look at the people I'm backing," Milken replied. "I'm backing people who have their own money at risk. Boone Pickens. Carl Icahn. KKR. They're not like Roger Smith at General Motors. I'm always going to do fine by these guys."

Again and again, though, Milken and his Drexel aides combined this can-do spirit with secret ruses, gouging some of their clients and granting others special favors that federal prosecutors later would characterize as akin to bribes. Without this chicanery, Milken and Drexel might still have sold billions of dollars of junk bonds and changed American attitudes toward credit. But it was easier—and a lot more profitable for Milken's gang—to control the junk-bond market by their own rules.

A favorite Drexel ploy was to pressure borrowers to sell more junk bonds than necessary, so that the spare cash thus generated could be used in the future to *buy* other Drexel bond issues. This practice was just barely legal, and it was distasteful to almost everyone involved. The rest of Wall Street carped about Drexel's "daisy chain," in which the firm's top clients doubled as lenders and borrowers to one another, creating a set of interlocking relationships that made Milken into the ruler of a new financial system. "Look at the world Mike Milken has created," *Forbes* magazine wrote at one stage. "It's almost as if he can print his own currency. A deal has problems? Refinance it through another client. . . . As long as those debts keep getting validated, as long as Milken can keep the machine running smoothly, everything is fine."

Kravis and Roberts say that Drexel never pressured them to boost artificially KKR's junk-bond borrowings and join the daisy chain. (Most proposed KKR junk-bond offerings were so huge that Drexel executives found it daunting to raise the mere minimum that KKR needed.) But on at least one occasion, the daisy chain was put to use for KKR's benefit. Internal Drexel records show that millions of dollars of Beatrice bonds were bought by other Drexel junk-bond issuers with spare cash on hand. Companies controlled by New York financier Ronald Perelman bought $3.8 million of Beatrice 15¼-percent bonds. Companies controlled by another New York financier and Drexel client, Nelson Peltz, bought $6.4 million of those same 15¼-percent bonds. Even one of Drexel's fastest-growing industrial clients, McCaw Cellular Communications, was prevailed upon to buy $2 million of the 15¼-percent bonds.

Also in the renegade category was what government investigators alleged was a Drexel tactic of offering secret personal payoffs to money managers who controlled large investment pools. In return, the money managers filled their portfolios with Drexel securities. To federal investigators, such practices amounted to bribes. A prime example involved the Storer underwriting in 1985. Some $50 million of bonds and preferred stock were bought by First Investors Management Co., a New York mutual fund group. Several years later, federal regulators discovered that First Investors' junk-bond portfolio manager, Benaldo Bayse, had been allowed to buy the much choicer Storer warrants "for his personal account at prices substantially below market value." Bayse lost his job at First Investors as a result—but KKR and Drexel had already benefited from his purchases.

If pressure tactics and payoffs didn't work, there was always sex. Some of Drexel's salesmen regarded every tycoon as a playboy at heart, and this led them to believe that Drexel could sell more bonds if it catered to prurient desires. A frequent New York lender to KKR described one visit to Beverly Hills, at which he expected to have a working dinner with a Drexel representative. "Instead, we went to see three hours of these girls mud-wrestling," the lender recalled in astonishment.

The lurid nature of Drexel's biggest gathering—an annual spring "research" conference better known as the Predators' Ball—was later made famous by author Connie Bruck. At the 1985 conference, Bruck wrote, Drexel invited its top sixty clients to a private party at Bungalow 8 of the Beverly Hills Hotel, where America's top raiders and entrepreneurs were surrounded by "extremely attractive" young women. Kravis, Roberts, and Kohlberg were too new as Drexel clients to attend the 1985 affair, but chatter soon spread on Wall Street that the women at the parties were, if not prostitutes, then models and secretaries selected for their looks rather than for their financial insights. Don Engel, the Drexel consultant who arranged these parties, regarded them as the right way to do business. He once told a corporate CEO: "How could I get all these guys to come if I didn't have the girls?"

In April 1986, Kravis, Roberts, and Kohlberg attended their first Predator's Ball. They were the heroes of the legitimate side of the conference—the men who had put together the giant Beatrice buyout that was being concluded even as the conference took place. And, inevitably, the three KKR partners were shown the seamy side of Drexel, too. The second evening of the conference, Drexel invited Kravis, Roberts, and Kohlberg to a private dinner at Chasen's, an upscale Beverly Hills restaurant. As the KKR partners walked into the upstairs dining room, their jaws dropped. For every businessman, there were two cute young blonds or brunettes in cocktail dresses. The KKR men were embarrassed and slightly offended. "We thought Drexel had come such a long way and then we encountered this," one KKR executive recalled. "I felt like I had walked into an underwear salesman's convention." Most disgusted was Kohlberg, the pillar of rectitude at generally prim KKR. Kohlberg and one of his longtime lawyer friends, Joe Flom, retreated to a corner of the room to talk quietly in private. "They were two of the most uncomfortable-looking men I've ever seen," a witness recalled.

Even after seeing the renegade side of Drexel up close, Kravis and Roberts chose to ignore it. They craved the financial power that Drexel provided. They liked the optimistic, pro-debt rhetoric that Milken and his lieutenants used. Milken "came up with an idea and worked very hard at it," Roberts said in 1989. Most of Drexel's ruses, Roberts asserted, were simply ways to fan investor excitement and create the appearance of scarcity that would help a bond issue sell quickly. Beyond that, Roberts said: "I don't know whether Mike did something right or wrong. He's been the victim of a lot of jealous competitors." To Kravis and Roberts, Drexel was simply a turnkey contractor, raising huge amounts of money in the junk-bond market without any need for meddling by the executives at the buyout firm. That arrangement kept the KKR men from learning too much about how Milken actually sold bonds—and from getting too tangled in Drexel's troubles.

Starting in November 1986, though, Drexel's troubles with the law became much more profound. On Friday, 14 November, one of Milken's newest allies, takeover stock speculator Ivan Boesky, agreed to plead guilty to insider-trading charges, pay a $100 million fine—and cooperate with government investigators. The moment the news hit the wires, Milken turned pale. He summoned one of his top bond salesmen, James Dahl, to work on Sunday, 16 November. Dahl later testified that Milken invited him into the men's room that Sunday, where Milken turned on the water and started to wash his hands. Then Milken leaned over and told Dahl: "There haven't been any subpoenas issued. So whatever you need to do, do it."

Cryptic as Milken's instructions were, the Drexel junk-bond chief had plenty to worry about. Drexel had secretly paid $5.3 million to Boesky earlier in 1986, which Boesky disclosed to the authorities once his Wall Street career ended. The implication: Boesky had swapped valuable and perhaps illegally disclosed information with Milken. Soon, legions of federal investigators began to close in on Drexel's world. In dozens of Drexel-financed deals, they saw traces of what looked like insider trading—with confidential takeover information being leaked to traders who thus gained an unfair edge on every other market participant. Milken's nominal bosses in New York began to sound worried, too. "We've been among the most aggressive firms, maybe the most aggressive," Drexel chief executive Fred Joseph said in an early 1987 interview. "We break new ground. Normally that's considered creative. Now, when it's under a microscope, I'm worried about it."

The most shocking disclosures about Milken and Drexel in the next two years went beyond insider trading, and cut to the heart of Drexel's financial role. As middlemen, Drexel had taken on grave responsibilities, both to borrowers such as KKR who wanted cash quickly at reasonable rates, and to lenders such as Fred Carr who wanted high yields on loans that weren't too risky. Milken had depicted himself as a driven, visionary man who worked superhuman hours to link his two sets of clients in ways that were fair to both sides. Buyers of junk bonds in particular came away with the impression that Milken wanted them to be the rich ones. Small details—such as Milken's ill-fitting toupee, his persistence in living in a modest Encino, California, home, and his fondness for ordinary activities such as basketball—left bond buyers with the impression that very little of the winnings from leverage were coming off in the middleman's hands.

It was a nice image for Milken to cultivate—but it was a lie. Far more than people realized, Drexel was gouging buyers of junk bonds. Secretly, Milken collected astronomical salaries at Drexel. Government investigators later discovered that Milken's pay totaled $295 million in 1986 and $550 million in 1987. Another of the ways that Milken grew so rich was to hijack the big equity stakes in buyout companies that had been set aside for bond buyers.

A full understanding of the nature of Drexel's maneuvers dawned slowly on KKR executives. In the fall of 1986, Kravis on a business trip bumped into a major insurance-company buyer of Beatrice bonds. By that time, it was becoming clear that the Beatrice buyout would be a big financial success for KKR, and that the post-buyout equity in the company would be tremendously valuable. Making small talk, Kravis said: "You must be feeling pretty good about those Beatrice warrants."

"What warrants?" the insurance man asked.

For the next few months, KKR executives speculated that Drexel had kept a small share, perhaps 10 to 20 percent of the warrants, while parceling most of them out to Beatrice bond buyers. But that hypothesis exploded in the spring of 1987 when KKR began preparing documents to sell a major part of Beatrice. Attorneys at Simpson Thacher began compiling the obligatory list of major Beatrice owners that had to be included in public financial filings. Were there any large warrant holders? Simpson Thacher attorney Casey Cogut asked Drexel. To Cogut's surprise, the answer was yes. Some 95 percent of the warrants were owned by various Drexel partnerships. Their value: an estimated $400 million.

KKR's younger associates turned furious, arguing that if bondholders didn't need the warrants, KKR and its limited partner investors should have been able to keep a larger ownership in the buyout companies. "We got screwed," KKR associate Mike Tokarz declared, as he banged heads with Leon Black, Peter Ackerman, and others at Drexel. Simultaneously, Ted Ammon harangued Ackerman about the Storer warrants. And Saul

Fox demanded an accounting from Ackerman about the Motel 6 warrants. Jerry Kohlberg even suggested that KKR sue Drexel.

None of KKR's sputtering drew apologies or any expression of shame from Ackerman, Black, or Milken. "It was the only time I felt like I saw the back of Ackerman's hand," Saul Fox said on the Motel 6 warrants. "I pressed him. I couldn't get anywhere with it. The guy was like a cornered mountain lion." Instead, Ackerman and other top Drexel officials insisted there was nothing wrong. All of KKR's big junk-bond offerings had seemed tremendously risky when Drexel marketed them. Drexel had assumed that warrants would be needed to entice bondholders. But the Drexel method of selling bonds involved guile, Ackerman cheekily explained to the KKR executives. The warrants weren't mentioned to prospective bondholders and were held in reserve. When it turned out—time after time—that the bonds really could be sold without equity, Drexel's top junk-bond professionals simply grabbed the warrants themselves.

Despite Kohlberg's suggestion of suing Drexel, Kravis and Roberts decided to let the matter drop. "There was only a 20-percent chance that we would win," Roberts later said. After all, KKR hadn't negotiated the return of unneeded warrants. More important, KKR wasn't done using Drexel's mighty junk-bond machine to serve its own ends.

The real outcries about Drexel's warrant grab should have come from bondholders. Veteran lenders like Prudential's Ray Charles knew that over the long run the only way that risky subordinated lending made sense was if lenders got to own a piece of buyout companies. That way, big profits from financially successful buyouts would offset the inevitable periodic defaults on loans gone sour. Drexel's clients had been denuded of that richly profitable equity—something that would cost them dearly later on.

But at the time, major junk-bond buyers viewed Drexel as a ticket to riches. Even the disclosure of the warrant caper didn't shake their faith. In the sunny market climes of 1986 and early 1987, in fact, First Executive, Columbia Savings, and other big Drexel clients kept posting big profits. Their junk-bond portfolios yielded 12 percent or more, making them appear smarter than cautious S&Ls and insurance companies that earned a mere 9 or 10 percent from portfolios full of home mortgages and other traditional investments. Fred Carr achieved his life's ambition of boosting First Executive from a tiny insurer to one of America's ten biggest. Tom Spiegel paid himself a whopping $9 million salary one year at Columbia, bought a Gulfstream jet, and hired an English butler for his offices. Magazines lauded Spiegel as the man running America's soundest

S&L. Listening to Milken's public pronouncements, many junk-bond buyers believed that the big promised yields from Drexel underwritings would be enough to make them rich. If Drexel skimmed profits from concealed warrants, these top investors figured, so be it.

The Drexel gospel gained fresh life in 1986 and 1987 as mutual-fund companies saw a profitable opportunity to link up small American savers with the junk-bond boom. Quarter-page advertisements in *Money* magazine beckoned small individual investors to DISCOVER HIGH INCOME. Toll-free phone numbers provided ways for ordinary investors to order prospectuses for junk-bond mutual funds round the clock. "Let [our] aggressive portfolio of higher yielding, medium to lower quality bonds start working for you today!" the biggest mutual-fund group, Fidelity Investments, told the public. "Start with just $2,500." In return, savers could look forward to rich yields that seemed so tempting at a time when safe Treasury bills paid 8 percent or less. "12.08%!" one magazine ad screamed at investors in giant type.

Small investors responded in the late 1980s with a stampede that astonished even Drexel's gung-ho financiers. A medical-supply salesman in Maine put $7,000 into a junk-bond fund to finance his children's college education. An eighty-nine-year-old widow in Florida switched most of her $250,000 savings into junk-bond funds. All told, ordinary American savers pumped more than $18 billion into junk-bond funds from 1986 through 1988. Money cascaded into the hands of mutual-fund managers faster than they could sensibly invest it. The path of least resistance was to channel cash into whatever new deal KKR or other leveraged financiers provided.

A classic speculative bubble was under way. The actual merits of each new bond offering began to matter less and less. The risk that junk-bond issuers would fail to pay their promised high yields and default on their debt was dismissed out of hand or ignored entirely. Instead, ordinary savers and Drexel's biggest clients relied on three things as they hurled cash into the junk-bond market.

The junk-bond buyers' first tenet of faith was in the virtues of extrapolation. Pioneers in junk-bond investing had undeniably made a lot of money, as Milken's early underwritings delivered the promised high yields and seldom defaulted. Rather than worry that this historic success might be about to end, optimistic buyers assumed it would never stop. First Executive's Fred Carr began arguing that investors' real folly wasn't in buying junk bonds. It was in *failing* to buy junk bonds, and instead owning high-grade bonds with skimpy yields.

Just as prized by junk-bond buyers was the virtue of companionship.

"So many smart people were putting money into deals," recalled Jim Upchurch, the chief investment officer at Columbia Savings. Investing alongside the smart money seemed like a winning strategy. In fact—in the classic sign of a speculative bubble—market participants began to fixate on other people's buying patterns as the key to success. Analyzing new bonds on their own merits was too tedious. Instead, the pros watched the mutual-fund inflows and tried to buy bonds ahead of the next wave of individual savers' cash. Small investors watched the pros. As Upchurch later put it: "People were caught up in the wave."

Finally, junk-bond buyers voiced an almost religious faith in Mike Milken, believing that he was a shepherd to the whole junk-bond market and could ward off any dangers. They swapped stories about how early Milken started his workday and how many facts about the bond market he could keep in his head at once. They emulated his phrases, filling their conversations and their annual reports with talk about new entrepreneurs, access to capital, and a financial revolution. "People believed in Mike," recalled David Scheiber, a portfolio manager at a California S&L that bought nearly $1 billion of junk bonds. "They thought he would take care of them."

Blessed with an instinct for market cycles, Kravis and Roberts repeatedly exploited the junk-bond hysteria of 1986 through 1988. They auctioned off businesses that KKR had acquired earlier—frequently attracting re-markably high bids from giddy new buyers bankrolled by Drexel. Cole National was sold just three years after KKR bought it, for $160 million more than KKR had paid. Amstar Corporation, a 1984 buyout acquisi-tion, also was sold within three years to a Merrill Lynch–led buyout group willing to pay a higher price for the same company. Ever dicier junk bonds were brought into being this way, as the same operating company strained to support a vastly increased debt load. But that wasn't KKR's problem. If reckless buyers wanted to pay KKR top dollar to get to own a business, Kravis, Roberts, and their colleagues were eminently willing to sell.

Not only was KKR indifferent to new buyers' ability to service debts; so, too, were the underwriters of the junk bonds involved. Profit margins from the junk-bond business were so huge that more than a dozen big Wall Street firms piled into competition with Drexel, battling one another to see who could underwrite the most daredevil junk bonds. Credit standards eroded tremendously in this period, as shown by the ratio of junk-bond issuers' operating earnings to their new interest expense. In

KKR's early days, a ratio of 6 to 1 was considered normal for an un-leveraged company; a ratio of 1.75 to 1 after a buyout was considered daring. As the junk-bond mania continued, however, average interest coverage ratios kept dropping. According to researcher Barrie Wigmore, they fell to 0.77 to 1 in 1986, and to 0.71 to 1 in 1988. Even if the money set aside for depreciation charges was figured in with the operating income—a more generous method of gauging a company's cash flow—interest coverage ratios on 1988 junk-bond deals had sunk to 1.23 to 1. At those levels, a borrowing company could hardly pay its debts from day one.

Ingenious junk-bond underwriters found a way to mask the fact that many leveraged companies couldn't meet their interest obligations. Deal-makers at Drexel, Merrill Lynch, and other Wall Street firms created remarkable new securities that "accrued" interest but didn't really pay it. Some of them were pay-in-kind, or PIK, bonds, that spewed out interest payments in the form of more bonds, rather than cash.* Others were "zero-coupon" bonds that didn't pay interest in any form at all. Instead, they were sold at a discount to their eventual maturity value in six to twenty years; the price difference provided something vaguely akin to interest income.

KKR benefited a second way from Wall Street's growing junk-bond rivalry. Whenever Kravis and Roberts needed to raise money in the junk-bond market for new buyouts, they pitted various underwriters in competition with Drexel, thus obtaining better terms from the eventual winner. High-handed at times, the KKR men sent back one preliminary bond-offering document to Drexel executives with notations appended at every stage. Next to the interest rate, they wrote "too high." Next to the price, "too low." Most of the time, Drexel fended off competitors and still won KKR's business. But KKR executives brought one assignment to Salomon Brothers in 1986, and another to Merrill Lynch in 1988.

One of the choicest KKR assignments, underwriting $1.1 billion of bonds for the Owens-Illinois buyout in early 1987, went to the most patrician firm on Wall Street: Morgan Stanley & Co. Formed in 1935 as a breakaway from J. P. Morgan & Co., Morgan Stanley had a reputation on Wall Street as a "white shoe" firm, a nickname that dated back to the early twentieth century, when the best-bred East Coast financiers wore white shoes to work. Junk bonds were an admittedly rough-and-tumble

---

*Those new bonds begat more new bonds for as long as eight more years. Eventually, it was hoped, the company's operating profit would have improved enough that all the PIK bonds could begin making cash interest payments.

new line of business for Morgan Stanley, but its investment bankers lobbied hard for the Owens-Illinois assignment. And Owens-Illinois's investment bank advisers, who were concerned at the time about Drexel's legal difficulties, urged the KKR men to use a non-Drexel underwriter.

Roguish as ever, Drexel executives decided immediately after KKR's Owens-Illinois announcement that it was time to nurture the KKR "relationship" and chide the buyout firm for straying from their fold. In April 1987, Ackerman and a half dozen Drexel colleagues hosted a private dinner for KKR executives at a small restaurant in Santa Monica, California. The Beatrice warrant caper was laughed off as quickly as possible; Drexel investment banker Alison Mass presented all the KKR partners and associates with Drexel's form of penance: a wall sign modeled after the ads for the movie *Ghostbusters,* in which the words *Equity Give-ups* were encased in a red circle with a slash through it. The Morgan Stanley connection was dealt with in similarly flip style. At the end of the meal, Ackerman rose to announce another prize for the KKR executives.

"We want to properly equip you for dealing with your current supplier of high-yield product," Ackerman told the roomful of KKR deal-makers. "Even though you are doing business away from us, we're still your friends. And we want you to be as well prepared as possible." With that, a pack of junior Drexel employees handed out large cardboard boxes to Kravis, Roberts, and the rest of the KKR team. Inside each box was a present from Drexel—a pair of shiny white shoes.

Within Drexel, meanwhile, the powerful financial machine that Milken had assembled in the early 1980s began to fall apart. Milken, who in his early years had represented himself as a watchdog for bond buyers' interests, became increasingly detached from his business and consumed with fighting the government's securities-fraud charges against him. Ackerman took over much of Milken's duties from late 1987 onward. Infused with a desire for quick success, Ackerman propped up Drexel's market-share statistics by selling a lot of bonds of dubious quality rather than limiting himself to sound underwritings of bonds that his clients would be glad to own a few years later.

The most telling example concerned Storer Communications, the television-station and cable-system operator that KKR had bought with Drexel's help in 1985. By late 1987, KKR decided that it wanted to break Storer into two pieces and sell them both. Broadcast properties of all types were fetching astonishingly high prices from new buyers. Although operating profits at Storer had risen a modest 20 percent in two years, bids for television stations and cable systems had climbed 30 to 50 percent. Itching to unload Storer, George Roberts and KKR associate Scott Stuart visited Drexel's Beverly Hills offices on 21 October 1987, just two days after the stock market crash of 19 October. Storer hadn't yet paid off its junk bonds, Roberts and Stuart acknowledged. But they wanted to assign the bonds to a buyer of the cable-TV segment of the company. Then they wanted to sell six of Storer's television stations to Memphis, Tennessee, entrepreneur George Gillett for $1.3 billion. Gillett would take on huge risks—including a yearly interest bill far beyond the cash flow of the TV stations at the time. But that was his problem. While KKR would keep a modest investment in the television stations, it would largely let Gillett worry about the extra debt.

Years earlier, Milken and Ackerman might have hesitated to under-write the new bonds that Gillett's company proposed to issue under the name of SCI Television. These bonds reeked of risk to investors. By the late 1980s, however, Drexel was peddling any bonds it could, no matter how risky. Hunger for fees, and the prestige of being the number-one junk-bond underwriter, had become the top priority for most of Milken's lieutenants. As for Milken himself, his priorities had become even more spectacularly distorted. In the midst of negotiations between Ackerman and Roberts, Milken popped in to share his latest thoughts—which had nothing to do with Storer at all. "I've been looking into Third World debt," Milken began. "There are great opportunities there. Take Mexico." For the next few minutes, Milken spun out a sweeping scenario in which he would buy up Mexican debt at a discount from U.S. banks, package it into new securities, and sell them to other investors. It would be a reenactment of his pioneering work in corporate bonds in the late 1970s, but on a scale a thousand times larger. Caught up in his own dreams, Milken blithely ignored $400 million of new junk bonds in front of him.

This madcap side of Milken puzzled Stuart, a twenty-seven-year-old New Orleans native who had joined KKR just fifteen months earlier, after graduating from Stanford Business School, and was still getting used to the foibles of America's most famous financiers. As Roberts and Stuart boarded an elevator to leave the Drexel building, Stuart gestured toward the conference room where Milken had been speaking.

"Is he always like this?" Stuart whispered. Roberts just shook his head and laughed.

Three years earlier, many of the KKR partners had regarded Milken as a genius. By the late 1980s, Milken had shrunk in their eyes to a much lesser role; now he was merely an eccentric ally running a powerful but unstable operation.

As Drexel and Milken slid into ever deeper trouble, the KKR partners disowned their once-warm association with the junk-bond kings almost entirely. When Milken was indicted on charges of securities fraud in early 1989, nearly one hundred top Drexel clients took out full-page ads in major newspapers and signed their names to a brief message that began: "Mike Milken, we believe in you." Conspicuously absent from that list were Henry Kravis, George Roberts, and Jerry Kohlberg. In the fall of 1990, after Milken had pled guilty to various charges of securities fraud and was about to be sentenced, KKR executive Ted Ammon testified against Milken concerning Milken's handling of the Storer warrants in 1985. Portraying KKR and its limited partner investors as casualties of Milken's maneuvering, Ammon said that if he had known how many Storer warrants ended up in Milken's hands, he would have pressed Drexel to lower its other fees and treat bondholders better. "We clearly anticipated coming back to the marketplace," Ammon said. "We wanted to have a happy group of bondholders."

With all the bitterness and sorrow of a spurned mistress, Drexel's top deal-makers watched KKR deny or tear apart ties that once had been so tight. Milken's defense attorney, Arthur Liman, pressed Ammon hard in cross-examination about how deep KKR's indignation had really run. Even if KKR had known beforehand that Milken would snatch as many Storer warrants as possible, Liman asked, "Would you have walked away from this transaction?" Ammon's reply was: No. Yet the overwhelming message from Ammon's testimony was that KKR now wanted to be seen as a victim of Milken's schemes, rather than as a confederate.

The ease with which the KKR men walked away from their Drexel relationship came as a jolt to Milken, Ackerman, and a few others among Drexel's top deal-makers. A few days after Ammon testified, a longtime Drexel executive said he found it "sad" that the KKR executives were publicly complaining that Drexel had mistreated them. He added: "I wish they understood what extraordinary results they got from their under-writer."

6
The Takeover Minstrels

Able to line up vast loans without creating a public stir, Kohlberg Kravis Roberts & Co. surfaced more than thirty times in the 1980s with high-priced takeover bids for publicly owned companies. Each time, bells went off in brokerage houses around the country, while Quotron terminals lit up with the news of the latest acquisition offer. The stock price of the target company would soar 20 percent or more in a matter of minutes. After a long silent pursuit, KKR would suddenly be in the headlines, offering a much higher price to acquire a company than investors just a few days earlier had thought possible. Shareholders would find themselves the lucky winners in an age of casino capitalism, about to collect quick profits from another jackpot in the takeover of a household-name company.

Once KKR—or anyone else—began a takeover bid, a spirited public drama of about six weeks' duration began to play out. High-paid lawyers jumped into corporate boardrooms and began scolding directors about their "duty of care" and "duty of loyalty" to the shareholders they represented. These lofty-sounding doctrines almost always translated into a duty to sell a company to the highest bidder. Meanwhile, an even higher-paid set of Wall Street advisers peddled takeover tactics to all interested parties. Some specialized in "defending" companies, others in advising would-be raiders. It hardly mattered. All the various advisers became pro-takeover conspirators as they barnstormed the country together, each serving predetermined roles in the others' maneuvers with corporate directors.

Time and again, takeovers turned into a stylized form of white-collar warfare. Wall Street in the late 1980s abounded with feisty combatants who specialized in lawsuits, shouting matches, and broken promises. The long-term impact of these takeover battles on America's economic strength didn't matter to any of the central participants at the time. The game itself was everything. Companies' advisers wanted to make money for shareholders and fees for themselves. Bidders wanted to outfox all rivals in takeover tactics, in order to claim another conquest at the end. KKR and its advisers displayed a dazzling cleverness in devising new tactics and weapons to obtain an "edge" in each new battle. And it was all perfectly legal.

In these showdowns, the KKR partners drew a lot of their success from a tactic no one else thought of: they stayed polite and composed throughout the most frenzied stages. Henry Kravis and George Roberts became known as America's number-one buyers of companies, and they played that leader's position to the utmost. Kravis was the salesman, bringing his natural ebullience into unfamiliar boardrooms in such a pleasant, cheerful way that nervous directors found him nearly irresistible. Roberts was the shrewdest gambler in town, showing unerring instincts for when to raise a bid, when to set a deadline, and when to walk away. Regardless of which cousin led the buyout firm's forays, the men from KKR kept their cool around big numbers even as other deal-makers got vertigo. Only Kohlberg, nearly a generation older than his two younger partners, found little to do; he played an ever smaller role as KKR's deals progressed.

As the central organizers of the biggest buyouts, Kravis and Roberts disbursed fees for dozens, even hundreds, of advisers. That meant that the KKR partners could bend Wall Street's top investment banks to their will by sprinkling advisory assignments around with great artfulness. Deal-makers at Merrill Lynch, Morgan Stanley, and a host of other big securities firms periodically took on lucrative assignments at KKR's request—and picked up hints that more fees lay ahead if their Wall Street firm continued to serve KKR's desires. Privately, investment bankers grumbled that Kravis and Roberts acted as if everyone on Wall Street could be bought. But most malcontents soon swallowed their pride and began looking for ways to get back onto KKR's fee queue. Intoxicated by the belief that they were "creating" shareholder wealth, deal-makers demanded rich rewards for making each takeover possible. For many top deal-makers, the prospect of winning a multi-million-dollar fee for a few months' work became a demon that drove them onward, and that governed their thinking about each new corporate client.

These powerful, roaming bands of takeover advisers left chief executives of takeover-prone companies flabbergasted and angry. "I got the feeling I was seeing a marvelous play," recalled one CEO, Smith Richardson of Richardson-Vicks Co., whose health-care company came under siege in the mid-1980s. "The actors were superb. They really had you convinced [that they were acting in the best interests of the company]. But it was all a charade." Years later, Richardson recalled with disbelief the performance of the advisers he hired to "defend" his company. For a few weeks, they jousted night and day with another set of advisers who were "attacking" his company. All the advisers billed for huge fees. And then the advisers recommended that Richardson-Vicks be sold to a third company. Richardson lost his job, his company lost its independent identity, and the various advisers collected more than $20 million for about six weeks' work. By the time Richardson-Vicks's old shareholders cashed their checks, the cavalcade of advisers was hard at work selling other companies across the United States.

Perhaps the most revealing glimpse of the takeover minstrels' priorities came in a moment of cocktail-party banter. In November 1986, KKR hosted a giant dinner in New York to celebrate its completion of the $4.2 billion buyout of Safeway Stores Inc. Among the guests was New York attorney Richard Katcher, who in theory should have viewed KKR as the enemy. For months, Katcher had worked on Safeway's behalf in an ultimately unsuccessful effort to avoid selling the company to any buyer. Nevertheless, he and his wife came to the party. Before long, Katcher's wife—who had never met any of the KKR executives before—briskly walked up to George Roberts and snapped: "So you're the guy who's taking away all my husband's clients!"

Trying to defuse any tension, Dick Katcher quickly interjected: "No, no. You don't understand. We get a fee that way."

Roberts's reply was much more enigmatic. "We're not bad guys," he said. "We don't go in when we're not invited."

America's takeover boom began in the early 1980s, several years before KKR became a significant financial force. At that time, leading companies in two mature industries—oil and food—began building up surplus cash flow, with no obvious way to reinvest these winnings in existing businesses and earn good returns. Rather than see these companies hoard their extra cash flow, or pay out much bigger dividends to shareholders, bold investment bankers urged the likes of Mobil Corporation, Kraft Inc., and other cash-rich companies to make giant acquisitions. Antitrust policy had been greatly relaxed since the Reagan administration had taken office, and many top executives believed they should exploit what might be a short-lived chance to snap up smaller competitors. Total U.S. takeovers, which amounted to $67 billion in 1981, nearly tripled by 1986, to $190 billion.

As deals grew ever bigger and more frequent, the accompanying pro-takeover machinery became ever more powerful. Specialized mergers-and-acquisitions departments at Wall Street firms swelled from almost nothing in the late 1970s to 300- or 500-person teams by the late 1980s. Frequently the M&A chief became a financial celebrity, better known and better paid than the securities firm's chairman. Best known was Bruce Wasserstein, a baldish, disheveled deal-maker at First Boston Corporation known for his booming voice and his lightning-quick grasp of takeover tactics. Nearly as prominent were about thirty other M&A advisers, all brilliant, ambitious Ivy League graduates in their late thirties or early forties. They vacationed together in the Hamptons, enrolled their children in the same nursery schools, and came of age together in the midst of a great bull market.

From the mid-1980s onward, the M&A specialists turned their attention toward leveraged buyout candidates. Takeover targets abounded: cash-rich, slow-growing companies with little existing debt and divisions that could be sold off quickly if needed. With so much ready credit available, acquirers didn't mind bidding far beyond prevailing stock-market prices to buy a company. They expected to recoup their high prices by selling pieces of the company to even giddier new buyers, by implementing quick cost cuts, or by exploiting the tax advantages of interest deductibility and increased depreciation. Asked why companies suddenly became worth so much more in takeovers, one financier in 1986 explained: "It's the leverage." He added, without any evident sense of self-parody: "What we're really doing is releasing value the way a sculptor releases a work of art from a block of stone."

And so the takeover minstrels swirled into KKR's life—starting with Beatrice. Several deal-makers later wryly referred to that buyout and its aftermath as "the Wall Street Full Employment Act of 1985–86." On KKR's side, a bevy of investment bankers from Drexel and Kidder, Peabody were joined by swarms of lawyers from Simpson Thacher and Latham & Watkins. Beatrice directors surrounded themselves with an equally large pack of Wall Street advisers from Lazard Frères & Co. and

Salomon Brothers Inc., as well as top-flight lawyers from Wachtell, Lipton, Rosen & Katz. On the fringes, investment bankers from E. F. Hutton and Goldman, Sachs tried—without much luck—to put together rival buyout offers. "There was this atmosphere of big-game hunting," recalled Fred Rentschler, a future Beatrice executive who attended one strategy session that was packed so tightly that advisers lined the walls of a KKR conference room two-deep.

KKR opened its public pursuit of Beatrice in mid-October 1985 with a takeover bid of $45 a share, or $5.6 billion, an amount rejected as "inadequate" by the food company's advisers. In the code language of Wall Street takeover battles, Beatrice's response meant: You need to raise your price. Taking his cue from Kidder, Peabody adviser Martin Siegel, Kravis two weeks later boosted KKR's offer to $47 a share. Beatrice's advisers still didn't accept the bid, and kept looking for rival suitors, but agreed to share confidential data on the company with KKR. Analysts quickly termed it "the beginning of the end" for Beatrice as an independent company. Soon afterward, Kravis won a chance to present KKR's case in person on Tuesday, 12 November, during a board meeting at Beatrice's downtown Chicago headquarters.

That morning, two close Kravis confidants say, was one of the few times they ever saw Kravis truly nervous. "Henry was anxious," recalled KKR associate Mike Tokarz. "He was pacing back and forth, thinking a mile a minute, trying to anticipate issues that might come up." But once inside the twenty-sixth-floor boardroom, Kravis owned the show. Standing at the edge of Beatrice's giant, five-sided board table, Kravis struck a tone that seemed reasonable and sincere. He began by jacking up KKR's offer to $50 a share, or $6.2 billion. He assured wary director William Karnes that KKR would treat small Beatrice shareholders fairly in a takeover, and protect workers' pension rights for years to come. When director Jayne Spain became so upset at the thought of selling Beatrice that she started crying, Kravis stopped his presentation and waited for her to calm down. With his big blue eyes and his trace of an Oklahoma accent, Kravis reminded one director of a prospective son-in-law asking for a daughter's hand in marriage. People who worked regularly with Kravis knew him as a financial Casanova, whirring from boardroom to boardroom every few months in search of a new conquest. But the Beatrice directors couldn't see that. "He was a gentleman," recalled Beatrice chairman William Granger. For one hour that Sunday morning, Beatrice's eighteen directors were the most important people in Kravis's life. They felt flattered. They felt relieved. That afternoon, the directors agreed to hand over Beatrice to Kravis, telling themselves, in Granger's words, that "it seemed like the best thing to do for shareholders."

Only a few Beatrice directors felt stampeded. Among the cynics was Alexander Brody, a top Ogilvy & Mather advertising executive who knew a lot about catering to a group's fears and desires. "We were progressing toward the inevitable," Brody later said. "The company had lost control of its destiny. After I was reminded fifteen times that I was liable, I had to go along. I was disappointed with our advisers at every level. Our advisers were much more concerned about getting a price that would stand the test of time than in looking for a way to keep the company independent. I wondered whose advisers they really were."

Within the KKR camp, too, the Beatrice deal triggered a distrust of Wall Street's roving investment bankers. Kravis at the time frequently relied on Kidder, Peabody's Siegel, a personable thirty-seven-year-old, to help develop bidding strategies that were supposed to stay secret. Quietly, though, Siegel was misusing that confidential information to tip off stock traders about KKR's plans. A crucial moment came in early January 1986, when KKR was forced to revise its bid slightly because of a misestimation of Beatrice's cash flow. The change ultimately made little difference; KKR simply reduced its immediate cash payment to Beatrice shareholders and substituted more preferred stock that would be turned into cash two years later. But on 8 January 1986, Wall Street was abuzz with talk that the Beatrice deal was in trouble. Siegel, it later turned out, had tipped off prominent Goldman, Sachs trader Bob Freeman about KKR's need to revise its bid—an action for which both he and Freeman would later go to jail. The full extent of Siegel's wrongdoing didn't become known until early 1987. But as KKR executives watched Beatrice stock plummet the morning of 8 January 1986, before any announcement about the revised bid was made, they became suspicious first of their Drexel advisers, then of Siegel. From that time onward, Kravis and Roberts still hired plenty of Wall Street talent to help them on takeover tactics—but the KKR partners became much warier about sharing confidential information with any outsider.

Over the next five years, takeovers, financial scandals, and glib advice swept across the country. Corporate advisers flew from city to city, counseling nervous directors about their options and arranging for more giant companies to be auctioned. The image of blue-eyed Henry Kravis stepping into a boardroom and politely explaining his latest billion-dollar offer became a symbol of an era. Shareholders collected an estimated $200 billion in gains, and advisers had a ball. Working breakneck hours on the biggest deals in history was "fun," Wachtell, Lipton's Katcher later acknowledged. As the deal tally mounted, most top advisers packed their offices with small, Lucite-mounted mementos of every merger or acquisition on which they had worked. Some of these collections stretched twenty across and five deep, filling entire credenzas. The tiny Lucite "tombstones," as these notices were known, became Wall Street's version of toy soldiers.

Amid all the clatter of these corporate auctions, one could almost hear a faint echo of Alex Brody's jaded question: *I wonder whose advisers they really are?*

Plenty of chief executives and directors did try to keep companies independent in the face of the 1980s takeover fever—with little luck. Laissez-faire markets meant that raiders could simply bid a high price, buy up all of a company's stock, and then oust both directors and management. Most "defensive" maneuvers were designed only to stall for time, to widen the circle of bidders for a company, and perhaps to locate a buyer more palatable to management than the original raider. A few maneuvers, such as the creation of exotic new securities known as "poison pills," were supposed to make a company almost impossible to acquire against the will of its directors. But these ploys seldom did much more than add 10 percent or so to the eventual sales price.

In mid-1986, Peter Magowan, the chief executive of America's biggest grocery chain, Safeway Stores Inc., discovered how inexorably this takeover mill operated. The grandson of Safeway's founder, Magowan was then in his sixth year of running the grocery chain. Articulate and boyishly handsome, the forty-one-year-old Magowan had done a good job of expanding Safeway's sales—but hadn't done nearly as well in improving its per share earnings. A perception grew on Wall Street that Safeway was "undermanaged" and might be a good takeover target. Before long, Safeway was stalked by the father-and-son raiding team of Herbert and Robert Haft, who bought a block of Safeway stock in the open market and began making takeover overtures. Determined to keep Safeway independent, Magowan hired Merrill Lynch and Wachtell, Lipton to prepare his defense. "We thought we were doing fine on our own," Magowan later said. Huddling at Safeway's Oakland, California, headquarters, the company's advisers studied all the standard defensive measures: selling pieces of Safeway, pleading with shareholders to ignore the Hafts, suing the Hafts, or impeding their bid. The mood within Safeway headquarters got ever angrier and more desperate. Merrill Lynch adviser Jeffrey Berenson briefly put forth a plan for Safeway to borrow heavily and pay an immense onetime dividend to holders. But even that seemed doomed. "We couldn't compete with the offer the Hafts had on the table," Berenson later observed. The Hafts had the tremendous advantage of being bankrolled by Drexel, which could raise more money faster than Safeway itself.

After a while, Magowan realized he could choose only the party to which he surrendered Safeway, not whether to surrender. "Meet with KKR," Magowan's advisers suggested. For years, Magowan had rebuffed low-key approaches by Roberts at Utah ski slopes and at fund-raising dinners for George Bush, telling Roberts that he wasn't interested in a buyout. But by July 1986, circumstances had changed radically. One afternoon, Magowan drove across the Bay Bridge and called on KKR's offices in San Francisco for the first time—and he liked what he found. Roberts was surprisingly calm and intimate. The two men settled into armchairs in Roberts's forty-fifth-floor office, overlooking the San Francisco Bay, and began chatting. "We believe in working with management," Roberts said, as he spelled out KKR's buyout creed. Talking without notes, Roberts covered all the familiar points. Management should own stock in a buyout; companies with stable cash flows were good buyout candidates; Magowan could talk to chief executives at other KKR-acquired companies if he had any questions about KKR's reliability and character. It was a set speech that the KKR partners had delivered in various forms for at least fifteen years, but to Magowan it sounded fresh and appealing. Roberts and one of his partners, Bob MacDonnell, then asked about Safeway's business and listened carefully to the answers. In the midst of the fury of fighting the Hafts' takeover bid, an hour with Roberts and Bob MacDonnell was like a cool breeze. "I never felt apprehensive," Magowan later recalled. "I felt they were straight shooters."

For a few moments in their get-acquainted session, Roberts turned stern, in a way that Kravis never did. There's some discipline involved in a buyout, Roberts warned. Some of Safeway's weaker regional divisions might have to be sold or closed. "You may have to make sacrifices, Peter, that you may not be prepared to make," Roberts added. A moment later, Roberts soothed his guest again. "We hear good things about you, Peter," Roberts said. "We think we'd be interested."

Coming out of that meeting, Magowan decided he had found his rescuer. The next day, he agreed to turn over confidential Safeway financial data to KKR—information that would help Roberts and MacDonnell greatly in bidding for Safeway. But Magowan alone couldn't declare the battle over. When KKR expressed interest in Safeway, the Hafts boosted their bid. Late in July 1986, Roberts made a formal takeover bid of $4.2 billion and told Safeway's advisers they had just thirty-six hours to accept. Otherwise KKR would drop out of the bidding, Roberts warned Wachtell, Lipton lawyer Dick Katcher, who was advising Safeway. With just hours left on KKR's deadline, Roberts and his advisers headed to Safeway's Oakland headquarters the afternoon of Friday, 25 July, expecting to sign a merger agreement. Unwilling to concede defeat, the Hafts and their lawyers at Skadden, Arps delivered a testy letter to Safeway's directors, demanding a better chance to compete with KKR.

At 4:45 P.M. that Friday, Katcher and Roberts began one of the takeover arena's great showdowns of the decade. Emerging from the Safeway boardroom, Katcher told the waiting KKR party that Safeway's directors wanted to extend the auction into the weekend. It was their obligation to shareholders. Katcher expected an angry outburst, which he could have handled easily. Instead, Roberts stayed still in his chair and began addressing Katcher in a slow, icy voice. "I've tied up my investment bankers," Roberts declared. "I've tied up Bankers Trust. I've tied up a lot of our people's time. I just can't ask them to spend more time on this." The conference room turned deathly still. Roberts's voice had sunk to a whisper; no one dared rustle a paper. "At five o'clock," he concluded, "we are walking away from this transaction."

Katcher turned pale. If KKR pulled out, Safeway's stock would plunge and the Hafts would never make a higher bid. Everyone connected with Safeway's "defense"—directors, investment bankers, and lawyers—would be sued for millions by angry shareholders. Roberts might be bluffing, but only a reckless fool would dare find out. Silently, Katcher turned around and walked back into the Safeway boardroom. Ten minutes later, at 4:55 P.M., Katcher emerged and announced that the auction of Safeway was over. KKR had won.

By being willing to lose a giant deal very late in negotiations, Roberts had beaten back the Hafts. It was a cagey gambler's maneuver, and over the next six weeks, Roberts clinched his triumph in face-to-face confrontations with both the Hafts' number-one emissary and the Hafts themselves.

Trying to salvage something from their Safeway bid, the Hafts sent a Drexel peacemaker—Peter Ackerman—to Roberts's Atherton, California, home the afternoon of Sunday, 27 July 1986. The Hafts weren't totally powerless after losing the auction; they still could try to impede KKR's takeover of the grocery chain through various last-ditch lawsuits.

Ackerman proposed that Safeway bid the Hafts farewell by selling some of its choicest divisions to the Hafts for the preferential price of $1 billion. "That's outlandish, Peter," Roberts replied. "Let's not even talk about it. Let's play tennis." For several hours, the two deal-makers swatted tennis balls back and forth on Roberts's private court, until dusk set in. (Ackerman won handily.) Still in tennis shorts as the evening grew chilly, Ackerman asked if he could step into Roberts's kitchen and phone the Hafts. "I'm afraid you can't," Roberts said. Instead he directed Ackerman to use a phone in an unheated shed by the tennis court. Shivering in his white shorts, pressed into the awkward role of fighting on behalf of a second-tier Drexel client even though his long-term interests lay with KKR, Ackerman told the Hafts his mission had failed. Roberts wouldn't budge. By this time, Ackerman was sweaty, tired, and cold. He didn't want to fight Roberts any more.

A few weeks later, the Hafts themselves stormed into KKR's San Francisco offices. They cursed at KKR's secretaries. They accused Roberts of violating securities laws. But their rage was impotent. As Roberts looked at the matching pompadours, one white, one black, of Herbert Haft and his son, Robert, a favorite Wall Street nickname for the two— "the poodle and the pup"—raced through his mind. Biting his lip, Roberts hardly said a word as the Hafts fumed. Then, at the end of one of the Haft tirades, Roberts sweetly inquired: "Does anyone ever do business with you a second time?" The answer was no. Truculent by nature, the Hafts made money by upsetting people. Eventually the Hafts extracted $59 million from Safeway, an amount Roberts thought was too much, but a small fraction of what the Hafts had pursued. The Hafts, in turn, ended their exclusive claim on Drexel's services for Safeway, allowing Roberts to hire Ackerman and his colleagues to sell Safeway's junk bonds.

Taken together, the Beatrice and Safeway deals lofted KKR into the most privileged position on Wall Street. No other acquirer had completed two giant deals so quickly, back-to-back. What's more, no other acquirer had ever sprinkled so many fees throughout the rest of the deal community. Together, the Beatrice and Safeway takeovers had generated fees for Drexel, Bankers Trust, Salomon Brothers, Lazard Frères, Merrill Lynch, Wachtell, Lipton, and a half dozen other firms, for a total of over $200 million. Simultaneously, smaller KKR transactions, such as the sale of paper-cup maker Lily-Tulip Inc. in 1986, had generated multimillion-dollar fees for other investment banks. When KKR divested several Beatrice divisions to help pay off the buyout debt, big fees rained down on Goldman, Sachs for helping with one piece; on Morgan Stanley for another; and on Salomon Brothers for a third. Such stipends bought KKR a lot of loyalty—or at least the appearance of loyalty—from almost all major investment banks.

Doling out fees so widely was "very deliberate," Kravis later said. "We said: Who are the people who can help us?" In its early years, KKR relied heavily on Kidder, Peabody as its main Wall Street adviser. But Kravis and Roberts found that if they channeled too much business to one Wall Street firm, the others stopped catering to KKR's desires. From the mid-1980s onward, Kravis said, he chose to spread the money around. Handing out fees, Kravis found, was a cheap way of making friends on Wall Street. At most, all the extra fees added 1 to 2 percent to KKR's deal costs—not enough to mean the difference between paying the right price for a company and overpaying. By sharing fees as if they were candy, Kravis explained, "Our hope was that we would be the first call on everybody's list."

Sure enough, as companies spun into the auction process, their advisers would respond, almost every time, by phoning KKR. "Would you be interested in bidding?" the advisers would ask Kravis, Roberts, or one of their colleagues. "We'd like you to take a look." Even when takeover prospects were hazy, Wall Street's investment bankers still kept ringing KKR's buzzer, hoping to stir something up.

In the spring of 1987, Roberts and Kravis decided to shore up their standing as the takeover kings of America. Other Wall Street firms such as Merrill Lynch and Morgan Stanley had begun forming powerful buyout departments of their own to compete with KKR. In private conversations, Kravis and Roberts talked about how to stay ahead of the competition. The best bet, they figured, was to raise a giant buyout fund from their pension-fund backers and other limited partners, and then pursue huge deals beyond anyone else's reach. KKR still had $1 billion of unspent commitments in its 1986 fund. Roberts, however, felt that wasn't enough.

In May 1987, all twenty of KKR's partners and associates gathered for dinner at Kravis's apartment, where many of them learned about Roberts's full strategy for the first time. The evening was meant to be a friendly social gathering, but Roberts quickly turned it into a closed-doors strategy session. Hundreds of people knew how to carry out a midsize buyout, Roberts declared. Even $1 billion acquisitions, which had once seemed huge, were becoming commonplace.

"A lot of the art has gone out of the business," he said. "The key to the business is going to be: Who has the most equity capital?" Superficially, Roberts was asking for his younger colleagues' advice about what to do next. But he barely paused for answers. KKR should have the biggest buyout fund, Roberts declared. A good fund-raising target: $3 billion to $4 billion. At the end of the dinner table, one of KKR's newest associates, Ned Gilhuly, gulped. He was just one year out of Stanford Business School, and now found himself immersed in giant sums. "I said to myself: That's fantastic if we can do it," Gilhuly recalled. "But Jesus Christ that's a big amount."

Within days, all of KKR's partners and associates were on the road, prospecting for cash. Roberts canceled a family vacation in China and instead spent June calling on the Oregon and Washington State pension plans. Kravis covered Japan, Europe, and state pension plans in the Eastern United States. Raether focused on university endowments. Before long, the money poured in. Washington State pledged $500 million. Michigan was good for $400 million. Roberts asked the Oregon Investment Council for $500 million and was told he could have an extra $100 million beyond that. (He took it.) Eight other state pension plans—from Illinois, Iowa, Massachusetts, Minnesota, Montana, New York, Utah, and Wisconsin—joined in as well. KKR also collected smaller pledges of $25 million or more from backers as diverse as the Salvation Army pension fund, Mitsui Life Insurance Co. of Japan, and the British Water Authorities pension fund.

One after another, pension and endowment fund officers scrambled to be part of KKR's success. Takeovers by this time had become the most exciting aspect of finance—and investing with KKR was the best way to join the drama. "The mood then was so ebullient," recalled Edward Hunia, the treasurer of Carnegie-Mellon University. His school pledged $15 million after only brief debate. When ITT Corporation's pension chief, Ed Ehrlich, was approached about joining KKR's buyout funds, he called some blue-chip financial institutions to ask their views on KKR. "The comments that came back," Ehrlich later recalled, were, " 'the best,' 'excellent,' 'highest recommendation,' 'the premier LBO outfit.' " Convinced that so many experts couldn't be wrong, Ehrlich entrusted KKR with $25 million.

In September 1987, the KKR executives wrapped up their campaign with a total of $5.6 billion. The firm now had even more money at its disposal than Roberts had aimed for. Flush with self-confidence, the KKR executives saw themselves as financial supermen. One sharp-eyed investor, Chicago banker John Canning, noticed that KKR had omitted a standard clause in its contract saying that no one buyout would consume more than 25 percent of the entire fund. "Is that a typo," Canning teasingly asked Kravis, "or do you want to buy IBM?" Kravis didn't laugh. "We want to keep our options open," he replied.*

The rest of the takeover business, meanwhile, at times bordered on mayhem. In June 1987, a small-time Cincinnati investment adviser, David Herrlinger, phoned the Dow Jones News Service to announce a $6.8 billion takeover bid for Dayton-Hudson Corporation, a major retailer. Investors had never heard of Herrlinger before, but that didn't stop them from bidding up the value of Dayton-Hudson's stock more than $500 million within minutes. Only a few hours later did it emerge that Herrlinger had been fired from his job and didn't have any financing for his bid. He was hospitalized for manic depression—a condition that seemed to afflict the entire takeover business.

The wackier the takeover business got, the better KKR looked. Investment bankers began to regard various small-time raiders and buyout boutiques as merely the stalking horses that would start takeover auctions. Such bidders, in Wall Street's eyes, weren't really destined to be the ultimate buyer of a company. That role was left to KKR, whose executives were reliable, polite, and capable of coming up with every nickel of the billions that they bid. In almost all the big takeover battles, "KKR was everyone's number-one choice for white knight," observed J. Michael Schell, a takeover lawyer at Skadden, Arps.

This yearning to crown Kravis or Roberts the winners of a takeover auction became especially apparent in the August 1987 bidding for a big Florida conglomerate, Jim Walter Corporation. KKR competed this time against eight other bidders, most of whom dropped out quickly. But one bidder—a neophyte buyout team from the brokerage house of Paine Webber—roared in with an offer of $69 a share, or $2.8 billion. That was a good $600 million above KKR's proposal. The more that Jim Walter's advisers probed the Paine Webber bid, however, the dicier it seemed. Paine Webber's lead commercial bank, Citicorp, voiced doubts in separate talks about how much Jim Walter was worth. Paine Webber's top investment banker, Kamal Mustafa, hadn't won the support of Jim Walter's top management. Other Paine Webber deal-makers confessed at one stage that they had double-counted the earnings of some Jim Walter

---

*Only Don Herdrich, the longtime KKR associate who retired in his mid-forties in 1986 so he could spend his money in peace, dared poke fun at his old colleagues' insatiability. As soon as word of the $5.6 billion total hit the headlines, Herdrich phoned up KKR's Raether and chidingly told him: "Nice job. I guess pretty soon now you'll be able to go out and raise the real Big Fund."

divisions, treating them both as businesses that could be sold at a profit, and as businesses that could be retained for continuing cash flow. At six P.M. on 12 August, Paine Webber took the rare—and embarrassing—step of *lowering* its bid for the company to $62 a share, of which only $52 a share would be paid in cash. "I didn't believe anything that Paine Webber said at that point could be credible," an investment banker handling the auction later said.

Even after Paine Webber's reduction, however, KKR's bid still lagged about 10 percent behind. Kravis, the KKR partner who had begun the bidding along with associate Mike Tokarz, had left the country for a sailing vacation off the Turkish coast. Roberts had flown in from San Francisco to take charge of the KKR team. Desperately anxious for a higher bid from KKR, Jim Walter's chief attorney, the omnipresent Dick Katcher of Wachtell, Lipton, called up KKR's chief attorney, Dick Beattie of Simpson Thacher, the evening of 12 August and asked for advice.

"Give George Roberts something to hit at," Beattie said. "Get him to bite. Tell him: If you can hit this, it's yours."

A few minutes later, Katcher and a Jim Walter director, Gene Woodfin, walked into a Simpson Thacher conference room where Roberts waited. If KKR could post an all-cash bid of $61 a share, Katcher and Woodfin said, the buyout firm could have the company.

Slouched in his chair, Roberts looked tired and listless. "I can't do sixty-one," he told Katcher. "Sorry."

"Well, I appreciate you seeing us," Katcher said. This time the Wachtell, Lipton lawyer was ready to try his own hand at billion-dollar bluffing. Without a further word, Katcher started to walk out of the conference room. Sure enough, as Katcher reached for the door handle, Roberts sprang to life.

"But I can do sixty!" Roberts chirped.

It was a deal. A few hours later, after haggling about some minor issues, Katcher, Woodfin, and Roberts signed a sale contract. KKR had clinched another giant acquisition, this time for $2.4 billion. Katcher had jousted a second time with Roberts with billions at stake—and had done far better than at the Safeway showdown the year before. Paine Webber was never heard from again in the deal.

Acquiring Jim Walter ultimately would prove to be one of KKR's worst mistakes. At the time, however, it was seen as just another indication of the buyout firm's cleverness.

As the takeover boom continued in 1988, some Wall Street firms set up specialty practices. Goldman, Sachs & Co., for example, became a virtuoso seller of businesses, particularly in elaborate auctions that pitted a dozen or more would-be buyers against one another. People on Wall Street began to talk about a "Goldman auction" the same way one would speak of a Verdi opera or a Patek Philippe watch. Goldman's diligent, low-profile investment bankers had the knack for drawing dozens of potential bidders into an auction, lured by the chance to see a confidential 100-page binder, or "book," about the target company. Soon, potential bidders found themselves egged on by a Goldman system that invited "indications of interest," then first-round bids, second-round bids, and then a long series of "final" bids. Goldman kept the results secret; bidders never knew precisely where they stood until the very end. But at every stage, Goldman investment bankers whirred among the various bidders, telling them such things as: "You're still in the running. But you're going to have to get your price up if you want to make the next round." Cynics began to wonder if Goldman serenaded even the number-one bidders this way—to make sure all parties raised their bids.

It was little wonder, then, that when Kraft Inc. decided in late 1987 to sell its Duracell battery business, the chairman of the big food company, John Richman, turned to Goldman, Sachs. Kraft had picked up Duracell six years earlier as part of another acquisition, but now securities analysts grumbled that Duracell didn't fit into Kraft's basic businesses. What's more, Kraft's stable cash flow, low debt, and easily salable units made it a ripe takeover target. Hoping that a Duracell sale might keep the raiders at bay, Richman invited Goldman partner John Golden to auction off the battery company.

At first, both Richman and Golden expected Duracell would sell for a little more than $1 billion, with the strongest bids coming from Japanese industrial companies. To their surprise, the Japanese yawned—while the chance to own Duracell enchanted at least a half dozen buyout boutiques. Duracell chief executive Robert Kidder, on a one-day swing through New York, met a series of excited buyout specialists, including one deal-maker at Salomon Brothers who waved off Kidder's attempts to explain the battery business. "Six and a half times EBITDA.* That's what we pay for companies," the Salomon man barked. "If we can get it for six and a half times EBITDA, we'll do it."

KKR started out in the back of the bidding pack, voicing a $1.2 billion "indication of interest" in February 1988. "These auctions always go on

---

*Earnings before interest, taxes, depreciation, and amortization—a measure of a company's cash flow used in calculating buyout bids.

for several rounds," KKR associate Kevin Bousquette later explained. "There was no reason to have our name attached to a high number at the start." He and Kravis expected plenty of time later to raise their bid. Predictably, auctioneer Golden called Bousquette shortly after KKR's initial bid and said: "You're too low. Unless you can bid higher than this, you won't make it to the next round."

Then, in April 1988, the stakes abruptly soared. Ted Forstmann, the senior partner at another leading buyout firm, Forstmann Little & Co., approached Golden with a $1.5 billion "preemptive bid." Forstmann had held long talks with Duracell's top executives and liked the company's prospects. In a bold tactical gamble, he hoped to cut the auction short by making a stunningly high bid that would expire if Kraft didn't accept it quickly. In a crowded field of eight remaining bidders, however, Forstmann's ploy didn't work. Although Forstmann asked Golden not to breathe a word of his offer to any other suitor, Golden wanted to see if the number-one buyout firm, KKR, could do better. Golden was an old business school classmate of Kravis's; he also had an obligation to seek the highest sales price possible for Kraft. Phoning Bousquette just hours after the Forstmann bid was made, Golden coyly asked the KKR associate: "Can you see a price of $1.5 billion or north of that?"

"I'm not prepared to hang a number on it," Bousquette parried. "But it's conceivable that's something we would look at."

"How fast can you do it?" Golden asked.

"This is KKR," Bousquette replied. "Timing shouldn't be an issue." A few hours later, Kravis made the decision official: Yes, KKR would be glad to keep bidding.

Any time a bidding war broke out between Henry Kravis and Ted Forstmann, it became thrilling sport for everyone else on Wall Street. The two men had snatched deals from each other for nearly ten years, most recently in 1986, in bidding for Lear-Siegler, an aerospace and car-seating company that Kravis examined and Forstmann got. Duracell was the choicest prize yet. It was the number-one maker of alkaline batteries, a fast-growing, highly profitable business with a good public image and few competitors. The more KKR and Forstmann Little saw of Duracell's internal data, the more they became convinced that the battery company could boost earnings hugely once it was free of Kraft. Top Duracell managers began talking about a buyout as a form of personal salvation—a way to break free of highly bureaucratic Kraft and run a much more profitable stand-alone company. Even friends would have dueled for the right to buy Duracell.

But Kravis and Forstmann seethed at the mere mention of each other's name. Tall and athletic, Forstmann routinely called Kravis and Roberts "the midgets." He railed about the moral issues of KKR's association with Drexel and junk bonds. Kravis would insist that he never noticed Forstmann—and then make odd quips, such as: "You know, I can see his office with a pair of binoculars from my office." Kravis and Forstmann had been business rivals as far back as their first jobs on Wall Street in 1970, when both tried to do deals at the tiny brokerage firm of Faherty & Swartwood. A founder of that firm, Marshall Swartwood, ventured that Kravis and Forstmann "actually were pretty similar in a lot of ways." Both raced ahead on energy and charisma, masking middling academic backgrounds. But they clashed incessantly, not only on business but also on intimate personal issues. First Forstmann and then Kravis had dated dress designer Carolyne Roehm in the early 1980s; she ultimately married Kravis.*

For Goldman, Sachs auctioneer John Golden, the blood feud between Kravis and Forstmann meant he had a great auction on his hands. Not only KKR but two other buyout firms, Clayton & Dubilier and Gibbons Green van Amerongen, told Golden that they, too, wanted to keep bidding for Duracell.

In an artful maneuver, Kravis took the auction out of Golden's control. He called Kraft chairman John Richman, the forgotten man in the auction, and invited him to KKR's offices. There, Kravis offered Richman an irresistible proposition. "We'll do this however you want," Kravis began. "We like Duracell and we want to put our best bid forward. But the only way it makes sense for us is if this is the last round." If Richman could close off the auction, Kravis said, KKR would make it well worth his while. To Richman, the auctioning of Duracell already was an astonishing success, beyond his wildest dreams. Eager to clinch a sale, Richman agreed to Kravis's gently couched proposal. "You have my word," he told Kravis.

Suddenly, the rules of the auction had subtly changed. Three of the four bidders still thought they were competing in a classic Goldman, Sachs auction—with untold rounds beyond the "final" round. Kravis

---

*In the winter of 1982, as Roehm later recalled in an interview, she told Forstmann she had just met someone new. "I think he does—it kind of sounds like what you do," Roehm said. "The managers of a company buy the company; they have incentives . . ."

"Who is it you're going out with?" Forstmann asked.

"His name is Henry Kravis," Roehm replied.

"Oh, yes," Forstmann archly replied. "He's the king of the business."

knew better. When the four finalists submitted their bids to Golden a week or two later, Clayton & Dubilier was at $1.55 billion, Gibbons Green at $1.65 billion, Forstmann at about $1.7 billion. KKR topped the list at $1.8 billion. "Congratulations," Golden told Kravis in a late-night phone call.

Forstmann was furious. He demanded a chance to bid again. Goldman auctions almost always had one more round, even after the "final" round. But this one didn't. Kravis had sewn up terms that greatly favored KKR—and Forstmann couldn't do anything except fume. As for Kraft, the announced sale of Duracell won the company a takeover reprieve of just five and a half months. Then Kraft was pushed into the M&A mill, too, as the target of a giant $13.4 billion acquisition bid by Philip Morris Cos.

Just as Philip Morris began stalking Kraft in October 1988, an even larger takeover took shape—an elephant of a deal that swept up all the takeover minstrels of the decade in their final, most frenzied performance. Up for grabs this time was RJR Nabisco Inc., the maker of Winston and Salem cigarettes, Ritz crackers, and Oreo cookies. Employees and customers knew it as one of America's biggest and most venerable companies. But for six weeks in late 1988, RJR Nabisco became a giant financial plaything.

The takeover show began on 19 October 1988, when RJR's flamboyant chief executive, F. Ross Johnson, told his directors that he wanted to take the company private for $75 a share, or $17 billion, in a leveraged buyout. Shearson Lehman would help orchestrate the buyout, Johnson said. But if Johnson thought his opening bid would prevail, he was deeply mistaken. "It's a lowball bid," George Roberts told Jerry Kohlberg in a phone conversation a few days after Johnson announced his opening big. "He's trying to pick up the company on the cheap." "You're right," Kohlberg replied. Within hours of Johnson's announcement, swarms of investment bankers, lawyers, and commercial bankers began scrambling for ways to get onto the RJR stage. Inevitably, their attention focused on KKR's New York office, where Kravis quickly convened top-level strategy sessions.

Trying to insinuate his way into the RJR deal, Kravis stumbled at first. He met the evening of Friday, 21 October, at KKR's offices with Peter Cohen, chief executive of Shearson, and argued that KKR—as the biggest, longest-established buyout firm—should play a role in the bidding. Cohen and his top aides scoffed. A few days later, Kravis was depicted as accusing Cohen of muscling in on KKR's "franchise." Kravis later denied using those words. But the impression of arrogance and ego on Kravis's part was hard to sweep away. KKR at the beginning was an unwelcome outsider, making even some of its own pension-fund backers nervous. "We generally don't support hostile bids," Michigan state treasurer Robert Bowman said at the time. "It's hard to say whether KKR's [interest in RJR] is hostile, but it certainly adds a new shade of gray to the painter's palette."

All the same, KKR had tremendous financial might at its disposal. Within thirty-six hours of jawboning with Shearson's Peter Cohen, Kravis began forming the nucleus of a giant bank group that would lend him billions. Out front was Mark Solow of Manufacturers Hanover, who had been itching for years to lead a giant KKR deal. Following right behind were top bankers at Bankers Trust, Citibank, and Chase Manhattan. Kravis didn't talk about specific fees with Solow but promised him: "We'll make it worth your while." Kravis also hired a raft of big-time Wall Street advisers, including Bruce Wasserstein, Eric Gleacher from Morgan Stanley, and Leon Black at Drexel. All told, those advisers would claim $100 million of the money that KKR planned to raise to buy RJR—while providing little useful advice. But to Kravis it was money well spent. He had prevented the shrewdest or most powerful firms from working for anyone else. Simultaneously, Kravis invited Roberts to fly to New York. In a rare pairing, KKR's two top partners worked side by side until the takeover battle was over.

The morning of Monday, 24 October, KKR jumped into the bidding with a $90-a-share bid for RJR. That bid, equal to $20.3 billion, was hailed as "staggering" and "the largest in history." Commentators predicted right away that it could begin a hard-edged battle.

For the next five weeks, a bizarre and unseemly auction of RJR unfolded. The sheer size of the giant RJR buyout—and the fees involved—brought out the crassest side of Wall Street deal-makers. During late-night talks the first week of November, Kravis, Cohen, and their respective advisers nearly made peace and agreed to buy RJR together for the reasonable price of about $90 a share. But then petulant fights broke out about which Wall Street firms would handle the eventual junk-bond underwritings associated with a buyout. "Drexel should do it," Kravis said. No way, the Shearson men replied. Shearson and some newfound allies at Salomon Brothers Inc. wanted the lead role instead. At stake were $300 million or more of fees, about 1.5 percent of the total money involved in the buyout, but the main prize in the eyes of Wall Street's top deal-makers. And there were bragging rights to contend for, too. Kravis,

Cohen, and Drexel's Peter Ackerman tried to devise compromises that would let as many as three firms share the junk-bond fees. But in one A.M. shouting matches, no one could agree which firms' names would get number-one billing on the austere tombstone ads that Wall Street firms bought to announce the completion of an underwriting. "This is crazy," Roberts whispered to Kravis after midnight one night as talks headed for collapse. "Everyone's interested in everything except doing a business deal. It's all jockeying for ego and position."

Circumstances got even more bizarre. Ted Forstmann twice tried to enter the bidding, only to be snubbed by Shearson and to a lesser extent by Ross Johnson. At one crucial juncture, Shearson chief executive Peter Cohen left Forstmann forgotten in a conference room for more than two hours. At another stage, a freshly hired outside lawyer interrupted Forstmann's efforts to negotiate directly with Johnson, telling him: "I am authorized to tell you to stop annoying [him]." Forstmann, a man who prided himself on his integrity, shot back: "I can tell now the lawyers have taken over. God help everyone."

The ultimate gaffe was made by Ross Johnson. Instead of proposing to share post-buyout ownership of RJR among as many employees as possible, Johnson began to circulate a "management agreement" that would allow the top seven RJR executives to own as much as 18.5 percent of the company for a mere $20 million. The value of that cheap stock was astronomical—$500 million at the outset and perhaps $2.7 billion after five years. Johnson would later insist that this plan was just a first draft, to be amended soon afterward to provide for much wider employee ownership—but whether it was a first or final draft, it was an explosive document once it was leaked to the press. *New York Times* reporter James Sterngold first disclosed Johnson's contract on 5 November, under a headline about "huge gains" for RJR Nabisco executives. A much more damning verdict came three weeks later, when Ross Johnson's face appeared on the cover of *Time* magazine, along with the headline A GAME OF GREED. In smaller letters, the magazine declared: "This man could pocket $100 million from the largest corporate takeover in history. Has the buyout craze gone too far?"

While the Johnson-Shearson team self-destructed, Kravis and Roberts showed ever surer footing as the RJR auction proceeded. They possessed the two crucial things needed to win: money and an aura of decency. KKR had the biggest bank syndicate, Drexel's unparalleled junk-bond power, and the largest buyout fund in the world. No one else could compete. KKR's toughest rival, Ted Forstmann, ran out of subordinated debt at a crucial stage in the bidding and couldn't raise his bids any higher. The Shearson-Johnson team began to fumble for all types of funding. Its bank syndicate wasn't as developed; its buyout fund was too small; its maneuverings in the junk-bond world were laughable.

Just as important, Kravis and Roberts stayed polite and calm to the people that mattered most: RJR's advisers and directors. Competing for the first time in the supercharged takeover arena, the Shearson-Johnson team turned shrill when unexpected irritations arose. At one point, Shearson's Cohen threatened to sue the special committee of RJR's outside directors who would ultimately decide the company's fate, simply because Johnson and Cohen thought the directors had allowed Forstmann a minor, supposedly unacceptable edge. (RJR director Charles Hugel wrote a testy note back to Johnson and Cohen, asking them to stop their "interference.") In stark contrast to their rivals, Kravis and Roberts dealt gently with the crucial directors and advisers. The KKR executives knew that every bidding contest was full of unexpected "deal-breakers"—crises that had to be overcome as smoothly and resolutely as possible. Familiarity helped, too; RJR's directors were being advised by Dillon, Read and Lazard Frères, which between them had already sold Storer, Beatrice, and Owens-Illinois to KKR. Furthermore, RJR's main law firm, Skadden, Arps, had worked with KKR as far back as the 1970s. Gradually, Kravis and Roberts sensed that the arbiters of the auction—RJR's outside advisers—were starting to come around. "We don't think of you as a hostile presence at all," the Dillon and Lazard advisers told Kravis and his number-one lawyer, Dick Beattie, in a late-November meeting. Those were magic words. Kravis and Roberts knew that, as long as they could stay calm and focused, as long as they could present a pleasant face to the RJR board and to Skadden, they could gain ground toward the acquisition.

After the fifth round of bidding, on 30 November 1988, the auctioning of RJR finally came to a close. Night and day, for more than a week, KKR and the Johnson-Shearson team had been nudged to boost their bids so as to meet a "final" deadline that soon gave way to yet another deadline. Exhaustion had set in; tempers were flaring on all sides. Partly for show, partly because of real frustration, Roberts repeatedly threatened to drop out of the bidding. At about nine P.M. on 30 November, Skadden, Arps attorney Peter Atkins finally wrapped up the drama. Emerging from the boardroom in RJR's New York offices, Atkins walked over to a waiting conference room full of the KKR executives and their allies, stopped in front of Kravis, and handed him a sheaf of papers. "Here's your signed contract," Atkins told Kravis. "Congratulations. It's yours."

KKR's victory reflected three time-honored strengths of the buyout firm—all three of which the outside world took some time to recognize. The first was financial cleverness. While Shearson's final bid of $112 a share was nominally higher than KKR's offer of $109 a share, the crucial question in assessing both bids was how to value the $6 billion or so of low-grade "cram-down" securities that would be pushed into the hands of RJR shareholders. Drexel's Peter Ackerman had tinkered with KKR's proposal until its cram-down bonds appeared far more likely than Shearson's to be worth 100 cents on the dollar. Late in November, RJR's top advisers at Dillon, Read and Lazard met for hours with Ackerman and came away impressed with his savvy. "Give Peter Ackerman a lot of credit for KKR's victory," a top Dillon, Read executive said after the auction finished.

Second, Kravis had attuned himself to the delicately voiced preferences of RJR's outside directors, who were running the auction. The RJR board had favored a buyout bid that would break up the company as little as possible. Kravis obliged, while Johnson proposed to hack off the entire food business to pay down post-buyout debt. Directors wanted assurances that workers' pay and benefits wouldn't be cut in the first two years. Kravis agreed; his rivals didn't. Directors wanted the investing public to continue to have some chance to own RJR even after the buyout. Kravis cooperated to a greater degree than his rivals. Alone, none of those gestures was decisive. But taken together, they nudged several RJR directors into picking the KKR bid over the Johnson-Shearson proposal.

Most important of all, handing over the company to Kravis and Roberts seemed like the most morally defensible choice. If the RJR buyout turned out to be a financial success, it would likely spew out billions of dollars in profits. There wasn't any publicly acceptable way for the Johnson-Shearson team to divide up that lucre. By the end of the auction, Ross Johnson was a villain, reviled on the cover of *Time* magazine. His Shearson partners were utter newcomers, a brash Wall Street firm trying to lay claim to a 100-year-old company for a few weeks of work. Directors were embarrassed to admit this at the end of such a giant, fiercely contested auction, but a big part of their decision was based on human chemistry and charm.

"We felt used and abused" by Johnson, one anonymous RJR director told a reporter in the fall of 1988. Selling the company to KKR might make Kravis and Roberts shockingly rich, too, in the years to come, but—thanks to the way that KKR set up the partnerships that acquired buyout companies—most of the eventual profits would be channeled to passive KKR investors such as the Oregon state pension plans, the Harvard endowment, and other "worthy" recipients. In the biggest battle ever for directors' loyalties, Kravis once again had come across as the most trustworthy man in a takeover battle gone mad.

Immediately after the conclusion of the RJR takeover battle, all the participants rushed to proclaim the company's shareholders as the winners. Even Ross Johnson talked about how well shareholders had done, getting $109 a share for stock that had traded below $50 just six months earlier. He sent roses to the RJR directors, along with notes congratulating them on the sale of the company. Advisers to the company professed that they had been motivated all along by shareholders' interests. There was a harried, desperate quality to their remarks, as if they had suddenly realized what bizarre excesses had just been carried out.

From a distance, the idea of fighting for the interests of people who owned stock in a company sounded like a worthy cause—much like standing up for "taxpayers" or "churchgoers." The giant companies that KKR sought to acquire often had 100,000 or more shareholders, representing a wide cross section of America. In RJR's case, many of its shareholders were retired employees, tobacco farmers, or North Carolina businessmen looking for a good long-term investment. Others were big institutions acting on behalf of ordinary people, such as the California teachers' pension fund. Altogether, shareholders' winnings from the RJR battle exceeded $10 billion, compared with about a $1.2 billion take for Wall Street and the banks from various deal fees.

As takeover battles progressed, however, mainstream investors benefited less and less. High-wire takeover dramas were simply too nerve-wracking for the public to stay in until the finish. When it periodically appeared that bidders might drop out, ordinary shareholders rushed to sell stock and take profits. In their place, a cabal of Wall Street's arbitrageurs, or takeover-stock speculators, stepped in to buy the shares. These aggressive traders shuffled in and out of takeover stocks, typically owning them for six weeks or less. They were wizards at their own game, monitoring stock prices by the second on trading screens, staying up to date on takeover rumors through constant phone chats with one another, and building huge stacks of all relevant financial documents at their desks. Graced with MBAs from some of America's best business schools, many arbitrageurs earned more than $1 million a year before reaching age thirty. Some ended up in jail because of insider-trading scandals; others were vilified in movies, novels, and cartoon strips. As mainstream shareholders disappeared, the last few bidding maneuvers in any deal were done in large part for the benefit of these "arbs."

No one saw the game-playing nature of these giant takeovers more clearly than Kravis and Roberts. In the final hours of their biggest takeover battles—from the Gulf bid in early 1984 to the RJR bid in late 1988—the cousins observed a ritual while waiting for companies' advisers to pick the winner. Sequestered in small, tense conference rooms, Kravis and Roberts would break out a pack of cards and begin playing poker with their top advisers, usually for pots of $100 to $300. Years later, those poker hands remained as vivid to the two KKR partners as the moment that a company's advisers walked out of a boardroom and said: "Here's your signed contract. Congratulations." At the end of the Beatrice vigil, Kravis told one interviewer, "I had just won a hand and was raking in the pot when the good news came." In the final hours of the RJR battle, everyone on the KKR team placed a $20 bet on what time it would be when RJR's advisers announced the winner.

The most telling incident dates back to the cold, rainy afternoon in Pittsburgh in March 1984, when Gulf Corporation slipped away from George Roberts. "I have two regrets about that deal," Roberts said years later. "One, we didn't get the company. And two, the poker game broke up when I was holding three aces."

7
The Mentor's Fall

Gliding from one giant deal to another during KKR's great ascent in the 1980s, Henry Kravis and George Roberts presented almost nothing of their personalites to the outside world. They seldom granted interviews. They kept even most of their business associates at a distance from KKR's inner workings. Journalists, groping for a way to describe two men they hadn't met, began depicting Kravis as a "ruler of a vast empire," as "King Henry," or as one of the "barons of the big buyout." Roberts was represented as "a publicity-shy family man," with "an astute mind." Their mentor, Jerry Kohlberg, seldom figured directly in KKR's post-1982 takeover battles or financing negotiations, yet—thanks to diligent image cultivation by his friends and a few acolytes—he was portrayed in the most flattering terms of all. He was said to be the prudent "senior statesman" of KKR: the veteran partner who didn't get involved in all the details but operated somewhere in the background, applying his expertise and good judgment to difficult issues.

These cut-and-dried images of KKR's three founding partners seemed sufficiently plausible that few people seriously questioned them as the buyout firm's power grew. On the rare occasions that outsiders probed for more details about how Kravis, Roberts, and Kohlberg really got along, the busybodies were politely shooed away.

The most closely kept secrets on Wall Street involve the inner workings of successful partnerships. Smart partners never speak publicly about quarrels within their firms or internal reallocations of power and profits. No matter how wrenching these issues might be, it is vital to keep them hushed up and to present a unified front to the world. Anyone who might have forgotten that lesson got a spectacular reminder in 1984 and 1985, when one of Wall Street's most respected old-line firms, Lehman Brothers, disintegrated because of a huge public row between its top two partners, Lewis Glucksman and Pete Peterson. Lehman Brothers became known as a "poisoned partnership." Its feuds were seen by chronicler Ken Auletta as a stark reminder that "human folly and foibles—not the bottom line of profits, not business acumen . . .—often determine the success or failure of an organization."

All the same, KKR in its glory years was wracked by its own angry words and growing clashes. As his importance at KKR waned, Kohlberg turned angry and then bitter toward his younger partners. Kravis, determined to take the lead in the New York office, began to elbow his former mentor aside. The partner in the middle, Roberts, bristled about Kohlberg's disastrous efforts to bring his oldest son into KKR—then, in a decisive moment, threw in his weight with Kravis. The fundamental culprit in these quarrels was something none of the men could change: the nineteen-year age gap between Kohlberg and his two younger partners.

In the early 1980s, the first signs of tension between Jerry Kohlberg and Henry Kravis were so peripheral to KKR's main business that no one paid much attention to them. Kravis liked fancy office trappings; Kohlberg preferred plain ones. Kravis voted Republican; Kohlberg voted Democrat. Kravis showed a boundless appetite for business travel, for meeting executives and pitching new deals. Kohlberg, as he entered his late fifties, began to take longer vacations and devote more of his energy to non-KKR tasks. One particular project, leading a search committee to pick a new president for his alma mater, Swarthmore College, consumed "half of Kohlberg's time for almost a year," a participant in the 1982–83 deliberations later said.

By and large, Kohlberg and Kravis coexisted comfortably as the firm's number-one and number-two partners in New York. They agreed on the most important business issues: what buyouts to pursue and how to pursue them. As Kravis gradually assumed more of the work-load, Kohlberg obligingly scaled back his ownership share in KKR each year—thus claiming a smaller share of KKR's future profits. When the three men went into business in 1976, Kohlberg had owned 40 percent of the firm, significantly ahead of the 30 percent each allotted to Kravis and Roberts. While all three partners gradually lowered their shares as more people joined KKR, Kohlberg absorbed the bulk of the cutbacks.

His ownership share shrank to 36.8 percent in 1979; to 32 percent in 1981.

In late 1983, Kohlberg began to complain of excruciating headaches. Doctors discovered an acoustic neuroma, a form of brain tumor that had to be removed. Kohlberg was stunned; he was a robust athlete who could beat tennis partners half his age, and had always regarded himself as blessed with excellent health. He had no choice, though, but to undergo several hours' surgery in January 1984 at Mount Sinai Hospital in New York. His prospects for a full, quick recovery seemed excellent. Then, several weeks after the operation, disaster struck. En route to his winter vacation home in St. Croix, the Virgin Islands, Kohlberg suffered a life-threatening blood clot in his lung. The plane landed at St. Croix and Kohlberg was rushed to a local hospital. After undergoing more medical treatment in St. Croix and New York, Kohlberg tried to return to KKR in May 1984, but found after a few weeks that he wasn't ready. All that summer he continued to recover at a second vacation home on Martha's Vineyard.

In September 1984, Kohlberg tried to return for good. Colleagues could see that he was in pain. He began drinking vast amounts of Coca-Cola, hoping the caffeine would ease his throbbing headaches. His memory, which had been flawless, now seemed spotty to colleagues at KKR. And while everyone else at the buyout firm worked twelve- and fourteen-hour days, Kohlberg found even an eight-hour day exhausting. "He was pushing himself to do things he should not have," recalled Paul Raether, then a KKR associate. "A lot of things were taking place around him. Jerry wanted to be part of the action. He's a very competitive guy." In the fast-paced markets of the mid-1980s, however, Kohlberg had trouble finding his footing. Bankers Trust's stunning lending clout and Drexel's junk bonds opened up vast new buyout possibilities for KKR. The pacing of buyouts was becoming drastically faster, too. Instead of taking months to execute mergers, George Roberts and Bob MacDonnell, beginning with the August 1984 buyout of food wholesaler Malone & Hyde, figured out much faster ways to acquire all of a company's stock through a tender offer, once directors and management approved a buyout. "The world just exploded," Raether observed. "Jerry couldn't catch up."

Two new associates had joined KKR in Kohlberg's absence, both picked by Kravis and Roberts. The newcomers—former bank attorney Ted Ammon in New York, and former Latham & Watkins associate Saul Fox in San Francisco—both were in their thirties and had worked with

KKR for years. Their arrival had expanded the firm's professional staff to seven, a ridiculously small number to most outsiders, but plenty big enough for the partners of KKR. Kohlberg, in fact, had never hired any associates at KKR; he was known as "Dr. No" when it came to proposals to expand the staff. "Why don't you just go out and hire twenty people?" Kohlberg once snapped when Kravis pushed several candidates too aggressively.

Then in the summer of 1984, Kohlberg phoned his partners from Martha's Vineyard to announce that he, too, had found a promising new associate for KKR: his twenty-six-year-old son, Jim. The young man was nine years out of high school in 1984, with a résumé better suited to a Jack Kerouac novel than a job at America's number-one buyout firm. Jim Kohlberg had made three one-year stabs at college, but hadn't yet earned a degree. He was an English major at the University of California at Irvine in 1975–76; an English major again at Northeast Louisiana University in 1976–77; and a finance major at Pace University in New York in 1983–84. For most of the years between college number two and college number three, Jim Kohlberg had lived in Connecticut while working as a tennis pro. At his peak, he had ranked number 830 on the world tour. After his tennis ventures, he had worked for about eighteen months as a commodities broker. Every now and then, he wrote lyrics for rock songs.

The idea of hiring Jerry Kohlberg's son horrified Kravis and several associates in the New York office. They had met Jim Kohlberg a couple of times, and regarded him as a good tennis player and a nice kid, but nothing more. "Jimmy shouldn't come in here," Kravis told Kohlberg. "He doesn't meet any of our standards." Yet Jerry Kohlberg believed in his son. He told friends that Jim had a clearer sense of purpose now, and was ready to come into the business. Jerry Kohlberg had the most normal urge of a father: to pass along some of his knowledge and success to his children. Besides, in Kohlberg's eyes, KKR was so small and close-knit that at times it could be viewed as a family firm. Bob MacDonnell was George Roberts's brother-in-law. Henry Kravis's father and one of Jerry Kohlberg's wealthy cousins invested with KKR. Bringing an adult son into the firm didn't seem different to Jerry Kohlberg.

Kravis began to realize that this was a big issue to the senior partner at KKR. Jerry Kohlberg wasn't at all vague or inarticulate about what he wanted this time. He was determined. So Kravis made a counterproposal. "If you want to hire Jimmy, why don't you have him finish school?" Kravis suggested. "Have him go to work at an investment bank and get five years of experience. Then let's bring him into the firm when he can stand on his own two feet. People are going to scrutinize him. He's got to be better."

Kohlberg wasn't assuaged. "Look, I've been sick," he told Kravis. "I don't want to wait five years to work with my son. This is important to me."

From San Francisco, George Roberts watched his two partners butt heads as never before. So he offered a different compromise. Jim Kohlberg could come to work in San Francisco. He would get a private office, the title of associate, and a chance to earn $100,000 or more. Roberts liked Jim Kohlberg; at one point when Jim hadn't been getting along with his father, he had stayed for several months at the Roberts home. But Roberts set tough ground rules. Jim Kohlberg's pay would be determined without any influence from his father; Jim Kohlberg could not work directly with his father; and Jim Kohlberg couldn't bring routine problems to Roberts for help, either. He would have to learn to work with Bob MacDonnell, Mike Michelson, and Saul Fox, the other professionals in the San Francisco office. On weekends, the rules would relax. Jim Kohlberg and George Roberts could have dinner together. But they would meet strictly as friends.

So in September 1984 Jim Kohlberg joined KKR's San Francisco office. He tried manfully to prove that he belonged, arriving at seven A.M. and working until eight P.M. He learned to operate sophisticated financial computer programs. But he had an impossible task ahead of him: to become a top-flight investment banker without any previous training and without special help from his colleagues. When Jim Kohlberg turned in financial projections, some of the numbers were wrong. "You had to double-check his work all the time," Roberts recalled.

To Jerry Kohlberg, it was galling to see his son struggling when Roberts had it within his power to help him much more than he was. Kohlberg called up Roberts and asked him why he was holding back.

"We've got these other guys," Roberts said. Mike Michelson at that point was shepherding Jim Kohlberg through a relatively small buyout in Oregon.

"Didn't I help you?" Jerry Kohlberg retorted.

"I know you did," Roberts said. "But life is different now."

In New York, different conflicts simmered. Henry Kravis's life style had always been more flamboyant than Jerry Kohlberg's, from grade school days onward. For years, each of the two men had coped mostly by ignoring what the other one did outside the office. By 1985, however, it was impossible to ignore Henry Kravis. He hobnobbed with the likes of developer Donald Trump; the Kravis name became a regular item on the society pages. Suzy chronicled his doings. So did Liz Smith and other gossip columnists. Every few weeks, the tabloids would report that Kravis was attending a glittering charity ball in New York or at a Long Island resort.

Kravis's romantic life began to be talked about, too. Since 1979, he had been separated from his first wife, Hedi. They finally got divorced in 1984, in proceedings so messy that some details spilled into the newspapers. As Kravis extricated himself from his first marriage, he began to see more and more of a tall brunette: the fashion designer Carolyne Roehm. She produced the lower-priced Miss O collection for Oscar de la Renta. But she had ambitions of starting her own fashion label. When Roehm first met Kravis in 1981, she thought of him as "just a moderately successful businessman." Then she realized that he was a rising star. Together, they set out to conquer New York. Roehm redecorated Kravis's bachelor apartment on East Seventy-second Street, replacing the drab white walls with much more lively reds and other bright hues. In return, Kravis helped Roehm set up her own dress-designing company, summoning KKR's number-one lawyer, Simpson Thacher's Dick Beattie, to handle the routine incorporation paperwork.

In each other's company, Kravis and Roehm shared a sprightly innocence. One of their first dinners together was at a Colorado ski resort, where Kravis spilled forth his thoughts on human destiny, telling Roehm that people were put on this earth with a certain set of building blocks, to use as best they could. She laughed and told him it was nonsense. In public, Kravis and Roehm enjoyed life with a lavishness that won them (and about fifty other New York couples like them) a place in what became known as "nouvelle society."

That sort of jet-set life galled Jerry Kohlberg no end. His wife, Nancy, made clothes, too, but they were never exhibited at nightclubs with fashion photographers all about. Instead, Nancy Kohlberg clipped wool from the sheep on their estate in Mount Kisco, New York, cleaned the wool, and dyed it. Then she knitted sweaters for members of the Kohlberg family.

Within KKR's New York offices, dozens of symbolic gestures underscored Jerry Kohlberg's status as the firm's leader. His was the first name in the partnership. He had the biggest corner office at the firm's early 1980s offices at 645 Madison Avenue. And before his illness, Kohlberg led the Monday-morning briefing and strategy session for all of KKR's New York partners and associates.

When Kohlberg fell sick, Kravis temporarily took over the running of the Monday-morning meetings. They became faster and less frequent. Even without a meeting, Kravis generally knew what was going on. Then in late 1984 Kohlberg returned to the firm, ready to resume his place at the head of the table.

"What's new?" Kohlberg regularly asked as the meetings began. "What are we going to talk about?" For the next ninety minutes, conversation meandered. Without any agenda, the meetings degenerated into bull sessions. "What's new?" became a favorite Kohlberg phrase. It was meant pleasantly, but it left Kravis seething. How could Kohlberg fumble so much? Kravis wondered. After a series of unfocused meetings, Kravis took Kohlberg aside.

"Quite honestly, this is a waste of time," Kravis said. "It reminds me of the meetings we used to have at Bear, Stearns. Jerry, why don't I run the meetings?" Kohlberg conceded the point. The next Monday's meeting was crisp and quick. "I went in with an agenda," Kravis recalled. "I knew what was important and what wasn't." The ceding of power was apparent to everyone at the meeting table. Forty-year-old Henry Kravis took the head chair now; fifty-nine-year-old Jerry Kohlberg sat by his side. As much as Kohlberg tried not to reveal any disappointment, colleagues could see it was wrenching for him.

About a month after KKR moved into elegant new Manhattan offices in early 1985, Kohlberg asked Kravis and Roberts to join him for breakfast away from the office. He had something important to discuss. The three men met at Kohlberg's private apartment in one of Manhattan's better hotels, the Carlton House, directly opposite KKR's old premises at Sixtieth Street and Madison Avenue. The meeting started out friendly.

Kohlberg spoke first. "I've been thinking," he said. "You guys have done a terrific job of running the firm while I've been away. I've been out of it for the last year and a half. But I feel better now. I feel good about my life."

Roberts and Kravis listened cheerfully. At any moment now, they figured, their old mentor would make a graceful concession speech. Kohlberg would acknowledge that the cousins were in charge for good— that it was time for him to cut back his role at KKR. Kohlberg might say something about wanting to take life easier, to spend more time with his family. Kravis and Roberts were already thinking of ways to honor

Kohlberg with a grand-sounding ceremonial title at KKR, such as chairman of the board.

Wrong. Kravis and Roberts had grossly misread the situation. Kohlberg wasn't about to pull back. "I want to make sure that we have a
nine-year partnership agreement," Kohlberg abruptly said, "and that our
interests all stay equal."

"What are you talking about?" Kravis snapped, his voice full of surprise and annoyance.

Kohlberg reiterated his plan. He owned 25.83 percent of KKR at the
time, entitling him to 25.83 percent of the firm's profits. That was just a
hair's breadth more than Kravis or Roberts owned. Since 1976, Kohlberg's percentage share had been shrinking faster than the two cousins',
as new partners and associates had been offered small ownership positions in KKR. If that trend continued, the very next partnership meeting
might cause Kohlberg's share to match or fall below the shares of Kravis
and Roberts. But Kohlberg didn't want to slip below the younger men.
Ever. "It's important to me," Kohlberg said. "Until I'm seventy years old,
we should be equal partners."

Now Roberts weighed in. His voice was calmer and more measured
than Kravis's. But his words were much more cutting. "I'm just dumb-
founded, Jerry," Roberts said. "We haven't done equal work in the past.
We aren't going to do equal work in the next nine years. Why do you feel
we should do this?"

"We all started the firm together," Kohlberg jabbed back. "If it hadn't
been for me, you guys would have been out on the street." Kohlberg
began to tick off some of his early actions in building up the buyout
business and the two younger men's careers. He had put up $100,000 in
1976, nearly all of the firm's starting capital. His contacts with Joe Flom
had helped bring in some of KKR's earliest fees. It was a long, impas-
sioned speech. "This is an institution now," Kohlberg lectured his two
younger partners, as he summed up his argument. "People do business
with us now because of the name of the firm, not the individuals." If
Kravis and Roberts lately had become the most active partners, Kohlberg
implied, that wasn't important. It never would be important.

After fifteen years during which the three partners had worked as a
team, sharing credit, something had snapped. Suddenly it was terribly
important who really had made KKR do so well. Kohlberg had his own
view. So did the two younger men, based on an entirely different perspective. Neither side could understand the other.

The breakfast quickly came to an end. No one had convinced anyone of anything. Kohlberg, Kravis, and Roberts silently walked the four blocks to KKR's new offices at 9 West Fifty-seventh Street. People returning from a funeral might have looked more cheerful. Kohlberg's attempt to win partnership parity until 1995 hadn't been officially rejected by Kravis and Roberts. But it was clear that they would never support it.

In the next few months, each side quietly talked about the dispute with close friends, asking for opinions. Kohlberg and the cousins each came away from such discussions more certain that their position was right.

Kohlberg spoke his mind with Arthur Aeder, a warm-hearted, morally upright accountant whom he had known since the mid-1960s, when Aeder used to visit Bear, Stearns to handle the partners' taxes. Aeder was every bit as pokey as Kohlberg—he was a stocky, bald man in his late fifties whose idea of an exciting vacation was to drive through New England in the autumn, watching the leaves change colors. But Aeder was a gentleman, and he knew KKR. From 1976 to 1980 he had been the firm's principal accountant, until Henry Kravis had decided that all of KKR's business should be routed to the much bigger firm of Deloitte, Haskins & Sells. Aeder had conceded that the switch was justified, even if it had cost him a lot of business. It didn't cost him a friendship, though. Aeder still kept close to Kohlberg.

How did big Wall Street firms handle partnership discussions? Aeder and Kohlberg asked each other. "They took three factors into account," Aeder later explained. First came the amount of capital each partner had contributed to the firm. Kohlberg believed he was way ahead on that score. Second was what each partner had done to develop the business over the years. In Kohlberg's mind, he was the leader on this factor as well. There was a final category, which Aeder called "the transactional part"—the contributions to profits during the past year or two. Only in that respect were Roberts and Kravis clearly ahead.

Those standards should be applied in that order, one-two-three, Kohlberg and Aeder told themselves. Fixating on recent accomplishments was a huge mistake. "I don't know any successful firms that are run solely on the latter principle," Aeder said. "If you do that, you just have a bunch of marauding joint venturers who argue about how to split up the booty. It's not a business."

To Kravis and Roberts, the future of the firm was indeed at stake—but for very different reasons. Kohlberg's proposal sounded dangerously wrongheaded to them. It seemed to deny reality, to deny that the two younger partners had overtaken their mentor. Kohlberg's plan would cost Kravis and Roberts a chance for a bigger share of the firm's profits in future years, but the cousins kept telling each other that money wasn't really the critical issue. This was a battle over fairness, over pride and recognition, over whose version of KKR's success was really true.

"Why do we have to carry Jerry?" Kravis kept asking Roberts. "It's just not right."

Kohlberg by early 1985 had slowed down tremendously from the hard-driving pace he had set in the 1970s. Of KKR's previous twelve buyouts, Kohlberg had played a dominant role in only one, the Fred Meyer transaction in 1981. Nearly all of KKR's major lenders and other investors—Bankers Trust, Drexel, the Oregon and Washington pension funds, Harvard, etc.—were ones that Roberts and Kravis had brought on board in the previous four years. Most of KKR's new business was being generated by the two younger men and the associates that they had hired.

"If Jerry was pulling his weight, if Jerry was finding deals and knocking on doors, if he had the contacts with banks, God bless him," Kravis later said. "We could have stayed even [in partnership shares] forever." But in Kravis's eyes, Kohlberg "wasn't doing anything."

"It was as if he came up with a patent and was entitled to royalties for seventeen years," Roberts later remarked.

None of Kohlberg's arguments budged his two younger partners. Yes, Kohlberg had put up $100,000 in 1976. But Kravis and Roberts regarded that money as incidental; they believed that KKR's real seed money came from the original seven investors of KKR Partners. Kohlberg had actively recruited only one of those investors, and had helped with two others. Even as far back as 1976, Kravis and Roberts believed, they were bringing in more business.

Kravis in particular wondered if other issues might be clouding Kohlberg's judgment. "Once Jimmy got into the picture, that's what got Jerry into this thing of: 'I've got to be even with you,' " Kravis later said. "He had to show Jimmy that he was every bit the equal of George and me. Otherwise he would look weak in his son's eyes."

To cave in to Kohlberg's plan was unthinkable. Kravis and Roberts were in the midst of hiring more associates, creating more partners, and pursuing ever bigger deals. They wanted to build a landmark, a firm that would last for more than just the next ten years. The new people should be given a chance to own part of KKR, the cousins felt, and to share meaningfully in a profit stream that exceeded $100 million a year. How could new people become owners if the existing partners didn't relinquish some of their share? Some time after the March 1985 breakfast, Kravis confronted Kohlberg with all these arguments. "We're going to destroy this firm if we don't compensate the younger guys the way they should be," Kravis told his former boss. "It shouldn't have to come out of George's and my hide solely." Kohlberg's hide was the prime target.

In their search for recognition, Kravis and Roberts could have ignored Kohlberg and instead boasted to the outside world about their deal-making triumphs. Yet doing so was unthinkable under the ethos of KKR. Partners in the tiny firm were expected to hide their egos from the outside world nearly all the time. Personal publicity was loathsome—a source only of trouble. If other deal-makers invited reporters into their homes and ended up on some list of "businessmen of the year," that was fine. As late as the mid-1980s, the partners of KKR took a weird delight in combining their firm's huge business success with almost total personal anonymity. Because they had cloistered themselves away from broad public recognition, the two younger partners cared, far more than they wanted to admit, what Jerry Kohlberg thought of them. They wanted the "senior statesman" to acknowledge that his younger partners had surpassed him, and deserved to have done so. The partnership shares would be the most telling indication of acknowledgment. Roberts especially wanted Kohlberg—his father–older brother figure of 15 years earlier—to acknowledge the younger partners' rise.

It was an acknowledgment Kohlberg never could grant.

New wounds opened quickly. In April 1985, KKR's San Francisco office completed the buyout of Red Lion Inns, a Portland, Oregon, lodging company. George Roberts and Mike Michelson led the buyout; Jim Kohlberg helped out. Soon after the transaction was completed, Jerry Kohlberg proposed to give some of his own interest in the deal to his son.

"You can't do that," Roberts said. "We've allocated a small percentage to him, because that's what we've decided to do."

Jerry Kohlberg protested: "Well, he worked very hard on it."

"I know," Roberts said, "but why treat him any different from anyone else? He's lucky to have a job here."

"Yeah," Kravis interjected. "He's a zero."

It was a ghastly choice of words, and Kravis knew it right away. Jerry Kohlberg was furious to hear his son insulted in such a fashion. Kravis tried to backpedal. The word *zero* had to be understood in context. Kravis said he had meant to say that Jim Kohlberg had started out as a minus to the firm, and now had worked his way up to neutral.

Jerry Kohlberg wasn't mollified. If anything, he was more determined than ever to protect his son from the ravages of an ungrateful firm.

A few days later, George Roberts tried to sort things out with Jim

Kohlberg himself. "Look, Jim," he said. "This isn't in your best interests to get ahead because of your dad. Don't you want to earn your own stripes?"

Roberts's appeal failed. Jim Kohlberg had been thrust into a demanding situation, and his youthful geniality was giving way to a new, much pricklier personality. "People have got to get used to the fact that I'm here," Jim Kohlberg said. He wasn't about to forfeit the opportunity that his father presented.

So in a series of telephone conversations, Roberts and Jerry Kohlberg thrashed over the issues once more. In the end, Jerry Kohlberg transferred part of his KKR ownership into a new partnership, Cabbage Hill Associates, that would be shared among all members of the Kohlberg family, including Jim. It was a roundabout way of solving the problem, and it didn't leave anyone happy.

New turf issues arose in New York as well. Some of KKR's associates began approaching Kravis, complaining that Kohlberg was burdening them with ill-conceived projects. As one associate put it: "Jerry is getting his 'out' basket confused with my 'in' basket." The associates on their own couldn't tell the firm's senior partner to bug off, but they thought Kravis might be able to solve their problem.

Kravis summoned up a tone that sounded reasonable to him, but doubtless seemed insolent to Kohlberg. "Jerry, please," Kravis said. "Let me coordinate the workload of these guys. One of us has got to do it. Either you do it or I do it."

At first, Kravis later recalled, Kohlberg conceded the point. "You're right. You know what's going on. You should do it."

Yet the next time Kohlberg spotted an interesting buyout candidate, he couldn't resist trying to recruit an associate to help him analyze the company. One particular project, an unsuccessful attempt to negotiate a buyout of Stride-Rite Corporation, a Boston shoe company, consumed more than a year of Kohlberg's time. KKR's younger associates found Kohlberg trying to rope them in on his projects even when they were already in the midst of three other deals, even when Kohlberg's buyout schemes were unworkable. Pressing on in the face of resistance was in Kohlberg's blood; his bulldog tenacity had survived all sorts of ups and downs since his early days at Bear, Stearns.

"This just isn't going to work," several associates told Kravis. Again and again, Kravis was forced to huddle with Kohlberg, and to confront the senior partner with the sad truth that he had fallen out of his own firm's mainstream.

All through the summer and early fall of 1985, the underlying owner-ship disputes among Kohlberg, Kravis, and Roberts stayed below the surface, unanswered. There were new buyouts to pursue; there was also a new buyout fund of nearly $2 billion that KKR was trying to raise. For a brief stretch, work alone occupied everyone's attention.

Then, on 21 November 1985, Roberts and Kravis came back with a counterproposal for Jerry Kohlberg. They had drawn up a schedule of the maximum permissible reduction in Kohlberg's ownership of the firm. According to this plan, his share could drop only a few percentage points each year, and it could never drop below a minimum threshold. Kravis and Roberts felt this was fair. The cousins would become the largest owners of KKR soon, but Kohlberg wouldn't be squeezed out.

Kohlberg abhorred the plan. He kept telling Kravis and Roberts that he was the "senior partner" of the firm. Senior partners always had the largest share of a firm. He reiterated his arguments about having started KKR. He again said that KKR's recent success reflected the firm's well-known name, rather than any extraordinary work by the younger partners.

Now the clashes began happening more frequently. On 18 December 1985, the three founding partners argued again. Their positions were dug in now; the attacks back and forth had a predictable quality. Nothing was getting through.

The next day, Roberts took an extraordinary step. In a five-page handwritten letter he poured out a message of anger and hurt pride to his former mentor. Using the most candid language he could, Roberts tried to tell Kohlberg why, for the first time in their friendship, the older man was grievously wrong. "I view our 20-year relationship with great pride, warmth, love and support," Roberts began. "For me you have been supporter, teacher, friend, role model (except for dress), 'anchor to the wind,' and athletic partner. I have always felt your support and genuine friendship, and knew that no matter how badly I screwed up, you would support me."

Then the blunt, painful message followed.

About a year ago, you told Henry and me that despite your diminished contribution over the past two years, you were now feeling better and strongly felt that our interest should remain equal over the next nine years, or until you were 70 years old. When I disagreed, you got angry ("miffed," as you stated). Thus began, in my mind, the problems we are having. Jerry, for some time now, you have not made an equal contribution to the success of the firm, and going forward I don't believe you will either. . . .

You said yesterday that all we had really done was to take over the contacts that you started, that KKR was now an institution (implying that people dealt with the firm and not because of the individuals here), and that you were very instrumental with your contacts when we started the firm. . . .

Listed below are the buyouts we have done since 1976. None of these deals walked in the door because of our name. Most of these deals had major problems in getting done; all had innovative financing structures which have been copied by others.

While I am reluctant to do this, maybe we should spend the time and re-hash the above when we are together.

Hopefully our new fund will reach at least $1.8 billion with about 45 participants. None of these walked in the door. Each has taken a lot of time, thought and effort to bring along. They invested because of our financial record, and because of the KKR people they met. Our financial track record did not just happen without a lot of work, worry, thought, planning and luck. And none were names of people you just turned over to Henry and me. Go through the list with this in mind.

I know from an ego standpoint, going below Henry and me must be difficult for you, as I am certain you worry how others both inside and outside the firm will look at you. You have also stated that you felt I undermine you with the others in the firm. That is farthest from the truth. You undermine yourself by not staying up on developments, not reading the memorandums, canceling meetings set up on your request, spending 15 minutes in a board meeting and then leaving, asking others to work on deals which 10 minutes of analysis on your part would show worthless. . . . When all of these criticisms have been voiced by the guys, I have staunchly defended your abilities and role in the firm. We have very intelligent and sensitive people at KKR. They see things for what they are and not for what you, Henry or I tell them. To the outside world, no one will know the difference.

Roberts renewed the 21 November proposal that Kohlberg's percentage share of the firm gradually be lowered. And then he closed by writing: "I still believe this is the fairest and best way to handle the problem. As I told you over the phone, for once you have a short-term view, and I have the long-term view. Let's try to solve the problem with the long-term view in mind.

"Love as always, George."

When Jerry Kohlberg got the letter, he told a friend that he had never felt so hurt in his life.

Kohlberg remained a general partner in KKR for the next fourteen months. From that point onward, however, the firm's destiny was entirely in the hands of the two younger men. Kohlberg's presence was hardly felt in the buyouts of Safeway and Owens-Illinois. His working hours remained greatly shortened, compared with the pace he had set ten or

twenty years earlier. In the summer, Kohlberg took a month off to go to
Martha's Vineyard; in the winter, a month to go to St. Croix. He was
sixty-one years old in 1986: a reasonable age at which to slow down a bit.
But KKR's younger professionals weren't about to accommodate anyone
who wanted to work at a slower pace.

Even outsiders could tell that things had fundamentally changed at
KKR. On the Beatrice buyout, investment banking advisers noticed that
Kravis ran the strategy sessions with an ebullience that left no doubt who
was in charge. Kohlberg skipped some meetings entirely. When Kohlberg
did show up, he sat in the back of the room and didn't say much. "The
world had changed so much from what Jerry knew," a Kidder, Peabody
investment banker later said.

On the Safeway transaction, Roberts and MacDonnell set the tone.
Jerry Kohlberg appeared in California for only one meeting. "I was very
impressed with the way that [Roberts and MacDonnell] treated Jerry," a
Morgan Stanley adviser later said. "Jerry didn't have a clue. He was out
of it. But they treated him with the proper amount of deference."

Within KKR, the sense of Kohlberg adrift grew much more vivid. At
times he would walk through the halls, without any clear purpose in mind.
Several KKR associates recall Kohlberg telling them: "You guys don't
utilize me enough. I can bring my judgment to bear on things." KKR's
young deal-makers, however, were zooming about at such a breakneck
pace that when they tried to involve Kohlberg in a project, only trouble
ensued. Powerful new Lotus computer software allowed KKR to spin out
ever more elaborate ways to make buyouts work. In the throes of a deal,
the KKR associates might revise their projections and analyses hourly.
Financing memorandums, which used to be 30 pages long in the early
1970s, now ran to 200 pages or more. Kohlberg acknowledged to some
associates that he didn't read the memos cover-to-cover. That required
the associates to give Kohlberg a detailed briefing on the buyout, so that
he would have enough facts on which to exercise his judgment. "Guys got
tired of that," Paul Raether recalled. "They were tired of bringing Jerry up
to date. By the time Jerry brought his insight to bear on a situation, we
were long past that point."

Kohlberg's ethics and sense of principles hadn't dulled one bit, however. If anything, his inability to maneuver in the forefront of KKR's
deals pushed Kohlberg into a new role—one he tried to create for
himself.

He would be the firm's conscience.

The key to a well-done buyout didn't lie on page 174 of a buyout memorandum, Kohlberg believed. Bigger issues were important. Was the management trustworthy? Were the negotiations in keeping with the standards for friendly deals that had been set in the 1960s and 1970s? Was everyone on the same side of the table?

The fast-paced new ways of Wall Street increasingly worried Kohlberg in 1985 and 1986. Many of the financial partners with whom he had dealt most closely over the years, such as Ray Charles at Prudential or Bob Judson at First Chicago, had retired by now. In their place were what Kohlberg perceived as fee-driven younger men who seldom asked the most important question of all: Does this deal feel right? Away from the office, Kohlberg told friends that he was troubled by the blurring between friendly and hostile takeovers. A new gray area was emerging: acquisitions that started out hostile but eventually won a company's reluctant assent. Deal-makers shrugged off the issues raised by the strong-arm techniques involved. Instead, they brazenly pursued huge fees—at least as Kohlberg perceived things. The fees that each adviser charged for takeover work weren't $1 million or so anymore; they had jumped to as much as $60 million. And everyone wanted a fee. The commercial banks wanted a fee. Drexel wanted a fee. KKR always claimed a fee. Investment bank advisers and lawyers weighed in, too. Was it really in a company's best interests to be paying so many fees?

In the new KKR, Kohlberg had trouble finding a forum for his concerns. People no longer came to him for advice. The old 1970s counseling sessions with Henry Kravis—in which Kravis would come into Kohlberg's office, propose a deal, and then field a series of skeptical questions from Kohlberg—were a thing of the past.

Once or twice, the old lion's roar could still be heard. In the early stages of the Beatrice buyout, some people argued in a large meeting that if the company's directors didn't want to talk to KKR, perhaps KKR should just approach Beatrice's shareholders directly, with an unsolicited tender offer for the company's stock. Doing so would be seen as openly hostile to Beatrice's board and management, but it might be a winning strategy.

"That's not the way of the firm!" Kohlberg thundered.

The chatter stopped. People listened to Kohlberg that time. George Roberts, who had been among the most interested in a tender offer, backpedaled and explained that he had only been exploring it as a theoretical possibility.

More often, Kohlberg's point of view failed to register with the authority that it had once had. When Kohlberg voiced concern about hostile deals, Kravis and Roberts retorted that the difference between friendly and hostile had never been all that clear. Hadn't Kohlberg himself pushed Fred Meyer's management aggressively in 1980 and 1981 before winning a merger agreement? What was so different about the new rounds of acquisitions? As for fees, Kravis and Roberts said, they simply charged the same percentage of the total deal cost that KKR had always charged, about 1 percent. Other parties' fees were about the same. Buyouts were much bigger now, so the dollar amounts of the fees had grown greatly. That should be a source of pride, not worry, the younger men argued.

In happier times, all these issues might have been debated until a peaceful agreement was reached. Kohlberg, Kravis, and Roberts never had been clones; they had clashed occasionally since the early 1970s. Throughout all these differences, they had always believed that no conflicts could tear apart their friendship and partnership.

By late 1986, however, Kravis had little patience for Kohlberg. And Roberts's unease about Kohlberg's son and the partnership shares made it hard for him to talk freely with his old boss. All three partners began to wonder if there was much friendship left to save.

The first casualty was Jim Kohlberg's job at KKR. The young man's work had improved, but Kravis and Roberts were not satisfied. As 1986 drew to a close, Jerry Kohlberg said he thought his son should be rewarded with a typical associate's bonus of about $1 million. Kravis and Roberts thought that was preposterous. KKR eventually paid Jim Kohlberg about $500,000—an amount that seemed far too generous to Kravis and Roberts, yet far too stingy to the Kohlbergs.

Immediately after the bonus argument, Jim Kohlberg said he wanted to transfer to New York for personal reasons. Roberts refused. "We're having enough trouble with the relationship with your dad," Roberts said. "The last thing we need is for you to go back there. You're not qualified to work there and it's become obvious to all the guys. Let's just keep your problem out here."

A few weeks later, Jim Kohlberg quit KKR and headed to New York anyway. His two years in San Francisco had left him with at least one permanent gain: an undergraduate degree at last, from Golden Gate University. In New York, twenty-nine-year-old Jim Kohlberg enrolled in an MBA program at a local university.

Jerry Kohlberg's final few months at KKR were painful for everyone. In late 1986, he, Kravis, and Roberts kept having talks about what they euphemistically called "reorganizing the partnership." Kohlberg by that time had conceded that his ownership interest would have to fall below the cousins' level, and that he would have to hand over most day-to-day authority to the younger men. But he wanted his ownership decline to be as gradual as possible. Moreover, he pressed for the power to veto any major action by KKR that he didn't like. From 1976 to 1982, each of the KKR founder partners actually had had such veto privileges. But when Bob MacDonnell became KKR's fourth partner in 1982, the veto provision had given way to majority rule.

Kravis and Roberts dreaded the idea of enabling Kohlberg to block their decisions. "It would have become a tyranny of the minority," Roberts later said. He and Kravis both felt that Kohlberg had begun searching for business issues on which to clash with them—just because of other underlying tensions.

In December 1986, before Jim Kohlberg's departure, Kravis and Roberts thought they had worked out an arrangement. Kohlberg wouldn't get his veto power, but the two younger partners also wouldn't be able to streamroller a decision through if Kohlberg objected. Instead, the matter would be put before all partners and associates of KKR for a group decision. It sounded cumbersome but just barely workable.

Then, in early January 1987, immediately after Jim Kohlberg left, everything looked different. Jerry Kohlberg had retained a high-powered lawyer, Todd Lang of Weil, Gotshal & Manges, to help negotiate his new agreement. John McLoughlin of Latham & Watkins acted for KKR. Roberts and Kravis presented their latest draft of a partnership agreement, filled with detailed clauses to cover all contingencies. Some of those terms irritated Kohlberg and Lang. They accused Kravis and Roberts of going back on earlier promises. A shouting match followed. The agreement collapsed.

By now, Kravis and Kohlberg were barely on speaking terms. Associates who walked past their offices on the forty-second floor of 9 West Fifty-seventh Street talked about "an icy chill" emanating from that corner of the building.

One afternoon in late January or early February 1987, Kravis phoned Roberts with something bigger in mind than just another gripe session.

"I'm fed up with this stuff with Jerry," Kravis said.

"Well, so am I," Roberts said.

"You know, what I think we ought to do is to give him an economic deal and just ask him to leave. Between Jerry and me, one of us is going to have to leave this firm. And it isn't going to be me."

"I think you're right," Roberts replied. "Before we do anything, let's sleep on it two or three nights and see how everyone feels about it."

Nothing changed. Both cousins were resolute. Kohlberg had to go.

Paul Raether, who had been elected a partner the year before, was brought into the conversations. So was Bob MacDonnell in San Francisco. KKR's associates weren't explicitly told what was afoot, but they could tell a showdown was imminent.

Raether briefly functioned as an emissary, trying to help Kohlberg realize how drastically things had changed. "Jerry, you're not listening to Henry and George," Raether said, with a pleading tone in his voice. "These guys are telling you they want a divorce. They want you to leave the firm, because you haven't been able to work anything out."

Kohlberg was stunned. For all the arguments and harsh words of the past year, he had never expected things would end with his being ousted from his own firm. But that's what was happening.

In a difficult lunch conversation a day or two later, Kravis told Kohlberg that the partners of KKR had reached their decision. The firm could no longer operate effectively with Kohlberg as a general partner. It would be best if he left. He could remain a limited partner, sharing in KKR's profits but not taking a role in its decisions. That seemed to be the way things were headed anyway. In sixteen years of knowing each other, the two men had come full circle. Their friendship had begun in December 1970, when Kohlberg hired Kravis at Bear, Stearns. It ended in February 1987, when Kravis told Kohlberg that it was time to go.

Kohlberg left the lunch angry and bitter. He also resolved to protect his own interests. For the next month, Kohlberg's lawyers negotiated a separation package so extensive that a KKR associate referred to it as "the biggest golden parachute ever." As of 13 March 1987, Kohlberg resigned as a general partner of KKR. Under the separation agreement, he could continue for nearly a decade to invest in buyouts on the same vastly preferential terms offered to KKR's own executives. Kohlberg's share of future buyout profits would sink slowly from 20.541 percent for deals originated in 1987 to 7 percent for deals originated in 1995. If KKR continued to do as well as it had in 1984 through 1986, Kohlberg could collect $200 million or more of future profits, without any active involvement in KKR's work. The agreement ran until 1995, a date carefully chosen by Kohlberg. It let him invest with KKR until age seventy, just as he had wanted all along.

Kohlberg also demanded a host of smaller concessions from Kravis and Roberts that had great psychological importance after the way he had been treated at Bear, Stearns. He insisted that KKR preserve his office for him, in case he ever wanted to use it, and he demanded that KKR pick up his $300,000 in legal fees for hiring Lang and other lawyers. He also won promises that KKR would pay his secretary's salary, wherever he kept his main new office, and would buy him a new Lincoln Town Car or its equivalent every year. KKR was even contractually obligated to pay for Kohlberg's driver—a perk that Bear, Stearns had denied him early in his career. (These various fringe benefits would last for about a year, at which point relations between Kohlberg and his former partners would become even more strained. In mid-1988, Kravis and Roberts would agree to make a lump-sum payment of $1.3 million to Kohlberg, and in return would be allowed to terminate their agreement to provide Kohlberg with the car, secretary, etc.)

Once the separation agreement was signed in March 1987, Kravis felt immense relief, according to his colleagues. Later on, he voiced some regrets about Kohlberg's departure, saying: "It was a very hard thing for me. I wanted to make things work. I had been with Jerry for a long time." At the time, though, Kravis vigorously returned to business without showing much remorse.

Roberts took Kohlberg's departure much harder. "The way I look at it, I came out worst of all," he said later. "I got a horrible economic deal, and I lost a very close friend."

All that remained was to tell the world. For private, reclusive KKR, that was surprisingly difficult.

The first public announcement came at the annual meeting of KKR's limited partners on 18 May 1987 at the Helmsley Palace Hotel in New York. Most of KKR's closest friends were there: Jim George and Roger Meier from the Oregon pension fund, John Canning from First Chicago, Ron Badie from Bankers Trust. A few people learned of Kohlberg's situation beforehand, but most came to the meeting unaware of the special news.

Jerry Kohlberg took the podium early in the proceedings and made a short speech. He said he was very proud of what KKR had accomplished, but deeply concerned about a breakdown in Wall Street's ethics. Kohlberg spoke of an "overpowering greed that pervades our business life." He didn't name names, but some people at the meeting thought Kohlberg was referring to Kravis and Roberts. At the end of the speech, Kohlberg said he was going to retire as a general partner of KKR and become a limited partner—just like all the people in the room with him.

After the speech, Michigan's pension chief, William Amerman, asked Kohlberg why he was stepping down. "Because of my health," Kohlberg muttered, and walked on. He was only a little more forthcoming with

Donald Stone, a New York Stock Exchange market-maker and longtime friend. "Youth will prevail," Kohlberg told Stone.

But a different version of Kohlberg's departure appeared in *The New York Times* on 19 June 1987. "There are some philosophical differences," Kohlberg told *Times* reporter Jim Sterngold. "I won't restrict myself to small transactions, but I'll stick with deals where reason still prevails." It was Jerry Kohlberg at his best. "Philosophical differences" was a lofty, ambiguous phrase that seemed to serve everyone's interests. Kravis and Roberts soon decided that it was far better for Kohlberg to voice a vague unease about KKR's way of doing business than to let outsiders know about all the human follies and foibles that had poisoned two longtime friendships.

For the next few years, all three of KKR's founding partners kept the real reasons for their breakup secret.

Immediately after leaving KKR, Jerry Kohlberg and his son Jim founded their own buyout firm: Kohlberg & Co. Their marketing pitch was an appealing one: They planned to return to the origins of the buyout business, to small, friendly deals. "We aren't going to do the biggest deals, the ones that hit the headlines," Jim Kohlberg explained in an interview. The father-and-son team rented offices on West Fifty-fifth Street in Manhattan that evoked memories of KKR's early premises in the Mutual Benefit Life building on Fifth Avenue. Floors were covered with gray wall-to-wall carpeting instead of the expensive Oriental carpets that Kravis and Roberts preferred. Conference rooms housed long tables covered with plastic laminate instead of expensive rosewood. And when the two Kohlbergs recruited a handful of young associates, they told the newcomers that they could stop by the senior partner's office for advice anytime.

In the hotly competitive deal market of the late 1980s, however, Kohlberg & Co. proved to be an also-ran. Jerry Kohlberg set out to raise a $1 billion investment pool from pension funds and banks, but got less than $300 million. Among those turning him down was William Amerman, Michigan's pension chief. "I thought he was tired but articulate at the Helmsley in May," Amerman later said. "When he came to see us about his fund, he was just tired." The Oregon and Washington pension funds said they didn't want to invest with Kohlberg & Co. either, citing a concern about "management depth." Jerry Kohlberg angrily told friends that he thought Roberts had sabotaged Kohlberg & Co.'s marketing efforts in the Pacific Northwest.

In its first three years, Kohlberg & Co. completed three modest-size buyouts, but drew scant notice in comparison with at least a dozen more powerful buyout rivals. In early 1988, Jerry Kohlberg tried to join the bidding for Stop & Shop Cos., but lost out to KKR. Kohlberg & Co.'s biggest deal, the $268 million acquistion of restaurant-equipment maker Welbilt Co., was largely negotiated by Tim Collins, an energetic young partner who joined Kohlberg & Co. from Lazard Frères. After a year at Kohlberg & Co., however, Collins returned to Lazard, telling friends that he saw little chance for career development in a setting where the Kohlberg father-and-son team occupied the top two positions.

As KKR's own deal-making grew more controversial, Jerry Kohlberg assiduously positioned himself as poles apart from his old buyout firm. In late 1988, he bought advertising space in *Euromoney* magazine to publish a thinly veiled critique of his old firm's new ways. Without naming names, Kohlberg complained that other buyout firms were chasing deals too aggressively because of a "need to prove their mettle to investors" and an "appetite for sizable fees." Kohlberg spoke scornfully of buyout firms that made "unsolicited bids" and said that all his deals would be "friendly." He railed against the practice of buying 4.9 or 9.9 percent of a public company's stock, just below the threshold amounts that would trigger various federal filing requirements, and then pressing directors to agree to a buyout. As it happened, KKR had just made two such "toe-hold" investments, in Texaco Inc. and Kroger Co.—investments that failed in their main goal of inducing a buyout but yielded big stock-trading profits anyway. Kohlberg vowed not to make toe-hold investments; he wrote that they "present a conflict of interest, a dilution of purpose and the potential for hostile overtures."

Such righteous language helped make Jerry Kohlberg into something of a hero in the business press. Kohlberg "had become uncomfortable with KKR's evolution from management partner to aggressive financial heavyweight," *BusinessWeek* suggested in a 14 November 1988 cover story about KKR. "By implication," *Fortune* magazine wrote in its own 1988 cover story, "the spiritual leader of the industry was saying: 'This is the right way to behave. KKR's is the wrong way.' "

Secretly, though, Jerry Kohlberg was racking up millions of dollars in profits—and the potential for even bigger windfalls later on—by investing heavily in every deal that KKR did after he left.

Some of Kohlberg's quickest profits, in fact, came from the toe-hold investments that he professed to despise. Internal KKR records show that from late 1987 to March 1988, Kohlberg invested $828,549 in a KKR partnership that bought 4.9 percent of Texaco, one of America's biggest oil companies. Whatever Kohlberg's general compunction toward toe-hold investments, he didn't have any qualms about pocketing a $5.4 million share of KKR's profits when that Texaco foray paid off. In fact, Kohlberg's accountant in the spring of 1988 complained to KKR that Kohlberg should have collected as much as $75,000 more in extra profits. Kohlberg had been allocated about a 17-percent share of the Texaco winnings under his 1988 profit-splitting formula, the accountant observed, when some of the Texaco winnings should have been paid out under the 1987 formula, which allowed Kohlberg a 20.541-percent cut. Kravis and Roberts thought the complaint was bizarre. Rather than argue, however, they credited another $75,000 to Kohlberg's account at KKR.

And while Kohlberg publicly criticized giant buyouts and hostile buyouts, in early 1989 he quietly invested millions in KKR's biggest, most combative buyout ever—RJR Nabisco. Internal KKR records show that Kohlberg pitched in $9,406,906, which allowed him to claim a 15-percent share of KKR's eventual profits from RJR. The money was channeled in through various blandly named Kohlberg investment vehicles, including a partnership known as Ariadne. That $9.4 million exceeded every cent that Kohlberg himself had put to work at Kohlberg & Co. through that firm's first three years. Jerry Kohlberg, in fact, became the third biggest individual participant in the RJR buyout, ahead of all of RJR's own managers, including the company's new chief executive, Louis V. Gerstner, Jr. Only Kravis and Roberts had bigger stakes. Kohlberg, on the sidelines, ended up with a bigger profit claim than Paul Raether, Ted Ammon, or any of the younger KKR executives who worked nonstop on the deal. Only a faint, almost invisible trace of Kohlberg's investment was disclosed to the public—a phrase buried deep in the 300-page prospectus for RJR's various bond offerings, saying that "current and former partners" of KKR had invested unspecified amounts in the buyout.

Two years after the RJR buyout was completed, Kohlberg had done remarkably well from this sketchily disclosed investment that ran so counter to his public pronouncements. His paper profits approached $100 million.

If money alone could have made Jerry Kohlberg happy after being ousted from KKR, he should have been ecstatic. But instead he remained a bitter man, brooding in isolation while his former partners branded their mark into the U.S. economy.

8
Ruling an Industrial Empire

At the apex of its power in the late 1980s, KKR controlled an industrial domain larger than Texaco, Chrysler, or AT&T. Companies owned by the buyout firm made Wesson oil and Ritz crackers, Winston cigarettes and Duracell batteries. Shoppers in the Western United States bought billions of dollars of groceries every year from KKR-controlled Safeway and Fred Meyer stores; shoppers on the East Coast patronized KKR-owned Stop & Shop supermarkets and Bradlee's department stores. Travelers who stayed at Motel 6, motorists who bought Auto Zone car parts, or television viewers who watched the local CBS station in any of a half dozen cities, all were trafficking indirectly with KKR.

The breadth of this buyout empire was so vast that it seemed impossible for KKR's twenty partners and associates to oversee so many enterprises in any detailed way. The buyout firm's holdings spanned almost every industry, from timber to tobacco, from pumps to pretzels. Nearly 400,000 adults worked for KKR-controlled companies, enough to fill two congressional districts. The cookie division of RJR Nabisco alone produced so many different products—more than 400—that Kravis freely conceded he couldn't keep track of them all.

Yet Kravis and Roberts shrewdly devised a way for KKR's tiny cadre of deal-makers to consolidate their power. At every company that KKR acquired, the buyout firm's partners quickly co-opted the top twenty-five to seventy executives by inviting them to buy a lot of risky but potentially valuable stock in the post-buyout company. Abruptly, these executives found half or more of their life savings tied up in the high-octane stock that KKR created. If executives met the financial targets that the buyout plans dictated, they could eventually sell their stock at a huge profit and retire rich. If they failed, corporate bankruptcy, a personal loss of wealth, and great shame awaited. Confronted with such drastically contrasting scenarios, executives did everything within their power to make the company's post-buyout stock more valuable. In the process, these executives began doing exactly what KKR wanted.

After some initial jitters, most buyout company executives decided they liked KKR's system. It bolstered their power and money-making potential far beyond what had been attainable in public companies. Executives relished the idea of being owner-managers of a business; it played to their pride and their desire for public recognition. They also liked KKR's willingness to leave them in charge of detailed decisions. Such executives as Safeway's Peter Magowan, Owens-Illinois's Bob Lanigan, and RJR Nabisco's Louis Gerstner didn't care whether KKR was motivated by trust or a disdain for everyday commerce. When Kravis, Roberts, and their colleagues politely pressed these executives, again and again, to look at the "cost side" of their companies, the executives responded.

Once part-ownership of a company was spread out among top executives, in fact, the KKR men needed to do very little. A system was in place that fostered KKR's interests. A new class of buyout beneficiaries had been created whose legitimacy and success depended on doing KKR's will. Magowan, Gerstner, and other top executives joined KKR in asserting that the overriding mission of a corporation was to make money for shareholders—a standard by which these men were unalloyed successes. Chiefly by cutting back inefficient old operations, executives preserved their own jobs and built their own fortunes. Eventually, the top executives at Safeway, RJR Nabisco, and other buyout companies came to sneer at sales growth for its own sake, which they had once cherished as their companies' main mission. Narrow self-interest turned these top executives into agents of KKR.

For the KKR partners, their overriding objective as owners of industrial companies was dead simple. KKR was out to make money. As early as 1978, KKR told potential participants in its buyout funds that it "would attempt to yield to the investors an excellent return on the equity investments made by the fund during a five-year period." That single-minded goal was reiterated and reinforced in KKR's great fund-raising efforts of 1987. In a memo to investors, the KKR partners defined their business mission at each acquired company as "monitoring and maximizing the value of the investment during the period it is held by KKR and its investors."

KKR's profit targets were fiercely ambitious. For most of the twentieth century, ordinary stock-market investors earned about 9 percent a year, counting both dividends and capital gains. Even the great growth stocks of the postwar era, such as Kodak, Wal-Mart, or Apple Computer, seldom racked up gains of more than 30 percent a year for long stretches. But to the KKR partners, 30 percent a year *was too low*. Their standard profit targets called for investors to reap five times their money invested over a five-year span, a profit rate that amounted to about 40 percent a year. And often KKR set its sights on even higher returns.

To rack up these outsize investment profits—especially at unglamorous companies whose basic prospects didn't begin to compare with the sizzling growth of an Apple or a Wal-Mart—the KKR partners counted on three things. First were the big tax breaks that came from loading up a company with debt and boosting its depreciation deductions. "Tax considerations play an important role" in increasing companies' cash flow after a buyout, KKR confided to potential investors in a 1982 fundraising memo. At RJR Nabisco, for example, the company's tax bill shrunk to just $60 million in the second year of KKR's buyout, down from $893 million the year before KKR acquired the company.

Just as important was the healing effect of debt reduction on a company's finances. In almost every buyout, the KKR partners expected the initial deluge of borrowings to be worked down over time—either by cash flow from operations or by selling pieces of the company for cash. As buyout companies shrank their debt, their interest bills dropped and much more of their cash flow would translate into net income. Like a runner discarding a suit of armor, such companies began to show tremendous acceleration in their per-share earnings growth, causing the value of their post-buyout stock to soar.

If the alchemy of leverage wasn't enough, the KKR partners could count on a third big source of investment profits: increased efficiency. Almost every big company was hidebound by excess overhead and bureaucracy, Kravis and Roberts came to believe. Headquarters staffs were too large. "I call them the people who report to people," Kravis often remarked. If most big companies could whittle down their overhead costs, the KKR partners believed, profitability could be greatly improved without the need for any sales growth. "Companies build up layers and layers of fat," Kravis told a newspaper editors' luncheon in 1989. "So many companies that we've bought have been so much better once we got them out of a corporate bureaucracy."

As Kravis became a more powerful and controversial figure in the late 1980s, the virtues of cost-cutting became almost a theological point for him. No one saw this more clearly than Jim Wilson, one of Kravis's old prep-school teachers. Every spring in the late 1980s, Wilson brought a busload of his students at the Loomis-Chafee School in Connecticut to New York for a day trip that culminated in a private dinner with their school's most famous alumnus, Henry Kravis. The first dinner, in 1986, was low-key, with Kravis spinning stories about his student days on Loomis's wrestling team. In later years, however, Kravis overwhelmed the students with a defense of the buyout business. "He's become an ardent believer that what he does is in the public interest," Wilson said in an interview. Whether the students asked questions or not hardly mattered. At the 1988 dinner, in one of the elegant banquet rooms of the New York Racquet Club, Kravis held forth about the virtues of buyouts for hours; it was past midnight when the students returned home.

For both Kravis and Roberts, this heartfelt disdain for corporate grandeur traced back to the values of their small-businessman fathers. Growing up in Tulsa, Henry Kravis got daily business pointers from his father, Ray Kravis, who founded and then managed a fifteen-person oil-reserve appraisal firm with the Kravis name on the door. Pursue big-name clients but keep your own overhead small, Ray Kravis taught his son. Farm out a lot of tasks to outside contractors. Own most of the business yourself, and share the rest with a few key employees that you trust. "He was a pioneer," Henry Kravis said later about his father. "I often think what guts he must have had."

George Roberts picked up a saltier version of those same values from his father, Lou Roberts, a small-time Houston broker of oilpatch deals. Lou Roberts's heroes were millionaire wildcatters with mud on their boots; his villains were the big oil companies with their legions of lawyers. One of the biggest negotiating coups of Lou Roberts's career was when he bought a piece of the great Permian Basin oilfield from a Cherokee Indian in the 1940s, after a protracted one-on-one negotiating session laced with whiskey and mutual insults. One of Lou Roberts's biggest mistakes was to sell that same field, much too soon, to an East Coast oil company for a pittance. During summer school breaks in the 1950s, Lou Roberts tried to pass on what he knew of business to his son. Other fathers lobbied to get their teenage sons summer jobs at big corporations.

Lou Roberts instead invited his son to drive with him along dusty Texas roads in the 1950s, traveling from Amarillo to Lubbock to Odessa, so George could see how a one-man brokerage firm lined up the next deal. "I used to ask him after every meeting: 'Why did you do this? Why did the other guy say that?'" George Roberts later recalled. "I learned a lot."

As much as Kravis and Roberts championed lean, efficient companies, they wanted to collect big profits without rolling up their sleeves and spending years transforming a company themselves. The KKR executives were deal men, eager to chase the next acquisition in a new town. The thought of lingering at one company for years to attend to nitty-gritty operating details seemed like torture to them. "Our attitude is: You run the business, and we'll help you with the financing," Kravis once explained. A top executive of Motel 6 learned the hard way about KKR's disdain for details, after he displayed several outdoor signs at a board meeting and asked Kravis and Roberts what would look best on a highway. The cousins came away shaking their heads. "Right after the meeting," Kravis later recalled, "I pulled George aside and said: 'We've got problems. Because if we, laymen as we are, have got to decide what the signs are going to look like. . . . That's dangerous.'" Within six months, the KKR executives had ousted that chief executive in favor of a new Motel 6 boss who could make decisions on his own.

Even the chief executives who thrived under KKR found that the buyout firm's partners politely shrugged off any interest in the operating details of their industry. Typical was the experience of Oran Robertson, the chief executive of Fred Meyer Inc., who tried fruitlessly to coax George Roberts and Mike Michelson into spending time at the giant dual-purpose grocery and department stores that he ran in the Pacific Northwest. "Come to Portland a day before the board meeting," Robertson urged. "Take a look at the stores. This is a unique concept in retailing." The answer from the San Francisco office of the buyout firm was: no thanks. Robertson was doubtless right about the wonders of his stores, but the KKR men were content to scan financial statements. Roberts and Michelson flew up to Portland the day of the board meetings, reviewed the company's finances, and flew back to San Francisco that night. Fred Meyer executives could look at the stores on their own.

Other executives found Henry Kravis just as diffident toward their businesses. Ed Mabbs, the chief executive of Incom International, an industrial-parts company controlled by KKR executives for a while, winced one time when Kravis described Incom as a bunch of "boring" businesses. "That's not fair," Mabbs replied. "Now some of the businesses, like industrial chain, may be boring. But others, like small lawn-mower engines, aren't boring at all." It was no use. To Kravis, Incom's businesses all were dull.

To make money without getting their shirts sweaty, the KKR partners urged companies' top executives to buy big stakes in their own companies alongside KKR and its limited-partner investors. Jerry Kohlberg had been the first to insist on this, in the early 1970s, as an important part of a well-conceived buyout. "We're all on the same side of the table," Kohlberg would assure executives. In the 1980s, Kravis and Roberts picked up a variant of that same message, offering stock to executives with as much reverence as they could muster.

At the start of every buyout, the KKR partners regularly set aside 10- to 15-percent ownership in a company to be acquired by that company's top management. Top executives already were accustomed to generous stock options that let them control 1 to 4 percent of a public company's stock as a group, but KKR's approach was radically different. The buyout would jack up top managers' stake in a company by three to ten times. Managers would pay hard cash for a sizable part of their stock—exposing themselves to financial loss if the company did poorly, a risk that options-holding executives seldom faced at a public company. "When a manager has his own money invested and it's his company," Kravis asserted in a 1984 panel discussion, "he's going to come in a little earlier in the morning. He's going to think harder about that capital expenditure. Does he need the limousine and the corporate jet?"

Artfully, the KKR men seized the moral high ground when it came time to allocate stock ownership, or equity, to top executives. One of the KKR partners—usually Kravis or Roberts, but sometimes MacDonnell or Raether—would sit down with the chief executive and deliver a buyout creed that went about as follows: *We expect the top management in a buyout to participate in the equity. We think of you as partners with ourselves in the buyout. We believe management should pay for its equity, at the same price as all the other investors. We like to see managers put a great part of their liquid net worth into a company. If this blows up, you'll get hurt. We all will. But if we're right about our hurdle rates, we all could make five times our money in five or six years. You stand to make a lot of money. We don't know exactly how many people should participate in the equity; we leave that up to you. But we want a lot of top management to participate.*

Chief executives melted at the speech. One after another, all the "buttons" that motivated a CEO had been pressed by the KKR partners; first pride, then security, then a chance to overcome danger—and finally, pure capitalist lust for wealth. The KKR men had to be careful not to rush the mention of profits too fast. On one occasion, in England, an investment banker working for KKR mistakenly raced ahead to mention the financial payoff before establishing the right spiritual tone, and was told: "Money does not concern me in the least." With that, the English chief executive ended the negotiations. When the message was delivered properly, however, the KKR men in these sessions both won a friend and recruited a chief executive to the buyout firm's way of thinking.

Top executives became the rajas in KKR's empire. Much like nineteenth-century Indian princes, they took charge of vast territories, with only modest obligations to their colonial masters. These executives were beneficiaries of KKR's largess; they were in line to make giant fortunes if the equity value of the company they managed soared. Curiously, the CEOs who had already built up fortunes of $5 million or more before a buyout—enough money to satisfy almost any other American—were the ones who scrambled the hardest to make even more money. It wasn't just that men such as Safeway's Peter Magowan or Beatrice's Don Kelly wanted third and fourth homes, yachts, and personal art collections, although some of them did. This endless pursuit of more wealth was the way the competition was played among top executives. The executives who made the most money, whether it was $1 million or $100 million, were the ones who merited the envy and admiration of their peers.

"Grab a man by his W-2 and his heart and mind will follow," KKR associate Don Herdrich once quipped. It was a throwaway one-liner for him, but a bedrock expression of how KKR operated. Some strong-willed executives, like Beatrice's Kelly or RJR Nabisco's Lou Gerstner, brought their own distinctive styles to a buyout company. That was fine with the KKR partners, who were prepared to do business with chief executives of all types—hands-on or hands-off, brash or self-effacing, it hardly mattered. The only obligation of a company's top executives was to deliver the financial results that KKR wanted.

The first big raja that KKR created was Don Kelly, a headstrong Chicago food-company executive who combined a folksy Irish-American manner with a razor-sharp attention to financial details. The son of a steel-company accountant, Kelly was a college dropout who had built his career at the Swift meat-packing company. When Kelly and Kravis began to get acquainted in 1983, Kelly was in his late fifties, managing not just Swift, but also a host of other businesses grouped under the Esmark Inc. banner. Kravis's and Kelly's first two attempts to do business together didn't work out. But then, in the prelude to the Beatrice takeover battle of 1985–86, Kravis approached a briefly out-of-work Kelly and asked if he would like to run the Chicago food conglomerate if KKR could acquire it. Yes, Kelly said—on the condition that he get 20 to 30 percent of the equity. KKR never allotted anywhere near that much, Kravis responded. For weeks, the two men dickered back and forth. "Why can't Don be reasonable?" Kravis plaintively asked his colleagues.

Eventually, KKR agreed to let Kelly buy about 1 percent of Beatrice's stock and acquire another 6.5 percent via options. In total, Kelly and various trusts that he administered came to control 10,040,000 Beatrice shares—a holding that cost Kelly just $5 million but ultimately proved worth $166 million. Other top Beatrice managers got to buy another 5 percent of the post-buyout stock. With that much valuable stock in their hands, Beatrice's new managers "have the same interest we have, to maximize return on invested capital," Kravis told a journalist in December 1985.

Sure enough, once Kelly took office at Beatrice in April 1986, he quickly began making the cuts that KKR wanted. He slashed by more than 15 percent the $975 million marketing budget that Beatrice allotted for promoting Tropicana orange juice, Fisher nuts, Playtex brassieres, and other products. (That marketing budget had grown so lavish that Beatrice bought television ad time in California to promote Fisher nut brands that it didn't even sell there.) Kelly and his aides dismantled a centralized bureaucracy that jacked up Beatrice's overhead costs to $211 million a year, some of the highest in the food industry. And Kelly canceled Beatrice's involvement in race-car sponsorship—a favorite hobby of previous chief executive Jim Dutt—which was costing Beatrice $40 million a year without any clear payoff. "A woman in the stands doesn't go out and buy a Playtex brassiere just because she sees a car going around with 'Beatrice' on the side," Kravis wryly observed.

Kelly wanted to make a personal mark at Beatrice, too. While KKR's partners thought only in financial terms, Kelly had another mission: to eradicate the highly controlled, bureaucratic style of Jim Dutt, a longtime rival of Kelly's. In the Dutt era, Beatrice executives could enter the boss's office only by a side door, and all visitors to Beatrice—no matter how powerful—were required to wear plastic visitor's badges. Kelly, on his first day at work, told subordinates to enter his top-of-the-building office any way they wanted, including through the window. And Kelly turned the badge issue into a personal crusade. Outraged at the sight of a distinguished Swiss banker wearing a peeling VISITOR badge at Beatrice's headquarters, Kelly issued an edict: No badges. When he noticed two days later that someone had pasted one of the hated badges on the suit lapel of a visiting attorney, Kelly hit the roof. "I put out a request that we get rid of visitor's badges, but apparently that hasn't got through," Kelly told his security chief. "So I'm going to give it to you in good old South Side Irish: Burn da goddamn tags."

"Yes, well, we can't do that for a while," the security manager said. "We have to change the instruction manuals."

"How long does it take to write: 'Don't give out badges'?" Kelly demanded. "I don't want people running around with badges. And that's the way it is."

On such matters of corporate style, Kelly had all the freedom in the world. "KKR doesn't tell me what to do," Kelly told the chief executive of a big East Coast food company in 1987. Even KKR associates Mike Tokarz and Kevin Bousquette learned never to visit Beatrice's Chicago headquarters without getting Kelly's permission first. On one unannounced visit, Kelly dragged the young associates into his office, telling them: "I expect you to let me know that you're here." Kravis's lieutenants were welcome to visit Beatrice's Chicago headquarters with an invitation, Kelly said. But he quickly added: "There is never a day that you're going to be allowed to do anything in this company of substance."*

All the same, Don Kelly's 7.5-percent Beatrice stake made him cut overhead and take other financial steps that were exactly what KKR wanted. "My job has been to constantly evaluate what is good for shareholders," Kelly told an interviewer in 1988. That was a huge relief to Kravis and Roberts, who had abhorred the wasteful ways of Beatrice before the buyout. And on the really big issues at Beatrice—as Don Kelly would later discover to his chagrin—KKR still called the shots.

At other KKR buyout companies in the late 1980s even deeper retrenchment was required. To the great satisfaction of the deal-makers at 9 West Fifty-Seventh Street in New York and 101 California Street in San Francisco, the top executives at companies such as Union Texas Petroleum and Owens-Illinois made the cuts that KKR wanted, even if they were agonizing decisions. Thinking like owners made the difference.

At Union Texas, a decisive moment came in early 1986, about eight months after KKR had acquired control of the company in a joint purchase with Allied Signal Corporation. Oil prices were plunging at the

---

*Kelly later told *Fortune* magazine about his early encounter with Tokarz and Bousquette, not identifying them by name but instead calling them only "a couple of the lesser lights in KKR's hierarchy." The description delighted Wall Street investment bankers, who promptly rushed over a shipment of 15-watt light bulbs to both Tokarz and Bousquette.

time, sinking as low as $10 a barrel, far below the $24-a-barrel level that
KKR and Union Texas had forecast. The dynamics of the oil market were
changing drastically; projects that had once seemed like sure money-
makers now looked like losers. Top Union Texas officials had already
drafted an "action plan" that called for big cutbacks in the company's
$300 million capital spending budget if oil prices continued to slide. But
at an early 1986 executive committee meeting in Houston, Union Texas
officials wavered on whether the full cutbacks would be needed.

"Would you spend $30 million of your own money at a time like this?"
Roberts crisply asked.

"What are you talking about?" Union Texas president Clark Johnson
replied.

"You and the rest of management own 10 percent of the company,"
Roberts reminded Johnson. "That's your share of $300 million."

The room went silent. Then Union Texas's top financial planners said
they wanted to look more closely at the company's "action plan." At a
subsequent meeting in March 1986, Johnson and his aides proposed to
spend just $230 million, the lowest amount in years. Union Texas em-
barked on a much more cautious strategy, weathering the oil slump but
not trying to add reserves aggressively. Some Union Texas officials missed
their old freedom to spend boldly—but to Roberts, that retrenchment
was a perfect example of how managers spent money more wisely when
they became sizable part-owners of a business.

At Owens-Illinois, corporate overhead came in for deep cuts. Once
again, top executives looked at their companies entirely differently once
they had $1 million or more of their own money tied up in ownership of
the company's stock.

The cost-cutting steps that Owens-Illinois chairman Robert Lanigan
and president Joseph Lemieux took weren't pretty, but they worked. First
the two men sacked 500 headquarters employees in March 1987. They
sold two Gulfstream G-1 executive jets that the company had bought a
few years earlier. Then Lanigan and Lemieux set about dismantling what
had been the pride and joy of Owens-Illinois's previous management—
the biggest, most lavish corporate headquarters in Toledo. Within three
years of KKR's arrival, the twenty-seventh-floor executive suite looked
gutted. Office after office sat utterly empty, without a stick of furniture
on the avocado-green carpet. A year before the buyout, Owens-Illinois
had boasted twenty-three vice presidents and a half dozen senior vice
presidents or division presidents. By January 1990, only five executives
still had jobs on the twenty-seventh floor. Entire departments, such as

those in charge of corporate strategy, human resources, and legal services, were shrunk to vestiges of their old selves and relegated to lower floors. Thanks to such cuts, Lanigan and Lemieux slashed corporate overhead by nearly two-thirds, to $13 million in 1990 from $32.4 million in 1986. Clerical staffing dwindled to the point where a single secretary served both president Joe Lemieux and vice chairman John McMackin. If the phone emitted a high-pitched ring, she answered: "Mr. Lemieux's office"; after a low-pitched ring, it was: "Mr. McMackin's office."

Altogether, those savings added perhaps $150 million to the value of Owens-Illinois's post-buyout stock—and at least $2 million each to the value of stock held by Lanigan and Lemieux. For that much money, they could get by without corporate jets, private secretaries, or even a receptionist.

Perhaps the toughest executive for KKR to win over to its way of thinking was Peter Magowan, the youthful, patrician head of the Safeway grocery chain. Magowan already was spectacularly wealthy before KKR arrived; his grandfather had founded Merrill Lynch & Co. What's more, Magowan had grown up in the grocery business, and had immense sentimental attachment to Safeway. Both his grandfather and father had been Safeway chairmen. Only forty-one years old when KKR arrived on the scene, Magowan had whizzed through a series of Safeway jobs since college days, doing everything from peeling lettuce in Houston at age nineteen to running the Oklahoma division as a fast-track young executive. "I knew a lot of people all over the company," Magowan later recalled. "They were my friends." In Peter Magowan's Safeway, profit and a rising stock price were important. But so, too, were growth, grandeur, and tradition at America's largest grocery chain.

"If we win this," George Roberts warned KKR's Bob MacDonnell during the July 1986 bidding contest for Safeway, "this is going to be a two-and-a-half-year project for you." Roberts and MacDonnell wanted to refocus Safeway drastically. Sales growth per se wasn't important to them. Higher profitability was. The KKR men wanted to sell off some of Safeway's weaker divisions entirely. They wanted Magowan and his aides to rein in capital outlays, halting a practice of spending millions to open more stores in low-profit areas. And the KKR men wanted Safeway managers to keep a much tighter rein on working capital, shrinking inventories so as to free up cash. After a week of so of studying the vastness of Safeway—with $20 billion a year of sales and 180,000 employees—Bob MacDonnell nearly threw up his hands. "What's the most important thing we can do if we want to turn this aircraft carrier around?"

MacDonnell later recalled asking himself. "How do we get these 180,000 people to do what we want? How do we get them to work in the interest of shareholders?"

The answer: a new pay system that injected KKR's priorities into the lives of thousands of Safeway managers.

To instill these values, Roberts and MacDonnell turned to an earnest, obsessively hardworking consultant, Steve Burd. The son of a North Dakota railwayman, Burd had come to work at the San Francisco office of Arthur D. Little & Co. There he became known as a relentless cost-cutter at companies in turmoil. "Transitions come with costs," Burd once explained in an interview. "Failure to make transitions comes with a higher cost. An enterprise can go out of business and die if it doesn't make changes." Around top executives, Burd mitigated that icy message with soft-spoken, polite manners. He was exactly the right emissary for KKR to send into a buyout company that needed radical change. Burd thrived on the nitty-gritty that the KKR men loathed. He knew how to handle the office politics and bureaucracy of a giant company, using skills that Kravis, Roberts, and their colleagues refused to learn. Preaching his message of cost-cutting and "transitions," Burd resembled nothing so much as an overseas missionary among the heathens.

At Safeway, Burd began by taking a drab, out-of-the way office in a dingy building across the street from Safeway's Oakland, California, head-quarters. He wasn't going to frighten anyone in Safeway's executive suites. From that office, Burd began to spin out a radical set of ideas. Safeway had missed its internal profit targets for seven years running, Burd noticed, yet most managers had still collected bonuses of 20 to 30 percent of yearly pay. That practice should stop, Burd argued. Bonuses shouldn't be tied to sales growth or tiny profit improvements over the previous year. They should be tied to Safeway managers' ability to meet ambitious profit targets, year after year. Managers who succeeded should get whopping bonuses—as big as 60 or even 100 percent of their salaries. Managers who missed those targets badly should be denied any bonus at all. *Grab a man by his W-2 and his heart and mind will follow.*

As Burd began privately testing out his new plan, senior Safeway managers balked at first. In one-on-one meetings with Burd, they argued that the new standards would be too hard, that managers would grow dispirited if they failed to win bonuses. But Burd persisted. Safeway managers would set the targets themselves, he said. Instead of prizing sales growth, they would center their plans on a new concept that he called "return on market value," or ROMV. The mechanics of Burd's plan were complex, but its purpose was simple. Regional managers who cut inventory or sold off unprofitable stores would score just as high—and maybe higher—than the old-style managers who prized sales growth above all. The Safeway managers who did what was needed to make KKR even richer would share in a small piece of the winnings themselves. In late October 1986, Burd presented his detailed new ROMV plan to Magowan and asked for permission to make it official. Let's do it, Magowan said.

In a poignant speech before about forty of his senior managers in early November 1986, Magowan embraced the KKR ethos in a way that gripped those in the audience. "Steve is going to present a proposal for how we might change management compensation," Magowan began. "Most of you know he's looking at fairly fundamental changes." Then Magowan reminded the audience that, for the past several years, he had been serving on the board of Chrysler, the carmaker that nearly went over the brink in 1981 and then fought its way back. Safeway, at that moment, was a lot like Chrysler, Magowan suggested. And Burd was the man to help start the recovery.

Converted to KKR's values, Safeway's managers went on to do everything that the buyout firm wanted. They slashed spending on new stores to just $228 million in 1987, down from $621 million in 1985. They shrunk inventory to $1.04 billion at year-end 1987, so that it turned over an average of seventeen times a year, much faster than the once-a-month average before the buyout in 1985, when warehouses had been kept packed with soft drinks, paper towels, and other goods to be sold in months ahead. Safeway's managers whittled down overhead and operating costs in the first two years of the buyout. They sold or closed more than 100 individual stores across the country that didn't meet Burd's new targets. Throughout Safeway management, the buzzword became ROMV instead of growth. Some five and a half years after KKR arrived in 1986, the value of the buyout company's stock had soared to $16 a share from an original $2—an even greater increase than KKR had predicted. Magowan's own 1.9 million shares of stock and options were worth $30 million. At least thirty of his top managers owned enough stock that they, too, were millionaires.

The chance to get rich from owning buyout equity drove Safeway's senior management team. "I do believe it changed their perspective on how they managed their jobs," Magowan said. Job cuts became much more tempting. "If we could do without, the value of the company was built in the process." Top executives stopped talking about competing with Cincinnati-based Kroger Co. to be America's biggest grocery chain. Instead, they focused their competitive drives on overtaking the most profitable chain, Albertson's Inc. of Boise, Idaho, regardless of whether that meant ringing up more sales.

Watching with pride in the background were MacDonnell and Roberts, the two KKR partners most involved in overseeing the Safeway buyout. "The more you can make guys understand that this is their business as much as ours, the better off we'll be," MacDonnell said in 1989. In the years before the buyout, MacDonnell added, Safeway executives dissipated nearly $1 billion on new-store construction that failed to make any meaningful contribution to profits. Under the more watchful eye of the KKR system, Safeway had switched its spending to the less glamorous but more productive area of store remodeling and upgrading, achieving robust 30-percent-a-year returns from the money spent.

In New York, KKR's top two partners, Henry Kravis and Paul Raether, began their own attempt in the late 1980s to reshape a giant U.S. company: RJR Nabisco. For years, the tobacco and food company had been an Augean stables of corporate waste. It supported ten corporate jets and allowed its chief executive's dog to fly for free across the United States, under the passenger name of G. Shepherd. RJR resorted to such excesses in part because its main tobacco business was both socially repugnant and incredibly profitable. Tobacco executives chose to be pampered pariahs, indulging themselves in perks that ranged from the corporate jet fleet to five-times-a-day mail delivery at the head office of the R. J. Reynolds tobacco subsidiary.

"Over and above any company I've ever seen, they had excesses in people and assets," Henry Kravis said in an interview right after KKR won control of RJR Nabisco. Kravis ticked off his list of irritants: membership in twenty-two country clubs, bloated headquarters staffs, top executives whose main business role seemed to be to cavort with former chief executive F. Ross Johnson on junkets. Kravis didn't want to fix those problems himself. But he was willing to spend lots of money— RJR's money—to hire someone who would.

Starting in December 1988, Kravis and Raether began searching for a take-charge, no-nonsense chief executive to replace RJR's Johnson, who had quit after the failure of his own buyout attempt. "If you get the right general," another KKR executive later explained, "the colonels and lieutenants will fall in line." First Kravis spent $500,000 to enlist big-league executive recruiter Tom Neff of Spencer Stuart Associates. Neff started with a list of twenty candidates, then quickly began to focus on the number-two executive at American Express, Lou Gerstner.

A onetime McKinsey & Co. consultant, Gerstner had such iron willpower that observers likened him to Gen. George Patton. When Gerstner was rushed to a hospital in the early 1970s after severing two fingers in a weekend lawn-mower accident, he badgered the surgeon treating the wound to finish up quickly, explaining: "I've got a meeting tomorrow that I need to get to." Only on doctor's orders was he kept hospitalized for three days. Gerstner didn't know much about the tobacco or food businesses, but his résumé had leadership and success written all over it. At age twenty-eight, Gerstner had been one of the youngest McKinsey associates ever named partner. At American Express, he had built the charge-card business into a nonstop growth machine. What's more, Wall Street chat was that Gerstner disliked being stuck in the number-two spot behind a relatively young Amex chairman. Gerstner was wary of KKR at first, telling Neff at one point: "Go away." But Neff persisted, sending a package of confidential RJR material to Gerstner's Connecticut home. Then Neff arranged for Kravis and Raether to pay a secret house call to Gerstner one Sunday evening in January 1989.

Sipping soft drinks in the den of Gerstner's home, the two KKR men put on a virtuoso performance. Kravis didn't brag for a moment about KKR's takeover prowess. Instead, he told Gerstner about how important it was for KKR to work as partners with managers who owned sizable parts of a business themselves. Raether and Kravis took turns providing an overview of RJR Nabisco's operations. Then Kravis wooed Gerstner with gentle talk about the tobacco and food company's promise. "Here's where we are today," Kravis said, as he briefly alluded to the hellish state of affairs at RJR—$25 billion in debt, gaping voids in top management, and a desperate need to cut costs and jack up operating profit. "Here's where we want to be in five years," Kravis continued. He sketched out alluring vistas of a company with less debt, expanding food businesses, and a soaring stock price. "All we need is the right CEO to get us there," he concluded.

Even for a savvy, skeptical executive like Gerstner, the images were irresistible. "Henry is a marvelous salesman," Gerstner said with a chuckle a year later. "He's so down-to-earth and straightforward. It's hard not to believe him."

Hooked on the prospects of running RJR Nabisco, Gerstner began meeting with the KKR men more and more. As talks grew serious, he began haggling about his pay and equity package, with a tenacity that

Henry Kravis in his East Side Manhattan apartment. He paid $5 million to live in the building that once housed John D. Rockefeller, Jr. *(Photo by Jonathan Levine/ONYX.)*

George Roberts in KKR's San Francisco offices. He and Kravis matched their elegant decor almost perfectly—with one exception: Kravis's New York offices had each painting identified with a little brass plaque. Roberts left visitors guessing. *(Photo by Eric Luse/San Francisco Chronicle.)*

Jerry Kohlberg's shyness and "wise uncle" demeanor made him very effective as a Wall Street deal-maker who appeared above the fray.

KKR's outlandishly complex method of financing the 1979 acquisition of Houdaille Industries was the butt of Wall Street jokes for a time. Then rivals realized how much money the upstart "buyout boutique" was making. Competitors stopped laughing and started imitating. *(Photo courtesy of Donald Herdrich.)*

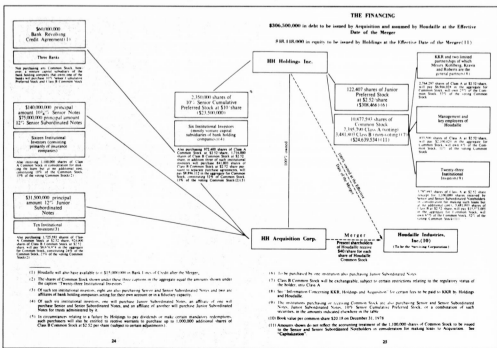

THE FINANCING

24   25

Three loan officers at the Los Angeles office of Bankers Trust—George Hartmann, Ron Badie, and Morgan St. John—built their careers by bankrolling KKR's buyouts. The T-shirts were mischievous souvenirs handed out at the completion of the $6.2 billion Beatrice buyout in 1986. *(Photo courtesy of Bankers Trust.)*

"We can help you," junk-bond specialist Peter Ackerman kept telling KKR executives in the early 1980s, as he linked the buyout business and his own firm of Drexel Burnham Lambert, Inc. Brilliant, shy, and temperamental, Ackerman helped KKR issue $15 billion of junk bonds—more than any other borrower in the United States. *(Photo by Amy Etra.)*

The rise and fall of Ackerman's boss, Michael Milken, kept the business community spellbound. At his peak in 1987, Milken earned $550 million and was seen as the next J. P. Morgan. In late 1990, Milken's Wall Street career ended for good when he was sentenced to ten years in jail for securities fraud. *(Photo courtesy of The Bettmann Archive.)*

Taking on more debt than any corporate acquirers had ever done before, Roberts and Kravis signed on February 9, 1989, the documents completing the $26.4 billion buyout of RJR Nabisco. It was seen as a happy moment. *(Photo by Michael Fairchild.)*

By acquiring RJR Nabisco, Kravis and Roberts got control of some of America's best-known cookie and cigarette brands, including Oreos, Ritz crackers, Winston, Salem, and Camel. A tiny shopping-cart trophy created by Wall Street advisers Bruce Wasserstein and Joe Perella paid homage to KKR. *(Photo by Jason Goltz.)*

Kravis's second wife, fashion designer Carolyne Roehm, began her own label in 1984 and won acclaim for her stylish dresses. Tall and slender, Roehm liked to model her own creations. *(Photo by Theo Westenberger.)*

Reveling in his wealth, Kravis in the late 1980s became a regular in society circles, attending lavish parties with his wife. One of their many chances to mingle with fellow celebrities came in 1989 at the seventieth birthday party of the late publisher Malcolm Forbes in Morocco. *(Photo by Ron Galella/Ron Galella Ltd.)*

Beatrice chief executive Don Kelly kept mementos in his office of all the deals in his career that topped $1 billion. That total reached eleven—five of them achieved with KKR's help. But on Kelly's twelfth try, the KKR men said no. *(Photo by Loren Santow.)*

Safeway chief executive Peter Magowan resisted a series of low-key buyout overtures from KKR's George Roberts in the mid-1980s. When unwelcome raiders stalked Magowan's grocery chain, however, an alliance with KKR began to look much better. *(Photo by George Steinmetz/ONYX.)*

Bob Kidder, chafing at the big-company bureaucracy surrounding him, ran Duracell for years as a division of Kraft. In late 1987, Kidder and his top aides secretly devised "The Exorcist Plan," a strategy for Duracell to break away in a buyout. He got his wish when KKR bought the battery company for $1.8 billion. *(Photo by Gary Spector.)*

Anxious to find a new boss for RJR Nabisco immediately after KKR won control of the tobacco and food company, Kravis in December 1988 asked an executive recruiter to draw up a list of thirty candidates. At the top of the list was Louis Gerstner, the take-charge president of American Express. *(Photo by Michael Mella.)*

More than any other chief executive, except Kelly, Gerstner haggled with the KKR men about his own stock and pay before taking the RJR Nabisco job. Kravis decided he liked that; it meant Gerstner knew what buyouts were all about. *(Photo by John S. Abbott.)*

KKR's partners and associates at year-end 1990. From left: Kevin Bousquette, Perry Golkin, Bob MacDonnell, Ned Gilhuly, Scott Stuart, Richard Kreider, Salvatore Badalamenti (rear), Henry Kravis (front), John Gerson, Paul Raether, George Roberts, Ted Ammon, Cliff Robbins, Tom Hudson, Saul Fox, Mike Tokarz (rear), Michael Chu (front), Jamie Greene, and Mike Michelson. *(Photo courtesy of Mary Hilliard.)*

Kravis hadn't seen since his 1985 battles with Don Kelly. If Gerstner left American Express, he would forfeit more than $10 million in deferred stock and pay, an amount so large that Amex figured its star executive would be unpoachable. "Why should I give that up?" Gerstner bluntly asked Kravis.

"We went back and forth, back and forth," Kravis later recalled. "I really thought for a while we weren't going to get him." But then Kravis gave in. RJR would pay Gerstner $14.5 million up front and at least $2.3 million a year—one of the highest guaranteed pay packages for a chief executive in America. Gerstner also won the right to buy $5.3 million RJR shares during his first four years at the company, including some at just one cent a share, the first time KKR ever let a chief executive buy stock at a preferential rate.

A few months later, Kravis decided he liked Gerstner's fighting spirit. "The harder a guy negotiates with us about equity, the better a CEO he is likely to be," Kravis later said. Such executives understood what buy-outs were all about.

For all the wealth that Gerstner had personally secured, RJR itself was about to become a lot more Spartan. Taking office at the tobacco and food company on 3 April 1989, Gerstner began by doing just what KKR wanted from all of its manager-owners—slashing wasteful spending. RJR stopped reimbursing executives for country-club memberships. It pared its headquarters staff from 400 to 150. Gerstner ordered that six of the company's ten private jets be sold, and that no executive use the remaining jets without Gerstner's written permission. Miles flown by RJR's corporate aircraft dropped 60 percent in the first year of the buyout.

This lean new ethos began to spread throughout RJR Nabisco. At the R. J. Reynolds tobacco division in Winston-Salem, North Carolina, internal mail deliveries were cut to one a day. The new tobacco chief, Jim Johnston, dismissed 1,525 workers in August 1989, shrinking the domestic tobacco division's payroll by 13 percent. KKR's favorite consultant, Steve Burd, spent several months at the tobacco division, helping install new management pay scales that rewarded frugal spenders.

At the company's Nabisco food divisions in East Hanover, New Jersey, senior executive John Greeniaus pared back advertising of well-known brands such as Ritz crackers and Oreo cookies by about 10 percent. American consumers were oversaturated with ads, Greeniaus argued; the cookies would sell just fine without quite so many commercials. And when RJR built a new headquarters in New York, chief administrative officer Gene Croisant skimped on every expense he could. Instead of Thai silk to cover the walls, Croisant opted for rayon from New Jersey. Hallways were covered with cheap, sturdy indoor/outdoor carpeting instead of the expensive marble and Oriental rugs that most big companies preferred. From beginning to end, Croisant spent just $18 million to build RJR's headquarters, about 30 percent less than Ross Johnson had spent for the company's previous offices in Atlanta.

Top RJR executives embraced austerity in large part because of the big stock packages that KKR liked to press on managers. Johnston and Greeniaus each spent $1.5 million to buy 300,000 shares of post-buyout stock in RJR Nabisco, and picked up options on another 1.2 million shares. That stock would be a total loss if the buyout failed financially; it would be worth $35 million or more if KKR achieved its usual financial target of a fivefold profit in five years. "Having the LBO perform and having our equity be worth something is the way we're going to be successful," Greeniaus said partway into the buyout. "This isn't about perks or climbing the old corporate ladder." In total, some 500 senior managers at RJR Nabisco were picked by Gerstner to own post-buyout stock. They became part of a lucky inner circle at the company, regularly receiving candid private letters from Gerstner that began: "Colleagues."

One after another, RJR Nabisco's new owner-managers canceled the grandiose projects that their predecessors had set in motion. The first to go was Premier, an ill-fated $1 billion attempt to develop a smokeless cigarette. As much as RJR hoped that Premier would revitalize the smoking market, the prototypes that Ross Johnson rolled out in 1988 were disasters. They required a blowtorch to light; the lungs of a racehorse to inhale. Kravis and his KKR colleagues didn't want to hear about faraway potential. They wanted results fast, and Premier didn't pass muster. The KKR men canceled that project even before Gerstner showed up.

Next to go was Cookieville, an ambitious, $2 billion plan to build two high-tech bakeries using robots and optical sensors, instead of human beings, to make cookies. It was ludicrous, Gerstner and Greeniaus decided. Even Cookieville's defenders couldn't see any way that the huge investment in the plant would pay off within ten years. In one instance, Cookieville planners wanted to install $10 million of robotics to eliminate three jobs held by forklift truck operators. Designers had gone amok, Gerstner and Greeniaus decided. Building high-tech bakeries might be fun, but it wouldn't make shareholders rich. Cookieville was zapped.

Such changes made RJR Nabisco a scaled-down, less ambitious company—but one that became a lot more profitable. After the buyout, RJR's operating profit margins climbed quarter after quarter, from a low of 17.5 percent of sales in the spring of 1989 to 25.2 percent of sales in the winter of 1991. Tobacco executives abandoned a long-held goal of holding one-third of the U.S. market, choosing to sell fewer cigarettes but market them at higher prices. "Our profit margins from 1988 to 1990 improved more than any other U.S. cigarette company," RJR tobacco chief Jim Johnston said. "That's because of a very strong emphasis on cost control."

As executives at dozens of buyout companies raced to wring efficiencies from their businesses, the KKR partners hardly needed to lift a finger. A few executives found it unnerving to see how much the KKR partners pulled back and let their system run its own course. Bill Jones, the president of Boren Clay Products, recalled phoning Kravis just to chat a couple years after the buyout of his brick company had been negotiated. "I'm beginning to feel like the lonely Maytag repairman," Jones told Kravis. "I never hear from you."

Politely, Kravis told Jones that this was the way KKR wanted it. "You know what I need," Kravis said. "You're delivering the numbers. We don't need to contact you. We know you're busy, and we've been busy too."

Most of the time, top executives loved the autonomy. They knew what to do. "KKR gave us a lot of freedom," Beatrice's Don Kelly recalled. He and his managers could raise prices on Hunt's tomato paste, change the advertising strategy for Orville Redenbacher popcorn, and make hundreds of other normal business decisions without needing KKR's approval. On most routine business issues, Kelly found, Kravis and his lieutenants played the same role that outside directors do at a public company. They wanted to be briefed on major developments, and to approve annual budgets, but they didn't want to micromanage a big food company. Timber executive Doug Westenhaver, machine-tool executive Phil O'Reilly, and brake-drum maker Ray O'Keefe all reported the same laissez-faire attitude from the KKR executives. In O'Reilly's words: "We didn't get much attention from KKR, and we never needed it."

Perhaps the happiest owner-managers were the top team at Duracell, the Bethel, Connecticut, battery company that KKR pried free from the big Kraft Inc. conglomerate in 1988. Duracell's top two executives, president Robert Kidder and U.S. operations chief Charles Perrin, both were gung-ho entrepreneurs in their early forties, itching to break free of a big traditional company. Kidder, in particular, found Kraft stifling. All his big spending decisions were closely second-guessed by Kraft administrators 900 miles away in the Chicago suburbs. Any factory addition at

Duracell costing more than $250,000 had to be ratified by Kraft executives; Kidder thought $5 million would have been a better threshold. Salary raises for the top thirty Duracell managers also needed to be cleared through Kraft. And when Kidder turned in a strong year's performance, instead of getting the stock or cash bonus that he wanted, he got crystal statues. By the final year of Kraft's involvement, Kidder's office was adorned with crystal elephants, crystal owls, crystal eagles, and crystal tetrahedrons. With little incentive to wring out the best possible results from Duracell, most of Kidder's lieutenants worked at three-quarters speed and padded their annual budgets so they could meet profitability targets without too much work. Kidder, by his own account, did little to stop their practices.

Then, as the Duracell buyout took shape, things changed. Kidder, Perrin, and a few other top executives met at Duracell's offices on Saturdays to draft what they called the "Exorcist Plan"—a defiant new business strategy that would take hold once they were free of Kraft. "We shed ourselves of the Kraft bureaucracy," Kidder later recalled. "Crystal statutes were no longer important. Cash was, and feeling of ownership." Midlevel managers were told to quit padding budgets, shrink inventories, and compete more aggressively against archrival Eveready and other battery makers. Kidder talked openly about 20-to-1 or 30-to-1 payoffs that managers could make from owning buyout stock if they achieved ambitious financial targets. On their own, senior Duracell managers volunteered gutsy spending cuts that they had resisted before. An overseas manager suggested closing twenty-three of thirty European warehouses to save costs. Kidder and Perrin decided to sell off a small, loss-making military battery unit. (Kraft executives had been pushing them to sell that unit for years, but Kidder had resisted, claiming that it was a unique window into military research.) When all the steps were added up, Duracell executives figured they could boost operating profit by more than 40 percent in the first year of the buyout.

KKR hardly needed to lift a finger. About once a quarter, Kravis and two KKR colleagues visited Duracell's headquarters for a three-hour board meeting. Prepped the night before by KKR associate Kevin Bousquette, Kravis usually asked an alert question or two. "Are you spending enough on R&D?" was a favorite. "What are growth opportunities in Eastern Europe?" was another. But mostly Kravis just listened, which was fine by the Duracell men. "KKR's strength is financial," Duracell U.S.A. president Charles Perrin explained. "We want them to understand the basics of our business, but we don't want them involved in the nitty-gritty."

Kidder and Perrin readily admitted that they were driven by the classic KKR motivator—huge stock holdings in their company, bought with most of their free cash. Kidder bought 200,000 shares for $1 million and had options on another 1 million shares. Perrin bought 160,000 shares for $800,000 and had options on another 800,000 shares. "You go from playing with Monopoly money to playing with real money," Kidder explained.

To John Richman, Bob Kidder's longtime boss at Kraft, the emergence of a roaringly successful new Duracell was both jarring and fascinating. For years, Richman had thought Kraft was getting the most it could from the Duracell management team. Suddenly, his ex-employees began pounding out quarterly earnings far beyond anything that Richman had ever thought possible. Duracell's sales soared; its market share climbed; it was a success story by any yardstick. Richman chafed at the defiantly anti-Kraft remarks that Kidder kept making, including one quip before a U.S. Senate committee that the "cheese burden" of working for Kraft had been greater than the "debt burden" of working with KKR. But Richman was calm enough to try to learn something from his onetime protégé. "Let's have dinner the next time I'm in New York," Richman suggested to Kidder in the summer of 1988. A few weeks later they met at Il Nido, a crowded Italian restaurant in midtown Manhattan, where Richman peppered his onetime aide with questions. "What's different?" Richman kept asking. "Why are you doing so much better?"

The secret, Richman decided, was big money, and the way it changed people's values. It was as if executives at buyout companies like Duracell played by different rules than the rest of American business. Most executives spent their lives juggling conflicting goals: keeping workers happy, holding to traditions, winning public recognition, and making money for stockholders. In a buyout, only the final priority mattered. Giant financial rewards induced managers to tear through companies in an all-out drive to improve profitability, regardless of the turmoil that such steps might cause.

"For every dollar that Bob Kidder and his people put in, they're likely to take thirty dollars out," Richman observed. "There's a tremendous power to such incentives. And there's no way you can do that in a public company."

9
The Discipline of Debt

From a distance, leveraged buyouts seemed like a tremendous force for efficiency in the U.S. economy during the 1980s. Study after study showed that worker productivity surged at companies taken private by financiers such as KKR. Operating profit at such companies typically climbed 20 to 30 percent in the first three years after a buyout, University of Chicago economist Stephen Kaplan found. All the while, capital spending held steady or diminished while operating cash flow jumped as much as 50 to 60 percent. Companies somehow seemed to get more done with smaller inputs. "The same managers with the same assets . . . are able to double the productivity and value of the enterprise," Harvard Business School Professor Michael Jensen told Congress in 1989. "It appears there is no explanation for the gains other than real increases in operating efficiencies."

In their public speeches, Kravis and Roberts gladly took credit for what scholars began calling "the discipline of debt." Buyouts "can help create more profitable, productive and focused companies, better able to compete for the long term in a changing business world," Roberts told an Oregon business group. Kravis was even more dogmatic. "Too many managers are not looking out for the shareholders," he complained in a business panel discussion in the mid-1980s. "They have more interest in their job security than in making the tough decisions." Buyouts time and again pushed managers into making those "tough decisions," he argued. Such Darwinist themes were routinely echoed by top executives at buyout companies, who portrayed themselves as economic miracle makers, working shoulder-to-shoulder with their KKR partners.

For hundreds of thousands of ordinary employees, however, watching buyout companies play by different rules was nothing to cheer about. Many of these workers spoke with fatigue and bitterness about struggling to meet financial targets set by unknown men far away. Glass-plant engineers in North Carolina forfeited their Christmas vacations to rebuild a sputtering furnace in record time. Motel managers in Texas and Florida scrambled to rent rooms to any guest that arrived—including prostitutes and thieves—just to achieve ever higher occupancy targets. Accounting clerks at every buyout company developed new bill-paying tricks to wangle a little more credit from their suppliers. Many of these steps did promote the efficiency prized by KKR and its academic supporters—but more than a few of the efficiency campaigns were unsustainable, or carried horrific social costs.

Worker frustrations ran deepest at those companies that struggled to keep their big debts under control. At times, the conditions at such companies regressed back sixty years or more, to a time when a few capitalist owners ignored the public welfare and instead chose only to maximize their own gain. More commonly, those workers and low-level managers who withstood the brunt of a buyout's austerity spoke about it with exhausted pride. Their big accomplishment was to survive. Most of them only faintly glimpsed what giant profits might be made by the people at the top. The rank and file certainly didn't share in the winnings. For ordinary employees, motivation came mostly from fear.

As these bittersweet and sometimes haunting efficiency stories were played out, Kravis, Roberts, and their KKR associates stayed surprisingly remote. They talked regularly with a few top executives. They arranged to see monthly financial reports from companies, which were studied closely at KKR's New York and San Francisco headquarters, but the KKR men didn't probe into how the financial gains were achieved. From the distant vantage of Henry Kravis or George Roberts, the hard work was done in the first few months of a buyout, when they installed both a system and a set of administrators that they regarded as trustworthy. After that, the KKR men ruled over their "efficient" new possessions like colonial powers, an ocean away.

At the beginning of any buyout, the KKR partners and the top executives of the target company jointly assembled a set of five- or ten-year financial projections. These documents became known as "bank books" because they were shared with the main banks lending money to finance the buyout. They spelled out dozens of financial goals, of which the most crucial were the company's yearly earnings before interest and taxes, or EBIT. Those earnings would be used in large part to pay down the immense debts accrued at the start of a buyout. At many buyout companies, the bank book took on a stature that was both awesome and terrifying to top executives.

Unlike other budgets that executives devised, the bank-book projections were ironclad. If executives met the targets for a few years, they could retire rich. If they fell short of those goals by much, defaults, bankruptcy, and personal shame would ensue. In the heady days of a takeover battle, as KKR was in the process of deciding whether to rescue top managers from an outside raider, many executives would promise ambitious EBIT growth in the years to come. Once the buyout was completed, it was time to make good on those promises.

The task of monitoring a company's monthly progress versus its bank-book targets was assigned chiefly to KKR's associates and junior partners—polite men in their late twenties to early forties whose résumés glittered with success. They were graduates of Harvard Law School and Stanford Business School, handpicked by Kravis and Roberts, and burning with ambition that they cloaked beneath a mantle of good manners. Each associate or junior partner was assigned to track one or two buyout companies—usually companies whose acquisition they had helped negotiate. Mike Michelson watched Owens-Illinois. Kevin Bousquette monitored Duracell. Saul Fox kept a close eye on Motel 6. Every couple of days, they phoned the company's chief financial officer to get a business update. Every month, the buyout companies sent Federal Express envelopes and fax transmissions with neatly typed data to KKR's New York and San Francisco offices. If the numbers were on target, the KKR associates and junior partners were as courteous as a private French tutor. The San Francisco associates tailored their schedules to the convenience of executives at East Coast companies, placing phone calls at 6:30 A.M. Pacific time from car phones on the way to work, simply because that was 9:30 A.M. in Toledo or New York and a good time for corporate treasurers or chief financial officers to talk. At the end of most calls, the KKR men finished with a closing line straight out of Emily Post: "If there's anything else we can do for you, let us know."

But KKR's good cheer turned icy if a company's financial performance faltered significantly. First the associates would start asking tough questions. "Why is this division underperforming? What are you doing to turn it around?" If the answers weren't reassuring, the associates would brief Kravis, Roberts, MacDonnell, or Raether. Then the KKR partners would demand answers from the CEO himself. And in the rare cases when a company continued to veer off track for six to nine months, one of the KKR partners would announce that he was coming to the headquarters city—and wanted to meet the CEO, alone, at an airport hotel. Abruptly, the KKR partner would ask for the chief executive's resignation. (KKR also would demand to buy back the executive's stock at cost, denying him the chance to make a single cent from the post-buyout stock that had seemed so precious earlier on.) Of the approximately sixty chief executives that KKR worked with in its first fourteen years, five proved so disappointing that they were asked to step down.

Even the executives who prospered in KKR's regimen knew that if their companies fell badly short of the bank-book projections, their wonderful rapport with the partners and associates of KKR could vanish. The chief executive and chairman of Owens-Illinois in the late 1980s, Robert Lanigan, described the underlying message from KKR as follows: "If you miss the targets, we don't want to know about the dollar, or the weather, or the economy." KKR wanted results, not excuses. "There are negatives if we don't meet those targets," Lanigan confided in an interview. He paused, as if afraid to say more. Then he concluded: "That's 90 percent of what drives us."

Under such circumstances, it was little wonder that Don Kelly, Bob Lanigan, and dozens of other executives at buyout companies were willing to fire their old friends and subordinates. The harsh penalties for missing the financial targets of the buyout—combined with the rich payoffs if those targets were met—dictated that chief executives must become ruthless champions of efficiency.

But for the corporate staffers getting pink slips, the notion that they were contributing to "efficiency" was no solace at all. In Toledo, a storm of protest broke out when Owens-Illinois terminated the jobs of 500 white-collar workers in Toledo soon after KKR took control of the glass company. "I don't like O-I anymore," an anonymous Owens-Illinois manager told the *Toledo Blade* in March 1987. "I don't feel proud of this place anymore. We're the money cow that will make this leveraged buyout work. And yet, we're being put out on the street. If someone came to me and wanted to do what KKR has done, I'd make them crawl over every mile of broken glass that I could."

The bluntest jolts of all came at Safeway, where more than 8,000 headquarters and regional employees lost their jobs in the first few months of the buyout. In Oakland, regional controller Robert Markell, a twenty-eight-year Safeway veteran, was told to interrupt his vacation and report to work at ten A.M. Monday, 18 August 1986. He arrived thirty minutes early—but wished he hadn't. "Because of the takeover by KKR, you are no longer employed at Safeway," Markell's boss bluntly told him. "You are terminated from Safeway as of today, but we will pay you through Friday." Some 300 other headquarters employees were sacked that day, less than a month after the Safeway buyout had been negotiated. Ousted employees were herded one after another into an "outplacement" meeting in a fifth-floor Safeway conference room, many with tears in their eyes. A consultant from Drake Beam Moran read a brief script telling employees that they would possibly feel "very angry" toward Safeway. People kept flowing into the room at such a pace that the consultant was forced to backtrack to the beginning of her script several times, before concluding her remarks with a promise of job counseling.

Several months later, many of the laid-off Safeway employees were still scrounging for new work. "I'm fifty-three years old and I'm in a position where I feel I have to prove myself to a new employer," former Safeway purchasing manager Raymond Trujillo complained. His old business contacts at Cummins Engine and International Harvester told him they were sorry to see him jobless, but couldn't help. In similarly tough straits was computer specialist Mary Ellen Lorray, who once earned more than $40,000 a year at Safeway. She sent out fifty résumés, but in her first few months of job-hunting, lined up only a part-time university teaching job for $1,300. "I've lost wages," Ms. Lorray said bitterly in November 1986. "I've lost a portion of retirement income. I've lost productivity. I feel emotionally drained."

As all these firings played out, the KKR associates and partners simply shrugged, if they reacted at all. "There was a lot of bureaucracy and overhead at Owens-Illinois," Mike Michelson observed several years into the buyout. Top management "took steps to lower costs and implement a new strategy." Bob MacDonnell praised Safeway managers for making "tough decisions." And Henry Kravis was outright boastful about the changes at Beatrice. "There was a complete layer of staff to get rid of," he said in an interview three years after the Chicago company made its cutbacks. Making them, in Kravis's eyes, had only positive implications: "It moved decisions out to the divisions, where they got made much faster." As far as the KKR executives could tell, those three buyout companies, and many others, ran every bit as well—and with lower costs—after the firings. The KKR men regularly endorsed this new austerity via long-distance phone calls to the top managers of buyout companies, without seeing any of the faces of people involved.

This sterile tone reflected a disturbing gap in the business experience of the KKR executives. Most of them had never dismissed anyone in their entire lives, except for the occasional antiseptic removal of a chief executive. They had never looked into the eyes of a longtime friend and employee who was angry and hurt, and heard that friend tell them: "I can't believe you are doing this to me." Even within KKR, Kravis and Roberts ducked confrontations and left it to their secretaries to fire inept receptionists or mailroom helpers. Only when they ousted Jerry Kohlberg in 1987 did Kravis and Roberts glimpse how painful a firing could be for people who had spent decades working together.

At most buyout companies, the discipline of debt quickly spread beyond headquarters to the factories, stores, and branch offices where most of an enterprise's work got done. There, mass firings were rare. In many cases, however, life at the shop-floor level grew more arduous.

Hourly workers and low-level managers often found themselves at the receiving end of harsh new directives meant to improve cash flow. These employees, hundreds of miles from headquarters, never were privy to the polite seductions by which the KKR men had won the trust of top executives. They never got to know the KKR executives as "Henry" or "George." They never got letters from their chief executive that began: "Colleagues." For the hundreds of thousands of company employees who didn't own equity in a KKR company, a buyout ushered in a period of fatigue and strain, in which people sweated hard and handed over the fruits of their economic output to a few remote owners. Often the people who worked the hardest got the most meager rewards.

The repercussions of this discipline of debt began to take shape in the early 1980s at Houdaille, the machine-tool, pump, and car-parts company that KKR had acquired with great resourcefulness in 1979. At the time that Kravis, Herdrich, and Kohlberg bought the company, optimism had abounded about prospects for U.S. heavy industry. Houdaille in 1978 posted record EBIT of $52 million, including more than $20 million from its five machine-tool businesses. Earnings for 1979 and beyond were expected to keep increasing, Kravis and Herdrich wrote in their financing memo for the buyout, thanks to "the underlying fundamental strengths of Houdaille's industrial businesses." Then came the twin recessions of 1980 through 1982, along with ferocious Japanese competition. The entire machine-tool group stopped reporting any operating profits at all, showing outright losses in the early 1980s even before taking Houdaille's big interest bill into account.

A year into the buyout, Houdaille's top executives began selling or closing factories that had little hope of generating acceptable EBIT any-time soon. The first to go were Houdaille's car-bumper plants in Ontario, Canada, and Huntington, West Virginia, which produced outmoded metal bumpers for Chrysler and American Motors cars. Losing orders rapidly to makers of lightweight plastic bumpers, the plants were doomed; they closed in 1980 and 1981. Also axed was a small machine-tool company in Minneapolis, Di-Acro, that couldn't withstand Japanese com-petition. Then a onetime star in Houdaille's machine-tool group, Burg-master Corporation in Los Angeles, began to stumble irretrievably. When KKR bought Houdaille, U.S. manufacturers had craved Burgmaster's popular turret-drilling machines so much that the subsidiary had boasted of an eighteen-month order backlog. Before long, however, strong Japa-nese rivals had begun capturing much of Burgmaster's old markets. Burgmaster's order book withered away, and the company began hemor-rhaging cash in 1985, losing as much as $1 million a month even before interest and taxes. After trying to sell Burgmaster but finding no buyers, Houdaille chief executive Phil O'Reilly in September 1985 proposed closing the plant. Kravis and other KKR executives quickly agreed. Its closure was a personal tragedy for machinists who had worked at the company for decades. Several of Burgmaster's largest machines, which had once been the company's pride, were auctioned off at less than 10 percent of their $200,000 cost—scrap value. But that wasn't KKR's problem.

Unable to cajole Houdaille's regular customers into buying more ma-chine tools, O'Reilly leaned on division managers to protect profit mar-gins the only way they could. Cut payrolls and "take a firm stance in union contract negotiations," Houdaille's top executives decreed.

Just south of Buffalo, New York, O'Reilly's austerity drive hit home for about 300 Houdaille workers at the company's Strippit machine-tool division. In the late 1970s, before the buyout, working at Strippit had been regarded as one of the best blue-collar jobs in the area. The pay was good, at about $10.50 an hour for electricians and technicians. The equipment was modern. And the metal-punching machine tools that Strippit produced were regarded as the best in America.

After the buyout, Strippit management turned first hard-nosed, then ruthless in an effort to keep profit margins from collapsing. First, Strippit division manager Kenneth Slawson tightened up admittedly lax rules about absenteeism and short hours. Workers began getting formal warnings about leaving their jobs ten minutes early or dawdling over lunch. Several that didn't catch on to management's new urgency were deemed "unemployable employees" and fired. Then Slawson put the screws on pay. Strippit couldn't instantly slash its wage rates—but it could make sure it never hired another worker on its old, generous terms. In a 1982 labor contract, Slawson and his negotiators rammed in a two-tier pay scale. New recruits for unskilled jobs would earn just $5.75 an hour, barely half of prevailing wage levels. Existing workers would get 3-percent annual raises, well behind inflation.

Even tighter terms followed. In 1985, Houdaille brought in a Florida consultant, Gilbert Pomar, to serve as chief negotiator. Sitting in a Strippit conference room, Pomar laid out plans to cut all workers' pay and benefits by 10 percent. "You can take it in benefits, or you can take it in hard wages," Pomar told union negotiator Gregory Stone. "Anyway you want to do it is fine." Stone blanched. "If I'm going to be shot, I'd just as soon not pull the trigger myself," he later said. For nine days, union negotiators tried to win any kind of pay raise, no matter how small, from Strippit. They failed. Ultimately Strippit and the union agreed on a three-year pay freeze—a contract that rank-and-file workers nearly rejected, but ultimately endured for fear of losing their jobs in a strike.

Such austerity helped Houdaille survive harsh economic times. When industry conditions finally brightened in the late 1980s, Strippit and other Houdaille machine-tool companies boosted EBIT back above $20 million. Top executives benefited greatly. O'Reilly's salary and bonus nearly tripled in the first seven years of KKR's tenure. Slawson was promoted to be head of the entire machine-tool group and became one of Houdaille's five highest-paid executives, earning $207,000 in 1986. These executives' closely held post-buyout stock did even better, leaping fourfold in value.

For Strippit machinists, however, there was only bitterness and despair. When Slawson's salary was disclosed in a Houdaille bond prospectus, workers at the Strippit plant "went crazy," recalled machinists' negotiator Stone. Men's room graffiti at the Strippit factory showed Slawson's face surrounded by dollar signs. Meanwhile, machinists watched helplessly as their earning power slipped year by year. "In 1980, this was one of the most sought-after jobs in town," Strippit machinist James Kollig recalled in late 1989. "It was legendary. Now it's below average." Kollig's pay had hardly inched up at all since his second year at Strippit, and under the two-tier wage schedule, new machinists were being hired at $8 an hour or less.

"You can't treat people like this," Kollig complained after ten years of working at a buyout company. "I wish the Japanese would buy us. I might get a raise."

As KKR began to take control of ever-larger companies, the austerity themes of the Houdaille buyout began to be played out on a vast, nationwide scale. At Safeway, for example, wage retrenchment affected many of the grocery chain's 180,000 employees. Before the buyout, Safeway had been a union stronghold, paying some of the highest wages in the grocery business. Safeway's 160,000 hourly workers liked that, but KKR didn't. Above-average wages of $14.64 an hour in 1986 made the company uncompetitive and hurt operating profits, Roberts argued. Bob MacDonnell, as the KKR partner most closely watching Safeway, took it upon himself to drive Roberts's message home. At executive committee meetings with Safeway chief executive Peter Magowan and a few top aides, MacDonnell kept asking: "What are you doing to achieve wage parity [with other chains in the regions where Safeway operated]?"

Soon enough, Safeway managers began to clamp down on pay. During the first two years of the buyout, average hourly wages inched up just 1.4 percent, or 21 cents an hour. In many regions, Safeway demanded and won pay freezes. In some districts, average pay actually fell. At a closed-doors executive retreat in Scottsdale, Arizona, three years after KKR bought Safeway, the grocery chain's vice chairman, Harry Sunderland, thundered: "We have been given a rare second chance to confront labor. . . . Only the radical surgery of the buyout and restructuring could give us the negotiating strength and resolve to rescue our core business from the insatiable appetite of the unions." To hold wages down, Sunderland added, Safeway needn't shy from strikes. The KKR partners would understand if a Safeway regional division incurred big losses one quarter from a strike, but won a cut-rate, long-term labor contract as a result.

For frustrated workers and union officials, Safeway's efficiency drive was harsh. In 1987, wages were cut 10 percent in the Denver area, and frozen in Oregon. Workers in Washington State staged an eighty-one-day strike in 1989 seeking higher pay; they got raises averaging just 2.4 percent a year over three years. "This settlement isn't everything you wanted," Seattle union leader Tony Abeyta told workers the day the strike ended. "But I had people coming up to me saying, 'Tony, I'm going to lose my car or house,' or 'I can't pay rent.' As your leader, I had to weigh prolonging the strike against winning another 5 cents an hour. I didn't think it was worth it."

Across the United States and Canada, Safeway began looking for ways to cut its reliance on high-paid veteran workers. Teenage "courtesy clerks," who traditionally had held only a few unskilled jobs, performing such simple duties as wheeling groceries to shoppers' cars, began getting more and more assignments that traditionally went to older workers earning higher wages. In Oregon, courtesy clerks earning $7 an hour began restocking shelves, bagging groceries, and intruding even in the highest-paid union job, meat-cutting. Veteran meat-cutters found themselves shunted from store to store in a series of part-time jobs that they began to suspect were designed by Safeway management to induce them to quit.

"Safeway pushes the contract language to the edge," complained Kathy Morris, a union official and former Safeway meat-cutter in Oregon. "We have an extremely difficult time dealing with them."

At other buyout companies, the discipline of debt spread beyond the hourly work force into the lives of low-level managers, too. The sheltering embrace of KKR's carefully rationed stock in a buyout company typically extended to only thirty to seventy top executives. Another couple of hundred managers might get periodic cash payments known as "phantom stock," matching the gains they would have achieved if they actually had been in the inner circle of equity owners. In the giant companies that KKR owned, however, with work forces of 50,000 or more, that still left a lot of salaried employees unprotected and vulnerable to the dictates of the bank book.

At Owens-Illinois, the discipline of debt slowly fanned outward from Toledo headquarters. During the initial buyout negotiations, the glass company's top two executives, Lanigan and Lemieux, had promised KKR they would push up EBIT from major divisions by 10.6 percent a year. One way to achieve that was by cutting costs and improving profit margins at Owens-Illinois's biggest division: glass bottle manufacturing. The midlevel managers who ran Owens-Illinois plants in towns such as Streator, Illinois; Clarion, Pennsylvania; and Winston-Salem, North Carolina, weren't consulted about these new financial targets. But they took on the burden of achieving these goals.

Typical of the managers straining to make the bank-book goals come true was Tom Waller, a round-faced man in his late forties who ran Owens-Illinois's plant in Winston-Salem. Waller had worked for the glass company for more than twenty years—long enough to remember the easy days when Owens-Illinois had sponsored sports teams and organized dances for its employees and basked in seemingly unending prosperity. But increasingly tough competition from plastic bottles—and the pressures of the buyout—combined to produce severe marching orders for Waller in 1987. Improve productivity 10 percent a year, he was told. Avoid wastage of molten glass that couldn't be turned into acceptable bottles. Expand output without hiring any new employees. Most of all, contribute to the 10.6-percent improvement in EBIT that Lanigan and Lemieux had promised to KKR's George Roberts.

Waller set to work. He discovered that if furnace operators tended more carefully to the company's ovens, and kept the temperature exactly at 2,450° F., the resulting glass output would be smoother and less prone to the tiny bubbles that led to defective bottles that had to be scrapped. It was a tough, unpleasant chore for a furnace operator to recalibrate the temperature every minute. But it was a tiny step toward cutting down on Owens-Illinois's scrappage rate.

When one of Owens-Illinois's furnaces needed to be rebuilt, Waller scheduled the work over the Christmas holiday, and instructed engineers to work in two ten-hour shifts, from seven A.M. to three A.M. It ruined everyone's holidays—Waller's included—but it got the furnace rebuilt in forty-five days, a good two weeks faster than anyone had expected. And that was a small step toward improving operating profit.

In the summer of 1987, however, word emerged from Toledo that Owens-Illinois was accelerating its program of shutting down inefficient plants. As much progress as Waller had made, his plant needed to do more to survive. Out of fear, many of the 270 people who worked for Waller volunteered their own cost-cutting steps. A packaging clerk discovered that if he stretched plastic wrap before putting it around truckloads of bottles, he could make the wrapping extend three times as far, and perhaps save $4,000 a year. A union steward in his spare time built a machine that automatically opened up cardboard cartons for six-packs of Miller beer, eliminating two jobs of unpacking cartons by hand.

And then Bob Stebbins, the longtime controller at the Winston-Salem plant, began taking on extra jobs. When the recycling manager quit, Stebbins added that assignment. When the purchasing agent retired, Stebbins assumed a third job as well. Three years into the buyout, Stebbins ended up with five different titles simultaneously—each of which had once represented a full-time job. Black plastic plaques attached to the door of his tiny office proclaimed him to be purchasing agent, controller, recycling manager, administrative services manager, and the chief industrial engineer.

For all his travails, Bob Stebbins didn't get any of the valuable Owens-Illinois post-buyout stock that KKR had parceled out among top executives. He didn't even collect a big bonus for a job well done. Asked what the benefits were from taking on so much work, Stebbins answered: "We get to keep our jobs."

That same mixture of pride, exhaustion, and fear registered in Tom Waller's voice several years into the buyout, as he talked about running the Winston-Salem plant. Even with an ever-shrinking payroll, Waller had ratcheted production to such high levels that in August 1988 his fifteen-year-old plant produced a record number of bottles in a 24-hour span. The next day, Waller broke into a rare smile, buying doughnuts and coffee with his own money and passing out the snacks to all his workers. A survivors' camaraderie took hold in the next few months, as many of the plant's workers began wearing navy blue o-i windbreakers that Waller had ordered. Lapel pins caught on, too, with a small, defiant slogan: ONLY THE BEST COMES IN GLASS. Yet Waller worried that no matter what he did, it wouldn't be enough. "I'd love to rest on our laurels a bit," Waller said one winter day, over a hurried paper-plate lunch of barbecued ribs. "But my boss isn't going to let me. He's going to want more."

Even when KKR wanted growth instead of cutbacks, the relentless pressure of a buyout's financial targets took its toll. Domineering executives leaned hard on their subordinates to deliver the numbers—no matter what the hidden price might be. Overly demanding executives weren't unique to buyout companies, of course. But the giant rewards of a financially successful buyout, and the giant penalties of a failed one, exacerbated the bullying tendencies in more than a few managers.

In the case of the Motel 6 buyout, some individual motel managers found their jobs turned far tougher when the company embarked on an expansion strategy. From a distance, KKR and Motel 6 chief executive Joseph McCarthy did all the right things. They doubled the company's spending on new motel construction. They decided to push for higher occupancy rates, by keeping room rates low while upgrading service with new features such as free phones and color televisions in all Motel 6 rooms. "We didn't tighten the belt; we loosened it," explained Saul Fox, the KKR associate who most closely watched over the lodging company. His goal: to expand Motel 6 quickly and position the company as America's number-one low-cost motel chain—a McDonald's of the lodging industry. But while the McDonald's hamburger chain generously shared profits with individual site managers, Fox and McCarthy did nothing of the sort.

Individual motel managers didn't get to buy the valuable equity in the buyout; that was reserved for about thirty top executives. Salaries for motel managers were kept low, at about $18,000 to $24,000 a year in the late 1980s. Motel 6, both before and after the buyout, offered free lodging on the premises to managers, a substantial economic benefit to the job. But living on site also meant that motel managers worked far more than an eight-hour day, often serving as their own desk clerks, handymen, and supervisers of maid service. Turnover among motel managers was high, with many lasting only a year or two before moving on to other jobs. The best candidates for motel managers, the company found, were retired couples willing to center their lives around their motels.

"There just weren't enough hours in the day," recalled Samuel Kemp, a retired Army intelligence specialist who began managing sites for Motel 6 in 1985 with his wife, Myrl. In the mornings, Mr. Kemp fixed broken washing machines and other appliances at the Fort Worth, Texas, Motel 6 that the two of them managed. In the afternoons, he was the desk clerk. And in the evening, Mr. Kemp was his own security guard in a high-crime neighborhood, patrolling the grounds with a stun gun or a can of Mace. On several occasions, Mr. Kemp stayed up nearly all night trying to keep panhandlers, prostitutes, and suspected drug dealers off the premises.

One of his biggest problems, Mr. Kemp later testified in a court case, was pressure from his district manager to jack up the motel's occupancy rate, even if that meant renting to unsavory people. When the Kemps took over management of the Fort Worth motel in February 1987, its occupancy rate averaged about 75 percent. Most guests were middle-class, including friends and relatives of people attending a nearby Baptist seminary. Mr. Kemp and his wife kept a "no-rent" list and refused to make rooms available to people who had been problem guests before. In mid-1987, however, Mr. Kemp later testified, a new regional manager told him that it wasn't Motel 6 policy to refuse a room to anyone. The no-rent list was confiscated. The occupancy rate at the Kemps' motel shot up—but so did trouble. One guest set fire to his room while freebasing cocaine. Several construction workers staying at the motel accused a prostitute of stealing money from them. A woman's purse was snatched. Mr. Kemp began pressing his district manager to add security guards, but was told that there wasn't any money budgeted for them. It took months even to get approval to build a fence around the motel. When the Kemps went on a brief vacation in June 1988, a relief manager achieved 100-percent occupancy of the motel—a prized senior-management target. Maids complained about marijuana smoke coming from some rooms, while a pack of motorcyclists stashed their bikes in the parking spaces that the Kemps usually set aside for handicapped guests. But that didn't seem to matter. When the Kemps returned from vacation, their boss commented: "I told you we could fill the motel up."

In July 1988, the Kemps resigned as managers of the Fort Worth Motel 6. "The motel was our home," Mr. Kemp later explained. "And we liked to have things the way that we would in our home."

The Kemps' bad luck may have reflected an unusually relentless push at a few motels for higher occupancy, regardless of the consequences. Just a few months after the Kemps quit, the district manager who pressured them to jack up occupancy rates was fired himself. For the overwhelming majority of guests and motel managers, Motel 6 did live up to its image as a wholesome, good-value budget chain. "The safety and security of our guests is of paramount importance," a Motel 6 spokesman affirmed in July 1991, after several lurid crime reports involving Motel 6 guests became public. But with the giant payoffs that buyouts offered to senior managers, there was every temptation to lean hard on lower-level employees to deliver higher occupancy rates and other desired financial results— no matter what the social cost.

From its remote perch, KKR couldn't even see this abuse of power, let alone try to stop it. At KKR's San Francisco headquarters, associate Saul Fox daily reviewed tidy fax-machine printouts from Motel 6 headquarters giving details about the chain's overall occupancy rate. He and KKR partner Bob MacDonnell periodically attended Dallas board meetings with the top few Motel 6 executives, where they approved expansionary marketing and construction budgets. The KKR men designed wonderfully ingenious limited partnership structures that let the lodging chain record robust operating profit without paying a dime of tax. But although Fox occasionally stayed at a Motel 6 himself, the KKR men didn't press hard to find out exactly what life was like at the chain's high-occupancy motels. During the buyout firm's five years of owning Motel 6, "I can't remember that security ever came up at a board meeting," MacDonnell remarked in July 1991.

The few times that Roberts, Kravis, and their colleagues were told about employees' frustrations and bitterness toward these efficiency drives, the KKR response was: That's business. Swarms of big American companies opted for tougher workplace conditions in the 1980s, whether they carried high debts or not. Efficiency was in. Coddling employees was out. Ford Motor Company, which kept a conservative balance sheet at all times, froze its workers' wages for a time in the early 1980s. International

Business Machines Corporation (IBM), which for decades had had a "no layoff" policy, began pushing early retirement programs with increasing vigor in the late 1980s, seeking to shrink its payrolls. And plenty of companies moved administrative departments out of the high-cost Northeast to low-wage Sunbelt locations.

"I don't see why we should be singled out," Roberts remarked at one stage. "You could just as easily criticize General Electric for getting rid of 100,000 jobs in the 1980s." Rather than being actively antilabor, the KKR executives and their manager-owner allies at buyout companies simply didn't give any special thought to workers' concerns. The two driving principles in any buyout were to pay down the debt and make the highly leveraged stock valuable.

From time to time, in a strange way, the discipline of debt actually produced consequences that workers welcomed. For all the exhausting conditions at Owens-Illinois's glass plants, the company's rising profit margins allowed its factories to stay open during a decade when two-thirds of all U.S. glassmakers either went out of business or were acquired by stronger competitors. For all of Safeway's harsh pay conditions, once its managers established the wages they wanted, the grocery chain became one of the industry's briskest hirers of additional labor, expanding its work force 18 percent during the buyout's first three years. The new Safeway jobs didn't pay especially well, but they were handy part-time work for students or mothers with limited hours available. At RJR Nabisco, meanwhile, the foregone wonders of the proposed Cookieville factories preserved a lot of reasonably well paying factory jobs that otherwise would have been eliminated by costly automation.

All the same, the twin motivators for top executives at buyout companies—alluring equity profits and frightening debt—combined to tilt the odds against workers' concerns. "KKR isn't in the grocery business," complained Kathy Morris, the former Safeway meat-cutter turned Oregon union official. "They're in the money business. They don't care what happens to union people. Anything that doesn't make money is sold." In northern California, Teamsters union official Ron Teninty voiced similar anxieties. He had never met Kravis, Roberts, or any of their associates. All he knew about KKR was what Safeway executives told him, what he read in the press, and what he saw firsthand in contract negotiations. And Teninty didn't like it. "Management says they want to maintain the union, but KKR is only interested in the bottom line," Teninty complained. In contract talks, Teninty said: "Management portrays KKR as the bad guys."

After several years of the discipline of debt, a weariness set in at many buyout companies. Workers felt it first. "I don't think management at Strippit cares about the typical American worker," machinist James Kollig protested in 1990. "They expect blue-collar workers should take all the pain. Then they don't understand why there's such hostility."

But top executives—especially those who announced long runs of layoffs and divestitures—felt a similar fatigue. At one midsize Los Angeles conglomerate, Norris Industries, chief executive Jack Meany and his top aides imagined themselves as combatants in an immense tug-of-war. They had taken on big debts in a KKR-led buyout in 1981; from that time onward, they had seemed locked in a struggle to lower Norris's debts and get the company's finances back on a sound footing. The tug-of-war image seemed so apt that Meany hired a local artist to draw a wall poster of Norris's top nineteen executives pulling on an orange rope that represented the company's debt. The resulting cartoon was half cute, half gruesome. It did show the orange line being dragged downward, quarter by quarter. But it also showed Meany's eyes shut and his jaws clenched as he tugged on the rope. Behind him, an equally grim-looking line of executives also strained to overcome the buyout debt.

In less fanciful imagery, Owens-Illinois's chief executive admitted to the same weariness three years into his company's buyout. "We're always cutting, cutting, cutting," Bob Lanigan said in an early 1990 interview. "There's the risk that you may cut out something that you really need. You might lose a marketing program that could have paid off. I don't think we've done that. But it's something I worry about."

Upholding morale was tough, too, Lanigan conceded, in the face of job cuts that descended on his employees with every budget cycle. Even valued employees kept their résumés handy at all times, and Lanigan found it hard to tell them not to worry. "If I were KKR," Lanigan confided, "I'd be concerned about whether the top five or six guys are capable of doing the entire job. It's a four-minute mile every mile."

To look at KKR's offices, no one would have conjured up images of tugs-of-war or four-minute miles. Thanks to the austerity of the buyout companies, the KKR executives could enjoy a life style so plush that each new day was filled with joy.

In San Francisco, a florist called on KKR's office every Monday at 8:45 A.M. with huge bouquets of cut flowers, to be distributed in every conference room. Winter or summer, tulips, roses, orchids, and lilies garnished every major conference table. In New York, KKR's partners and associates were graced with a different perk: a gray-haired shoeshine man who arrived most days at lunchtime. Kneeling before Kravis or any needy associate, the shoeshine man would buff their loafers and oxfords while the KKR men worked or chatted.

Each of the KKR associates, even the ones in their twenties, boasted a private office with a mahogany desk, an Oriental carpet, and a personal secretary. Monitoring companies' performance and looking for new deals was hard work—often stretching from seven A.M. to seven P.M. or later and spilling into weekends. From their windows, however, Kevin Bousquette, Mike Tokarz, and the other New York associates could look out on a panoramic, forty-second-story view of New York's Central Park. In San Francisco, Saul Fox, Ned Gilhuly, and their colleagues were soothed by a sweeping, forty-fifth-story view of the San Francisco Bay and city skyline. Desktop buzzers in conference rooms summoned kitchen crews, ready to cater to the associates' snacking preferences. Some opted for cookies after lunch; Saul Fox preferred fresh-pressed carrot juice at four P.M.

Living best of all were Kravis and Roberts. Each of them bought a private jet in the 1980s, even as they insisted that buyout companies sell their planes. Kravis picked up a helicopter, too, and incorporated his own airline, East-West Air Inc. It served only two passengers—himself and Roberts—but that was enough. Kravis and Roberts each acquired fine oil paintings, even as companies such as Owens-Illinois sold off their corporate art collections to raise cash. On the walls of KKR's New York offices were small brass plaques identifying each painting for visitors' convenience. New England seascapes in the outer rooms gave way to nineteenth-century portraits in the main conference rooms, and then to Kravis's favorites in his own office: eighteenth-century horse-and-rider masterpieces by the English painter George Stubbs.

Cocooned among so many creature comforts, the KKR executives never grasped the grim side of debt. Most of their contact with buyout companies was by phone, by computer printout, or in elegant boardrooms and private dining rooms. Kravis and Roberts seldom visited factories or stores or warehouses. Their associates did go on brief plant tours of companies that KKR owned. But the young men didn't linger long enough to hear what was really on workers' minds.

With wonderment, several senior Owens-Illinois executives recalled the first time that George Roberts visited Toledo to talk with the glass company's top managers. It was the winter of 1987; KKR's buyout had just been negotiated. The firing of 500 employees was still secret, but about to be announced. The stern orders to improve profit margins at every glass plant were about to be issued. A gritty determination had already taken hold among the survivors, which Roberts tried to stoke.

"We're all in this together," executives remembered Roberts saying. "If you can meet the bank-book projections, we at KKR will be very, very satisfied.

"And have fun," Roberts added.

10
Cashing Out

For all the industrial power that Kravis and Roberts wielded, KKR's mission of achieving truly big investment profits required the buyout firm to cut each company loose before long. The crux of the buyout firm's money-making ability lay in the strategy of loading up companies with tax-deductible debt, wringing some quick efficiencies from the business, and then paying off the borrowings. That was the financial engineering that generated 40- to 60-percent annualized profits for investors in KKR's buyouts. Once the high debt was paid down, the KKR partners lacked any great ideas for making additional money from a company's operations. Even if company managers had their own brainstorms, the payoff from almost any new growth strategy was too slow for KKR's lofty profit targets. The firm's only recourse, once debt levels began to shrink, was to seek what KKR executives quaintly called an "exit strategy."

Buyout companies, in whole or in part, had to be sold off—typically within five to seven years after KKR acquired them. "The longer you hold, the more your returns will decline," Kravis told a magazine interviewer in 1986. There wasn't a single piece of their industrial empire that Kravis or Roberts cherished so much that they wanted to keep it forever.

Selling companies brought out skills in the KKR men that mirrored the ones they utilized in buying businesses. Kravis, Roberts, and their colleagues could be cheerful, ingratiating, or even sly for short periods, if they thought that would help stoke a buyer's appetite. But beneath their good manners, the buyout firm's executives stayed as cool and disciplined as ever. They didn't deeply care who ultimately acquired parts or all of a buyout company: foreigners, management, industry rivals, or other LBO firms. Their overriding mission was to make money for themselves and their limited partner investors—which the KKR executives did very well.

As KKR acquired vast, sprawling companies such as Beatrice or Safeway, the buyout firm ended up pursuing breakup strategies remarkably similar to those of corporate raiders. Various fringe subsidiaries of these companies were sold, one after another. Poorly performing units were dumped so that the company could concentrate on its core business. Sometimes star performers were sold quickly, too, if a buyer wanted to pay a high price. Unlike corporate raiders, who accomplished their breakups by tossing out old management and running the companies themselves, the KKR executives worked hand-in-hand with top management to make these divestitures happen. For executives such as Safeway chief executive Peter Magowan, there was all the difference in the world between civil George Roberts and abusive Herbert Haft, the raider who had stalked Safeway in early 1986. To workers at the divisions being sold, however, the difference between raider and KKR was so subtle as to be insignificant.

Once KKR had sold a company and faded away, a fresh set of buyers began a whole new business cycle. Most of these acquirers started by pumping cash back into businesses that had endured the discipline of debt. The new owners made amends for the tightened capital spending and socially hostile conditions that KKR may have introduced. In doing so, buyers often reinstalled some of the "corpocracy" that KKR had cut.

For all the profits that KKR reaped from briefly owning major companies, these financial detours often came with hidden penalties for the companies themselves. Several giant companies became such habitual playthings of the takeover world that their managers spent too much time shuffling assets, and let prize operations be sold because of misplaced priorities. Lost in the process was any chance of achieving the visionary quality of America's best companies: the ones that pursue big, exciting goals and achieve them. KKR's method of dismantling companies often took a badly assembled conglomerate and turned it into a reasonable collection of free-standing businesses in new owners' hands—but KKR repeatedly missed opportunities to create a great company.

As far back as the mid-1970s, the KKR partners tried to negotiate the skillful sale of each buyout company at a profit a few years after it was acquired. "Henry Kravis was the consummate salesman," recalled Jack

Valentine, a Connecticut businessman who bought Advo-System, a small junk-mail outfit, from Kravis in 1976. "He was articulate, bright and gracious."

Kravis needed all his charm for that sale; Advo-System had stumbled under four years of ownership by Kravis and his colleagues, and had briefly been considered for liquidation. But when Kravis started talking with Valentine, there were no problems, only opportunities. "Henry held out this carrot of great potential for the business," Valentine recalled. "All it needed was someone to manage it." Unable to resist that invitation, Valentine bought the company for $100,000 plus assumption of debt. And to Valentine's delight, Advo-System proved eminently rescuable, expanding its sales more than tenfold over the next decade.

Just as forceful in pressing for a money-making sale was Jerry Kohlberg. In April 1980, he convened a board meeting of Incom International Inc., an industrial-parts company that KKR owned. Incom president Ed Mabbs had done the cutting that KKR wanted; now he wanted to build the company into a Fortune 500 industry leader. But detailed Incom board minutes show that KKR had other plans. "We have called this meeting to discuss the sale of Incom," Kohlberg began. "The time is right to pursue this sale cooperatively, deftly, and professionally."

It was vintage Jerry Kohlberg. He had stepped into a delicate issue and quickly created the appearance of a happy consensus—on his terms. By speaking calmly and leaving out any inconvenient facts, Kohlberg came across as the most reasonable man in the room. Anyone who wanted to oppose the sale would be forced to sound quarrelsome. Mabbs, who wasn't the easiest executive to push around, was boxed in before the meeting was two minutes old. Futilely, Mabbs protested that Incom had "plenty of unrealized potential." It was no use. KKR soon sold Incom for $112 million to Italian industrialist Gianni Agnelli, a price that yielded the KKR partners and other buyout investors a twenty-two-fold return on their original $5 million investment in the company in 1975. Incom's new Italian owners began grumbling a year later that the company's plants were aging and hadn't got enough investment under KKR's tenure. Mabbs, in turn, clashed with the new owners and resigned a few months after KKR sold the company. But for Kravis, Roberts, and Kohlberg, the sale of Incom was a dazzling success. Each of them collected at least $2 million on the sale, which vaulted them from mere prosperity to the status of multimillionaires.

Over time, the KKR partners discarded each of the little companies they had acquired when they were just getting started in the 1970s. The very first KKR buyout in 1977, A. J. Industries, was sold to First Chicago's buyout group in 1985 for vastly more than KKR had paid. The Florida conglomerate that Kravis and Kohlberg had acquired with such daring in 1979, Houdaille, was sold to a British company, TI Industries PLC, in 1986. Many of Houdaille's plants had been sold or closed amid hard times in the machine-tool industry. The company's chief executive, Phil O'Reilly, was weary and ready to retire after a futile five-year battle in Washington against Japanese imports. But Houdaille had diversified wisely with a $220 million acquisition partway through the buyout, and had paid its debts all the way through. The KKR investors made 22 percent a year on their money. (Many of them got a second chance to own Houdaille's businesses when KKR reacquired two-thirds of the company from TI in 1987 and renamed it Idex Corporation.) Glossing over all that had gone wrong, KKR in a 1989 briefing book described the original Houdaille buyout as a success, chiefly because "superior returns were realized by the investors."

Even companies that other people might regard as never-to-be-sold treasures were shed by KKR with relentless efficiency when it looked like the price was right. For several years in the early 1980s, KKR owned Golden West Broadcasting, which operated television station KTLA in Los Angeles. Roberts had bought the station from singer and businessman Gene Autry in 1983 for $245 million. Just the mention of KTLA could cause misty eyes among people in broadcasting. It was the first U.S. TV station west of the Mississippi, founded in 1947. It was where stars as diverse as Bob Hope and sportscaster Dick Enberg had begun their television careers. But to the KKR executives, it was just another business that generated about $50 million a year in cash flow. "I don't think you should ever fall in love with anything except your wife and kids," Roberts later explained, when asked why he let go of KTLA. "To do otherwise is looking for trouble."

Attentive to takeover cycles, Roberts put the Los Angeles station on the market in early 1985. Buyers were then paying fat prices for television stations elsewhere, he observed. KTLA's profits and ratings were healthy, but programming costs had begun climbing fast. If someone else wanted KTLA, they could have it. Roberts hired a young Morgan Stanley investment banker, Steven Rattner, to market the Los Angeles television station for him. Executives at Cox Broadcasting were interested, but the chief executive of Chicago's Tribune Co., Stanton Cook, was most interested of all. Adroitly, Rattner played to Cook's appetites. "If you're going to be in the independent [TV station] business," Rattner told Cook, "you've got to own this."

Determined to win KTLA, Cook bid $510 million, the highest price ever paid for a single television station at the time. When his bid was announced as the winner, it left both sides happy—for very different reasons. Cook took pride in building an empire, adding a Los Angeles station to Tribune's stations in Chicago and New York. If it hurt per-share earnings for a year, he didn't mind; the chance to expand was what thrilled him. Roberts and KKR associate Mike Michelson found joy in something entirely different. Their limited partner investors had tripled their money in two and a half years—a 77-percent annual gain that amounted to one of KKR's best showings ever on a sizable buyout. The new owners, even if they worked miracles, couldn't hope to do so well.

As KKR took control of some truly giant companies in the mid-1980s, takeover activity of all types entered a period of explosive growth. Second-tier buyout firms prowled about, looking for acquisitions in the $100 million to $600 million category. Chief executives of big corporations "restructured" and "redeployed" assets by buying and selling midsize divisions as if they were baseball cards. And ever-growing armies of investment bankers toured the United States, pitching acquisitions to any CEO who would listen. A steadily surging stock market caused almost every acquisition to look like a bargain two years later.

As a result, the KKR executives—who ultimately were sellers of everything—found themselves in the lucky position of being able to dangle pieces of their big companies before fresh buyers eager to pay top dollar. The prices offered were so high, in some cases, that the KKR executives convinced themselves that they had an outright duty to break up the companies they owned. Rather than pass on an entire corporation, intact, to the next owner, the KKR executives found they could make more money ("realize more value" in their argot) by dismantling a company in stages.

The great case in point was Beatrice, the sprawling Chicago conglomerate. When KKR took control of Beatrice in April 1986, divestitures were only a small part of the game plan. Banks had insisted that $1.5 billion of peripheral businesses be sold in the first eighteen months, so as to reduce debt. But both Kravis and Beatrice chief executive Don Kelly publicly declared that, aside from those divestitures, their goals were to expand the business. Once the early asset sales were over, Kelly told an interviewer in November 1985, Beatrice was as likely to buy companies as to sell them. Kravis was even more emphatic. "We will continue to grow Beatrice," Kravis declared in the 2 December 1985 issue of *Business-Week*. "There will be a stronger, more efficient, streamlined Beatrice three years from now and eight years from now."

What actually transpired at Beatrice—and what became of Kelly's alliance with KKR—is a poignant story of what happens when promises and profits collide.

Immediately after taking control of Beatrice on 10 April 1986, Kelly plunged into the task of selling some fringe businesses. Just three weeks into his new job in Chicago, Kelly auctioned off Beatrice's Avis Rent a Car subsidiary, awarding it to the buyout firm of Wesray Capital for $275 million. The Friday before the sale was announced, KKR associate Mike Tokarz hectored Kelly over the phone, asserting that the Avis sale was going too fast. With a little maneuvering, Tokarz thought, a slightly higher bid might emerge from KLM, the Dutch airline. But Tokarz got nowhere, even when he asked Kravis to intercede. "Let's pass on picking the fight," Kravis told Tokarz. It wasn't worth jeopardizing KKR's relations with Kelly, Kravis explained.*

Within a few months, Beatrice announced two more sales that, all told, raised more than the $1.5 billion needed for bank-loan repayments. On 16 June 1986, Beatrice agreed to sell its Los Angeles Coke bottling business to Atlanta-based Coca-Cola Co. for more than $1 billion. Coca-Cola at that time wanted to regain more control over its bottlers, which had operated independently for decades; the Beatrice divestiture provided it a perfect way to do so. And in early August 1986, Beatrice agreed to sell its Playtex brassiere and tampon unit to the subsidiary's own management in a $1.25 billion buyout.

In Chicago, Kelly began dropping hints that he would like to take Beatrice public and start looking for acquisitions. About 75 percent of the original Beatrice remained; the company's debt level had become manageable. But within KKR's Manhattan offices, thirty-six-year-old associate Michael Tokarz began to devise a drastically different fate for Beatrice.

An energetic, blond Midwesterner, Tokarz was known on Wall Street

---

*The Avis buyout proved to be one of Wesray's biggest coups, yielding $750 million on a $20 million equity investment. Years later, KKR executives winced to think that they had let such a money-maker slip out of their grasp too cheaply. Tokarz habitually blamed Kelly. But the person with the best perspective on the whole issue, Avis treasurer Gerard Kennell, suggested that the real oversights were on KKR's part. It took a lot of intricate study to see ways that owning Avis in a buyout could pay off, Kennell said. Wesray executives did the work. With the exception of one brief visit from Tokarz, no one from KKR ever came to Garden City, New York, where Avis was based, to learn the car-rental company's story in detail.

as one of KKR's Young Turks. He worked some of the longest hours at the buyout firm, regularly arriving at seven A.M., competing with fellow associate Kevin Bousquette to see who could get to work first. Tokarz had joined KKR just a year earlier, coming over from Continental Illinois in September 1985. But he had already taken on a series of big assignments, raising the giant Beatrice and Safeway bank loans and assuming day-to-day responsibility for Houdaille/Idex. As Tokarz worked into the evenings analyzing Beatrice financial data, he became convinced that this had the potential to be the biggest money-making buyout of all time—if KKR played it right.

The winning move, Tokarz told his KKR colleagues one morning, was to sell off more pieces of Beatrice as quickly as possible. "Gentlemen, we're fools not to do it," Tokarz declared. The stock market was climbing that autumn, as the Dow Jones Industrial Average approached 2,000 for the first time. Food stocks, usually a laggard, had turned into glamour issues that soared even more than broad market averages. Economists warned of a possible recession in 1987, but food-industry takeovers proliferated anyway, and small food companies were being acquired at some of the highest multiples of operating profit seen in years. Ticking off all these reasons, Tokarz began lobbying with KKR for the breakup of Beatrice—a campaign that he later remembered with considerable pride.

"I made this huge, three-month pitch," Tokarz recalled. "I worked each guy [within KKR]. I was very aggressive. I told them: 'You bought this company. You're fiduciaries for these investors. If you think the right thing to do is to sit on this company, let me show you why your fiduciary duty is to sell the company.' Businesswise, maybe I'm too icy cold, but that was the way it had to be done."

Over and over, Tokarz played through his calculations, showing what a profit windfall KKR could achieve if it kept selling pieces of Beatrice until the whole company was gone. He found a vital ally in San Francisco: George Roberts, who agreed with his analysis. The holdout, for a time, was Kravis, who had personally recruited Kelly for the top job at Beatrice, and who worried the most about keeping the Chicago company's top management happy. It was Kravis who publicly had stated a year earlier that KKR wanted to expand Beatrice. Before long, though, Tokarz and Roberts together persuaded Kravis to change his mind.

The next time Kelly came to New York, Kravis tried to broach a bit of KKR's plan to the Beatrice chief executive. Kelly hated it. The strong-willed, blustery Chicago executive had already staked out his strategy:

trimming Beatrice's debt a bit more and then hunting for acquisitions. In Kelly's eye, there wasn't any reason to budge. "Henry understood from day one that if he wanted to call all the shots, I'd be gone," Kelly later said. By the fall of 1986, Kelly had already confronted the KKR executives with three threats to quit when decisions didn't go his way—and had won at least part of what he wanted each time. The KKR men couldn't afford to have their best-known operating company chief executive storm off in a huff. It might hurt Beatrice; it certainly would hurt KKR's standing in the business world.

"Kelly used to call me up and threaten me," Tokarz later complained. "He wanted to be the kingpin of the deal."

So Tokarz hatched a plot. He decided to create the financial equivalent of a small raft, put Kelly aboard it, and float Kelly off to sea while KKR continued the disection of Beatrice. The small raft would be called E-II Holdings Inc., and would consist of about one-eighth of Beatrice—chiefly the company's nonfood businesses such as Samsonite luggage and Culligan water-treatment systems. Those businesses would be sold to the public, with Kelly in charge as a major shareholder and chief executive. Meanwhile, Kelly would cede his top job at Beatrice to food executive Fred Rentschler, a well-respected but less confrontational executive. KKR would then be free to peddle the remaining Beatrice units as it saw fit.

All that was necessary was for Kelly to believe that E-II was his own idea. And Tokarz saw a way of achieving that. KKR's closest contacts at Beatrice were in the Chicago company's finance department. In detail, Tokarz began talking with Beatrice treasurer Bert Corcoran about E-II. Corcoran liked the notion. "Our objective was to reward shareholders, and here was a way to do it," Corcoran later recalled. So in late 1986, Tokarz prepared a thirty-page computer analysis of exactly how such a spinoff would work. Then—in a moment of guile—he sent the printout in a plain manila envelope to Corcoran's home. No one except Tokarz and Corcoran would know whose idea it was. A few days later, a modified version of Tokarz's plan took shape within the Chicago company, to be presented to Kelly as an internal Beatrice idea, totally free of KKR meddling. Best of all, the new company would allow Kelly to make acquisitions free of KKR's intervention. "That's what sold Don on the idea," Corcoran recalled.

A few months later, in May 1987, Beatrice announced that it was spinning off E-II and putting Kelly in charge of the new company. Always a master of small gestures, Kravis had tried to get the right to name the new company Esmark—something that would have had great sentimental appeal to Kelly. Years earlier, Esmark had been a big conglomerate, run by Kelly until it disappeared in a takeover. By 1987, the Esmark name was the property of entrepreneur Byron Hero, who owned the Danskin hosiery business. Kravis tried futilely to pry the Esmark name away from Hero, offering him as much as $2 million. Kelly and his aides, unaware of KKR's real role in the creation of E-II, thought it was very sweet of Kravis to try so hard to accommodate Kelly's whims.

Once in charge of E-II, Kelly vowed to make his new corporate name famous. Full of bravado, he told reporters that he hoped to make a multibillion-dollar acquisition within a year. "Nine billion dollars doesn't scare me," Kelly blustered.

The launching of E-II marked high tide for KKR's efforts to break up Beatrice profitably. In one of the giddiest junk-bond deals ever, Drexel raised $1.5 billion for E-II, telling bondholders only that the company would use the money for unspecified acquisitions. Public investors paid $420 million to buy stock in E-II, even though the company's big debt bills doomed it to hefty losses for at least its first few quarters.

Within KKR, Tokarz and Bousquette figured that a fabulously profitable liquidation of Beatrice was assured. In a moment of exuberance, Tokarz and Bousquette valued Beatrice in a KKR fund-raising memo as if the company had been entirely sold, for proceeds of triple what KKR's equity partnerships had paid for their stock. That amounted to a 192-percent annualized return, KKR bragged—by far the best showing ever on a giant buyout.

But hubris had got the best of Tokarz, Bousquette, and their bosses at KKR. The tail ends of Beatrice proved hard to sell. Many of the businesses that remained, such as Hunt's tomato paste and Swift meats, weren't as fast-growing or glamorous as what had been sold. Potential buyers also were scared off by Beatrice's messy tax situation. Beatrice had paid minimal taxes on some profitable divestitures years before KKR arrived, and the U.S. tax authorities didn't like that. The company's books were under federal review, and if Beatrice lost, it could owe the IRS $500 million or more.

After Kelly left, the KKR men hacked off three more pieces of Beatrice for $2.5 billion. Rentschler wasn't about to try to block them. Kelly was busy with E-II. They had an open field.

Pushed onto the block was Beatrice's Tropicana fruit-juice unit, which had been one of Kelly's delights. Normally uninterested in day-to-day business details, Kelly during his time at Beatrice had nurtured Tropicana as if it were his favorite child. He had made it a priority to visit

Tropicana's operations in Florida and learn about the concerns of on-site managers. When Tropicana managers asked for $30 million to be spent on new computer systems and refrigerated railcars, Kelly told them: Fine. Cash might be scarce in a highly indebted buyout company, he explained, but there was still money for Tropicana. "Kelly told us: 'I'm proud to have you on my team,'" Tropicana executive vice president George Zulanas later recalled. "He gave us the confidence to go ahead and do the right things."

In early 1988, however, Seagram Co. offered $1.2 billion for Tropicana—a huge premium beyond the $500 million at which KKR had valued the juice company in 1985. Tropicana's sales and profitability had grown greatly in the intervening three years, aided by frost-free winters in Florida and the new spending programs that Kelly had approved. Seagram officials urgently wanted to diversify from their main liquor business, where consumption was declining year after year. For $1.2 billion, Kravis and KKR associate Kevin Bousquette decided, Seagram could have Tropicana. It was a great business, the KKR men agreed—but at the right price, everything was for sale.

Just about the time that the Tropicana sale was announced in March 1988, Kelly returned to Beatrice. He had kept a board seat at the conglomerate when he embarked on his E-II adventure, as well as a claim to the number-one job at Beatrice if E-II ceased to exist. Sure enough, E-II lasted less than a year. Kelly's first big acquisition target, American Brands Inc., had turned the tables and acquired E-II instead. Returning to Beatrice's headquarters at 2 North La Salle in downtown Chicago, Kelly took back the top job from his understudy, Fred Rentschler, and began looking for ways to grow the company again. His first choice: to spin off Beatrice's meat, cheese, and bakery operations into a new company called E-III and go hunting afresh for acquisitions.

Once again, Kelly and Tokarz began to clash. The Chicago executive—now sixty-five years old and looking at what would probably be the last giant deal of his career—wanted E-III to start out with little debt and a big war chest with which to make acquisitions. Tokarz balked at empowering Kelly another time; so did Roberts. Their top priority was to sell all of Beatrice at once, most likely to Unilever, the Anglo-Dutch food giant. And if E-III were to exist at all, the KKR men wanted it to be on their terms. In their version, Kelly's new company would go deep in debt so it could channel $500 million or more directly to Beatrice. That arrangement would pep up KKR's profits from the Beatrice investment, even if it left Kelly in charge of a heavily indebted company.

Eager to avoid outright war between Tokarz and the most important chief executive in KKR's stable of companies, Kravis called in a mediator. Investment bankers at Salomon Brothers were told to analyze all proposals from Kelly's team and from KKR's associates, and then report to Kravis, Kelly, and the rest of the ten-member Beatrice board on which proposals were best for the company's shareholders. It seemed like a wise way to defuse tension. But the evening before Salomon's team was due to make its presentation, Tokarz and KKR colleague Paul Raether stormed into Kravis's office, upset. Kelly was leaning too hard on the Salomon investment bankers to adopt Kelly's method of calculating values, Tokarz complained. "Henry, you've got to do something about it," Tokarz pleaded.

The morning of 5 May 1988, the face-off began. Kelly arrived at KKR's offices, grim-faced and silent. In his hand was a yellow pad, something Kelly brought to meetings when he expected sparks and wanted a record of who said what. Trailing behind Kelly were a half dozen of his Chicago lieutenants. Tokarz tried to shake Kelly from his confrontational mood with a chipper "Good morning, Don!" that was half friendly, half sassy. Kelly just grunted and sat down.

Before Salomon investment banker Bill Rifkin could begin his presentation on Beatrice's seven alternatives, Kelly asked to speak. Someone had been meddling with Salomon's calculations, Kelly said, and it wasn't him. "Mike Tokarz changes all the numbers to get the results he wants," Kelly charged. And then Kelly looked at Kravis and said: "I think you should know that the way we have done the numbers, there's only one alternative that management will support." That choice, Kelly said, was alternative number four: a stand-alone E-III without much debt.

Kravis turned red. "Don, we agreed that we were going to have Salomon Brothers review all the alternatives," he said in a slow, cutting voice. "I haven't been through the presentations, and I'd like to hear them before I make up my mind."

And then Kravis attacked. "This is a partnership," he told Kelly. "It's clear you don't want to be a partner, you don't want to act like a partner. If you're not prepared to behave as a partner, we're going to make decisions without you."

The room went deadly quiet for a few moments. Then, quivering inside, Salomon's Rifkin got up and began running through his formal presentation, discussing chart after chart for forty-five minutes. All the options were very close in value, Rifkin said, but selling Beatrice might be the surest bet. A veneer of normality existed, as KKR's Raether periodically asked Rifkin a technical question. But the two most powerful people in the room didn't seem to be hearing a word that Rifkin was saying. Kelly sat red-faced, with his blank yellow pad in front of him, looking like a beaten man. Kravis stared straight ahead, gripping the mahogany conference table. To one witness, he seemed like a man trying to regain his composure after a fistfight.

At the end of the Salomon presentation, Kravis walked over to Kelly and gingerly tried to make peace. Alluding to a dinner that the two men had previously scheduled, Kravis politely asked Kelly: "Don, are we still meeting tonight?"

"At dinner or at twenty paces?" Kelly responded. The whole room burst into laughter. And at that moment, Kelly capitulated. Despite the entourage that Kelly had brought with him, he was outnumbered and outmuscled. Of the ten Beatrice directors, six were KKR partners or associates. The remaining directors—Kelly and three of his subordinates—were in the minority. "If you want to sell the company, we'll sell it," Kelly conceded.

Three months later, in August 1988, as it became clear that KKR was determined to liquidate Beatrice, Kelly resigned as chief executive. "You don't need me anymore," he told Kravis. "I'll end up bored, and you'll wonder what you're paying me for." E-III never came to be, but Kelly did stay on as a Beatrice director. When the Unilever sale talks fell through, he tried to encourage KKR to hold Beatrice awhile and grow the company. "I could sit for ten years with these businesses," Kelly declared in an interview in late 1989. It was no use. In June 1990, KKR sold the remaining pieces of Beatrice for $1.3 billion to ConAgra Inc., a giant Omaha, Nebraska, food company.

That final sale left Kelly disappointed and wistful. At a 7:30 A.M. board meeting in KKR's offices to approve the ConAgra deal, Kelly said he would vote for the sale, but wanted a few minutes to address the board first. "It was tough emotionally for Don to see the business sold," a witness at that board meeting later recalled. "Don had really tied up a lot of his identity with the business." Chagrined, too, was Fred Rentschler, then serving his second stint as Beatrice's chief executive. As KKR entered its final negotiations to sell Beatrice, Rentschler lined up a new job running Northwest Airlines. Publicly, he said he was simply switching to a more attractive job—but friends said that Rentschler found KKR's buyout priorities bewildering. "Fred was a good operating manager caught up in a world of trading companies as if they were baseball cards," one investment banker asserted.

To the KKR men, everything at Beatrice had worked out almost perfectly. The original $407 million of equity that KKR's limited partnerships had invested in the company had grown nearly fivefold in four years, counting the proceeds from the E-II deal and the ultimate ConAgra sale. The extinction of the Beatrice corporate name—a Chicago landmark—didn't trouble them. New owners such as Seagram, Coke, and ConAgra were developing Beatrice's old subsidiaries better than KKR or Beatrice's previous owners could have done. On a percentage basis, KKR's investors had earned about 50 percent a year, smack in the middle of the 40- to 60-percent range for which KKR aimed. "We're damn proud of the deal," Bousquette told an outsider the evening that the final Beatrice sale was announced.

Tokarz was even more exuberant. He had spotted profit opportunities that no one else had seen, dared to pursue them, and succeeded. "We put $407 million into the company and took out $2.2 billion," he said, spilling happy laughter. "We made more than 50 percent a year for our investors. I'd do it again—and again—and again."

For nearly all of KKR's partners and associates, there were a few cherished moments in their careers when they suddenly spotted the ideal money-making strategy in a buyout. For Mike Tokarz, such a moment arrived early in the Beatrice buyout, as he began the computer runs that led him to devise the E-II divestiture and the breakup of Beatrice. For Bob MacDonnell, the number-two partner in KKR's San Francisco office, a similar sort of flash occurred in July 1986, when Safeway executives sent a carton of confidential documents to KKR's offices, to let the buyout firm get a better understanding of the grocery company.

MacDonnell for years had been the Ringo Starr of KKR: the fourth member of a group best known for its two or three most talented, flamboyant members. He had joined KKR's San Francisco office the day the firm was founded in 1976, as the first employee other than the three founding partners. Six years older than Roberts or Kravis, MacDonnell nonetheless had started work as an associate, and had risen to the rank of partner only in 1982. People who worked with him in business knew him as a tough negotiator, a creative financier, and a gentleman outside the office. On Wall Street, however, he was known mostly as Roberts's brother-in-law (their wives were sisters). During the late 1960s, Roberts had dragged his taller, mustached brother-in-law along on business calls, not so much because he wanted MacDonnell to say anything, but because Roberts wanted the presence of someone older-looking on his team. On the Safeway buyout—after twenty years of tailoring his career to Roberts's—Bob MacDonnell fully came into his own.

As MacDonnell opened up Safeway's carton in July 1986, he found confidential figures that were the grocery chain's secret shame—and KKR's delight. As profitable as Safeway was overall, huge chunks of its territory were operating deep in the red. Oklahoma lost millions of dollars. Utah did even worse. Kansas was hopeless. Nearly all of Safeway's profits were coming from just two-thirds of its territory, chiefly along the Pacific Coast from Los Angeles to Seattle, and throughout Canada. None of this had been disclosed to Safeway's public shareholders; it didn't have to be. Instead, Safeway was pursuing a strategy common to many big public companies: quietly draining off cash from its strong businesses to subsidize its weak ones.

The moment MacDonnell saw those figures, he knew what a big part of KKR's mission at Safeway would be. The roughly 600 stores in those weak divisions should be sold as soon as possible. Whatever price they fetched would help pay down debt without hurting Safeway's earning power. "We were just astounded" at the opportunities, MacDonnell later recalled. "We said to ourselves: If we can sell these nonearning assets, that's $800 million or $900 million."

That summer, MacDonnell and Roberts jointly began nudging Safeway chief executive Peter Magowan to embrace this radical new strategy. It wasn't easy. A builder and an optimist by nature, Magowan was proud of running America's largest supermarket chain. He conceded that a few of the weakest divisions should be sold, but he argued that, given time and more money, the others might turn around. A paternal company, Safeway wasn't used to taking drastic steps to deal with loss-making divisions.

This time, no secret envelopes were sent to anyone's home. Instead, Roberts asked Magowan to size up Safeway's seventeen regional divisions and divide them into profitable ones that should be kept, borderline ones, and unprofitable ones that should be sold. The fate of vast divisions that employed 10,000 people each and rang up $1 billion of sales a year would be decided partly by Magowan's memo, and partly by what Roberts and MacDonnell decided to do with it. When he turned in his memo, Magowan said he hoped to keep most of the divisions in the first two categories. But Roberts had other ideas. "Tier one was where he wanted to concentrate," Magowan said. "He felt that was the guts of the company." If Safeway clung to too many borderline divisions, Roberts argued, strong divisions would be starved of the capital they needed.

Before tackling the U.S. divestitures, MacDonnell decided to sell what had long been Safeway's prize overseas division: its British operations. Safeway had operated in Britain for more than twenty years, ever since Magowan's father opened stores there in the early 1960s. In all the time before KKR arrived, no one at Safeway would have dreamed of selling the U.K. unit, which was renowned for its profitability and its top-tier image among shoppers. But MacDonnell figured that KKR and Safeway could fetch $1 billion for the British business, selling it at a lofty twenty-six times annual earnings. That would go a long way toward reducing Safeway's bank borrowings; it would start the crucial cycle in which a buyout company pares down debt and makes its highly leveraged stock more valuable.

Traveling to London in January 1987, MacDonnell brought with him Safeway vice chairman Harry Sunderland, a hardheaded executive who viewed the grocery chain in terms similar to KKR's. The two men started talks with the only British grocery concern for which a Safeway U.K. acquisition truly made sense: Argyll Group. The opening bid from Argyll Group was less than $700 million, much lower than MacDonnell wanted. There wasn't any other buyer that could keep the auction going. But MacDonnell set in motion—and Sunderland abetted—an audacious bargaining strategy. Safeway did have other options, they cheekily told Argyll president Alastair Grant. If he didn't raise his bid, Sunderland explained, Safeway would spitefully sell its British supermarkets, a handful at a time, to each of Argyll's toughest regional competitors. "Now, I've been an investment banker for twenty-five years, so it's easy for me to posture," MacDonnell later said. "But for a guy from the supermarket business, to look these guys right in the eye and bluff like a master. . . . It was just terrific." Cowed into bidding against himself, Grant boosted his bid to about $1 billion—the price that KKR wanted. MacDonnell and Sunderland headed home as, in their own eyes, heroes.

Then came the hard part. Most of the U.S. divisions that Safeway wanted to sell paid the highest wages in their regions. It was a point of pride to the food workers' union that they had bargained so successfully over the years with America's biggest grocery group. In Dallas, for example, where nonunion chains paid only $5 to $7 an hour, Safeway's wages averaged $10.64 an hour. As Safeway's internal profit numbers had shown, however, lower-paying nonunion chains were crushing Safeway in many inland states. MacDonnell didn't like that, and, the more they thought about it, neither did the top Safeway executives.

KKR was about to blast away the old high-wage contracts. When the buyout firm was done, more than 30,000 Safeway employees would be working at lower pay for owners other than KKR. Workers would seethe and union officials would wring their hands and talk about living with "new realities," but the KKR men would stay resolute. In their eyes, this was the right way to run a business. Safeway's stock value would climb, and divisions that might have died from uncompetitiveness would be given new life.

Once again, MacDonnell and Sunderland teamed up to start selling divisions, joined this time by KKR consultant Steve Burd. First they tried selling Safeway's 142-store Dallas division to archrival Kroger Co. Those talks fizzled, though, as Kroger expressed interest in only a handful of Dallas-area stores. Safeway dropped hints that it wanted to cut the Dallas workers' wages on its own, but the grocery clerks' union resisted. Rumors of a sell-off swirled among Safeway's Texas employees, hurting morale and contributing to widening losses. In early April 1987, Safeway announced a drastic step: it closed the Dallas division, putting 8,600 employees out of work and preparing the way for the stores to be sold strictly for their real estate value. Safeway's Dallas employees were horrified and angry about their fate. At one store, they threw their Safeway uniforms into a pile in the parking lot and burned them.

The Dallas catastrophe wasn't exactly what MacDonnell wanted. It was bad business and too wrenching even for his tastes. But KKR wasn't about to pull back on its divestiture strategy. MacDonnell was certain that it was the right course to pursue. He and Safeway's top executives merely decided to be a little more flexible in union negotiations—and to warn the unions that if wage-cut talks broke down, another Dallas could happen to their workers. Tragic as the Dallas closure was, MacDonnell later said, "It taught us a lesson and it taught the unions a lesson."

For the next six divisions that MacDonnell, Sunderland, and Burd put on the block, grocery union officials were offered a deal. If unions agreed to accept wage cuts as deep as 20 or 30 percent, Safeway would look for other buyers among leveraged buyout groups who would be willing to keep union representation. If not, Safeway would open up the bidding to buyers determined to run nonunion grocery stores. Choosing the lesser of two evils, union officials agreed to accept wage cuts. "The question is, What price will protect our people and keep the company in business?" a top food workers' union official, William Olwell, told a reporter in 1987.

Before long, Safeway's underperforming divisions in Oklahoma, Arkansas, Houston, El Paso, Utah, and Kansas were peddled to new buyers who could slash pay. Typically, workers who had earned $10 an hour were rehired at $7.50 an hour. Buyers in total paid nearly $1 billion for Safeway operations that had hardly earned anything before the buyout, but would now become money-makers—at workers' expense. "Nobody likes the process," conceded Martin Dubilier, head of a New York buyout firm that bought Safeway's Oklahoma stores for $180 million. But once wage cuts were instituted, Dubilier believed, the Oklahoma stores could become competitive and grow again.

By late 1987, KKR's intended whittling-down of Safeway was essentially complete. Roberts's strategy had prevailed over Magowan's; just about all the borderline divisions had been sold, leaving Safeway with just its choicest, tier-one divisions. All told, the asset sales had raised $2 billion, enough to pay off more than one-third of the company's buyout debt. Safeway had shrunk from America's biggest grocery chain to number three. As compensation for that loss, the company's debts were manageable again, and its operating profits were robust.

Unexpectedly, however, MacDonnell got a chance to make one more sale—a deal that came to be regarded as extremely clever within KKR, and that was viewed with some bitterness within Safeway. It involved one of Safeway's most promising units: the 172-store southern California division. While Safeway historically hadn't done well in southern California, as the smallest of five major competitors, the division's financial results had rapidly improved in 1986 and 1987 under the guidance of a spirited new division manager, Don Gates. In his hands, the southern California unit had ended its losses and begun boosting operating profit, and had made it into the seemingly protected territory of tier one.

For the right price, however, KKR was willing to sell even one of Safeway's stars. The number-two southern California grocery chain, Vons Cos., had quietly contacted MacDonnell in 1987 to ask whether KKR was interested in selling Safeway's local division. No, MacDonnell had said at first. Then after a few months, he made a counterproposal. The southern California unit wouldn't be sold for cash alone, he said. But if Safeway could emerge with some cash and a big ownership stake in Vons, it might be possible to do a deal. That possibility intrigued Vons chairman Roger Stangeland. Before long, MacDonnell and Stangeland began meeting secretly in San Francisco and Los Angeles to discuss a deal that they code-named "Sunday Supper."

Masterfully, MacDonnell played to both Stangeland's hopes and fears. At one moment, the KKR partner talked about what a powerhouse a combined Vons/Safeway would be in southern California, able to command more advertising space, negotiate better with suppliers, and generally enjoy a market leader's role. "That should be worth a lot," MacDonnell said. A little while later, MacDonnell played to Stangeland's anxieties, reminding him that KKR could just as easily sell to another southern California grocer and leave Vons in much worse competitive shape. After a few months of negotiating, MacDonnell got Safeway exactly the deal he wanted: $325 million in cash and 35-percent ownership in Vons. Bargaining once again from a difficult position, MacDonnell had achieved far better terms than a seller had the right to expect.

Left in the dark as talks progressed were all employees of the southern California unit, including Gates. KKR didn't want Gates or his workers to slack off, believing they wouldn't be accountable to Safeway anymore. Only a day or two before Safeway planned to announce the deal did KKR consultant Steve Burd finally phone Gates and break the news to him. It meant, among other things, that Gates would lose his California job and have to angle for whatever transfer Safeway could offer. Gates was furious, Burd later recalled, and asked how in the world Safeway could sell out his division when he was in the midst of such an impressive turnaround. "Why can't I stay and finish the job?" Gates asked.

Over and over, Burd kept coming back to KKR's driving rationale for every major business decision: This deal would push up the value of Safeway's stock. Three years later, Gates said he endorsed the strategy wholeheartedly. That evening, he didn't.

Right before Christmas 1987, angry Safeway division managers blasted MacDonnell at a Hawaii retreat for ripping apart their company. "Things were awful, morale-wise," MacDonnell recalled. He was pelted with one question after another about why KKR was breaking up Safeway. Over and over, he assured division managers that KKR really was done with its selling this time. The Safeway buyout wouldn't result in an outright liquidation as in the case of Beatrice. Besides, MacDonnell kept pointing out, the sales were achieving KKR's ultimate end of making Safeway a more valuable company. The southern California divestiture alone had boosted Safeway's stock value so much that many of the division managers in the room with him were millionaires now. All they had to do was think like owners, and it would look a lot better.

Four years after that confrontation in Hawaii, MacDonnell could say that KKR had remade Safeway exactly as it wanted. The grocery chain hadn't sold any more divisions; instead it had grown the ones it kept. Reduced to a lean, efficient core business, Safeway reported bigger operating profits from 1,400 stores than it had from 2,200 before the buyout. Safeway's wage costs had been reined in for the first time in years.

The price for KKR's success had been steep. The famous Safeway name had been taken down in a lot of cities. Safeway's hourly workers hadn't shared in the financial gains; their earnings had lagged behind inflation, and none of them had been allowed to buy stock in the company at the start of the buyout. People outside the equity circle got nothing. And when a merger took place in southern California—the nation's biggest, fastest-growing grocery market—Safeway had pulled out instead of acquiring a competitor.

By the yardstick that meant the most to KKR, however, the Safeway buyout was a big winner. In the first five and a half years of the buyout, its stock had soared from $2 a share to $16.

As thousands of companies were tugged through buyouts in the 1980s, economists periodically tried to assess the net gain or loss to society at the end of it all. Had buyouts brought greater efficiency through managerial empowerment and the discipline of debt? Or had paying off large borrowings caused enterprises to skimp too much, hurting companies in the long run and weakening America's competitiveness?

No sweeping answers emerged; none is likely to. Merely deciding what amounts to corporate "success" or "failure," the economists quickly discovered, is a surprisingly slippery task.

In a survey of fifty-eight companies acquired in buyouts from 1977 to 1986, University of Chicago economist Abbie Smith found that companies showed remarkable efficiency increases in the first few years after a buyout, as measured by statistics such as cash flow per employee, which frequently rose more than 20 percent a year. Buyout companies also turned over their inventory faster than average companies did, and collected bills due more quickly. But buyouts tended to bring a modest slowdown in capital spending—a crucial indicator of a company's long-term growth prospects.

Such mixed results over the short term led to efforts to evaluate buyout companies' performances over a period of ten years or so, to determine whether the efficiency gains in the first few years of a buyout came at the expense of long-term weakness. But researchers soon found that any long-term study became hopelessly muddled by an ever-growing list of extraneous factors. Mergers, recessions, and the vastly varying skills of subsequent owners made it impossible to isolate a buyout's effects over the long haul. Scholars went dizzy trying to assess Playtex, for example, which started as part of publicly traded Beatrice in 1985, was reshaped in three successive buyouts in the next three years, and then finally was bought in large part by another food conglomerate, Sara Lee Corporation, in 1991. Following the progress of a drop of water in a city reservoir would have been be an easier task.

A clearer answer comes from executives who bought companies from KKR. Their verdict: The buyout firm amounted to a good renter of the businesses that it owned for a few years. KKR and the top executives working for it generally maintained a company's operating strengths. In some cases, as in the Motel 6, Duracell, and A. J. Industries buyouts, KKR even encouraged expansion-minded executives to grow their businesses. Most of the spending plans that KKR approved, however, amounted to safe, predictable extensions of a company's existing business. The debt burden and limited time horizon of a buyout argued against taking the kinds of big, bold gambles that build great companies.

One thoughtful buyer of properties from KKR, ConAgra president Philip Fletcher, recalled that, when he first considered acquiring the Beatrice food businesses in early 1990, he worried that KKR might have skimped on capital spending or product marketing. "The very pleasant surprise was: No, they had not." But Fletcher saw plenty of room for improvement. Beatrice's managers "knew over the past five years they were in sort of a boarding-room situation," he told *Advertising Age* in late 1990. "They knew it wasn't long term." With ConAgra, Beatrice's managers suddenly were pushed to expand sales and augment product lines, rather than simply pay off debt, trim inventories, or meet other buyout goals. The oft-traded Beatrice units had finally found what was likely to be their long-term corporate home. Observed Fletcher: "Being with a fast-growing food company turns them on."

During the frenzied buyout years, KKR shuffled companies in and out of its portfolio with the speed and determination of a gin-rummy player steadily building toward a better hand. The buyout firm's executives never felt compelled to worry about lost opportunities at units such as KTLA, Tropicana, or Safeway's southern California division. Every few months, as *Fortune* writer Carol Loomis observed in a mid-1988 article, KKR bought something vastly bigger and more exciting than the companies it had just shed.

Then, starting in the spring of 1989, all the coalitions that had made KKR so powerful began to come unstuck.

11

"We Don't Have Any Friends"

For the first few months after buying RJR Nabisco in February 1989, the KKR executives actually thought their record $26.4 billion acquisition might be a stepping-stone to even larger deals. When *Fortune*'s ranking of America's 500 largest companies appeared in April 1989, George Roberts opened up the magazine at his desk in San Francisco and quickly scanned the rankings, looking for acquisition targets. "There are two or three companies in the top ten that might make good buyout candidates," Roberts calmly told a visitor that spring. Companies as immense as Exxon, Ford Motor, and IBM filled the upper reaches of the list. But Roberts was as unruffled as if he were flipping through a Sears catalog, picking out lawn furniture. The acquiring power of KKR had been growing so fast, for so long, that from the forty-fifth floor of 101 California Street, nothing seemed impossible.

Rather than a prelude to future $50 billion takeovers, however, the RJR acquisition turned out to be the buyout era's abrupt culmination. The reasons had little to do with the financial wisdom or folly of that deal itself—and much more to do with public sentiment toward a small financial firm that had grown so powerful so fast. Suddenly KKR was in the spotlight and controversial. In Congress, in boardrooms, and in ordinary conversation, people expressed uneasiness about buyouts and especially about the acquiring grasp of the most visible KKR partner, Henry Kravis. Satirists took aim at Kravis, likening him to Peter Pan and worse. Passersby in Manhattan began spotting Kravis on the street, and not all of them were friendly. "I can't tell if people want to shake my hand or stab me," Kravis remarked at one point. Fame, in his case, quickly turned into notoriety.

KKR was particularly vulnerable to this change in public sentiment, because its business depended so much on the compliance of hundreds of allies. Piece by piece, the KKR coalitions began to fragment in 1989. The first to back away were chief executives of big public companies, who had watched with fascination and horror as Ross Johnson ruined his career at RJR Nabisco. Abruptly, other big-company executives swore off any notion of taking their companies private and becoming manager-owners. Boards of directors and the powerful Delaware courts, meanwhile, retreated from the doctrine that companies should be auctioned to the highest bidder. Congress began to modify parts of the tax code that greatly favored buyouts. Members of another part of the KKR jugger-naut, the investment bankers and lawyers who had helped carry out so many jumbo deals, turned surly or defected to go into business as com-petitors to KKR. And finally, factory workers and low-level managers, who had largely been ignored in the great takeover stampede of the 1980s, began to find effective—even heartrending—ways to speak out against the loss of jobs associated with the onset of a buyout.

Only gradually did Kravis and Roberts realize that their world was coming undone. Immediately after their RJR triumph, they still had billions of dollars at their disposal in the Big Fund. Their Rolodexes brimmed with contacts, contributing to a supreme confidence that bor-dered on arrogance about their skills as deal-makers and impresarios. At a Harvard Business School dinner in May 1989, Kravis told an overflow crowd of more than 1,000 people that buyouts deserved high praise as a tactic to "free U.S. business from the paralyzing clutches of hidebound corporate bureaucracies and increase our competitive position in the world economy."

Yet a warning of trouble had already registered in the KKR inner circle even before the battle for RJR was finished. During the Thanksgiving holiday in 1988, Kravis left New York to go skiing in Colorado with his wife and a few friends. The weekend gave Kravis a chance to clear his mind and figure out KKR's next move. The afternoon of Saturday, 26 November, Kravis and a lawyer/investment banker friend, Peter Tufo, pulled off the ski trail for a few moments, looked out on the town of Vail below them, and talked about what might happen if the buyout firm actually won history's biggest takeover battle. The KKR partners would forever lose their comfortable anonymity, Tufo said. There would be new visibility for the buyout firm, new responsibilities, a series of attacks from new enemies. "Your life is going to change," Tufo warned. Caught up in the excitement of the deal, Kravis hadn't begun to think about its broader impact. For a few moments, he digested Tufo's remarks, and then he conceded: "You're right."

What unfolded in the next eighteen months, however, was far more jarring for KKR than either Kravis or his friends expected.

By late 1988, the riches flowing into the hands of Kravis and Roberts had become so vast that heads started to turn. *Forbes* magazine estimated the cousins' wealth at $330 million each in mid-1988, rising at a pace of nearly $100 million a year. Each new buyout was designed to enrich the KKR partners in a variety of ways. First came an acquisition fee for KKR, which didn't have to be shared with the limited partner investors at all. The biggest deal of all, RJR Nabisco, produced a $75 million fee for six weeks' work. Then came directors' fees, management fees, and a fee for overseeing unspent money in KKR's buyout pools. Finally, each time an older buyout company was sold, the KKR executives skimmed 20 percent of the owners' profits for themselves, before dividing the remaining 80 percent among pension funds and other passive investors.

Like a gourmand growing hungrier with every bite, the KKR partners found that each new burst of wealth only heightened their desire for more. When the RJR buyout was completed, executives within KKR seriously considered billing the company for a *$300 million* fee—equal to the buyout firm's standard 1 percent of the deal. That would have amounted to about $89,000 an hour for the seven KKR partners and associates who worked on the deal, but the KKR men didn't see anything wrong with that. "I never wanted to be paid by the hour," George Roberts once remarked, when asked how he could justify such giant fees. Kravis and Roberts scaled back their bill only after pressure from their lawyers and other advisers, who said such a giant fee would be widely seen as "obscene" and could cause political trouble for KKR in the months to come. Even so, the $75 million fee—the biggest ever charged on Wall Street—fit many people's definition of obscene.

This rapid buildup of wealth began to taint KKR's carefully nurtured image in the business community. One of Kravis's most appealing representations to chief executives was the notion that the CEO's success would come first; that KKR was merely a helpful ally in the background. "Nothing would make me happier than for you to be the rich man at the end of this," Kravis had assured brick-company president Bill Jones in 1974. As far along in KKR's development as the Beatrice and Safeway buyouts, it still was possible for the KKR partners to convince corporate executives that the real winners in a buyout would be the managers of the companies, not the string-pulling financiers.

By the late 1980s, Kravis had adopted a Gilded Age life style that made a mockery of those buyout promises. His clothing tastes, never spartan to begin with, now included such luxuries as four-ply cashmere cardigans that cost $825 each. His housing tastes turned even more lavish. He owned a $5 million apartment on Park Avenue in Manhattan and a huge country home in Southampton, New York. A second country home in Sharon, Connecticut, included its own heliport, a nearby farm acquired for $2.6 million in 1989, and an indoor horse-riding track. When those weren't enough, Kravis could head to his ski lodge in Vail or other property that he owned in England. Six servants kept the silverware tidy and shuttled his possessions among his various homes. His second wife, dress designer Carolyne Roehm, hosted parties for 200 people at New York's Metropolitan Museum, at which music was provided not by anonymous local performers but by world-renowned Japanese prodigy Midori.

Longtime friends of Kravis, who had known him before he became so grand, began to chide him about his new airs. On one New York visit, Bill Jones, the brick-company president, stopped in the Saks Fifth Avenue department store to admire some of Roehm's $3,000 dresses. Jones's wife bought her clothes off the rack for a tiny fraction of that amount. "You must be cleaning up with her business," Jones told Kravis.

"No. Oh, no," Kravis replied. "It's very competitive. The only way you make money in that business is by licensing out the designer name."

Jones's face lit up. He had an idea for Kravis. Two weeks later, a hefty brown packing case from Pleasant Garden, North Carolina, arrived at KKR's Manhattan offices. Inside the case was a present from the kilns of Boren Clay: six bricks, each branded on the side with the name CAROLYNE ROEHM. In the glittery world of $3,000 designer dresses, Jones decided, there must also be room for designer bricks.

Other executives found Kravis's extravagance unsettling. Ironically, one of them was Ross Johnson, the ill-fated head of RJR Nabisco before its buyout. In October 1987, a year before the RJR takeover battle, Kravis, Johnson, and Beatrice chief executive Don Kelly met at Kravis's apartment for a private dinner to talk about buyouts. Overwhelmed by the wealth around him, Johnson at one point asked Kravis about a giant, nine-foot-high oil portrait of an English nobleman that hung on the back wall of Kravis's dining room. It was a $1 million painting by John Singer Sargent, which Kravis had bought in London and then transported to

New York via a cargo plane, because it was too big to fit in the baggage hold of a passenger jet. To the astonishment of Johnson and Kelly, Kravis began to explain how much trouble he had had getting the painting inside his apartment. It was too huge to fit through his doorway, he said, so shippers were obliged to hire a crane and stop traffic on the street below. They removed the casement on one of his windows, and hoisted the painting seventy feet in the air so it could be pulled through the cavity where Kravis's largest windows normally fit. Johnson came away from that dinner shaking his head. A day later, he called Kravis and said that for a variety of reasons, he didn't think they could work well together.

Before long, New York's society press seized on Kravis, depicting him as the tycoon that America loved to hate. An unreflective man, Kravis never figured out why photographers wanted to shoot pictures of him grinning in the middle of his sumptuous living room, or posed in suit and tie in front of one of his Stubbs masterpieces. A month or two later, when articles popped up in society magazines or *USA Today,* they appeared on the surface to be flattering. But subtle barbs were thrown in along the way. Kravis was "born into a life of privilege," one writer observed. "He's in it for what the money can buy," another suggested. A surprisingly large number of bankers and lawyers—the upper-middle-class allies whom Kravis needed to complete his deals—began collecting such articles with horrid fascination. They started asking themselves: Is all our hard work on buyouts really just a way to pay for Henry Kravis's next bauble? Various commentators fueled this unease, notably former investment banker Michael Thomas. In a series of columns in *The New York Observer* in 1989, Thomas fixated on Kravis, always referring to him by the derisory epithet "the Li'l King."

As one example after another of ostentatiousness spilled forth, Kravis and his KKR colleagues found that corporate chief executives weren't so eager anymore to entertain the notion of a buyout. "I heard some of the rumors" about Henry Kravis, said one Midwestern food-company executive who hesitated to do business with KKR. When the KKR men tried to schedule get-acquainted chats with top executives, they were met with delays and excuses. Even trusted intermediaries for Kravis and Roberts, such as Roger Meier, the longtime chairman of the Oregon investment council, found the buyout firm's image deteriorating in 1989. At one point, Meier tried to interest a major East Coast company in considering a KKR-led buyout. Meier thought his chances were pretty good; he knew two of the directors from his own circle of contacts. But when he started serious prospecting, the company's top executives slammed the door in his face. Chagrined, Meier reported: "When you ask them if they want to talk to George or Henry, it's as if you asked them if they wanted to put their hand on a hot stove."

In a rapidly changing business climate, KKR couldn't sell security anymore. Its partners and associates whipped across the country faster than ever, telling their story to top executives wherever they could. But the sales calls throughout 1989 were one strikeout after another.

"Before RJR, the number of absolutely huge companies willing to discuss an LBO with their boards was absolutely stunning," a top Goldman, Sachs partner observed. Chrysler Corporation chairman Lee Iacocca, in fact, had gone so far as to ask three of his directors who knew KKR well—Safeway chief executive Peter Magowan, Owens-Illinois chairman Robert Lanigan, and RJR director Paul Sticht—to make a special presentation on buyouts to the car company's board right around the time of the RJR buyout. While no one formally broached the idea of a Chrysler buyout, Iacocca's curiosity clearly had been whetted. By the summer of 1989, however, executives like Iacocca had changed their thinking entirely. "The moment RJR and all the news about Ross Johnson came out, everyone stopped doing anything," the Goldman, Sachs partner observed. "Executives decided they had missed a window of wealth, and now simply didn't want to lose respect at their company." Confidential buyout studies suddenly were shredded and forgotten.

Two other important underpinnings of the 1980s takeover boom—the courts and the tax laws—also began to change to KKR's disadvantage. For years, the buyout firm had been greatly aided by legal doctrines that practically dictated the sale to the highest bidder of companies receiving properly financed takeover bids. In mid-1989, however, directors of Time Inc. turned down a $12.2 billion takeover offer from Paramount Communications, saying they would rather merge their company into Warner Communications. Paramount tried to block Time's maneuver in Delaware courts, but failed. In a landmark ruling, Delaware judge William Allen said that the "business judgment" rule allowed directors to turn down takeover offers well above the current stock price if they felt that the takeover wasn't in the long-term interests of a company's shareholders. With one stroke, Judge Allen had taken away much of the power of corporate raiders—the stalkers who had generated much of KKR's business in the 1980s. Thanks to the advent of this new "just say no" defense, directors at companies under siege could resist a raider without resorting to a buyout. They could continue on their course and let the financial harpies fade away.

Just as damaging to KKR's prospects were several little-noticed changes in the tax laws. Several times in the late 1980s, Congress curbed an acquirer's ability to boost a company's depreciation charges after a buyout. That cut back one of KKR's favorite ways of reducing a company's tax bill, which had allowed the firm to pay well above current stock prices for its acquisitions. Congress also whittled away the ability of buyout firms to avoid paying big taxes when breaking up a conglomerate. Until 1988, buyout firms had been free to carry out acquisitions by using a variety of shell companies, much as KKR had done on its Houdaille buyout. Some of those shell companies, known as "mirror subsidiaries," allowed the new owners to sidestep capital-gains taxes that otherwise would need to be paid on divestitures. Mirror subsidiaries were first restricted, and then disallowed outright as Congress became concerned about the loss of tax revenue and the fact that rampant use of mirror subsidiaries was making every conglomerate a breakup target.

In the wake of these legislative changes, the tax system from 1989 onward still favored high-debt buyouts, but in a much less compelling way than before.

Legislators reined in these tax incentives in part because of public pressure to "do something" about Wall Street's wave of takeovers. "The numbers and trends are very alarming," the chairman of the House Ways and Means Committee, Representative Daniel Rostenkowski, declared on 31 January 1989, as he began the first of nine congressional hearings into the buyout boom. Some legislators, echoing their constituents, charged that buyouts brought layoffs and the breaking up of long-established corporations. Other members of congress said that they were upset about buyouts' tendency to shunt huge profits into the hands of a few deal-makers. Even a relatively pro-business senator, Finance Committee chairman Lloyd Bentsen, said he feared that a future recession "could be deepened and lengthened by a massive move to debt."

A flurry of House and Senate committees tried to lure Kravis—the man who personified Wall Street's buyout power—into giving public testimony in early 1989. Don't do it, a top Washington attorney, Ken Levine, advised Kravis. "You'd just be a target," Levine explained. "You'd be eaten up by the media." The high visibility of the RJR buyout and the movie *Wall Street* made Levine especially nervous. Kravis, he feared, would be seen as a real-life version of the movie villain Gordon Gekko for members of congress to savage. So Kravis instead offered influential legislators as many private meetings as they wanted, on his terms. These would be small gatherings in Washington offices and clubs, without any media coverage. To KKR's great relief, legislators acceded.

In a series of closed-door breakfasts in early 1989, Kravis and Roberts tirelessly laid out their pro-buyout arguments: that these deals pruned back corporate excess, revitalized executives, and made the U.S. economy more efficient. But because of KKR's own taste for splendor, many of these arguments sounded hollow. Companies such as Safeway, Beatrice, Owens-Illinois, and RJR indeed had shed some private jets soon after KKR acquired them, and had adopted more Spartan ways in their executive suites. A careful reader of Beatrice's financial statements, however, would have found that two of the food company's jets didn't venture outside the buyout firm's circle. One was bought by Beatrice chief executive Don Kelly for his personal use. Another, a top-of-the-line Gulfstream III, was snapped up by KKR partner Bob MacDonnell for $10.3 million.

At one breakfast, North Dakota Representative Byron Dorgan slyly interrupted Kravis in the midst of a diatribe against entrenched corporate managers who used corporate jets as their personal playthings. "How did you get down here?" Dorgan asked.

"We flew down in one of our planes," Kravis replied. A couple of congressmen began to smirk. "But that's different," Kravis earnestly continued. "We own our jets."

Several Democratic congress members found that answer much too haughty for their tastes. And even though Congress ultimately dropped the buyout issue in mid-1989 (partly because a vast savings-and-loan crisis clamored for much more immediate attention), a distaste for KKR's line of work lingered in Washington. "These are people who want to make as much money as they can, as quickly as they can," Dorgan said in an interview in early 1990. "They take things apart rather than put them together."

On Wall Street, too, the takeover minstrels who had long aided KKR's deal-making desires began to back away. Some, like powerful lawyer Marty Lipton, decided that their loyalties (in public, at least) lay with traditional corporate clients instead of high-debt buccaneers. "We are overleveraging American companies and forcing them to focus on short-term results," Lipton wrote in a widely circulated memo to clients on 28 October 1988. "The only remedy is effective legislation. Investors . . . cannot be allowed to force American business to be denuded of equity and operate with unsustainable levels of debt."

One of Wall Street's most politically savvy executives, Lazard Frères partner Felix Rohatyn, sounded similar themes in testimony before the

House Ways and Means Committee in March 1989. "Management can be highly motivated without mountains of debt to make them more efficient," Rohatyn argued. Buyouts "are the effects of imbalances created in the economy . . . and a generally highly speculative environment fostered in the 1980s." Rohatyn periodically liked to speak out against Wall Street practices, positioning himself as a financial expert who could see the bigger economic picture. In disowning buyouts, Rohatyn acknowledged that his stance might mean less business for Wall Street and his firm. But, in a pious summation, he said: "If it results in a healthier economy, it will benefit the markets as well as our clients and our business."

Other New York investment bankers still craved the giant fees that KKR could provide, but they chafed at being so dependent on one fabulously successful client. Among them was Jeff Beck, an eccentric deal-maker who periodically claimed to have worked for the CIA, to have fought in Vietnam, and to be the heir to a huge fortune. Beck had helped bring Kravis and Kelly together for the Beatrice deal. He went on to play a minor role in advising KKR on its big RJR Nabisco acquisition, but was booted off the team in late October 1988 after Kravis became convinced that Beck was leaking details of KKR's bidding intentions to the press, a charge that Beck vigorously denied. A year later, homebound because of a severe leg injury, Beck's biggest deal-doing hopes still involved KKR. When it briefly looked like Campbell Soup might be a takeover target, Beck jumped on the phone to Kravis, pitching a possible buyout of the food company. "You're already the preeminent player in food-company deals," Beck purred into the phone. "You really ought to look at this." Yet less than ten minutes before that call, Beck had loudly told a visitor that Kravis's high living was simply "too much."

Rather than grumble, plenty of other investment bankers simply stopped serving KKR and went into the buyout business for themselves. The most successful was Donald Brennan, the Morgan Stanley executive who in early 1987 had helped KKR sell the forest-products division of Owens-Illinois. Immediately after that transaction, Brennan took over leadership of Morgan Stanley's own buyout group. He and several colleagues raised a $2 billion buyout fund and bought nearly a dozen companies. In late 1989, Brennan could point to a wall chart of Morgan Stanley's buyout holdings and declare that, taken together, they amounted to the twentieth largest industrial enterprise in the United States. No longer did he need to be a mere KKR adviser. He was a full-fledged competitor to Kravis and Roberts.

In vain, Kravis protested to top executives at Morgan Stanley that he didn't like their firm's growing focus on doing its own buyouts. The profit potential from running a buyout department was too great for the Morgan Stanley men to be dissuaded by a few clients' grumblings—even from a client as powerful as Kravis.

After the RJR acquisition, much of the deal-doing drive at KKR switched to the firm's San Francisco office, and George Roberts. Unlike Kravis, Roberts did a good job of hiding his wealth. On family vacations in Hawaii, Roberts strolled the beaches in worn chinos, looking like any other tourist. When he skied in Colorado, he borrowed the keys to Kravis's chalet; there wasn't a string of auxiliary Roberts homes across the United States. Well known in top business circles, Roberts was practically invisible to the broader world—which was just the way he wanted it. One of the nice things about living in northern California instead of New York, he once remarked, was that he could take his children to the movies and not be recognized as anyone special.

For all his shy, self-effacing ways, however, Roberts continued hunting for mega-deals. In KKR's early years, Roberts's San Francisco office had accounted for as much as 60 percent of the firm's buyouts, outpacing the combined efforts of Kravis and Kohlberg in New York. In the heady first few months after the RJR acquisition was negotiated, Roberts hinted to several of KKR's big pension fund backers that he might lead the buyout firm in making several more truly giant acquisitions. A favorite Roberts dream involved a turn of events that would culminate in his buying Chevron, the San Francisco–based oil giant that had beaten KKR in the bidding for Gulf in 1984. Such an acquisition might cost a total of $30 billion, which even at 10-to-1 leverage would exhaust the money remaining in the giant $5.6 billion buyout fund that KKR had raised in 1987. But Roberts had the solution. Before long, KKR would raise an even larger pool of capital from its pension fund backers. The next buyout fund might truly be the Big Fund, Roberts told confidants, perhaps reaching $10 billion.

Right at the peak of KKR's power, however, Roberts's tactical touch began to falter. The first misstep came in late 1988, when KKR tried to acquire Kroger Co., a giant Cincinnati-based supermarket chain. Twice before, KKR had made supermarket acquisitions for $1 billion or more, picking up Safeway in 1986 and Stop & Shop in 1988. In both cases, top executives of the grocery chains had embraced KKR after hostile takeover overtures from the Haft family of Washington, D.C. So when the Hafts stalked Kroger in September 1988, Roberts quickly lobbed in his own acquisition proposal. Kroger chairman Lyle Everingham, however, showed no desire to traffic with KKR. He wanted to keep Kroger independent, even if that meant embarking on a massive recapitalization in which Kroger borrowed heavily and paid a huge dividend to shareholders.

Frustrated by Everingham's resistance, Roberts tried to storm Kroger. He began contacting Kroger's directors on his own, ignoring the grocery chain's chairman. In a chilly letter to Kroger's directors dated 4 October 1988, Roberts put forth a $5 billion takeover proposal. "Our revised proposal is far superior to your restructuring plan in all respects," Roberts declared. For the next five paragraphs, he ticked off financial considerations, concluding with the observation that KKR's bid was "28 times the company's earnings for the last 12 months." Utterly missing from Roberts's letter were all the soothing hallmarks of a typical KKR offer. There wasn't a word of praise for Kroger's existing management. There was no talk of wanting to grow the company, take care of employees, or otherwise be a good corporate citizen. KKR, which had done so well in the 1980s by selling itself to top executives as a palatable alternative to corporate raiders, now was behaving exactly like a raider itself.

Kroger executives bristled. "Our company isn't for sale," Everingham told reporters. Selling to KKR "wouldn't be in the best interests of Kroger, its shareholders and affected constituencies." Faced with an unequivocal no, Roberts retreated only a few paces. He decided to abandon KKR's takeover bid, but he arranged to buy 9.9 percent of Kroger's stock, which KKR later sold at a substantial profit. In Roberts's eyes, the whole adventure had been a money-maker and caused little damage to the buyout firm's reputation. But almost everyone else on Wall Street and in corporate America saw it as a shabby turn of events for KKR. "They got singed a little on Kroger," a leading investment banker later observed.

A few months later, KKR stumbled in another takeover attempt. For years the KKR partners, particularly Roberts, had wanted to buy a major bank. The entire banking industry seemed bloated and in need of the financial discipline that the buyout regimen provided. Besides, as one of the most tightly regulated industries, banking had the lure of forbidden fruit. Most people thought it would be impossible for a firm like KKR, which controlled so many industrial companies, to maneuver around the Depression-era Glass-Steagall Act, which was meant to keep banking and commerce separate. Roberts, however, kept looking for openings. He briefly considered investing in Seattle-based SeaFirst bank in 1983, but backed off in the face of a preemptive bid by Bank of America. Then Roberts and KKR associate Mike Tokarz, a former banker himself, secretly explored possible acquisitions of First Chicago and a major New York bank in 1988, but didn't get very far.

In early 1989, Roberts and Tokarz thought they had found the prize deal that would make up for their early losses. One of Texas's largest banks, Mcorp, began to slide into serious financial trouble. Federal regulators took over the bank and announced that they were willing to sell it to any qualified U.S. or foreign bidder. KKR pounced. Teams of Deloitte accountants on KKR's payroll fanned out through Texas, evaluating Mcorp's branches so thoroughly that they carried out a county-by-county economic analysis of Texas. No one at KKR personally knew how to run a bank, but that wasn't seen as a problem. If Mcorp's old management was found wanting, which seemed likely, KKR could simply "go out and hire" one of the best bankers in America to run the Texas bank, a KKR adviser declared. The lure of a top-dollar pay package from the buyout firm was supposed to pry any banker from his or her job. In all, KKR poured about $5 million of its own money into its evaluation of Mcorp— the most it had ever expended on a deal without having signed an acquisition agreement.

Competing against five big commercial banks from the United States and Scotland, Tokarz and Roberts thought they had the inside track. They devised an intricate ownership structure that just barely let KKR skirt around Glass-Steagall restrictions.* Then the KKR men submitted an opening bid to the Federal Deposit Insurance Corporation, which was running the auction for Mcorp. Tokarz hinted to the FDIC that he was willing to raise his price if necessary. Midlevel staffers at the FDIC found Tokarz's presentation convincing. On 27 June 1989, the agency's staff in a private memo recommended selling Mcorp's main businesses to KKR for $517 million. Such a sale would have given KKR control of $13.1 billion in banking assets, making it the third largest bank in Texas. And it could well have been a stepping-stone toward even greater financial power. "Mcorp would just be a base upon which to begin buying other banks," one KKR adviser publicly declared.

KKR, however, hadn't counted on the opposition of Robert Clarke, a onetime Houston lawyer who was both comptroller of the currency and an FDIC director. A longtime free-market advocate who was beginning to have second thoughts about how well the banking system

---

*KKR itself proposed to buy only about 4.9 percent of the bank, within the ownership limits allowed by Glass-Steagall. But KKR's traditional limited partners would each buy stakes as high as 4.9 percent, too. In toto, the KKR investor group would control the bank.

was holding up without much regulation, Clarke decided he didn't like KKR. In a closed-doors FDIC board meeting on 28 June 1989, Clarke decried KKR as a "leveraged buyout junk-bond artist" that was likely to break up Mcorp and sell off the pieces in a "short-term transaction to maximize KKR's profits." Another FDIC director, C. C. Hope, Jr., questioned KKR's lack of "any experience or expertise in banking." The next afternoon, the agency's directors voted to award Mcorp to an expansion-minded Ohio bank, Banc One Corporation, instead of to KKR. In sheer dollar terms, Tokarz and Roberts had put together the best bid. But the FDIC directors—breaking with a decade of purely capitalistic auctioning of companies—decided that paying top dollar alone wasn't enough to win.

As if Kravis and Roberts weren't creating enough trouble for themselves, their old partner, Jerry Kohlberg, found a way to attack them publicly in the summer of 1989. In the first two years after Kohlberg left KKR, an uneasy truce had prevailed in which Kravis and Roberts in effect bought Kohlberg's silence by paying him sizable alimony. After his departure, Kohlberg had continued to invest in all of KKR's deals on favorable terms; he also continued to collect a total of about $200,000 in annual directors' fees from companies that KKR controlled. Kohlberg skipped most board meetings, regularly attending only those of Fred Meyer, the Portland retailer he had known for decades. Otherwise, he was a phantom—but he cashed his directors' checks anyway. All of the money that flowed from KKR to Kohlberg, however, was not enough to soothe the ex-partner's wrath at the younger men who had shunted him aside.

On 21 August 1989, Kohlberg sued Kravis and Roberts, accusing them of "breaches of fiduciary duty" and "appropriation of partnership assets." His main complaint: He didn't like the way that KKR had recapitalized several small buyouts from the late 1970s and early 1980s. The firm had cashed out part of Kohlberg's stake at a profit after he left KKR and reduced his ownership going forward. The two main cases cited in the suit involved Houdaille, the pump and machine-tool company that later was renamed Idex, and Marley Co., a maker of cooling towers.

To Kravis and Roberts, Kohlberg's complaint was ludicrous. All the original equity investors had made a lot of money from the Houdaille and Marley buyouts, including management, KKR executives, and their limited partner investors. Kohlberg himself had raked in $1.3 million from his original $219,563 investment in Marley, as well as the chance to roll over his winnings in exchange for 17.625 percent of KKR's future gains at Marley. Kohlberg had more than quadrupled his money in Houdaille, too. The recapitalizations had been mainly a way for KKR and its investors to collect profits to date and then put more debt on the companies' books so that the alchemy of leverage would work anew. The only reason that Kohlberg's ongoing share in the buyouts was dropping was to make room for new KKR executives—including associates Ned Gilhuly and Mike Tokarz, who had taken over much of the day-to-day responsibilities for Marley and Idex, respectively.

Unsure how to fight their old mentor, Kravis and Roberts decided to do almost nothing. They issued a brief statement saying: "We believe he is wrong both as to the facts and his interpretation of the agreement between us." Otherwise, the KKR partners stayed quiet and hoped the suit would go away. They weren't so lucky. Kohlberg had been quietly seething about his former partners for more than two years, his rage building each time he read another article that described Kravis's flashy, cock-of-the-walk life style. After a two-hour lunch with Kohlberg in early September 1989, rival buyout specialist Martin Dubilier reported: "He believes Henry Kravis is a manipulative, self-serving bastard."

With his attack on KKR, Kohlberg managed to touch a chord of sympathy in the wider world. "Is hubris about to catch up with Henry Kravis?" *The Economist* asked in its article on the suit. Other publications quickly latched onto the notion that KKR had done something wrong. The tiny buyout firm had made so much money, so fast, that its gains seemed somehow suspect. Kohlberg's publicist, Davis Weinstock, assiduously pushed an anti-KKR view on any reporter who would listen. Before long, people who had never read Kohlberg's suit closely began muttering about fraud and cheated investors. Some six months later, Kravis and Roberts quietly settled the suit with Kohlberg, boosting his stake slightly in Marley but leaving his stake untouched in Idex. All told, Kohlberg got extra buyout ownership stakes worth a bit less than $1 million at the time. Both sides claimed victory and agreed not to discuss the suit further.

Much harder for KKR to quiet down, though, was the long-suppressed anger of workers and their union leaders who felt badly treated by buyouts. In testimony before the Senate Finance Committee in January 1989, AFL-CIO president Lane Kirkland asserted that 90,000 union members had lost their jobs in the previous decade because of leveraged buyouts and other takeovers. While financiers profited, Kirkland asserted, "It is the working Americans who pay the price with the loss of their livelihoods and the debasement of their communities." Sen. John Danforth of Missouri challenged Kirkland's job-loss figure, citing a study by KKR's accountants at Deloitte. In that survey, KKR-controlled companies had expanded their payrolls by 4.4 percent a year after buyouts, significantly faster than payrolls had expanded at those companies before they were acquired.*

Rather than argue about statistics, prolabor forces found that the fastest way to shape the public's attitudes toward buyouts was by anecdotal horror stories. First the son of a machinist at Houdaille's old Burgmaster unit, Max Holland, chronicled the demise of Burgmaster in his 1989 book, *When the Machine Stopped*. In his account, KKR was simply a profiteering firm uninterested in the health of basic business. Holland's themes were echoed by union officials in dozens of state legislative hearings. Tom Climo, a former union official at the Amstar Inc. sugar company, asserted at one Massachusetts hearing that payrolls were shrunk, refineries closed, and safety standards allowed to lapse after KKR acquired Amstar in 1984. Kravis and Roberts tried to fight back with statistics-filled speeches about buyouts' contributions to American efficiency. Cutbacks at companies such as Burgmaster and Amstar were really just parts of overall retrenchment in those industries, the KKR men argued, rather than anything related to buyouts. But public sentiment was swayed much more by tales of trampled workers than by figures. When *Time* magazine surveyed Americans in February 1990, some 68 percent said they thought the takeover wave of the past decade was "not a good thing."

Perhaps the most powerful blow on behalf of ill-treated workers appeared on the front page of *The Wall Street Journal* on 16 May 1990, under the headline THE RECKONING. With example after example, *Journal* reporter Susan Faludi told about the Safeway workers who had fared worst in that buyout. A fired Dallas trucker had committed suicide. A laid-off baker had ended up living in a homeless shelter. A Soviet émigré engineer who had saved Safeway $1.6 million by inventing a new cooling system had also been fired. He had gone jobless for four years, and had turned into a recluse. He complained: "I am ashamed. I am like an old thrown-out mop."

These haunting portraits stretched out for twelve columns, in the *Journal*'s longest news story ever. The article generated more than 200 letters, and ultimately won a Pulitzer prize. It also jolted some of the

---

*That Deloitte study included more than a few estimates and projections, as well as actual job counts. It also treated divestitures and acquisitions somewhat inconsistently, at times giving KKR credit for job growth when buyout companies made acquisitions, but not penalizing them for divestitures. At the time, however, it was seen as an effective rebuttal to the AFL-CIO's contentions. Researchers who later looked at both KKR and union data were left to conclude that the actual job tally was somewhere in between the two sides' estimates, with definitive numbers proving elusive.

people closest to KKR. Scott Sperling, a Harvard University investment specialist who had helped bankroll KKR for years, read the article and voiced dismay at what his buyout dollars appeared to have caused.

In vain, top KKR and Safeway executives protested that the *Journal* article was unfair. Most Safeway workers had kept their jobs; additional new workers had been hired, too. None of the things that were important to KKR—higher cash flow, debt reduction, better teamwork among top Safeway executives—had appeared in the *Journal*'s article at all, except under a brief heading: "The Winners." Roberts couldn't believe that a *Journal* reporter had set out to interview him for a major feature story without having read Safeway's prospectuses or financial statements in detail. Faludi couldn't believe that the architect of the Safeway buyout could be so detached from all the stories of human suffering she had unearthed.

The day after the article ran, Roberts declared that he was "disgusted" with *The Wall Street Journal.* For months to come, Roberts and Kravis found that they carried a new burden in their sales calls on corporate executives, lenders, and pension fund backers. They had to prove that buyouts didn't kill people.

As public scorn toward KKR piled up, the deal-makers at the tiny buyout firm grew nervous and suspicious toward outsiders. For years, KKR had been the toast of Wall Street, the firm that everyone tried to flatter. Press coverage of buyouts had always been somewhat skeptical, but most articles had been too brief, obscure, and sketchy to make much of a difference. Suddenly, KKR was being depicted as the firm that epitomized the unacceptable face of capitalism. No one, it seemed, wanted to do business with such a financial ogre. After the RJR acquisition was completed in February 1989, the buyout firm went through the rest of 1989 without announcing a major acquisition—its longest period of inaction since 1982. Trying to keep his spirits up, Kravis told interviewers that KKR had plenty of work to do with its existing portfolio of companies, even if the buyout firm never did.

Within the halls of 9 West Fifty-seventh Street and 101 California Street, KKR executives began theorizing that even the people saying nice things to their faces might be scoffing behind their backs. "You get paranoid in this business," Bob MacDonnell told a caller in the spring of 1990, just after KKR was forced to lower its asking price in an attempt to sell Safeway stock to the public. Wall Street underwriters had assured him that the deal would go well, then reported late in the process that buyers had disappeared. MacDonnell complained: "You start to think there's a cabal out there, trying to get together and break you."

Associate Saul Fox began to wonder whether KKR had really ever built up more than just a series of transient alliances, bonded only by a desire for money. "We don't have any friends," Fox remarked with some bitterness in early 1990 as he surveyed the buyout firm's troubles.

Earnestly, the KKR partners—Kravis especially—tried to adapt to the demands of a harsher world. Kravis reined in his social life from mid-1989 onward, attending fewer parties and keeping photographers away from his money. He told his wife, Carolyne Roehm, to cut back her publicity, too, after business friends began muttering about the sight of her in a *Fortune* magazine cover story about chief executives' second wives. Well-mannered even in defeat, Kravis wrote gracious notes to competitors when they achieved buyout successes that KKR might have wanted. "Congratulations," Kravis wrote his longtime rival Ted Forstmann, when Forstmann Little & Co. sold a major buyout company at a big profit in early 1990. "Keep up the good work. It's great for all of us in the business."

A few chief executives, who had endured their share of public scorn, reached out to Kravis. After one barrage of media criticism, Houston oil executive Robert Allen sent Kravis a small plaque with a quote from Teddy Roosevelt: "It's not the critic who counts, not the man who points out how the strong man stumbled or where the doer of deeds could have done them better. The credit belongs to the man who is actually in the arena, whose face is marred by dust and sweat and blood." That plaque became one of Kravis's most cherished possessions—something he showed off to visitors instead of his oil paintings or the Lucite financial "tombstones" that chronicled giant deals of years past.

Restoring KKR to its old status as a palatable financial partner would be a long struggle. Enough skepticism about Kravis and his colleagues had been engendered in the business community that most executives would think twice about doing business with the buyout firm. "I can't imagine why any chief executive would want to talk to them now," longtime KKR watcher John Canning, the head of First Chicago's venture capital group, commented in January 1990.

The tough new realities of courting CEOs registered when executives of the buyout firm began calling on Tony Millar, the chairman of a fast-growing British food-service business. His company, Albert Fisher Group, needed $200 million or more in late 1989 to finance expansion. While Millar wasn't interested in an outright buyout, he was willing to sell part ownership in Albert Fisher to an American financial firm. That intrigued KKR executives. Several associates began prospecting with Millar and arranged for him to meet with Kravis. In December 1989, however, Millar decided to do his deal with a different American group: an affiliate of Lazard Frères known as Corporate Partners.

KKR executives say the talks faltered because of their own doubts about how desirable an investment in Albert Fisher would be. But Millar cited a different reason. According to an investment banker who worked on the transaction: "He couldn't get comfortable with KKR as people."

12
Credit Crunch

" 'A s long as the money doesn't run out, luck will follow,"
George Roberts periodically told KKR's younger associates in 1989,
whenever they grumbled about minor setbacks. That poker player's epi-
gram became a Roberts favorite during the jarring months after the RJR
buyout. It wasn't any fun for the KKR men to find themselves attacked
from all sides—but at least most of the assaults were short-lived. An
opponent would voice some harsh words, then disappear. Gradually, the
somewhat thin-skinned executives at the buyout firm learned to shrug off
criticism. They still had their big buyout fund. They still possessed financial links that could command billions of dollars of loans. Eventually, the
period of public scorn would pass, and KKR could embark on giant deals
again.

From mid-1989 onward, however, the money started to run out.

All the lending alliances that had made KKR so powerful began to
disintegrate. For years, buyout firms had borrowed billions of dollars of
other people's money on the basis of financial projections, guarantees,
and assumptions that ultimately came down to one simple tenet: trust.
The deals were going to work. But that trust proved remarkably fragile.
A handful of buyout companies began having trouble paying their debts
in 1989 as overall economic growth slowed significantly for the first time
in seven years. With a weak economy, the prospect of more financial
failures loomed. Quickly, lenders and regulators began to tear apart the
network of easy credit that had been built up in the previous ten years.
Before long, the risks of bankrolling heavily indebted companies—which

had been ignored or denied as late as 1988—became an increasingly big worry for bankers and junk-bond buyers. The giddy optimism at the peak of the lending cycle subsided. In its place came a new wariness and distrust.

Just as rampant speculation had fed on itself for years, so too did the new skepticism. From 1989 to 1990, banks' loans to buyout companies skidded 86 percent, to their lowest level since the early 1980s. The junk-bond market collapsed even more drastically. Lenders at mutual funds, insurance companies, and S&Ls all took a hard look at the types of deals they had been bankrolling. Cash began fleeing the junk-bond market at a rate of billions of dollars a month, as onetime lenders blinked, cursed their folly in putting money into unsound deals, and then swore never to be so reckless with their cash again.

KKR's executives, to their great dismay, were helpless to do anything but watch. For the first few months of the 1989 credit retreat, Kravis, Roberts, and their longtime lending allies refused to believe that they were beholding anything more than a "pause" in the lending boom they had come to know and love. Month by month, however, the retreat picked up speed. In a futile effort, Roberts at several stages tried calling on bank chairmen, urging them to loosen up their lending again. They received him politely but made no promises. Many were too worried about the survival of their own banks to think of doing a favor for a client—even one as powerful as KKR. As evidence of rising defaults and greedy practices spilled forth, the pullback in lending intensified. Before long, the U.S. economy sank into its first recession in nine years. And then no new loan, good or bad, seemed to merit the risk.

As all the financial and economic upheaval of the Age of Leverage played out in the 1980s, one powerful group had remained oddly silent: the financial regulators in Washington. Benign neglect had prevailed, thanks to the Reagan era's emphasis on free-market thinking. "There was a feeling that the government should keep its hands off," recalled George Gould, undersecretary of the treasury in the mid-1980s. "The market would sort things out." About the only area in which financial authorities used their muscle was in prosecuting insider trading associated with takeovers—a relatively minor economic issue compared with the impact of piling an extra $1 trillion of debt on corporate America's books.

By 1988, however, even Treasury and Federal Reserve officials could see that market discipline had vanished. In 1987 and 1988, Wall Street firms and commercial banks banged out ever riskier buyouts and high-debt financings at breakneck speed. There didn't seem to be any mechanism to rein in lending as risks got greater. Instead, a speculative frenzy took hold, fueled by big loan-origination fees and the ease with which most risky loans could be passed off on naïve or unthinking investors.

Only the spectacle of a company as huge as RJR Nabisco being swamped with debt caused the first faint stirrings among regulators. In December 1988, Comptroller of the Currency Robert Clarke declared that buyout loans should be "carefully considered" before being made by banks. He added that banks might soon be required to carry higher loan-loss reserves for such loans. His remarks at the time were considered more of a trial balloon than a serious switch in policy. The Federal Reserve, the FDIC, and the comptroller of the currency divided up oversight of major banks, and it was usually the Fed that spoke with the most authority.

Before long, Fed chairman Alan Greenspan made his presence felt. In February 1989, the Fed followed up with guidelines that for the first time defined loans for highly leveraged transactions, or HLTs. All major banks would be required to report their HLT exposure to shareholders once a quarter, the Fed decreed. Such loans would get "greater scrutiny" from regulators, the agency added. In addition, regulators warned small banks about buying pieces of buyout loans from big banks without carefully analyzing the borrowing company's creditworthiness themselves.

For the first time, the elaborate daisy chains created by Bankers Trust, Citibank, and other big banks began to be called into question. In late 1988, Bankers Trust executives had breezily admitted originating $60 billion in buyout loans over the past few years, while hanging on to just $2.7 billion themselves. The remaining 95.5 percent of the loans had been shoveled into the portfolios of foreign banks, regional banks, insurance companies, and other loan buyers. As the Fed challenged such arrangements, the second-tier players began to perk up and ask themselves: Is this really a sound loan? Should we be adding it to our portfolio? Gung-ho loan syndicators at the big banks found it wasn't so easy anymore to promise a $500 million buyout loan, quickly skim off the up-front fees, and then peddle 90 percent or more of the loan to little banks. The big banks indulged in one last lending frenzy in the summer of 1989, showering $30 billion of loan commitments on the high-debt acquisition of Time Inc. by Warner Communications Inc., when Warner wanted only $11 billion. After that, bankers retreated for good.

The disappearance of second-tier lending banks became frightfully clear in October 1989 with the proposed buyout of UAL Inc., the parent of United Airlines. If ever a business was badly suited for leveraged buyouts, it was the airline industry, where cash flow was wildly unpredictable—veering up and down depending on fuel prices, the economic cycle, and even threats of terrorism. Capital spending needs for new planes were sizable every year, and they couldn't easily be postponed just to help service debt. A high-debt airline could be vulnerable to a cash squeeze or a loss of consumer confidence. Yet UAL chief executive Stephen Wolf, a die-hard optimist hungry for more riches, proposed a $6.8 billion buyout of UAL, anyway. Two big banks, Citibank and Chase Manhattan, together agreed to lend Wolf nearly half the money he needed, and to try to corral other banks for the rest. In loan meetings, Chase and Citi executives dangled the usual lures before other banks: up-front fees of 1.5 percent of any loans made.

This time it didn't work. American banks balked: the UAL buyout was "one of the worst buyout proposals we've seen," a banker at First Chicago declared. Then Japanese banks, which had begun providing as much as 50 percent of U.S. buyout loans in 1988 and 1989, refused to participate. Airlines are "a cyclical industry," a Japanese banker observed. "All the projections that the banks are working off are straight up." In the eyes of Japanese banks, the proposed UAL loans were too reckless to be made. Finally, at 2:54 P.M. on 13 October 1989, UAL issued a terse statement saying that after three months of efforts to complete the buyout, funds committed by various banks "are not sufficient."

The stock market panicked. In the next sixty-six minutes, the Dow Jones Industrial Average plunged 191 points, or 7 percent. Traders began to fear that the grand, glorious wave of takeovers that had made investors so rich was about to come to an end.

At first, KKR executives watched the UAL wipeout in bemused, I-told-you-so fashion. They hadn't joined the bidding for the airline; KKR associate Kevin Bousquette had quickly dismissed the deal as ill-conceived and had told Kravis not to look into it any further. As the failure of the UAL bank syndicate crossed news tickers, Kravis sat in his office spinning tales of his childhood for the benefit of journalist Anthony Bianco. But as the stock market crashed in earnest, KKR colleagues darted into Kravis's office to brief him on the calamity. The interview with Bianco dragged on for another thirty minutes and then Kravis, forcing a smile, asked his visitor if they could continue at a later date. "I think I'd better get back to work," Kravis nervously said.

Simultaneously, in 1989, the junk-bond mania began to dwindle, then collapse. For years, Drexel's Mike Milken and his acolytes had recruited new investors by preaching that defaults on these wonderfully high-yielding securities would be too rare to make a difference—perhaps 2 to 3 percent a year. From the mid-1970s through the mid-1980s, financial history appeared to bear out that view. In early 1989, however, the reckless underwritings by Drexel and its Wall Street imitators began to implode. Junk-bond companies began to default on their debts at a brisker pace. Eastern Airlines, Integrated Resources, and nearly a dozen other companies all failed to pay interest on their bonds in 1989's first half.

At first, Drexel loyalists tried to dismiss the pickup in defaults as a brief aberration. In April 1989, Fred Carr, the chairman of First Executive and the number-one buyer of junk bonds, declared: "The high-yield bond market continues to do very well. Each credit will stand on its own." But other money managers and economists saw greater cause for worry. The immense credit boom of the mid- and late 1980s had created legions of KKR imitators—tiny buyout boutiques able to borrow billions of dollars to pursue their acquisition dreams. Huge swaths of American industry had been swamped with debt, according to the dictates of second, third, and fourth waves of takeover artists. More than a few of these companies, it was becoming clear, lacked the means with which to pay off their debts. It would require only a modest pickup in defaults to transform junk bonds into truly horrid investments for S&Ls, insurance companies, and mutual funds.

By the fall of 1989, the junk-bond retreat turned into a rout. Combined assets of all junk-bond mutual funds peaked at $35.2 billion in June 1989. They inched down slightly over the next two months, then tumbled more than $4 billion in the last four months of 1989. Investors, reading about the pickup in defaults, began to pull their money out. Those who left their money in found that the value of their junk-bond holdings declined week after week.

Savings and loan associations, some of which had been voracious buyers of junk bonds, began to run for the exits, too. As part of an S&L bail-out bill passed in August 1989, Congress required federally insured thrift institutions to sell their junk-bond holdings by 1994. Many started their selling right away. As a result, the great Drexel financing machine, which had once pushed junk bonds into the hands of willing buyers, began to sputter. At an investors' conference in late 1989, Drexel executive Joseph Bencivenga conceded to investors: "You can't be force-fed something you're not hungry for."

The more sentimental types in the junk-bond market felt sure that if

Milken had remained in his powerful position at Drexel, the junk-bond boom might have kept going a bit longer. In March 1989, however, after a two-and-a-half-year government investigation, Milken was indicted on ninety-eight counts of racketeering and securities fraud. Vowing to fight the charges, he resigned from Drexel and formed his own firm. All the same, Milken conceded that the pressure of government prosecution had left him powerless in the financial arena he once had dominated. Asked in May 1989 about his influence in the junk-bond market, Milken sheepishly replied: "I've been away from that for a year."

For KKR, the growing signs of a credit crunch meant trouble. Even though the buyout firm wasn't seeking to finance any new buyouts in 1989, its existing portfolio began to take a pounding. An early casualty involved KKR's plans for Beatrice, the Chicago food conglomerate, which hadn't yet been sold. Beatrice in late 1989 proposed to issue $300 million of junk bonds so it could pay a big dividend to KKR and its investment partnerships. A year or two earlier, bond buyers would have salivated for the chance to own more securities linked to KKR's good name. This time, however, bond buyers balked. With most of the proceeds going into KKR's hands instead of for plant expansion, "You get concerned about the purpose of such a deal," said a top portfolio manager at an Illinois insurance company who declined to bid for the bonds. KKR and Beatrice eventually managed to complete the financing, but were forced to pay higher interest rates than they wanted.

Other credit troubles begin to nibble at the KKR portfolio. In the summer of 1989, the smallest company in its buyout portfolio, Seaman Furniture, fell far short of its operating-profit targets, and faced defaults on its debt. KKR had paid too much to buy Seaman in 1987, KKR partner Paul Raether readily admitted to reporters. Having made that brief mea culpa, however, Raether and associate Cliff Robbins shunted most of the blame onto Seaman's management and the weak Long Island, New York, economy where Seaman operated. The KKR men let the retailer's chief executive resign, hired a replacement, and restructured Seaman's debt. The KKR partners also pumped in an extra $7 million of their own money, a measure that helped keep Seaman afloat for another two years; it finally filed for bankruptcy in January 1992.

Even as Raether and Robbins dealt with the Seaman mess, another problem buyout clamored for attention. It was SCI Television, a spinoff from the 1985 Storer Broadcasting buyout that KKR executive Ted Ammon had negotiated. By mid-1989, KKR had already made a fortune from selling the various pieces of its Storer buyout. The buyout firm was willing to write off much of its $100 million tail-end investment in SCI Television, of which 55 percent was owned by broadcast entrepreneur George Gillett and 45 percent was owned by KKR. Some junk-bond holders, however, who had lent $400 million to finance the SCI Television deal in late 1987, weren't so amenable. They had been drawn to the transaction in part because of KKR's glittering reputation—and if there were financial problems, they wanted KKR to pay.

The most strident SCI Television bondholder was Stan Phelps, a bald Yale graduate with mottled teeth who operated a small "vulture fund" that invested in distressed securities. Other people bought bonds directly from Drexel at 100 cents on the dollar in big syndicates; Phelps was a loner who waited until troubled companies' bonds had sunk to 10 or 20 cents on the dollar, then snapped them up from frustrated holders. He specialized in making life hell for companies that couldn't pay their debts. Shortly after SCI Television missed an interest payment on 15 November 1989, Phelps threatened to push the company into bankruptcy proceedings and have it liquidated—a process that would put cash in his hands and leave zero for KKR. Then Phelps began bombarding Gillett and KKR with blistering letters and phone calls. "You reneged on your contract to pay interest," Phelps wrote Gillett. "You, Drexel, Kravis, and Milken are entitled to nothing." In other letters, Phelps lambasted Kravis as "a junior partner of a convicted felon," Drexel Burnham Lambert.*

Kravis couldn't believe a small-time bondholder like Phelps needed to be taken seriously. Yet with fascination and dread, Kravis silently listened to Phelps's harangues on each conference call. "Don't forget, George Gillett and Henry Kravis are working for me now," Phelps scolded KKR's junior man on the project, associate Scott Stuart. And in a narrow legal sense, Phelps was right. After protracted negotiations, KKR and Gillett just barely managed to restructure the company's debts and avoid bankruptcy. But the price for KKR was humiliating. Its ownership stake dropped to 19 percent from 45 percent. Kravis was forced to resign his board seat at the company. Bondholders like Phelps got new bonds, while KKR was forced to write down to zero some $100 million of SCI Television preferred stock held by its limited partner investors.

Then much bigger trouble struck at one of KKR's major buyouts: Jim Walter Corporation. At first, the problems seemed to have nothing to do with the sudden tightening of credit. They involved what to KKR was an

---

*Drexel in December 1988 had pled guilty to six felony charges of violating U.S. securities laws, most pertaining to its activities in the junk-bond and takeover markets.

obscure side issue: the company's liability for asbestos-injury claims relating to insulation that one of Jim Walter's subsidiaries had sold in the 1950s and 1960s. Before long, however, the asbestos issue became tangled up with the ugliest creditor dispute KKR had ever encountered.

At the time KKR had negotiated to buy Jim Walter in 1987, the Florida conglomerate was posting robust earnings from its main divisions, which built homes, mined coal, and sold pipe. The one blight on the company's record was its Celotex building-products subsidiary, which, although it posted more than $25 million a year in operating profits, was deluged with more than 60,000 personal-injury claims relating to the asbestos insulation it once had sold. Even a top Jim Walter adviser, investment banker Steven Waters, conceded that Celotex probably had "substantial negative value" to the overall corporation. Still, Mike Tokarz, the KKR associate doing most of the work on the Jim Walter deal, was itching to bring a buyout to completion. For months, he looked for ways to slough off the asbestos problem. "We're still researching mechanics, etc., on the isolation of Celotex," Tokarz wrote in a fateful work memo in early 1987. Eventually, he thought he saw a way. KKR agreed to buy the entire Jim Walter company; but on the evening that the transaction closed, Tokarz spent four hours signing documents on behalf of twenty-nine new companies. Many of those entities—in best KKR tradition—existed for only a few hours. When the signing was done, all the valuable parts of the old Jim Walter Corporation were regrouped under a new banner: Hillsborough Holdings Corporation. Shunted to the side was the old corporate shell of Jim Walter, which didn't take on any of the buyout debt and ended up owning only one operating business: Celotex. In the spring of 1988, KKR sold Jim Walter/Celotex to entrepreneur Gary Drummond for just $5 million in cash and another $95 million in notes with lenient payment terms. Less than two and a half years later, Celotex ended up in bankruptcy proceedings, unable to handle its torrent of asbestos claims. But Tokarz didn't think KKR needed to worry any more about Celotex's fate.

Tokarz was wrong.

On 13 and 14 September 1989, Kravis, Roberts, and Tokarz found themselves in a place they wished they had never seen: the drab nine-story state courthouse in Beaumont, Texas. All three KKR executives were being sued as part of a giant, $3 billion suit against KKR, Hillsborough Holdings, Drexel, and several other powerful entities. The impetus for the suit: Celotex's unwillingness after leaving KKR's hands to pay compensation to asbestos victims. Celotex was still solvent at the time, but its purse strings had tightened greatly. A well-organized pack of attorneys for asbestos victims decided that if Celotex wouldn't pay, someone else should. In a suit filed in July 1989, the attorneys went after all major parties connected with the Jim Walter buyout, contending that the deal and the subsequent Celotex sale were a "fraudulent conveyance."

Leading the Beaumont assault was flamboyant Houston attorney Stephen Susman. Susman had never met any of the KKR executives before, but in a preliminary hearing on a KKR motion to be dropped as defendants, Susman decided to depict Kravis and Roberts as villains. In his opening remarks, Susman denounced "people who sit in their offices in New York and pull invisible strings to move huge sums of wealth and commerce around." Before the court, Susman portrayed himself as the selfless champion of 81,000 victims of asbestosis. At one point, he pulled out a tattered bag of asbestos made by a Celotex subsidiary years earlier. And he thundered: "This LBO, which put hundreds of millions of dollars in the defendants' pockets and involved in excess of $2.5 billion—this LBO didn't take care of us. In fact, it left us out in the cold, and we want to do something about it."

The KKR men were stunned and horrified by Susman's ability to whip up anti–Wall Street sentiment. Scornfully, Susman referred to KKR's shedding of Celotex as "magic" and "a seriously complex series of transactions." For the next two days, Susman and other lawyers depicted KKR, Hillsborough, Jim Walter Corporation, and Celotex as part of a seamless industrial combine. Kravis, Tokarz, and Walter bristled, but there wasn't much they could do. Tokarz contended that KKR had acted properly all along, separating Celotex from the rest of Hillsborough because of bank financing requirements and tax reasons. When one of KKR's own attorneys from Simpson Thacher asked Tokarz in court if there had been any desire to short-change the asbestos claimants, Tokarz responded: "Absolutely not." But the labyrinthine nature of KKR's regrouping suggested otherwise.

Then Susman began to sting Kravis and Roberts about their immense wealth. When Roberts insisted that he had owned no significant property in Texas since leaving the state as a teenager, Susman began ticking off details of $1.7 million that Roberts had invested in a Houston real estate partnership. After insinuating that such amounts were insignificant to a man with Roberts's fortune, Susman said: "I just need to find out whether maybe something slipped your mind."

The next day, Susman grilled Kravis in the same fashion about the Jim

Walter buyout itself. "Now did KKR & Co. receive any fees in this transaction?" Susman asked Kravis at one point.

"Yes," Kravis replied.

"What fee did they receive?"

"One fee we received was a $35 million fee for putting the transaction together." A moment later, Kravis owned up to a second fee: $500,000 a year for monitoring Hillsborough after the buyout.

Quickly, Susman contrasted those amounts with the mere $1.5 million that the KKR partners themselves had invested in the post-buyout company. "Now what kind of return is that?" Susman snapped.

"That's a fairly good return," Kravis conceded.

"I would say so. Now, in fact, you haven't even told us the whole picture yet, have you, Mr. Kravis? I want you to tell the court how much money you're receiving each year from those forty or fifty institutional investors."

The "standard" fees, Kravis replied—1½ percent a year of the money committed to KKR. Kravis didn't complete the math, but Susman had made his point. KKR's annual fees from its limited partners at that time totaled about $50 million. The way the Hillsborough buyout had been set up, the KKR partners couldn't help but profit, no matter how the company fared. For the first time in their careers, Kravis and Roberts realized how ugly all their success could be made to look. It wasn't at all appealing to be so rich in a contentious setting.

Two weeks later, Susman and the asbestosis victims' attorneys won the first skirmish of what looked to be a long battle with Kravis and Roberts. Beaumont judge Gary Sanderson denied the KKR partners' request to be dropped from a long list of defendants in the overall Celotex suit. The entire case should go to trial at a later date, Judge Sanderson wrote.

For the KKR men, the prospect of a Texas trial was terrifying. One of America's biggest oil companies, Texaco Inc., had ended up in bankruptcy proceedings just a few years earlier after losing an $11 billion lawsuit in a Texas court. All of KKR's artful 1987–88 maneuvering with Celotex might hold up in a federal court, or a Florida court. But Texas state court was another matter entirely.

Before long, the Beaumont debacle started to turn into financial torment. In his preliminary ruling, Judge Sanderson barred KKR from selling off any more pieces of Hillsborough—impeding the buyout firm's main strategy for realizing profits. Hillsborough in September 1989 reported weak quarterly operating results and had to dip into cash reserves to cover its quarterly interest payments. The company's junk bonds started to slump in price, dropping to about 80 cents on the dollar in October 1989 from 101 cents on the dollar just two months earlier.

Ordinarily, bond price fluctuations didn't matter to KKR; it had already borrowed the money it needed. In the case of Hillsborough, however, wiggles in the bond prices had life-and-death impact for the buyout firm. Hillsborough had issued what were known as "reset" bonds. These securities' interest rates were due to be adjusted every year so that the bonds would continue to trade at 101 cents on the dollar. That reset feature, concocted by Drexel in the late 1980s, was meant to be a boon to bondholders. In theory, bonds that stumbled in price could be restored to full value by having Drexel reset their interest rates at higher levels. In the case of Hillsborough, bonds yielding $14\frac{5}{8}$ percent could have their rates adjusted to 16 percent, 20 percent, or even higher. Once the bonds started to plummet in price, however, the reset mechanism would turn into a financial death trap. Simple arithmetic suggested that truly giant interest rates would be needed to get the bonds back up to 101 cents on the dollar, yet paying such interest rates, of 25 percent or more, could quickly bankrupt any company—no matter how healthy it was before hand. Then the bonds would collapse again. In extreme cases, no interest rate, no matter how high, would be able to make good on the promise of such reset bonds.

In the first week of December 1989, Drexel investment banker Alison Mass called Tokarz from California with grim news. The bonds can't be reset, she told him. Some 2,500 miles away, Tokarz sputtered in rage. "You gave us a head fake," he snapped. "You said it could be done, and then it couldn't."

Tokarz called up Mass's longtime boss, Peter Ackerman, to fume at him, too. Ackerman was chillingly calm. "It's the market, Mike," Ackerman said. Sometimes market conditions were friendly, and Drexel could get low rates for its clients. Sometimes conditions were harsh, and deals couldn't be done so easily. Mighty as KKR was, it couldn't fight the entire junk-bond market.

With Mass's phone call, Hillsborough had fallen into what Tokarz later called "a technical abyss." If KKR couldn't reset the bonds' interest rate as promised, the bonds would come due years ahead of schedule. Bondholders would be entitled to get all $624 million of their money back on 2 January 1990. The guarantee on pages 91 and 94 of the bond prospectus was iron-clad. But Hillsborough couldn't keep that promise. Hillsborough had at most $100 million in ready cash. The Beaumont court had effectively blocked Hillsborough from selling any more assets to raise funds, and the mounting credit crunch left KKR with no hope of arranging bank loans to pay off the bondholders. Hillsborough was in deep trouble. The only faint hope of avoiding default, Tokarz believed, was to persuade bondholders to swap their reset bonds for new securities that KKR could brew up in a hurry.

Feverishly, Tokarz began to shuffle together financial ideas. Maybe Hillsborough's coal unit could issue some more bonds. Kravis and Roberts anxiously spurred him on. But bondholders were leery. When Tokarz, Hillsborough executives, and Drexel representatives set out to visit bondholders in Chicago, Boston, and Los Angeles, they were met with distrust and scorn. "KKR wasn't forthright in its road show," said Ken Urbaszewski, a portfolio manager at Kemper Insurance Co. and a major holder of Hillsborough junk bonds. "They stretched the truth by a wide margin."

The wariest bondholders were at Fidelity Investments, the big Boston mutual-fund complex that for years had been a faithful buyer of KKR-sponsored junk bonds. In the late 1980s, Fidelity had used toll-free phone numbers and ads in *Money* magazine to lure some $1.5 billion from ordinary Americans into junk-bond mutual funds. Fidelity had already plunked more than $30 million into Hillsborough bonds. In late 1989, however, Fidelity's top executives began having a serious change of heart about the junk-bond market.

Leading the resistance at Fidelity was Gary Burkhead, the firm's forty-eight-year-old chief investment officer and a part-time vestry member of the Episcopal church. Everything about Burkhead projected an air of rectitude: his three-piece navy blue suits with watch chain, his crisply parted, close-cropped hair, and especially his desk. Other people might leave papers strewn about; Burkhead stacked all his work into neat piles and then perched glass paperweights atop each bundle, protecting this tidy order from any disturbing breeze. In the fall of 1989, with all the earnestness of a Jimmy Stewart character in a Frank Capra film, Burkhead stepped forward to do battle.

"Bondholders should be very firm in dealing with people who borrow," Burkhead later said. "They are debtors. They have obligations." He spoke frequently of fairness, and obligations, and promises that had to be fulfilled. It was a language that KKR had seldom heard since such old-time lenders as Prudential's Ray Charles had retired in the early 1980s.

A showdown was building between the people who had built up fortunes with leverage, and the people who had lent them the money.

Gadflies like Stan Phelps were now being joined by mainstream investors like Gary Burkhead. All these lenders were growing angry and bitter, convinced that they had been financial dupes who got little of the profits when things went well, and took most of the losses when deals soured. "Bondholders and banks have provided a lot of money for LBOs," Burkhead explained in an interview. "It's important that when things change, they assert their rights as strongly as possible."

Having set Fidelity's strategy, Burkhead needed a street fighter to carry it out. He found his man in Josh Berman, a feisty New York lawyer at the firm of Kramer, Levin, Nessen, Kamin & Frankel. Day after day, Berman poked at Tokarz with a picador's skill. Berman adopted a tone of exaggerated friendliness in their phone calls, beginning nearly every sentence with a boisterous "Michael!" Then he would sneer at Tokarz's proposals to retire the reset bonds by issuing new securities to Hillsborough holders. KKR wasn't doing enough, Berman kept insisting. KKR should surrender 20-percent ownership in Hillsborough to bondholders. Or else KKR should guarantee to pay off all of Hillsborough's junk bonds within six months, regardless of various contingencies that Tokarz kept citing.

Tokarz grew frosty and peeved at this taunting. Berman's demands struck him as outrageous. "There's nothing I can give you," Tokarz told Berman in a phone conversation in early December 1989.

But the picador wouldn't stop. "Michael!" Berman jabbed back. "KKR didn't get to be KKR by being unresourceful or unimaginative. Think of something! There must be something you can do."

Simultaneously, the asbestosis victims' attorneys began hammering on KKR even harder. In mid-December, top Hillsborough executives and KKR associates Mike Tokarz and Perry Golkin met with a half dozen of the asbestos lawyers at an Atlanta airport hotel, in the hopes that the lawyers might settle their Celotex claims on terms that KKR could tolerate. A few minutes into the talks, Tokarz and Golkin realized that peaceful negotiations would be impossible. One after another, the lawyers lashed KKR for its conduct. Several of them proclaimed that Texas was a great state in which to bring cases to trial, and said that they were looking for a knockout. "We're going after all your assets," one of the lawyers declared at one point. "We're going to take the paintings off your walls."

Tokarz was furious. Golkin was shocked. No one talked to KKR like this. But the asbestosis victims' attorneys made their living by taking on giant companies and fighting by whatever means they could. That was how they won millions for asbestosis victims—and millions in contingency fees for themselves. One of the scrappiest attorneys, Pittsburgh lawyer Tom Henderson, had helped plunge one major asbestos maker into bankruptcy in 1982. Seven years later, he proudly told a reporter, it was still there. And the way the courts were set up, with every suit entitled to a full trial, the KKR men seemed almost powerless to stop Henderson and his fellow lawyers.

Deeply frightened by the idea of a full trial in Texas, the KKR executives in early December asked their top lawyers at Simpson Thacher and Latham & Watkins if there was any way out. Yes, the KKR lawyers answered, but it was a bleak solution. If the asbestos lawyers wouldn't back off, and if bondholders wouldn't agree to Tokarz's swap proposal, Hillsborough could file for bankruptcy protection in its home district, back in Florida federal court. Doing so would jeopardize the value of Hillsborough's equity and be a huge blow to KKR's prestige. In one swift stroke, however, it would move all the asbestos litigation out of Texas— where it was conceivable that KKR and Hillsborough could be obliterated—and into Hillsborough's home territory. Florida state law was much more favorable to the company on asbestos issues; and a hometown judge in Tampa, Florida, might look on the buyout a bit more benignly than Beaumont's Judge Sanderson. "I don't think KKR wanted to file for bankruptcy," Simpson Thacher attorney Richard Garvey later said. "But once they knew it might be necessary, they started to appreciate the advantages of filing."

The most forceful argument in favor of a bankruptcy filing came from George Roberts. "Did you ever see the movie *Platoon*?" he asked colleagues. "Well, there's this scene at the end where the captain's troops are being overrun in Laos. There's no way he can get them out. So he ends up calling an air strike on his own position, knowing that it will stop the enemy. Then at least he can get some of his men out. That's what we're doing," Roberts concluded. "Tough times call for tough things."

Within a week, KKR's air strike began. Kravis and Tokarz called a meeting of all the bondholders on 19 December at Simpson Thacher's Lexington Avenue offices in New York. They met in a thirtieth-floor office, just across the hall from the giant conference room where Kravis and Roberts ten months earlier had signed the documents that completed history's biggest takeover, the RJR Nabisco buyout. On that occasion, hundreds of people had sipped champagne, drunk toasts to one another, and hailed the KKR partners as conquering heroes. This time, there was no celebration.

First Tokarz, then the chairman of Jim Walter Corporation, sixty-six-year-old Jim Walter himself, and finally Henry Kravis explained that Hillsborough really might file for bankruptcy protection if bondholders didn't agree to the exchange offer. "I've been with this company forty-three years," Jim Walter said. "This is a hell of a way to go out. But if that's the way it has to be done, then it will be done."

Kravis was equally blunt. "Don't think that we won't file Chapter 11 because of what it will do to our business," he said. "We're willing to bear that risk."

The two sides broke for lunch, then met again around two P.M. One last time, Kravis tried to cut a deal, falling back on the same language he had used as a young investment banker in the 1970s. "Look," Kravis told the bondholders that remained. "Business is based on trust and confidence. If there was something we could do for you now, we would. But we can't. Trust us that if by June 30, if you're not out of the bonds—we can't say we'll do something. But trust us." Then Kravis turned to the bondholders' leader, Fidelity lawyer Josh Berman. "Will that do it?" Kravis asked.

A decade earlier, even six months earlier, the answer would have been yes. The warmth and sincerity of Henry Kravis had opened doors everywhere. Bankers and pension officers and presidents of brick companies had believed in the ebullient Oklahoman with the sunny smile and the big blue eyes. For most of the 1980s, people around the globe had jumped at the chance to do business with a group as successful as Kravis and KKR.

But times had changed. "That's not my call," Berman said. "I can take it back to my people. If you want to talk directly to them, you can. But I suggest we negotiate and work something out."

Kravis refused. He had already made one direct approach to Fidelity's top brass a week before, and had been snubbed. Fidelity chairman Edward "Ned" Johnson wouldn't return Kravis's phone calls. Johnson's number two, Gary Burkhead, did talk to Kravis, but his message was chilly. KKR's proposals were "inadequate" and "off the mark," Burkhead had told Kravis. If Kravis wanted to push Hillsborough into bankruptcy, that was his business.*

---

*Just before the Christmas holidays, Tokarz and Berman sniped at each other one last time. On the final Friday before Christmas, Tokarz sent the Fidelity lawyer a bottle of Chivas Regal Scotch, with a hopeful card reading: "Looking for Peace and Happiness in the New Year—Michael Tokarz." Berman wasn't appeased one bit. "Anyone who knows me knows that I don't like liquor," Berman later said. He immediately sent his secretary to the corner liquor store to buy a slightly

At eight P.M. on 27 December, lawyers entered the federal courthouse in Tampa to do something they had never done for KKR before—put a Fortune 500 company into Chapter 11 bankruptcy proceedings. KKR's final attempt to placate bondholders had failed. The buyout firm had wanted 80 percent of Hillsborough's senior noteholders to agree to Tokarz's latest swap proposal; 79 percent had done so. It had wanted 89 percent of senior subordinated holders to agree to the swap; 76 percent had done so. Several bondholders had seen signs that, in the last two weeks of December, Kravis and Tokarz had stopped trying to win over recalcitrant bondholders. The troubles facing KKR and Hillsborough were so vast that Florida bankruptcy court actually seemed like sanctuary.

For a few weeks, Hillsborough had the shameful distinction of being the biggest buyout company ever to file for bankruptcy. But on 15 January 1990, it was surpassed by the retail empire of Canadian developer Robert Campeau, which collapsed with more than $6 billion of debts. In a wild acquisition spree in the late 1980s, Campeau had used borrowed money to buy the companies that owned prestigious department-store chains such as Bloomingdale's, Ann Taylor, and Jordan Marsh. As strong as those companies were, the debt loads that Campeau took on were lethal. His bankruptcy filing sent shock waves throughout the financial community.

Then, in early February, the firm most closely associated with the Age of Leverage—Drexel Burnham Lambert—found itself fighting for survival. Drexel's own financial health had been sapped by the collapse of the junk-bond market, which eroded the value of $1.5 billion of junk bonds that the firm itself owned. Its cash reserves were drained even more when Drexel's top management, in a bizarre decision, decided in January 1990 to pay more than $250 million in bonuses to the firm's top deal-makers—as if Drexel still were as profitable as ever. Finally, on 12 February 1990, Drexel ran out of cash. The banks and other securities firms that provided it with routine short-term loans in the commercial-paper market said they wouldn't lend Drexel any more money. Drexel chief executive Fred Joseph pleaded with top officials at the New York Fed to intercede and arrange emergency loans to his firm. He was refused.

---

costlier bottle of Scotch. By return messenger, he sent his countergift to KKR's offices six blocks away, along with a note reading: "Looking for Prosperity and Good Fortune in the New Year—Josh Berman."

On 13 February 1990, Drexel itself filed for bankruptcy protection from its creditors.

People at KKR were stunned. All the vital pieces of KKR's world were falling apart, much faster than Kravis, Roberts, and their associates could fully comprehend. Until Drexel's announcement, the KKR men hadn't imagined that such a powerful firm, and such a longtime ally, could perish so quickly. "It's as if Drexel was vaporized with a laser gun," Roberts said in disbelief. The afternoon that Drexel went bust, one of the KKR associates phoned a Drexel investment banker and innocently asked: "What is this going to do to our relationship?"

"You don't understand," the Drexel banker replied. "There is no relationship left."

A few months later, almost all traces of Drexel had been obliterated. In June 1990, liquidators moved into the New York headquarters of Drexel Burnham Lambert and put up for sale all of the firm's property, from computers to coat racks. Some 6,000 shoppers and curiosity seekers streamed through hallways where some of the legendary deals of the 1980s had been put together. College students in shorts and T-shirts rifled through abandoned desks, picking out business cards for the fun of it. A thick blue volume of deal-maker Leon Black's confidential papers found a new use: as a doorstop in the sixth-floor men's room. For investment bankers and casual browsers alike, the dismantling of Wall Street's most powerful firm of the 1980s was a sobering and melancholy sight. Walking through Drexel's empty corridors, a security guard commented: "This is like an estate sale after a funeral."

Surrounded by the wreckage of his financial era, Henry Kravis became a very vulnerable man. Even when talking to his closest allies—KKR's limited partners—Kravis felt pushed onto the defensive. Trying to organize his thoughts for a speech to the limited partners in the spring of 1990, Kravis drafted a speech that, some colleagues believed, was meant to answer the unspoken question: "Is Henry out of control?" In his remarks Kravis tried to spell out reasons why the answer was no, why his financial backers still should like him and trust him.

For much of 1989, Kravis had handled success badly, coming across as too flamboyant and arrogant for the tastes of people with whom he needed to do business. Big parts of the business community that had found KKR's rise incomprehensible and frightening now yearned for the firm's collapse. Newsletter writer James Grant, a scathing critic of high-debt finance who was sometimes described as Wall Street's version of H. L. Mencken, went so far as to prepare a mock newspaper advertisement proclaiming that all the assets of KKR had been sold in bankruptcy proceedings for $57,894. The purported buyer: Kravis's longtime rival Ted Forstmann. If Drexel had crashed, it seemed only a matter of time before its number-one borrowing client, KKR, would be headed for oblivion, too.

Within KKR, however, the firm's associates began to see a remarkable change in Kravis. In the face of adversity, a humbler, more stoic side of Kravis began to emerge. When Seaman, SCI, and Hillsborough went sour, Kravis didn't try to blame Robbins, Ammon, and Tokarz—even though the three associates were most directly responsible for KKR's troubles on those deals. Instead, one Monday morning, Kravis pulled together all the firm's partners and associates at a conference table so he could pin some of the blame on himself.

"All of us at the firm approved these deals," Kravis declared. "And that begins with George and me. We're all responsible. And we're all going to do what we can to fix them."

In the next few weeks, KKR's partners and associates took their cue from Kravis and began huddling together far more than ever before. They swapped ideas on how to salvage their deals, and reassured themselves that they were doing the right thing even if a hostile outside world was destroying much of the firm's handiwork. Morose about his failure with Hillsborough, Mike Tokarz in particular drew reassurances from everyone within the firm, from Kravis and Roberts to the secretaries and receptionists.

At many other citadels of high-debt finance, a vicious form of infighting took hold in late 1989 and early 1990. One of KKR's oldest rivals, the nineteen-year-old buyout firm of Gibbons Green van Amerongen, fractured into two firms as its partners blamed one another for various failures. Wesray Capital—the firm that had become the pied piper of the buyout business with its 100-to-1 payoff from the Gibson Greeting acquisition in 1983—turned practically moribund after its two founding partners quit. Buyout departments at Merrill Lynch, Shearson Lehman Brothers, and other Wall Street firms were racked with defections. Proud, defensive deal-makers dodged responsibility for failure and instead tried to blame every setback on one another. In so doing, they sped the collapse of their own firms. KKR, at least, was free of such finger-pointing.

Before long, KKR's cohesion would face its ultimate test. The biggest buyout ever, the $26.4 billion purchase of RJR Nabisco, was in serious trouble.

13
Fear, Humbling, and Survival

Until about 3:10 P.M. on the afternoon of Friday, 26 January 1990, everyone at KKR believed that RJR Nabisco was winning the battle against the big debts imposed by its buyout. The KKR executives were so confident that the company's financial picture was brightening that on that afternoon they invited three Wall Street firms to "the Fishbowl"—the main, glass-enclosed conference room at RJR's Manhattan headquarters—to talk about ways that the tobacco and food company might refinance its debt more cheaply. Brisk, upbeat talk filled the air.

People barely noticed when RJR's chief financial officer, Karl von der Heyden, was summoned out by a phone call during the Goldman, Sachs presentation. When von der Heyden returned, however, everyone could see instantly that something had just gone terribly wrong. Instead of quietly taking his seat, he stopped at the doorway and stared straight ahead. His face was slack. Catching the group's attention, von der Heyden relayed the jarring message he had just been told moments earlier.

"You're not going to believe this," von der Heyden said. "But our bonds have been downgraded by Moody's."

Indignant voices rang out. "That's terrible." "Preposterous." "Shit." "How could they do that?"

Struggling hard to stay focused, von der Heyden spelled out the bad news. A week earlier, top RJR executives had briefed Moody's Investors Service, one of the top two credit-rating agencies, on RJR's finances. The meeting hadn't gone as well as RJR executives had hoped. A young Moody's analyst, Gloria Vila, had kept peppering RJR executives about their company's ill-fated efforts to launch Uptown, a cigarette meant to be marketed mainly to blacks. A firestorm of public protest had forced RJR to kill the Uptown project. Von der Heyden had tried to explain that, despite all the embarrassment, the Uptown mess had had almost no financial impact on RJR. Vila had kept pressing the issue, however, and now after taking a week to reach her decision, she had just phoned von der Heyden to announce that Moody's was lowering the credit rating on RJR's bonds. "Marketing risks are evident" in the tobacco business, Vila declared in a four-page press release. RJR's cash flow and its ability to service its debts might suffer.

A year or two earlier, KKR and von der Heyden could have laughed away Moody's action. No one had cared back then about credit ratings; few corporations had bothered pursuing Moody's top ranking of triple-A. The big money was made by financiers who invited dicey, "speculative" ratings of double-B and lower for their debt. But in the nervous financial markets of early 1990, Vila's report filled junk-bond investors with the terror of a police siren wailing outside an after-hours nightclub.

Moments after von der Heyden sat down, the top member of the Goldman, Sachs team, vice chairman Robert Rubin, was yanked out of the meeting by another phone call. Moody's had just disseminated its downgrading of RJR on the news wires, he learned, and the news was causing the junk-bond market to crash as never before. Fearful that RJR might be headed for default, panicky investors had decided to dump junk bonds of all types. They could ask questions later. Bond prices had dropped 10 percent or more within twenty minutes. In many cases, frightened sellers couldn't find buyers for their bonds at any price. To Goldman's bond traders, this was Armageddon.

When Rubin stepped back into the meeting room, he too was shaken. "Please excuse me," he told RJR's chief executive Lou Gerstner. "I'm needed downtown at the firm. I apologize, but I have to leave." The meeting collapsed in disarray, as KKR executives headed to a Quotron terminal and watched with disbelief and horror the free-fall in RJR's bond prices. By the end of that day, RJR's biggest junk-bond issues had sunk to trade at just 66 cents on the dollar. The next Monday the bonds skidded even further, to 56 cents on the dollar. Brazilian bank debt was worth nearly as much.

At first, the KKR executives couldn't believe the storm of trouble that descended on them. They angrily blamed the financial cataclysm on Vila, calling her "inexperienced" and worse. Unwilling to believe that anyone savvy could question RJR's financial health, Kravis and Roberts conjured up psychological theories to explain why the young Moody's analyst might bear a grudge against America's second-largest tobacco company. Within KKR, denials of any serious trouble filled the hallways, as did expressions of contempt for outsiders. This time, however, it was KKR that was out of touch. Asked to choose between Gloria Vila or the juggernaut that KKR commanded, investors overwhelmingly believed the thirty-one-year-old analyst with the four-page report.

For the next six months, Kravis and Roberts would battle against financial disaster. Imbedded in the RJR buyout, which the KKR men in late 1988 had regarded as some of their cleverest work, was a catastrophic design flaw involving reset bonds. In dire echoes of the Hillsborough Holdings dilemma, the KKR men again confronted the financial poison of bonds that might not be resettable. Instead of gliding easily toward more riches on their biggest buyout ever, the KKR executives would struggle through the first half of 1990 to avoid a wipeout that could have produced the largest U.S. corporate collapse in history.

As the reset drama played out in the winter and spring of 1990, Kravis suffered one humiliation after another from the onetime facilitators of the buyout firm's vast desires. Junk-bond buyers openly hissed at one of his speeches. A commercial banker suggested that Kravis stand in the lobby of his bank each morning and shower the bank chairman with gold coins, as a gesture of KKR's desperate need for new bank money. In the most terrifying snub of all, prominent takeover lawyer Marty Lipton, whose firm had smoothed the way for so many of KKR's giant acquisitions in the 1980s, warned Kravis in a private lunch that a bankruptcy filing by RJR might be KKR's only option.

Humbled at every turn, Kravis, Roberts, and their associates rallied together and looked for a way out. Executives at the buyout firm ran financial models through their personal computers at such a rate that they sketched out more than 200 scenarios aimed at rescuing RJR from its financial plight. Associates Ted Ammon, Scott Stuart, and Cliff Robbins filled entire offices with stacks of gray and blue binders, analyzing every possible scenario. "We're going to solve this together," Kravis stoically told the people within his firm. At a time when many of Wall Street's 1980s buccaneers wrecked their careers and spitefully turned on each other, the KKR men kept their unity. "This was our future," Kravis later said. "If this didn't work out, there would go fourteen years, out the window."

Dick Beattie, the veteran Simpson Thacher lawyer who had advised Kravis since the early 1970s, expressed the stakes for KKR even more bluntly. "Don't let anyone kid you," Beattie later said. "This was about the survival of the firm."

From Gloria Vila Day onward, it became taboo within KKR to breath even a word about the origins of the lethal RJR reset bonds. And with good reason: The bonds existed only because of a weird, accidental chain of events in the midst of the frenzied takeover battle for RJR. Most of the time in the autumn of 1988, the KKR negotiating team had controlled its decisions masterfully. But there was one crucial slip—a mix-up between KKR executive Ted Ammon and Drexel's Peter Ackerman.

Partway through the November 1988 bidding for RJR Nabisco, the outside investment bankers running the auction began dropping hints about what kind of bid would win. One message was to be wary of financing a bid by using junk bonds that would be pushed into sharehold-ers' hands in exchange for their RJR stock. The two investment bankers most actively shaping the auction, Lazard Frères partner Felix Rohatyn and Dillon, Read executive Franklin Hobbs IV, both viewed such "cram-down" junk bonds with disdain, believing that many such securities simply weren't worth anywhere near 100 cents on the dollar. "We were tired of hearing investment bankers' bull about why 70 cents of paper should be regarded as a dollar," a Lazard partner later said. "Cash is king," the Dillon and Lazard men repeatedly told bidders.

The trouble was, KKR liked issuing junk bonds. It had used them aggressively from 1984 onward as part of its bidding arsenal. So part-way through the six-week-long bidding for RJR, Drexel deal-maker Peter Ackerman and KKR executive Ted Ammon tried to keep junk bonds in the game while soothing the RJR auctioneers' concerns. The week of 14 November 1988, Ammon and Ackerman told a midlevel Lazard executive, Jonathan Kagan, that KKR wanted to issue at least $3 billion of cram-down junk bonds, but that KKR might be willing to recalibrate those bonds' interest rates in a year or two. Kagan was in-trigued. If ever a financially solid junk bond could be created, this sounded like the right approach. Ammon didn't outright commit KKR to all of Ackerman's proposals, but Kagan thought this point was worth negotiating some more.

Then, on the morning of Saturday, 19 November 1988—in bizarre circumstances—the terms of KKR's junk bonds were crystallized. The night before, KKR had submitted a formal $94-a-share bid for RJR. On Saturday, a twenty-person KKR negotiating team arrived at the offices of Skadden, Arps, Slate, Meagher & Flom, RJR's law firm, to explain its bid.

Drexel's Ackerman was supposed to talk about the junk bonds, but in a scheduling goof, someone had told Ackerman the day before that he wasn't needed. Set free, Ackerman had promptly flown back to his home in California. Frantically, arrangements were made at Skadden's offices to summon at least the voice, if not the body, of Ackerman. In a detail reminiscent of *The Wizard of Oz,* the Drexel deal-maker's voice was piped into the conference room via a small metallic speakerphone perched on the middle of the conference table. Speaking only a few hours after his cross-country plane trip, Ackerman was remarkably calm and persuasive. He ticked off the virtues of KKR's bid, saving the best for last. "Besides, we have a reset feature on our paper," the Drexel deal-maker declared.

KKR's lead attorney, Dick Beattie, was flabbergasted. Sitting in the midst of the KKR team, Beattie felt sure he knew all the details of the buyout firm's bid; the afternoon before, he had drawn up a six-page term sheet. That document hadn't mentioned any reset. Grabbing a piece of scratch paper, Beattie frantically wrote: "Do we have a reset?" and passed the note to the nearest KKR executive, associate Cliff Robbins.

"I don't know," Robbins quickly wrote back. "I guess we do now."

Robbins was right. The Lazard and Dillon investment bankers seized on resettable junk bonds as a vital part of any winning bid. At last they thought they had a way to minimize the junkiness of any bonds pushed into shareholders' hands. If the bonds sagged in price after they were issued, the interest rate could simply be pushed up to make the bonds more valuable again.

While KKR embraced the idea of reset bonds, the other main bidder for RJR, the Shearson–Ross Johnson team, balked. Shearson managing director James Stern told Lazard that he could tolerate a reset provision only if the maximum possible interest rate was capped at 17½ percent, nearly double the rate RJR historically paid on its debt. Shearson wouldn't take chances on paying anything higher, Stern said. In contrast, the KKR men spent little time worrying about how high a rate reset bonds might lead to; they smugly expected that a reset provision would let them *lower* RJR's bond interest rate in a year or two. As Ammon later pointed out, nearly every KKR buyout had grown financially stronger over time, allowing companies such as Beatrice to cut borrowing costs a few years after KKR acquired them. Neither Kravis nor Roberts even attended brief talks on 29 November 1988, when the idea of an upper limit on the bonds' reset rate was considered and rejected. "There were ten thousand things going on at the time," KKR associate Scott Stuart later recalled.

"This just seemed like one of them. How were we to know how important it would become?"

For months after acquiring RJR Nabisco, the KKR executives toyed with the idea of quickly setting a new, permanent rate on the company's reset bonds—much as a homeowner might decide to lock in a fixed rate on an adjustable-rate mortgage. At every meeting, however, advisers argued that there was no need to rush. KKR had until February 1991 to reset the bonds. Several advisers, led by Merrill Lynch & Co.'s Jeffrey Berenson, asserted that the longer KKR waited, the sounder RJR's finances would become; this would result in lower interest rates. RJR's $6 billion of reset bonds had begun trading with an interest rate of 13.71 percent, and on three occasions in the summer of 1989, KKR passed up chances to lock in a new rate of 14 percent. Only Drexel's Peter Ackerman dissented. "If I were you, I'd start the reset process now," Ackerman counseled at one meeting. "No one can predict the future. The good news is already out about RJR, and the company has $6 billion of paper outstanding. If you can do it [the reset] now, you ought to do it."

Months later, people replayed Ackerman's remarks in slow motion, suspecting that he had been trying to warn KKR of giant troubles ahead. At the time, people dismissed the Drexel deal-maker as ornery.

By late January 1990, the reset crisis had begun. Once the Moody's downgrade sent RJR's junk bonds crashing, it wasn't clear that any new rate, no matter how high, could fulfill the bonds' reset obligations. Just as with Hillsborough, a financial wrecking ball now loomed before a KKR-controlled company. Jacking up the interest rates on the RJR bonds to 25 or 30 percent might superficially seem to restore the bonds' promised value to investors—but at those interest rates, RJR's balance sheet would rapidly disintegrate, as the tobacco and food company ran uncontrollable losses because of its vastly larger debt bill. Before long, RJR might be forced to default on all its debt, reset bonds included.*

Aware that his firm's entire future had suddenly become tied up in the fate of the junk-bond market, Kravis decided in early February 1990 to

---

*The RJR reset bonds did differ from Hillsborough's bonds in three modest ways—all of which gave KKR a glimmer of hope. They didn't need to be reset as quickly; KKR could request that they be adjusted at any time before 9 February 1991, two years after the original buyout. Also, the penalties for failing to achieve a reset weren't as clearly spelled out as in the Hillsborough case, though they were widely believed to be dire. And unlike the cash-paying Hillsborough bonds, the RJR bonds were "pay-in-kind" bonds, paying interest until 1994 in the form of more junk bonds. That meant they wouldn't immediately impose a cash drain on RJR, no matter what their new interest rate. But if reset at a rate of 25 percent or more, the bonds would spew out new "baby bonds" at a frightening pace, eventually leaving RJR with an overwhelming interest bill.

venture outside KKR's offices and talk to bondholders himself. At the invitation of Merrill Lynch's deal-makers, Kravis agreed to address a giant junk-bond conference at the Phoenician, a lavish Phoenix, Arizona, resort built by savings-and-loan operator Charles Keating. Bondholders were rumored to be furious about their big paper losses on RJR bonds. But Kravis thought he could soothe them. Sitting down with a speechwriter at the public-relations firm of Kekst & Co., Kravis prepared what he hoped would be an inspirational, confidence-building speech.

It was a disaster. A few people hissed as Kravis took the podium at the Phoenician. Looking out on an audience of nearly 500 powerful bond-holders, Kravis proved too shrill and condescending for the disgruntled creditors before him. "Financial panics are almost always the result of a herd mentality run amok," Kravis scolded his audience. "No one wants to stand in front of a rush of oncoming cattle, not even Merrill Lynch." No one laughed at the joke. In fact, the cattle analogy offended some bondholders. Kravis went on to insist that KKR's junk-bond perform-ance had been "superb," though nearly everyone in the audience had recently been bruised by the financial troubles of Hillsborough, Seaman, and SCI.

Partway through the speech, an undercurrent of fear crept into Kravis's remarks. "We are confronting a reset problem," he said. "KKR has $1.5 billion at risk in RJR. . . . We are well aware of the problem and its ramifications for RJR, its equity value, the future of the high-yield market and very importantly, the future of KKR." Kravis concluded by urging that bond buyers work together with equity investors like KKR. In the hostile climate of the time, Kravis's plea fell flat. The insurance company analysts, mutual-fund managers, and savings-and-loan execu-tives in the audience weren't in the mood to be charmed by Kravis. Most of these portfolio managers were frightened by the abrupt drop in the value of their clients' money, and feared they might lose their jobs. They knew all too well—thanks to lavish magazine articles about Kravis's high living—that Kravis had salted away a vast fortune during the great lever-age boom. "A lot of people were jealous," recalled Merrill Lynch's Beren-son. Many were outraged that Kravis offered no specific remedy while the RJR bonds were tumbling so badly.

The next day, Kravis walked the hallways of the Phoenician, futilely seeking reassurance. More than any of the other KKR executives, Kravis craved glory and public recognition. This time, he was shunned. "Kravis was talking down to us," a junk-bond mutual-fund manager later said. "It wasn't like a Milken speech," veteran San Diego money manager Jim Caywood opined.

The few bondholders that came up to Kravis taunted him. "Don't forget: We made you in the RJR deal," one bondholder told Kravis. "We gave you the money to do it." Kravis and the bondholder sparred for a bit before Kravis retorted: "No one institution has ever made us. We get help from everyone."

On Sunday, KKR associate Jamie Greene arrived from San Francisco to join Kravis for the rest of the conference. Still stunned by his frosty reception at the conference, Kravis dodged Greene's every attempt to talk about the bondholders. For a few hours, at least, Kravis just wanted to blot out all memories of a terrible speech. All the hallmarks of Kravis's charm—the blue eyes that opened a little wider when he made his promises, the attentiveness to how comfortable other people were in their chairs—were useless amid 500 cynical creditors. "The bondholders were pissed," Greene later said. "They thought we'd do nothing. They didn't realize Henry's sincerity.

"Granted," Greene added, "I'm not sure even Henry knew what we were going to do."

As if bondholder troubles weren't bad enough, the KKR executives soon found they were in dire straits with RJR's main lending banks. In late January, Greene had proposed what he believed was a routine contract change in RJR's $7 billion of bank borrowings. KKR had altered its timetable slightly for repaying RJR's debt. In a modification known as the seventh amendment, Greene wanted to loosen up some restrictions in the bank-loan documents accordingly. In KKR's boom years, such bank amendments had been won readily.

This time the banks mutinied. KKR was too "arrogant," one banker complained. Other bankers said the Fed's tough new guidelines about leveraged-company loans had greatly changed their willingness to do business on KKR's terms. The precise terms of the seventh amendment called for erasing the banks' claim to $2 billion of overseas RJR collateral, and granting the company more leeway in repaying $5 billion in bank debt due 9 February 1990. That might be handy for KKR, but it didn't help the banks.

The loudest protests came from American loan officers at Dai-Ichi Kangyo Bank, a giant Japanese bank that KKR hardly knew. Dai-Ichi had only begun LBO lending in 1987, but it had pumped in $650 million toward the original RJR buyout. To the embarrassment and dismay of

Dai-Ichi, their bank already had suffered in the collapse of Robert Campeau's retail empire in January 1990. Lured by the glamour of Campeau's elegant properties, such as Bloomingdale's department stores, many Japanese banks had stepped up lending to his retail group just as American banks were shedding their Campeau loans in 1988 and 1989. Once burned, the Japanese banks weren't about to err again.

A couple of RJR's main bankers at Citibank and Chase Manhattan tried to mediate. They urged Greene to include an "amendment fee" for the banks as part of KKR's proposal. The bankers never named their amount, but later said they envisioned about $8 million to keep the banks happy. It would have been a small but significant payoff on KKR's part, a way of acknowledging that the banks had the upper hand. Greene dismissed the idea out of hand.

"We paid a shitload of fees a year ago," Greene told Chase banker Edward Crook. "That should take us through a year."

"That was then," Crook replied. "This is now."

Greene held his ground. Proud of the KKR name, he couldn't believe that the world's major banks would thwart the buyout firm that had brought them the biggest, richest leveraged deals of the 1980s.

On 2 February 1990, Greene got bad news. KKR's lending banks had failed to grant the 51-percent approval needed for the seventh amendment. Only about 35 percent of the banks had agreed to his terms. The next week was "agonizing," Greene recalled. If the seventh amendment didn't pass, RJR would technically default on its main bank-loan agreement, with only a ten-day grace period to fix the default before other credit agreements also would come unstuck.

Bankers didn't really want to push RJR into a wave of defaults; doing so would ruin the soundness of their own giant loans to the company. Some banks were willing to play a giant game of financial "chicken," however, betting that KKR would capitulate to their terms to avoid financial ruin. "We were a long, long way from bankruptcy, but we were on a slippery slope," a Bankers Trust lender recalled.

Finally, on 7 February, the banks blinked. Taiyo Kobe Bank, Hokkaido Kokushoku Bank, and seven other small lenders sent fax messages to RJR's lawyers at White & Case, announcing that they would ratify the seventh amendment. KKR now had 54-percent acceptance for Jamie Greene's terms. Within hours, other banks acquiesced in the now-inevitable approval. Only Dai-Ichi Kangyo remained a holdout.

Default, in at least a technical sense, had been less than forty-eight hours away.

Ostracized by the rest of the financial world, KKR's executives hud-dled in New York for much of February 1990 to talk about how to handle the reset. Even though they still had fourteen months before RJR's junk bonds absolutely had to be reset, time had become their enemy. If they couldn't come up with a solution reasonably quickly, there was no telling how far the bonds might sink.

"There were some dark, dark moments," KKR executive Ted Ammon later recalled. Kravis and Roberts both woke repeatedly in the middle of the night, their heads spinning with fears and financial schemes. One of the worst sufferers from insomnia was thirty-one-year-old KKR associate Cliff Robbins, a graduate of Harvard University and Stanford Business School, who up until then had enjoyed uninterrupted success in life. A year earlier, confident that the RJR buyout would someday make him a millionaire, Robbins had pumped practically all his savings into an invest-ment stake in the tobacco and food company. Now he was confronting the likelihood of his first serious failure. On weekends, Robbins stared into space, obsessed about the reset. Several times, his fiancée had to shake him to bring him back to reality. "It was tougher than any acquisi-tion," Robbins later said. "We couldn't walk away from it, no matter how bad things got."

Before long, a wartime-style camaraderie took hold within KKR. Rob-erts emerged as the strategist in San Francisco, phoning KKR associates at their homes on weekends for long, wide-ranging conversations. Every Saturday morning, Scott Stuart got an hour-long phone call from Roberts. Every Sunday afternoon, it was Ted Ammon's turn.

In New York, Kravis was the optimist, picking out themes that he hoped would keep his colleagues' spirits up. The basic RJR business is doing well, Kravis kept saying. Markets eventually turn around. RJR's own general counsel, Larry Ricciardi, teamed up with Simpson Thacher's Beattie and another partner, Rob Spatt, to look for ways that KKR might be able to skirt around some of the most onerous language in the reset obligations.

In the broadest terms, KKR had only two routes it could follow. Either the reset bonds had to be bought back and retired, or they somehow had to rise in price to a point where the bonds could be reset at a bearable interest rate. Both paths were blocked. Debt-laden RJR lacked the spare cash to buy back more than a handful of its reset bonds. RJR's borrowing capacity was tightly hemmed in by dozens of covenants. Raising cash by hacking off pieces of RJR's food businesses wouldn't work either. The Planters peanuts and Lifesaver candies unit might fetch $2 billion or more. Yet under terms of the original buyout loans in 1988, money from divestitures could only be used to pay off bank debt; it couldn't be freed up to repay the bonds.

As the entire $200 billion junk-bond market disintegrated, KKR was helpless to make the RJR reset bonds rise in price. "It was like trying to push a rope uphill," Kravis later said. Even when RJR reported a 35-percent increase in first-quarter operating profits, the bond prices perked up for only a few hours before resuming their downward slide. "Nothing that we tried worked," Robbins said. For KKR, which had lived a charmed life for years, the reset mess was agony.

Early in March 1990, Roberts began to focus on KKR's only real hope of extricating itself. The remedy wasn't ideal, but it was the only option that didn't bump into a dead end right away.

RJR needed a lot more equity. The company's original cantilevered financing—of which Kravis and Roberts had been so proud in 1988—was dangerously wrong for 1990. KKR had pushed too far into the high-risk, high-reward world of immensely leveraged companies. A creditors' mutiny was threatening to tear the company apart. It was time for a strategic retreat toward something much closer to a conventional company's financial structure.

As early as mid-1989, Roberts had lobbied for cutting RJR's debts by putting more equity into the company. His first proposal had been fanciful: a public offering of stock at $10 a share. By early 1990, Roberts had turned far more realistic. Selling stock to ordinary public investors was unthinkable; RJR was still reporting big net losses after its interest bills, and investor nervousness about the company's prospects was too great. It was possible, however, to turn to KKR's giant buyout fund for money. Some $3.2 billion remained untapped, there for Kravis and Roberts to spend in whatever way they thought was appropriate.

In essence, KKR's limited partners would have to buy RJR a second time.

This time, KKR would use its partners' cash to shrink RJR's excess debt. Roberts hoped that the limited partners' spending power could be stretched further by fresh bank loans to what would be a financially stronger RJR. By combining the limited partners' cash with bank loans, KKR could hope to retire half or more of the reset bonds—and reset the remaining ones at a bearable rate.

As RJR became a much less leveraged company, some extravagant profit targets would perish. In the giddy days right after the buyout of RJR

Nabisco, Drexel investment banker Leon Black had whispered that the deal might pay off at 60 percent a year for KKR's investors. That lofty target was about to become a chimera. But the financial health of the company and KKR would be shored up greatly. At his desk in San Francisco, or at his home on weekends, Roberts sketched out new capital structures for RJR and shared them with his associates, chiefly Ted Ammon. Pretty soon, Roberts and Ammon came to believe in this new idea. With an equity infusion, the two men decided, a financially safer KKR could sidestep the reset morass and still deliver a 25- or 30-percent annual profit to its owners.

In New York, KKR associate Scott Stuart started plugging in exact numbers for Roberts's proposals. A slender, recent-vintage graduate of Stanford Business School, Stuart was one of the "numbers jocks" at KKR, able to analyze any company's finances in thirty- to forty-page computer printouts that were Wall Street's version of "simultaneous equation" math problems. This time, Stuart was tackling the toughest set of simultaneous equations KKR had ever faced. Tinkering with any single piece of the proposed refinancing—the size of the bank loans, the amount of new equity, the likely new interest rate on the reset bonds— drastically changed all the other parts. Several times each day, Stuart and fellow associate Cliff Robbins came into Ammon's office to talk about their latest analysis in detail. Meanwhile, Merrill Lynch's investment bankers bombarded the KKR associates with dozens of gray binders crammed full of Merrill's own financial models. The stacks of computer paper around Ammon's office grew more than a foot high. "You name the permutation, and we tried it," Ammon later said.

Only Roberts kept his analysis ruthlessly lean. Every week or two he flew into New York and reviewed his single sheets of paper with the KKR associates. Sometimes his customary yellow tablets gave way to scraps of stationery from his favorite Manhattan hotel, the Carlyle. "When things got really tough," Stuart recalled, "George started using one and a half sheets."

As KKR's ideas took shape, the next step was to see whether banks would play along. In late March, Kravis and KKR associate Jamie Greene started test-marketing. The two men called on the vice chairmen or presidents at three of RJR's lead banks—Manufacturers Hanover, Chase Manhattan, and Citibank. (The fourth lead bank, Bankers Trust, was assumed to be loyal enough to KKR that a special visit wasn't needed.) Kravis's central question was a simple one: Would the banks lend RJR

more money? The top bankers' response was polite but guarded. "Everyone said they wanted to be helpful," Kravis recalled. "But you couldn't
tell if that was a canned answer or not."

Concurrently, Greene began much tougher talks: hardball negotiations
with the midlevel bankers at Chase, Citi, Manny Hanny, and BT who
would make the real decisions. As recently as the seventh amendment
debacle in early February, Jamie Greene had epitomized the proud, efficient, and slightly arrogant ways of KKR at its peak. He had called
meetings for three P.M. and let the bankers caucus alone until he arrived
at five. He had called bankers "Eddie" and "Jimmy," even if no one since
grade school had addressed them that way. "Hey guys, come on!" Greene
would exhort the bankers whenever negotiations stalled for a moment.
Yet all through the spring of 1990, Jamie Greene ate humble pie. Bank
lending for buyouts had atrophied to virtually nothing, as the commercial
bankers reminded him at every instance. Bank of Boston was pulling out
of leveraged lending entirely. Canadian Imperial Bank of Commerce was
withdrawing. Securities analysts and economists were warning the world
about the dangers of lending to companies deeply in hock.

No one was blunter than Jim Ferguson, a short, fiery executive at
Manufacturers Hanover. Ferguson had been a crucial lender to KKR as
far back as the Beatrice deal in 1985. If any one banker possessed the
stature and track record to talk back to KKR, it was Jim Ferguson. And
he didn't hesitate. "You need us," Ferguson lectured Greene at one big
meeting. "There isn't anywhere else that you can raise money. The other
capital markets are closed off. You and Henry Kravis should be standing
in the lobby of our bank every morning, showering [bank chairman John]
McGillicuddy with gold coins as he gets on the elevator. You need us."

Jaws dropped. No major lender had ever talked to KKR like that
before. "He was bitter about a whole decade," Scott Stuart recalled. "He
was especially angry about the size profits that Drexel made. His attitude
was: I don't think there will be any more LBO business. The hell with
relationships. Tell KKR to screw it."

Another time, Ferguson turned his wrath on KKR's advisers from
Merrill Lynch. "With all the money you're getting paid and you can't tell
me the value of the company?" Ferguson sputtered in disbelief. "What
the hell are you getting paid for? You think, just because you get paid so
much money, that you're so smart. Well, you're not."

As Ferguson's tirades unfolded, bankers from Chase Manhattan and
Bankers Trust rushed to intercede, assuring Greene and the Merrill Lynch
men that they weren't nearly so hostile. Secretly, though, the other bank-

ers loved Ferguson's scoldings. "The way he said it was outrageous," one banker later remarked. "But Jim said some things that needed to be said."

The gravity of KKR's predicament hit home in early April, when Kravis got his biggest jolt of fear and outrage since the Hillsborough asbestosis attorneys threatened to seize the paintings from KKR's walls. This time the messenger of doom was Marty Lipton, the number-one partner in the Wachtell, Lipton law firm, who was advising Lazard Frères—one of the arbiters of the whole reset situation. In a private lunch with Kravis at KKR's offices, Lipton said he had been doing some thinking about KKR's alternatives. There were ten options, nine of which might be unworkable, Lipton said. The tenth choice was a bankruptcy filing by RJR.

"My jaw dropped when he said that," Kravis later recalled. "I thought he was kidding at first. But he wasn't. He was dead serious." Playing through Kravis's mind were a series of harrowing realizations: *My God, can you imagine what that does to the financial institutions of America? And the world for that matter? Certainly KKR is out of business.*

But Lipton matter-of-factly pressed his solution as KKR's best hope. In bankruptcy proceedings, he said, KKR might be able to get bondholders to accept less than 100 cents on the dollar for their claims. "This is probably the best way and the most expedient way to do it," Lipton continued. And he finished with a delicate taunt. "I'm sure this comes as no surprise to you. You have excellent counsel in Dick Beattie, and I'm sure he has already considered this."

"There's no way we'd do that," Kravis shot back.

Think about it, Lipton replied, as the lunch drew to a close. His law firm had some excellent bankruptcy specialists that KKR could meet with. Wachtell, Lipton's partners had made many millions of dollars in the mid-1980s by "defending" companies against takeovers and then running auctions that nudged the companies into KKR's hands. If KKR was about to crash and burn, it seemed only logical that Wachtell, Lipton's lawyers should once again find a money-making angle.

Desperate to prove Lipton wrong, KKR in early May sounded out Dillon, Read and Lazard about a new attempted solution to the reset mess. Kravis and Ammon asked two of their advisers from Merrill Lynch, Jeff Berenson and Ray Minella, to convey a proposal that KKR inject $1 billion of equity into RJR, buy back some junk bonds, and reset the remaining bonds at a rate of 17 percent or so. The response was humiliating. That's unacceptable, the Dillon and Lazard partners said. It's so far off the mark we won't even negotiate with you. To make sure the point sank in, Lazard partner Luis Rinaldini reminded the KKR emissaries that Lazard was a private partnership in which individual partners like Rinaldini were personally liable for any mistakes. "I don't want to be sued for this," he remarked. If an inadequate reset solution were enacted, angry bondholders would quickly take the Lazard partners to court, seeking many millions in damages. "We're talking about the money for my little girl's education," Rinaldini snapped.

KKR had hit bottom. Between the angry banker from Manufacturers Hanover, bankruptcy-minded Marty Lipton, and Rinaldini's little girl, America's number-one buyout firm was slowly being crushed.

One hope remained for KKR in mid-May: to return to the banks and the firm's longtime pension fund backers with open hands in an attempt to assemble a much bigger rescue package for RJR. "We were getting ready to step off a cliff," recalled KKR's Jamie Greene. "No one knew if our parachute was going to open, or if we would crash on the ground." Over dinner at a California country club on the evening of Sunday, 19 May, Roberts spelled out the precise details of his plans to KKR's other sixteen partners and associates. The next day, all of KKR's limited partner investors from Oregon, Michigan, Harvard, and other big institutions would gather at the elegant Portman Hotel in San Francisco for their annual review of the buyout firm's entire portfolio. For most of the two-day meeting, KKR would do everything possible to impress and soothe its backers. Then, on day two, Roberts would take the podium and talk about RJR.

For twenty-four hours, KKR's fortunes hung in the balance. On paper, Kravis and Roberts had unlimited freedom to call for their limited partners' money. But if the limited partners viewed the proposed RJR infusion as throwing good money after bad, they might fight the buyout firm every step of the way, even taking court action to block KKR's access to their cash.

The first day of the San Francisco conference, KKR strained to project an image of success, ignoring the past year's body blows. Duracell's Bob Kidder was picked to be the lead-off speaker; he told an upbeat story of his company's progress and left a free orange-and-green pack of AA batteries on every attendee's chair. Safeway's Peter Magowan wrapped up the first day's session with another financial success story. At every stage, Kravis and Roberts were gracious to a fault, chatting at length with minor backers and handing out a "tribute to our partners"—Cross pens—at dinner. But all through the first day, worrisome undercurrents popped up. Kravis bristled about the press, posting security guards at the Portman

Hotel's entrance and warning investors that reporters might sneak into the conference disguised as waiters. Late in the day, Hillsborough executives delivered a morose talk about their company's status in bankruptcy. And the after-dinner speaker the first night, Harvard economist Michael Jensen, struck a somber note with a talk about "the politics of finance," suggesting that small-minded politicians were trying to hound financial creators like KKR and Drexel out of business. Investors in the audience sensed a nervous, scared side to Kravis that they had never encountered before.

Then came the showdown. At 9:30 A.M. on the second day of the conference, Roberts stepped to the podium and began the highest-stakes sales pitch of his career. "I know you want to know what we're going to do about RJR," Roberts began. He spoke without any notes; his voice was as calm as ever. "We've been looking at stacks and stacks of proposals. If you piled them up, they would fill up this entire stage, three feet high. Well, we've sifted through them and picked through them. We're down to a stack about this thick." He held up his thumb and forefinger, about an inch apart.

"What we're looking at calls for putting more equity into the company. I know a lot of you are concerned about making LBO investments in the current environment. But where else in the world could you duplicate this kind of investment? This company owns Ritz crackers, which as a 58-percent share of the cracker market. It owns Oreo cookies, which has a 48-percent share of its market. It has fourteen number-one or number-two brands in their categories. Where else in the world could you own what we in this room own together? You can't duplicate it. We're doing everything we said we'd do in RJR. Regardless of what anyone else in the press or in Washington says, we feel what we're doing is good and successful and productive. We're going to grow it and protect it."

A few minutes later, Roberts gently wrapped up his speech. "We may be coming back to you very soon for some money to put into RJR," he said. "It's likely to be substantial." The investors nodded calmly. For one tense moment, Roberts braced for hostile questions from the audience, for an insurrection. Without the money, KKR was sunk.

A hand shot up in the audience, from an investor eager to ask the first question. It was Roger Meier, the former chairman of the Oregon Investment Council, who was retired now but still invested some of his own money in KKR deals and liked coming to the conferences. Could KKR fix its financial problem a slightly different way? Meier wondered.

No, Roberts replied, but we've looked at it.

The next few questions were equally sympathetic. The breathtaking moment of tension had passed. The investors weren't going to mutiny; they were willing to let the rescue of RJR proceed. "George did an excellent job with his speech," the new chairperson of the Oregon Investment Council, Carol Hewitt, later said. "I came out of the meeting wanting to buy RJR bonds." As for KKR's younger associates, they were so proud of Roberts's speech that they wanted to burst into applause.

Certain now of drawing as much of the limited partners' money as would be needed, the KKR executives returned to negotiations with Bankers Trust, Chase, Citibank, and Manufacturers Hanover. Roberts's blueprint for patching up RJR called for about $2 billion of bank loans and a $1.6 billion offering of preferred stock with a modest 10 percent annual dividend to accompany an equity infusion of $1.5 billion or more. Together, fresh bank loans, the preferred stock, and the new equity would pay for retiring more than half the loathsome reset bonds. KKR associate Jamie Greene put a detailed loan proposal before the banks and waited for their response. Even in the antileverage climate of spring 1990, Greene believed, a company like RJR that was strengthening its balance sheet could simultaneously borrow more from the banks. He just didn't know how expensive additional credit would be.

Chase banker Maria Beechey taught Greene the price. A crisp, polite Englishwoman in her thirties, Beechey had been chosen by other bankers to be their spokesperson that spring in dealing with KKR. Never outright rude, Beechey began a crucial late-May meeting at RJR's headquarters by assuring Greene that everyone wanted to work together to deal with "a difficult market." Then she pummeled him with the banks' bill. The banks wanted an amendment fee of $50 million to make any new loan. They wanted commitment fees, origination fees, and facility fees that would total 5.5 percent of the loan—far beyond the usual 1 to 3 percent. Beechey didn't take the math any farther, but Greene did. The banks wanted nearly $200 million in fees.

Greene listened in stunned silence. "You gotta be kidding me," he muttered to himself. Another banker watched to see if Greene would vomit. But Greene did his best to respond in the crisp, correct tone that Beechey had set. KKR would take the proposal under advisement, Greene said. He would be back with an answer in a day or two.

At first, the rest of KKR's executives voiced outrage and disbelief. "We knew it was going to be expensive," Kravis said. "But this is outrageous." Then a few days later, the KKR men caved in. "The banks said: 'Take it or leave it,'" associate Scott Stuart recalled. "We had to take it."

For fourteen years, commercial banks had helped make Kravis and Roberts very, very rich. Now the banks were about to even the score. The financial climate had changed drastically from the glory days of the mid-1980s, when bankers fought for the privilege of lending to Kravis or Roberts. Now KKR's name was a liability, a symbol of overreaching. Kravis and Roberts needed to pay a fortune in fees to get banks to rescue them from their reset morass.

Aptly, there was no windfall for the firm that usually let its meter run the highest: KKR itself. All through the 1980s, Kravis and Roberts had shamelessly pressed for the biggest transaction fees ever, setting world records with fees of $60 million for the Safeway buyout and then $75 million for RJR. In the spring of 1990, however, KKR had lost its nerve. Both Kravis and Roberts told their associates that it "wouldn't be appropriate" to charge a fee for solving a problem that KKR had helped create.

In early June, KKR made its formal money call to its limited partners. Fax requests for cash arrived at the state treasuries of Oregon, Michigan, New York, and a half dozen other states. As it had signaled at the San Francisco conference, KKR wanted $1.7 billion—the firm's biggest equity investment ever—to inject into RJR. Loyally, the limited partners relayed the money to KKR's special account at Manufacturers Hanover. KKR had asked its partners to keep the money infusion confidential, but with more than seventy partners involved, there was no way to keep it secret for long. In a string of articles from 13 June to 26 June, *The Wall Street Journal* began spelling out details of KKR's rescue plan, explaining that RJR Nabisco "would be shielded from a potential debt crisis," though "KKR's potential profits would be curtailed." As news stories emerged, the reset bonds jumped about 20 percent by the end of June, to 85 cents on the dollar. Bondholders began to think a reprieve to their troubles might be taking shape. Even so, the bonds traded well below the levels that KKR needed to achieve.

From mid-June onward, clinching the bank loans became KKR's most crucial task. Greene took the lead, with Roberts constantly pressing him to speed up, for fear that delays would hurt KKR's chances. In late May, Greene said it might take ninety days to complete the RJR refinancing, though a much simpler deal could be done in three weeks. Two days after he told Roberts about his timetable, Greene found a package awaiting in his office. It was a present from Roberts: a homemade calendar. On a huge white sheet of construction paper, Roberts and his secretary had marked off twenty-one days in big black letters. The final day, in late June, was circled in red.

As Greene hurriedly canvassed twenty-five leading U.S., Japanese, and European banks, he found that the loan's big drawing points were the strength of RJR's basic business—and the giant fees involved. As this reporter disclosed in the *Journal* on 26 June 1990, RJR ended up budgeting a whopping $250 million in fees to get the refinancing done. (Banks shrunk their demands slightly, but lawyers, printers, and investment bankers added more than $50 million to Beechey's original bill.) Top executives at RJR were aghast. "That's more money than the Planters/Lifesavers division [of RJR] earns in a year," Gerstner told the KKR men. Every week since taking the helm at RJR, Gerstner and his managers had scrounged to cut costs. They had pared back the company's investor-relations staff from twenty to three. They had saved pennies on things as picayune as carpeting and corporate stationery. Abruptly, Gerstner was being told to dissipate all the cash from those savings—and far more as well—on a financial rescue plan he had never bargained on. "It's horrifying to think that people could charge fees like that," Gerstner told Greene. Yet the big bank fees were unavoidable if the deal was going to get done.

One by one, the world's banks began voicing support for RJR's refinancing package. Daily logs kept at Citibank showed how stiff resistance gradually shaded into indifference, then curiosity, and finally excitement about lending money once more. For one last hurrah, KKR had revived some of the old magic. On Friday, 6 July, KKR wrapped up its bank loan with $7 billion in bank commitments, triple what it needed. Jamie Greene had missed his twenty-one-day deadline by about two weeks, but Roberts didn't mind. RJR quickly borrowed $2.25 billion, the maximum allowed under various restrictions in the tobacco and food company's existing credit agreements. The surplus loan pledges were a big psychological boost to the battered KKR partners and associates.

Thanks to chatty bankers, details about KKR's refinancing plans steadily trickled out to the wider world in late June and early July. Nearly two-thirds, or $4.4 billion, of the reset bonds would be bought back, using a mixture of the bank loans, the equity money from KKR's partners, and an issue of new preferred stock. As investors digested the details, the reset bonds rose as high as 88 cents on the dollar. The vicious circle of reset trouble feeding on itself had been broken. While it wasn't precisely possible for KKR to predict what new rate Dillon and Lazard would set, it was clear that it wouldn't take a giant rate boost to get RJR's bonds back to a trading price of nearly 100 cents on the dollar.

Slowly, bondholders' cynicism gave way to a willingness to sell their reset bonds on KKR's terms—and let the deal proceed. A few bondhold-ers, like portfolio manager Hillel Weinberger at CNA Insurance, even began to purr the old phrases of the Milken era. "There's one thing you have to understand," Weinberger told a questioner in late June. "The deal is going to get done. It's very important to KKR that they carry it out." For him, at least, faith alone was reason to buy once more. Other bondholders, though, stayed wary. The refinancing was likely to repair their immense losses on RJR bonds, but it wasn't going to net them a fortune.

On Monday, 9 July, Kravis and Roberts were ready for the final step. Simpson Thacher attorney Dick Beattie called investment bankers at Lazard and Dillon and said that KKR was prepared to do the reset the following weekend.

For some time, Kravis had been briefing Dillon, Read's Franklin Hobbs and Lazard partner Damon Mezzacappa about KKR's plans. After months of disastrous attempts to negotiate with bondholders en masse, Kravis at last had returned to the kind of discussion at which he excelled. These were closed-door talks among just a few people, where politeness and self-confidence mattered once more. Working from Rob-erts's refinancing package, Kravis would spell out just what KKR wanted.

In an intricate process, the new reset rates would be set by the com-bined efforts of Dillon, Read, Lazard Frères, and KKR's main Wall Street adviser at the time, Merrill Lynch. If the various parties differed, a fourth investment bank would figure out how to bridge the gap. By the night of Saturday, 14 July, the advisers had pulled to within about 1½ percentage points of one another in their assessment of what new interest rates would be needed to make RJR's junk bonds trade at full face value again.

On Sunday, 15 July, everyone huddled at one of Simpson Thacher's conference rooms for the final day of talks. RJR's Lou Gerstner flew in from a brief vacation in Nantucket, arriving in a sport coat. Everyone else, Kravis and Roberts included, showed up in slacks and open-necked shirts.

At one P.M., the Lazard and Dillon men reported back with their recommended reset rates: 17½ percent for one class of bonds, 18 percent for another. Merrill Lynch, in line with KKR's analysis, countered that 16½ percent for both classes of bonds would suffice. The gap between the investment bankers' recommendations was small enough that KKR could live with whatever compromise rate emerged. To split the differ-ence, all sides turned to Donaldson Lufkin Jenrette Securities Corpora-tion, a midsize Wall Street firm with a lot of junk-bond expertise. DLJ also could claim to be independent; it was about the only sizable Wall Street firm that hadn't done at least one project for KKR in the previous two years. Working from DLJ's downtown Manhattan offices, DLJ investment banker John McMahon and a few colleagues began their own deliberations about what interest rates to pick.

As Sunday afternoon wore on, the executives from KKR, RJR, and their lawyers each pulled out $100 from their wallets and began an impromptu office pool. Under the grand name of "Reset-O-Rama," nearly thirty people bet on the interest rates that DLJ would pick, and on the price at which RJR's bonds would trade the next day. It was reminiscent of the final vigils during the auctioning of Gulf Oil or Beatrice or RJR, when Kravis, Roberts, and their friends would break the multibillion-dollar tension with poker games or with tiny side bets. This time, however, Kravis and his colleagues weren't trying to pull off another giant acquisition. They were trying to save KKR's biggest deal from disaster.

After eight hours of deliberation, DLJ's McMahon phoned Simpson Thacher's offices at 9:15 P.M. He had split the difference almost exactly in half, shading slightly toward the higher Dillon/Lazard analysis. The new interest rates on RJR's reset bonds would be 17 and $17\frac{3}{8}$ percent, McMahon said.* The vigil was over.

Around ten P.M., Kravis, Roberts, Raether, and three of the KKR associates headed to Kravis's home for dinner. All of the buyout king's brazen splendor surrounded them—the giant Sargent painting, the horsehair-upholstered chairs, the immense silver candlesticks on Kravis's main dining table. This wasn't a fancy celebration, however. It was a shirtsleeves meal of pasta, eaten at a small table off to the side of Kravis's main dining room. Turning to his younger colleagues, Kravis offered a kind word for each one. "Job well done," he said to Ammon, to Robbins, and to Stuart. For a few moments, the KKR team played through the six-month drama once more, annoyed that Dillon, Read and DLJ had decreed such high interest rates on the bonds. But the overriding tone of the meal was one of fatigue and relief that the harrowing days were over.

By the end of the reset drama, KKR had lost the seemingly effortless grace of its golden years. Kravis, Roberts, and their colleagues had strug-

---

*Kravis and Roberts proved to be bumblers at Reset-O-Rama. After both made their wagers, Kravis decided he didn't like his first choice and wanted to change it. "You can't do that," KKR executive Ted Ammon lectured him. "You have to buy a second chance." Unable to budge Ammon—a lawyer by training—Kravis put in a second $100. Neither of his two bets were any good. At the end of the evening the two most accurate guessers, Jamie Greene and RJR chief executive Lou Gerstner, split the pot.

gled to achieve a less-than-perfect reprieve from an unexpected financial crisis. They hadn't wanted to buy RJR Nabisco a second time. They hadn't wanted to accept a high reset rate on the junk bonds. They had begrudgingly let go of expectations that they could still make 60-percent-a-year profits for their investors; the more conservatively capitalized RJR would be lucky to do half so well.

"We had given away a lot to get the deal done," a top adviser to the buyout firm later said. But KKR had survived.

From July 1990 onward, Kravis and Roberts kept pursuing new buyouts, though they did so without the old fire in their eyes. Their fourteen-year obsession with setting new records, with constantly topping their largest deal to date, finally seemed over. Even in their jokes, the two men showed a contented, giddy side that few people had seen since the cousins' college days together.

One morning shortly after the reset drama finished, KKR's two dominant partners broke into giggles over breakfast at the firm's New York offices. "Have you heard?" Kravis asked a visitor. "We're going back to Bear, Stearns."

"Yeah," Roberts said. "We're going to work for Ace Greenberg. He always said he'd be willing to have us come back."

"Only we're going to start at the bottom," Kravis added. "We'll be associates."

14
Debt Is Out, Equity Is In

Until the RJR Nabisco crisis changed their lives, it was easy to tell what Henry Kravis and George Roberts had brought to the world. For the first fourteen years of KKR's existence, the buyout firm's hallmark could be expressed in one word: *debt.*

Both dangerous and tempting, debt was a financial force that Kravis and Roberts always felt they could harness to their advantage. Early in his career, Kravis pitched high-debt buyouts to reluctant corporate executives by telling them: "Take a look at this! It may seem a little scary at first. But it will work!" Roberts turned classic lender-borrower relations inside out in the mid-1980s and made bankers think they were lucky to have the opportunity to lend to him. As KKR grew ever more powerful, Kravis and Roberts derived their economic clout from a single fact: They could borrow more money, faster, than anyone else. Leading a vast leverage movement, the two cousins helped change the way that American business felt about borrowing money. It defied belief that $50 billion of loans could be orchestrated by a firm so small that all its employees could fit into a few station wagons. Yet for a few years, Kravis and Roberts made once-loathsome levels of debt seem alluring and even compelling.

As a new decade got under way, however, a series of hammer blows had reduced the high-debt financial world to rubble. Defaults had become so widespread that some 38 percent of all junk bonds issued in 1988 failed to pay interest punctually. The U.S. recession that began in July 1990 revealed just how vulnerable leveraged companies could be when their earnings withered and their interest bills stayed high, month after month. Tax-law changes took a further toll, making debt-based acquisitions much less attractive than before. To make the demolition of the old order complete, public revulsion toward the profiteers of debt now made it impossible for anyone, even Kravis or Roberts, to borrow billions in breezy style.

Yet KKR—the firm that soared the highest on the way up—was one of the few to survive the collapse intact. Its partners didn't go broke or get indicted. They didn't scatter to other firms or jobs, as many of KKR's old allies did. Other leveraged deal-makers grew so disenchanted that they opted for retirement in their forties, choosing to start their own small businesses or head to new destinations as varied as a Wyoming ranch and a London political-science institute. Not the KKR men. Kravis, Roberts, and their associates stayed put and tried to figure out how in the world they could do new deals and make more money.

Opportunists by nature, the KKR executives soon invented a new role for themselves. If they couldn't prosper anymore by creating debt, they could make money by eliminating it. From early 1990 onward, KKR ceased to be America's biggest corporate borrower—or even a borrower of any size. Instead, in a remarkable reversal, KKR became Wall Street's number-one issuer of stock. In rapid-fire succession in 1990 and 1991, the KKR executives raised more than $2.5 billion by taking their best-performing portfolio companies public. One after another, Safeway, Duracell, the AutoZone division of Malone & Hyde, RJR Nabisco, Stop & Shop, and Owens-Illinois began trading on the New York Stock Exchange. Most of these offerings were carried out at big premiums to the prices that KKR's investors paid for their stock. And nearly all the proceeds were used to whittle down the giant borrowings that had once been a KKR hallmark.

The Age of Leverage, surprisingly, was being erased by its creators. The harsh "discipline of debt" abated as companies' balance sheets returned to more normal levels. The immense erosion of corporate creditworthiness in the 1980s began to reverse course, too. Analysts at Standard & Poor's reported in mid-1991 that, for the first time in years, credit-rating upgrades were becoming more common among U.S. corporations; downgrades were becoming rarer.

As the KKR partners began undoing their handiwork of the previous decade, their own significance started shrinking. The apprehensions and excitement of a few years earlier—when magazine cover stories talked about "enormous power lodged in the hands of relatively few Wall Streeters" and the "eclipse of the public corporation"—now seemed greatly overblown. No longer were Kravis and Roberts the lords of an ever-expanding industrial empire, accountable to no one but their friendly circle of ninety or so passive investors. Instead, new public stockholders began to share control of RJR Nabisco, Safeway, Duracell, and the other major KKR buyout companies. Independent directors joined the boards of what had been purely KKR-controlled companies. The entry of fresh public shareholders pushed down the KKR partnerships' ownership stakes in companies from as much as 90 percent to just 30 to 60 percent. Kravis and Roberts turned their attention away from deal-making and toward an important, but less controversial new role: functioning as powerful outside directors of the companies they controlled.

KKR's orderly retreat was widely seen as good news. It was welcomed on Wall Street, where buyout companies' publicly traded shares performed well, and it was quietly cheered at the operating companies themselves. Peter Magowan, the chief executive of Safeway, had reluctantly accepted KKR's discipline of debt in 1986, and watched as it drastically reshaped the grocery chain. After growing $30 million richer in the process, Magowan had tried hard from 1988 onward to convince outsiders that KKR's intercession had been a good thing. It was easier for him to feel that Safeway was on the right course after KKR encouraged the supermarket operator to be a public company once more. Safeway was committed to "expanding and improving our store system," Magowan declared in the company's 1990 annual report to shareholders. Selling stock was one of the best ways to finance that growth. Even as Safeway announced plans to go public, in fact, Magowan rolled out a five-year, $3.2 billion spending program for new and remodeled stores, his company's biggest such outlay ever.

At RJR Nabisco, senior executives were delighted to see their company's high-debt era come to an end. In the spring of 1991, chief executive Lou Gerstner had privately voiced a little testiness about RJR's financial obligations. "The cards were dealt when I got here," he had said in an interview. "There was a chair that I was supposed to sit in and play those cards. The cards said: You must sell assets. You must refinance senior debt. There were five or six things that KKR created in its financial structure. They weren't mine to change."

As KKR kept shuffling the deck, Gerstner and his fellow RJR managers began drawing better hands. The tobacco and food company's July 1990 refinancing turned out to be the first of four major steps over the next eighteen months to pump more stockholders' money into RJR and ease its debt burden. "Debt was out; equity was in," Kravis explained in the spring of 1991. "We had to bite the bullet. The right thing to do for the company was to put more equity out there." By the end of 1991, vast amounts of RJR Nabisco stock had been pushed into the hands of bondholders, new public investors, and KKR's partnerships, quadrupling the company's equity to $8 billion. Total debt had been shrunk greatly. At last, Gerstner told his managers, the company had the cash it needed to invest more aggressively in new products, marketing, and research and development. RJR's immense cash flow didn't need to be diverted so overwhelmingly toward debt repayment. As RJR grew more creditworthy, the company also no longer had to submit all its big spending plans to 100 lending banks for approval. RJR's managers, who had been frustrated for months by drawn-out bank reviews that hampered their ability to make quick acquisitions in Hungary, Mexico, and other emerging markets, let out a sigh of relief.

Once RJR regained much of the financial health it had had before the buyout, KKR's role at the company began to fade. By the end of 1991, KKR's partnerships owned just 41 percent of the tobacco and food company, down from more than two-thirds in early 1989, right after the buyout. Most of the rest of the stock was in public hands, including some that RJR's bondholders had picked up for just $5 a share in November 1990. Public investors applauded this debt reduction by rapidly bidding up the price of RJR's common stock when it began trading on the New York Stock Exchange in early 1991. Even Moody's, the credit-rating agency that had terrified investors with its downgrading of RJR's junk bonds in January 1990, declared a year later that the company was on the right course and deserved an upgrade.

At Duracell, the high-debt era came to an end just as decisively. In the spring of 1991, chief executive Robert Kidder declared that his Exorcist Plan was history. Most of the financial targets set three and a half years earlier in that document had been met; some had been greatly exceeded. Duracell had survived a buyout and even thrived. In May 1991, the battery company sold stock to the public at $15 a share, triple what KKR, Kidder, and his managers had paid. In the summer of 1991, Duracell used its stock-offering proceeds and some new bank loans to retire every cent of its junk bonds outstanding, ten years ahead of schedule. Except for KKR's 53-percent ownership of Duracell, the battery maker didn't resemble a typical buyout company one bit. It added jobs every month and was poised to receive a healthy single-A credit rating, the strongest of any company that KKR had ever owned. Duracell also reported double-digit growth in sales and operating profit. Portfolio managers began comparing

Duracell to other fast-growing consumer-products companies like Gillette and even Coca-Cola.

Denied the choice of buying America's biggest companies on credit anymore, Kravis and Roberts devised less dramatic approaches, to keep KKR active on a smaller scale. They sent KKR associates to France, Australia, and Hungary to look for acquisitions abroad. They used as much as $1 billion of their limited partners' money to buy minority stakes in publicly traded companies.* And Kravis, in particular, arranged for KKR to start bankrolling acquisition-minded entrepreneurs in radio, publishing, and cable television. This time, Kravis explained, KKR would start from scratch and build up new companies by small acquisitions.

Initial progress was fitful. All the same, Kravis convinced himself that the combination of KKR's money and an entrepreneur's talent could produce more winners. His brightest hope was K-III Holdings, a publishing venture that three former top executives of Macmillan Inc. had started from scratch in 1989. K-III grew to about $1 billion a year in sales by 1991, buying such diverse publications as *Soap Opera Digest* and *National Hog Farmer.* A worldwide rival to the largest media combines it wasn't. Yet Kravis gushed with paternal pride anytime he was asked about K-III.

The graying of Kohlberg Kravis Roberts & Co. became most evident in the makeup of the firm's partnership. In the mid-1980s, power had been concentrated almost entirely in the hands of Kravis and Roberts. They had done most of the work; they had commanded most of the profits. The ouster of Jerry Kohlberg had only reinforced the cousins' importance; the appointment of Bob MacDonnell, Paul Raether, and Mike Michelson as additional partners in 1982, 1986, and 1987 had lessened the cousins' hold on the firm only slightly. As Kravis and Roberts grew older, though, their priorities shifted greatly. Personal control wasn't as important anymore. Permanence was.

"They don't want to be Donald Trumps—flashes in the pan," said KKR executive Saul Fox in late 1990. "They want to build something that will last beyond them."

Roberts, in particular, became an outspoken booster of the younger men at KKR, telling them they were good enough to line up deals on their own. At the end of 1990, Kravis and Roberts voted to expand KKR's partnership circle to seven, promoting Fox and fellow associate Ted

---

*KKR didn't show much aptitude at such investing, incurring paper losses as large as $353 million at one stage. By the end of 1991, its portfolio had recovered to show a small gain overall, but still lagged behind broad stock-market averages.

Ammon. Kravis and Roberts reduced their claim on KKR's profit stream to about 20 percent each, allowing the firm's eighteen other executives to hold stakes ranging from 0.5 to 8 percent apiece. Year by year, the gap narrowed between the two men with their names on the door and everyone else. "Eventually, we'd like to make everyone a partner," Roberts said in 1991. Kravis said he hoped KKR would end up like Wall Street's most durable partnership, the nearly 100-year-old firm of Goldman, Sachs & Co. "You don't see Mr. Goldman or Mr. Sachs there anymore," Kravis observed. "But the firm is still going strong."

As much as Kravis and Roberts adapted to changing times, the crises of 1989 and 1990 had sapped their acquisition power. The cousins had lost two great sources of clout: an ability to win over the chief executives, directors, and advisers who controlled a company's destiny, and an ability to borrow billions in a hurry. The sturdy portfolio of companies that KKR had acquired in the late 1980s would allow the buyout firm, in effect, to live off its inheritance comfortably for some years to come. But KKR's executives could no longer breeze through the Fortune 500 rankings as a shopping list for new acquisitions.

A telling moment came in early 1991, when KKR began its fifth attempt to buy a major bank. Up for sale were $14 billion in healthy assets of the Bank of New England, a major Boston-area bank, which had been rendered insolvent by problem real estate loans and now was being auctioned off by federal regulators. KKR wanted to bid. After some early soundings with regulators, however, KKR executive Mike Tokarz decided that the only way to proceed was to link up with a banking-industry partner. "We felt that we would have another Mcorp experience if we bid on our own," a KKR executive later said. "This would keep the regulators off our back."

Investment bankers at Salomon Brothers suggested that the KKR team visit J. Terrence Murray, a chatty, expansion-minded Rhode Island banker who ran Fleet/Norstar Financial Group. "I'd heard my share of aspersions about KKR," Murray later told a reporter—but when Murray, Kravis, and Tokarz finally got together in February 1991, a bit of the buyout firm's old charm still worked. The KKR men came across as "gentlemanly, insightful, seasoned people who picked things up very quickly," Murray later recalled. "I walked away saying: 'I could work with these guys.'"

For the next two months, Tokarz and Kravis pushed themselves as far into the background as they could. "This is really a Fleet/Norstar bid," Tokarz told inquirers. KKR was putting up much of the money and proposing most of the bidding tactics, but Tokarz, well aware of how controversial KKR had become, chose to minimize his role in the face of outsiders' questions. His strategy proved wise. A $625 million acquisition bid from Fleet/KKR won approval from federal regulators in April 1991, edging out rival offers by Bank of Boston and BankAmerica. The joint purchase wasn't nearly as grand as KKR's first few attempts to crack into banking. In a much-changed world, however, it signaled a realistic scaling back of the buyout firm's ambitions. After years of commanding marquee billing on all its takeovers, KKR now assumed a modest supporting role: the behind-the-scenes provider of patient capital, aiding someone else's acquisition.

As the Age of Leverage wound down, so, too, did much of the pizzazz associated with KKR. Kravis's second wife, Carolyne Roehm, announced in the summer of 1991 that she was closing down her dress business to spend more time with her husband. The business had been unprofitable for years, but family friends said money wasn't the issue. Rather, they said, both Kravis and Roehm had been deeply jolted by the death of Kravis's oldest son in a car accident during a Colorado vacation. The games and gambles of the fashion world hardly seemed worth the trouble after a death in the family.

In the buyout business, a dismantling began of the vast financial network that had once played such a big role in making KKR's dreams come true. If there weren't any deals anymore, there wasn't much reason for bankers, accountants, lawyers, and other members of the entourage to stick around. Many of them drifted to new pursuits, like miners leaving a boom town after the ore veins were largely played out. Some quit with giant fortunes, several went bust, and a few went to jail. Others lingered to work a last little pocket of business, but did so with a sense that the glory years had come and gone.

In Los Angeles, one of the gung-ho members of Ron Badie's lending team, Morgan St. John, took six months off at age thirty-five to travel through the Pacific. High-stakes finance had been thrilling, he explained, but he wanted a change of pace. Badie remained in charge of the Los Angeles office, but stopped chipping in a remarkable 10 percent of Bankers Trust's worldwide earnings. The days of rushing to the airport in pursuit of a new deal (and buying clean shirts along the way for the next day's meeting) were over, too. Most big banks, including Bankers Trust, had entered a period of serious retrenchment because of losses on problem loans. Badie's group had fared better than most; but in 1991, he had to make staff cuts for the first time in years.

In Beverly Hills, the white office building that had once been Michael Milken's citadel of power became just another empty property after Drexel filed for bankruptcy-law protection. Milken himself in early 1991 began serving a ten-year jail term for securities fraud. Drexel's biggest junk-bond buyers—who had helped bankroll KKR and other buyout specialists—were hard hit, too. The two biggest buyers of junk bonds, insurance executive Fred Carr and S&L executive Tom Spiegel, both lost their jobs and watched helplessly in late 1990 and early 1991 as their institutions, First Executive and Columbia Savings and Loan, ended up in Chapter 11 bankruptcy because of big losses on their junk-bond portfolios. Mutual-fund companies all but disowned their junk-bond funds, ceasing ad campaigns, firing their portfolio managers, and telling clients to put their money in normal stock and bond funds.

On Wall Street, a retinue of advisers still called on KKR, but the lineup was noticeably sparser than before. Merrill Lynch deal-makers Jeff Berenson and Ray Minella resigned from their firm in 1990, after running up giant losses by sponsoring some non-KKR deals that went sour. Onetime KKR adviser Martin Siegel in 1990 finished a three-month prison sentence for insider trading, but was barred from ever coming back to work on Wall Street. Bruce Wasserstein, the one-time star of First Boston's mergers department, opened his own firm of Wasserstein, Perella & Co., but found it difficult to attract clients. Only Wachtell, Lipton, the law firm with an angle for everything, continued to thrive.

Surprisingly, most of Drexel's tacticians and advisers landed on their feet. Leon Black, who had often functioned as KKR's conduit to Milken in the 1980s, opened a firm that bought distressed companies' junk bonds at cut-rate prices. He quickly attracted more than $1 billion of backing from a major French bank. Alison Mass, the Drexel adviser who got in a shouting match about Hillsborough's problems with KKR's Mike Tokarz in late 1989, moved to Merrill Lynch. There she became a star investment banker again—promoting stocks instead of junk bonds.

The most remarkable career switch was performed by Drexel's Peter Ackerman, the "absentminded professor" who first started wooing Roberts in 1982. After Drexel collapsed in early 1990, Ackerman severed most ties to the U.S. financial world, took up residency in London, and became a visiting scholar at the prestigious International Institute for Strategic Studies. "I have a lot of suppressed intellectual interests," Ackerman told a confidant in mid-1990. He began wearing jeans and sport coats instead of tailored suits to work, studied political manifestos instead of prospectuses, and offered economic advice to the breakaway Soviet republic of Lithuania. This new career paid dismally; Ackerman's main employer was the Praeger publishing house, which advanced him just $800 to write a scholarly book about civilian resistance movements. But money didn't matter: Ackerman had earned as much as $165 million a year at Drexel, and most of that was safely stashed away in U.S. Treasury bills at Citibank.

Only one part of KKR's grand coalition survived the 1989–91 credit crunch without much upheaval: state pension funds. As a result, Kravis and Roberts in late 1990 turned to these traditionally loyal passive investors, looking for more money. In due time, the KKR men contended, opportunities to carry out big buyouts would arise again. It would be prudent to build up a war chest early. Starting in October 1990, KKR executives barnstormed America, looking for $1 billion to $2 billion as a "supplement" to the nearly depleted $5.6 billion Big Fund of 1987.

Ultimately, KKR collected a respectable $1.8 billion from its limited partners—but the buyout firm also ran into some flak along the way. Old-time loyalists such as Roger Meier in Oregon, John Hitchman in Oregon, and William Amerman in Michigan had either retired, moved to new jobs, or been voted out of office. Their successors still respected KKR, but had a lot more questions to ask. KKR's fees became objects of contention. So did the social impact of buyouts. Nearly half of KKR's longtime backers, such as Harvard University and New York State, ultimately decided not to invest in the supplemental fund. Others, such as Washington State, pledged money but did so only after prounion investment board members berated KKR partners about their responsibility to workers.

Roberts came away from KKR's cross-country tour muttering that "politics" had intruded into state pension plans' investment decisions. Each new opponent irritated him. After all the money that KKR had earned for Washington State's pension system, it bothered him that state union leader Gary Moore would condemn KKR's style of investing as "too risky." After all the money that the buyout firm had earned for Harvard's endowment, it irked Roberts that Harvard investment officer Scott Sperling occasionally criticized KKR in the press. "The next time we go out and raise a fund," Roberts said, "we'd like to do it with a smaller group of guys that we know are really behind us."

What Roberts dismissed as "politics," nearly everyone else regarded as the public interest. The buyout business had touched too many people's lives—often in unsettling ways—to be regarded as just a takeover technique that was the preserve of Wall Street. Some 2,300 American companies had been swept up in 1980s buyouts; as much as $180 billion had been lent to finance those transactions. New billionaires had been created; a relentless push toward corporate efficiency had been championed; an unnerving number of bankruptcies and defaults had occurred.

As leading figures at a time of runaway profiteering, Roberts and Kravis had become answerable for the era's shortcomings as well as its strengths. The two cousins weren't obscure young pioneers anymore, driving a rental car into Worcester, Massachusetts, or Hartford, Connecticut, as they had done in the early 1970s, seeking small insurance-company loans to finance trifling acquisitions. The partners of Kohlberg Kravis Roberts & Co. had staked out such an important economic position that their work invited—even demanded—public scrutiny. And as the pace of new acquisitions slowed down, the fundamental issues and consequences of the buyout movement became ever clearer.

In broad economic terms, the biggest surprise about buyouts was how transient they turned out to be. They instigated dangerous, thrilling journeys for companies over a span of several years. At the end of the cycle, however, many businesses found themselves surprisingly close to where they had been at the start. Debt was piled on, then taken off. The headquarters staffs that had been pared back so greatly were repeopled again. Marketing and capital-spending budgets were once again drafted according to the indulgent principle of "What would we like to have?" rather than the short-lived, draconian principle of "What do we absolutely need?" Rapid-fire divestitures became a thing of the past; expansion came back in style.

Buyouts were neither the economic curse nor the cure that ideologues of various stripes had once insisted they must be. They did make a difference in some key respects, by helping American efficiency for the short run, by crimping slightly the capital spending that any vibrant company needs to ensure long-term growth. Over longer time spans, however, buyouts became just a detour in the history of public companies.

The Age of Leverage was profoundly important in a political and moral sense, however, because of the way it caused society to divide up its wealth. For the first time in more than fifty years, the gap between rich and poor widened significantly in the United States. In a society that had long prided itself on a progressive income tax, free public universities, and a host of other social policies designed to broaden the middle class, suddenly only an elite seemed to matter.

An implicit promise of the American way of doing business had been broken. The making of great fortunes has ordinarily been tolerated, even encouraged, on the belief that the wider public benefits from the goods, services, or property on which such wealth is based. When the public embraces new billionaires as business heroes, it welcomes pioneers who create something for the rest of society—such as Sam Walton, the founder of Wal-Mart stores, or Bill Gates, the inventor of Microsoft computer software. The buyout specialists, for all their daring, hard work, and charm, never produced anything comparable. Instead, a new class of financier-industrialists grew astonishingly rich in the 1980s while having almost no lasting effect for good or bad on industrial progress.

When pressed about what they had really done to change society, the buyout movement's champions most frequently pointed to deeds of omission. Unneeded factories weren't built; poorly performing divisions were sold off; excess managers were let go; wasteful advertising was canceled. These cutbacks did serve a purpose, at least in the short run. In their pre-buyout days, big corporations like Beatrice and RJR Nabisco had turned into sprawling bureaucracies, squandering shareholders' money and filling executive suites with aimless intrigue. Buyouts provided a legitimate means by which new owners could hose down such enterprises until they worked properly.

The executives who administered the discipline of debt, however, to a remarkable degree used other people's sacrifices as a means of financing their own gentrification. The fate of the Beatrice corporate jets, for example—which ended up being sold to a KKR partner and to Don Kelly—makes it very difficult to regard the men behind buyouts as true champions of economic efficiency. Widespread pay cuts—such as the ones for tens of thousands of Safeway workers, which helped add $30 million to the chief executive's net worth—make it impossible to reconcile buyouts with the sense of fairness that is at the heart of democratic capitalism.

Currently, whatever efficiency gains buyouts brought are overwhelmed by the carnage of financial losses at the end of an era of rampant speculation. As Federal Reserve Board chairman Alan Greenspan put it in testimony to Congress at the end of 1991, "the nation's balance sheet has been severely stretched" by excess borrowing at all levels. While businesses, consumers, and even the federal government struggle to pay down debts and show more financial control, the healing process is likely to entail longer recessions and weaker recoveries than usual.

Some of the images of the 1980s—Mike Milken chattering about Mexico while his junk-bond empire crumbled, or bankers leaping from their seats to lend $400 million even before a borrower could finish explaining his business—are likely to enter folk wisdom as cautionary tales, much like the accounts of shoeshine boys buying stocks with borrowed money just before the crash of 1929. As the new stories spread, and become myths of their own, it is unlikely that any credit cycle for decades will be as drastic as the swing from the giddiness of 1987 to the panic of 1990. Chastened lenders can be counted on to avoid a precise repeat of the follies of the 1980s for a long time.

All the same, the pro-debt ideology that fueled the Age of Leverage may yet have its day again. Credit conditions are unendingly cyclical, producing new peaks of optimism every generation or two. Bankers, after all, are paid to take risks. And take them they will.

Proud of their own record, Roberts and Kravis see nothing to apologize for. Their buyout firm became one of the great capitalist success stories of the century, generating more than $7 billion of investment gains in its first fifteen years. The tug-of-war between free-market efficiency and democratic fairness never much concerned KKR's partners, and probably never will. Instead, Roberts and Kravis judge themselves by much narrower standards. As pioneers who kept working very hard even after achieving great riches, the cousins contend they deserve every cent of the profits they collected. They obeyed the securities laws in an era when dozens on Wall Street cheated. They handled easy credit skillfully when others didn't. Bristling at the suggestion that KKR was just a lucky winner in an age of casino capitalism, Roberts in late 1991 began ticking off a list of all the difficult—seemingly impossible—deals that he and his partners had completed over the years. "There's a lot of sweat equity that went into this firm," Roberts declared. "There still is. We didn't just bet $1 million on eight the hard way and walk away winners."

Yet when college students periodically ask Roberts for career advice, he comes very close to repudiating the path he has followed for the past twenty-five years.

"I tell them, 'You ought to take engineering and marketing courses,' " Roberts explains. " 'Don't take finance courses. A lot of the easy stuff [on Wall Street] has already been done. The market has already taken care of it.' And after college, I tell them: 'Go out and learn how to run a business. Get into manufacturing. Get into marketing. Get that experience. And then go out and buy something and make it better. The way you're going to add value isn't by being a paper shuffler or an agent of Wall Street. You'll do it by adding expertise.' "

Appendix

KKR's Buyouts

Since its founding in 1976, Kohlberg Kravis Roberts & Co. has completed thirty-eight buyouts, spending a total of $60.3 billion. The companies acquired are listed below, along with the following statistics concerning each buyout (from left to right): the purchase price paid by KKR; the percentage of this price paid by KKR's equity funds; the length of time KKR owned the company; the financial payoff for the ownership group (before KKR's fees); and the annualized profit rate (before fees) for investors over the life of the buyout. In cases where KKR has not yet sold at least half of its original investment in the enterprise, the last two columns, concerning investors' profits, are omitted.

A. J. INDUSTRIES INC. (1977)

$26 million	6.5%	8 years	44:1	58% a year

Los Angeles–based maker of jet-refueling equipment, truck brake drums, and industrial heaters. Reagan-era defense buildup helped company expand greatly. Sold in 1985 to First Chicago buyout group.

L. B. FOSTER (1977)

$106 million	1.7%	12 years	6:1	14% a year

Pittsburgh-based maker of oil-drilling pipe. Taken public in 1981 at big premium to price paid by KKR investors. Company's fortunes later collapsed as oil-industry slump set in. KKR distributed common stock to its investors in 1989, when stock was at $4 a share.

U.S. NATURAL RESOURCES (1977)

$22.3 million	4.4%	7 years	20:1	51% a year

Portland, Oregon, producer of coal, lumber-milling machinery, and air condi-tioners. Sold to KKR executives, certain original investors, and company man-agement in 1985. Second-round buyout has yet to be sold.

HOUDAILLE INDUSTRIES INC. (1979)

$355 million	2.6%	7½ years	4:1	22% a year

Fort Lauderdale, Florida, maker of machine tools, pumps, and car bumpers. More than half its operating companies were sold or closed during KKR's tenure. Company redeployed assets, buying Crane Packing Co. for $200 million in 1981. TI Industries of Britain bought Houdaille in 1986; half the company was soon reacquired by KKR executives and some outside investors. Second-round buyout, renamed Idex Corporation, was taken public in 1989.

SARGENT INDUSTRIES (1979)

$40 million	1.2%	5½ years	6:1	38% a year

Los Angeles maker of valves for nuclear submarines, garbage trucks, and other users. Sold to Dover Corporation in 1984.

F-B TRUCK LINE CO. (1979)

$12.8 million	5.6%	6 years	Total loss on equity

Salt Lake City, Utah, trucking company. Immediately after buyout, it was hit hard by recession and increased competition caused by industry deregulation. Assets liquidated.

EATON LEONARD CORPORATION (1980)

$13.5 million	8.5%	5½ years	Total loss on equity

Carlsbad, California, maker of machine tools. Performance slumped in 1980 and 1982 recessions. Filed for Chapter 11 bankruptcy protection in 1986.

ROTOR TOOL CO. (1981)

$27.5 million	6%	6 years	8:1	42% a year

Cleveland maker of heavy-duty tools, principally for the car industry. Sold in 1986 to Integrated Resources.

AMERICAN FOREST PRODUCTS (1981)

$425 million	22%	7 years	Break-even

San Francisco–based timber company, acquired from Bendix Corporation at peak of lumber price cycle. Subsequent industry downturn hurt results. KKR was forced to restructure debt in 1986. Investors' losses were offset by unique tax benefits in timber industry. Most assets were sold to Georgia-Pacific for $228 million in 1988.

MARLEY CO. (1981)

$354 million	2.9%	6½ years	2:1	13% a year

Shawnee Mission, Kansas, maker of water-cooling towers, heating systems, and pumps. Restructured in 1988, allowing investors to cash out. KKR executives and some original investors own company in second-round buyout.

LILY-TULIP INC. (1981)

$151 million	19.8%	5 years	7:1	53% a year

Augusta, Georgia, maker of paper cups. Cut corporate overhead during KKR's tenure. Sold to Fort Howard Corporation in 1986.

PT COMPONENTS INC. (1981)

$150 million	4.1%	5 years	7:1	52% a year

Indianapolis, Indiana, maker of Link Belt power transmissions. Cut work force, closed unprofitable plants during KKR's tenure. Sold to company's own management in 1986.

FRED MEYER INC. (1981)

$225 million	29.1%	10+ years

Portland, Oregon, retailer. Expanded sales about 10 percent a year after KKR buyout, chiefly by opening new stores. Went public in 1986 at $14.25 a share, four times price that KKR investors paid in 1981. KKR investors remain major owners; stock traded in late 1991 at about $22 a share.

FRED MEYER REAL ESTATE (1981)

$200 million	37.1%	10+ years	3:1	23% a year

Portland, Oregon, owner of Fred Meyer store sites. Most real estate was sold in stages after buyout.

NORRIS INDUSTRIES INC. (1981)

$420 million	4.8%	3 years	7:1	87% a year

Los Angeles–based maker of Thermador stoves, Premier faucets, car hubcaps, missile casings, and other industrial products. Cut headquarters costs during KKR's tenure, benefited from defense buildup. Sold to Masco Corporation for $460 million plus debt assumption in 1985.

PACIFIC REALTY TRUST (1983)

$53 million	36%	5 years	2:1	15% a year

Portland, Oregon, real estate trust. Sold in 1988 to PacTrust Realty, a company owned by its management, KKR executives, and some outside investors.

DILLINGHAM CORPORATION (1983)

$350 million	13.9%	4½ years	3:1	20% a year

Honolulu-based construction company, with interests in propane gas distribution, barges, and towing. Liquidated in stages by KKR.

GOLDEN WEST TELEVISION (1983)

$280 million	23.2%	2½ years	5:1	77% a year

Los Angeles operator of television station KTLA. Sold to Tribune Co. of Chicago for $510 million in 1985.

AMSTAR CORPORATION (1984)

$451 million	11.3%	3 years	5:1	82% a year

New York–based sugar company with interests in machine tools. Closed inefficient sugar refineries during KKR's tenure. Sold to Merrill Lynch buyout group in 1987.

WOMETCO ENTERPRISES INC. (1984)

$856 million	15.8%	4 years	3:1	39% a year

Miami, Florida, conglomerate with interests in television stations, cable TV, Coca-Cola bottling, movie theaters, food service, and vending machines. Largest television station was sold to General Electric Co. in 1987; bottling and cable-TV businesses were sold in 1986.

MALONE & HYDE (1984)

$550 million	19.2%	8+ years	11:1	46% a year

Memphis, Tennessee, food retailer and operator of auto-parts stores. Food business was sold to Fleming Cos. in 1988; AutoZone chain grew rapidly after buyout and was taken public by KKR in 1990.

COLE NATIONAL CORPORATION (1984)

$318 million	26.1%	3 years	3:1	44% a year

Cleveland operator of Child World toy stores and other retailing chains. Sold to management and Drexel Burnham buyout group in 1987.

PACE INDUSTRIES INC. (1985)

$1.3 billion	15%	5 years	3:1	34% a year

New York conglomerate involved in magazine printing, business-form production, and water-heater manufacturing. Several major units were sold by KKR to Japanese buyers in 1988.

RED LION INNS (1985)

$600 million	30%	7+ years

Vancouver, Washington, lodging chain, operating about 60 hotels, chiefly in Western states. Acquisition was made by Washington and Oregon pension funds and KKR executives themselves, rather than by KKR buyout fund. Ten hotels were sold to the public in a limited partnership offering in 1987.

MOTEL 6 INC. (1985)

$881 million	14.2%	5 years	5:1	38% a year

Dallas-based motel chain. Grew rapidly after buyout; converted to master limited partnership and went public in 1986. Never paid a dime of taxes because of innovative partnership structures. Sold to Accor S.A. of France in 1990.

M&T INC. (1985)

$110 million	24%	2 years	2:1	21% a year

California real estate and construction company. Sold in 1988 to PacTrust Realty, which is owned by management, KKR executives, and some outside investors.

UNION TEXAS PETROLEUM INC. (1985)

$1.6 billion	15.4%	6½ + years

Houston-based oil and gas company. KKR acquired 45% of Union Texas from Allied-Signal Corporation, which continued to own the rest. Earnings were hurt by 1986 oil price slump, but recovered afterward. Company was taken public in 1987; stock has traded around $18 a share, about triple what KKR's partnerships paid.

STORER COMMUNICATIONS INC. (1985)

$2.5 billion	8.8%	3 years	4:1	61% a year

Miami-based television and cable-TV company. KKR sold Storer's television stations to entrepreneur George Gillett in 1987. Storer's cable-TV business was sold to a joint venture of Comcast and Tele-Communications Inc. in 1988.

BEATRICE COS. (1986)

$6.2 billion	6.6%	4 years	3:1	50% a year

Chicago-based food company, known for its Tropicana juices, Hunt's tomato paste, Wesson oil, and Swift-Eckrich meats, as well as Avis Rent a Car, Samsonite luggage, and Playtex underwear. Broken up and sold off in stages over four years. Major buyers included ConAgra (for food businesses), American Brands (for nonfood businesses, known as E-II Holdings), and Seagram (for Tropicana).

SAFEWAY STORES INC. (1986)

$4.2 billion	3.0%	5 + years

Grocery chain, based in Oakland, California, the largest in the United States when KKR acquired it. Weaker-performing divisions were sold to buyers who could implement wage cuts. Remaining divisions increased earnings by adding high-profit departments such as delis and florists, while holding down labor costs. Taken public in May 1990; stock has since traded at eight times what KKR paid.

OWENS-ILLINOIS INC. (1987)

$3.7 billion	4.7%	4½ + years

Toledo-based maker of glass and plastic bottles. Cost-cutting after buyout increased profit margins in a stagnant industry. Company went public in December 1991 at $11 a share, slightly more than double what KKR's partnerships paid.

JIM WALTER CORPORATION (1987)

$2.4 billion	6.0%	4+ years	Valued at total loss

Tampa, Florida, homebuilding, coal-mining, and pipe-making conglomerate. Filed for Chapter 11 bankruptcy protection in December 1989 because of asbestosis litigation and inability to meet "reset" obligations on junk bonds.

SEAMAN FURNITURE CO. (1987)

$290 million	13.1%	4+ years	Valued at total loss

Uniondale, New York, furniture retailer. Furniture sales weakened immediately after buyout; company fell far short of financial projections made by management and KKR. Seaman in 1989 handed over part-ownership to creditors in return for scaling down its debts. It filed for bankruptcy in January 1992.

STOP & SHOP COS. (1988)

$1.2 billion	8.2%	3½ + years

Boston-based grocery chain and operator of Bradlee's discount stores. Company expanded grocery-store division after buyout, and increased profitability at Bradlee's. Company went public in November 1991 at $12.50 a share, nearly four times what KKR's equity partnerships paid.

DURACELL INC. (1988)

$1.8 billion	19.4%	3½ + years

Bethel, Connecticut, maker of alkaline batteries. Company increased market share, expanded abroad after buyout. Went public in April 1990; stock has since traded above $30 a share, more than six times what KKR's equity partnerships paid.

RJR NABISCO INC. (1989)

$26.4 billion	5.6%*	3+ years

New York–based tobacco and food company, maker of Winston, Salem, and Camel cigarettes, Oreo cookies, Ritz crackers, and Planters nuts. Survived major scare involving "reset" bonds in early 1990. Boosted profit margins by cost-cutting and price increases. Taken public in early 1991; stock has since traded above $10 a share, about double what KKR's equity partnerships paid.

K-III HOLDINGS INC. (1989)

$1.2 billion	37.5%	2+ years

New York publishing company, run by former Macmillan executives. Started from scratch, with pool of capital for acquisitions. Has bought diverse magazines, ranging from *National Hog Farmer* to *Seventeen.* Also owns book clubs and Funk & Wagnalls encyclopedia.

BANK OF NEW ENGLAND (1991)

$625 million	45.3%	1+ years

Boston-based bank, held by federal regulators after big losses associated with problem loans. Healthier parts of bank were acquired by Fleet/Norstar Financial Group Inc. in a joint bid with KKR investors, who supplied capital.

*Original equity investment in February 1989; later raised to 12.1 percent in July 1990 refinancing.

Notes

Some 243 people were interviewed in person for this book, many in multiple sessions at various times in 1989, 1990, and 1991. Several hundred additional sources were interviewed by phone. The three subjects of this book—the founding partners of Kohlberg Kravis Roberts & Co.—shared their recollections and private files to a considerable degree. Jerome Kohlberg, the least cooperative of the three partners, sat for a two-hour interview in May 1989, answered additional questions in writing, and granted access to his friends and his speeches. Henry Kravis was interviewed in person ten times from May 1989 to October 1991. George Roberts was interviewed seven times over the same period. In addition, competitors, lenders, Wall Street advisers, and limited-partner investors spoke at length about their experiences with KKR. So did regulators, top executives, and rank-and-file workers at buyout companies. Both KKR and the buyout business have been many things to many different people. The sourcing for this book reflects this diversity.

In cases where dialogue has been reconstructed, the notes that follow identify the principal sources for each exchange, the dates when those sources were interviewed, and any significant variances in participants' accounts. No additional dialogue has been invented or synthesized.

Documents, both public and private, played a vital role in every chapter. Financial data on KKR-controlled companies comes from prospectuses, bond offerings, and 10-K annual reports filed with the Securities and Exchange Commission (SEC). Internal documents of KKR, Kohlberg & Co., Prudential Insurance Co., Drexel Burnham Lambert Inc., and

Citicorp are cited where appropriate. Various lawsuits—whatever else they have accomplished—have brought a wealth of usually private information into the public record. Those suits are identified by plaintiff, defendant, year, and court. Board minutes and private letters are cited by date and source.

Newspaper and magazine articles provided valuable snapshots of people's views in a fast-changing era. The most frequently cited sources are *The Wall Street Journal* (*WSJ*) and *The New York Times* (*NYT*). *Institutional Investor, Forbes, Fortune, BusinessWeek, The Portland Oregonian, The Washington Post,* and the *Los Angeles Times* have been valuable sources as well.

Introduction

page xiii: ". . . you see a miracle": *Toledo Blade,* 30 August 1941.

page xiv: adding more than $2 trillion: The Wilshire 5000 index, the summation of the market capitalization of the top 5,000 U.S. stocks, totaled more than $3.4 trillion at the end of the 1980s, up from $1.03 trillion at the beginning of the decade.

page xiv: Deloitte's largest client: interview with Michael Cook, chairman of Deloitte & Touche, 19 January 1990.

page xv: Taylor's visit to KKR: interview with KKR associate Jamie Greene, 17 April 1989.

page xv: "learning to love leverage": Beth Selby, "Learning to Love Leverage," *Institutional Investor,* December 1986.

page xvi: "natural tension": William Greider, *Secrets of the Temple* (New York: Simon and Schuster, 1987), p. 11.

page xviii: "We were hoping . . .": interview with Henry Kravis, 18 June 1991.

page xix: "Never fall in love . . .": phone interview, July 1991.

page xx: "The eclipse . . .": That title was used by Harvard Business School professor Michael Jensen for an overview of the buyout business in *Harvard Business Review,* September-October 1989.

Chapter 1: Courting CEOs

page 1: Bill Jones's troubles: interview with Bill Jones, 10 February 1990; interview with former Boren Clay accountant Tom Hudson, 11 April 1991; phone interview with former Boren Clay banker James Melvin, May 1989; phone interview with Simpson Thacher attorney Richard Beattie, November 1991.

page 2: Kravis's appearance: interview with Bill Jones, 10 February 1990.

page 3: Purchase price and fee: internal documents of Prudential Insurance Co.; internal memoranda of Bear, Stearns & Co., including thirty-four-page memo on proposed acquisition dated 5 March 1974; letter from Kravis to Milan Resanovich of Prudential, 29 March 1974.

page 4: "Nothing would make me happier . . .": interview with Bill Jones, 10 February 1990.

page 5: Bear, Stearns's 1960s ambience: phone interviews with nine current and former Bear, Stearns executives, March through June 1989.

page 5: Kohlberg's career track: interview with Kohlberg, 22 May 1989.

page 6: Shyness became an asset: interview with former Bear, Stearns executive Ron Shiftan, 17 July 1989.

page 6: "I liked the long-term . . .": interview, 22 May 1989.

page 6: Luftman as the more engaging: interview with Theodore and James Stern, sons of Sterndent executive H. J. Stern, 2 May 1989. "To me, Jerry Kohlberg was a little bit of an enigma," recalled James Stern. "He said very little in meetings. Others said the words for him. He would be at the edge of the room. His associates would be up front, talking." Similar recollections were voiced in an interview, 15 September 1989, with Leon Prince, a long-time executive of Bally Case & Cooler, a company acquired by Luftman and Kohlberg in 1967.

page 7: Devised a third way: interview with Luftman, 17 May 1989; interview with Kohlberg, 22 May 1989; initial public offering prospectus for Stern Metals Corporation, 23 September 1965.

page 8: ". . . just financings": phone interview with June Lawyer, June 1989.

page 9: "We talked . . .": interview with Kohlberg, 22 May 1989.

page 10: Roberts typing letters: phone interview with Alan Sergy, Roberts's senior-year college roommate, June 1989.

page 11: Kravis copying phrases: interview with former Bear, Stearns executives Ron Shiftan and John Sheehy, 17 July 1989.

page 12: Roberts's departure from Bear, Stearns: interview with Roberts, 7 September 1989.

page 13: Kravis's ouster: interview with Kravis, 3 May 1989.

page 14: Early KKR ambience: interview with ex-secretary Peggy Coiro, 26 May 1989; phone interview with Richard Wakenight, former Vapor Corporation treasurer, March 1989.

page 14: MacDonnell's "plinking" episode: interview with MacDonnell, 17 April 1989.

page 15: "All the money's . . .": phone interview, April 1989, with David Street, former First Chicago Corporation banker who financed early KKR acquisitions.

page 15: O'Keefe's travails: interview with O'Keefe, 10 April 1989.

page 16: A. J. board meetings: minutes of A. J. Industries Inc. directors' meetings for 31 August 1976 and 30 September 1976.

page 17: Kravis at the golf course: interview with Bill Jones, 10 February 1990.

page 18: Boren's restructuring and sale: internal Prudential Insurance Co. files for 6 February 1987.

Chapter 2: The Growing Allure of Debt

page 19: Saltarelli background: phone interview with Saltarelli, February 1990.

page 21: Senator Bacon's concerns: *Congressional Record,* 1 July 1909, p. 4007.

page 22: Professor Graham's warnings: Benjamin Graham, David L. Dodd, and Sidney Cottle, *Securities Analysis* (New York: McGraw-Hill, 1962), p. 543.

page 22: Professor Jensen's outlook: Michael C. Jensen and William H. Meckling, "Theory of the Firm," *Journal of Financial Economics,* Autumn 1976.

page 23: "You have to structure . . .": *NYT,* 1 August 1976.

page 25: First KKR-Houdaille meeting: reconstruction is based on phone interview with Philip O'Reilly, in March 1989; interview with Kravis, 3 May 1989; interview with Don Boyce, Houdaille's treasurer at the time, 5 June 1989; phone interviews with Peter Sachs, August 1989 and May 1991; phone interview with Gerald Saltarelli, February 1990.

page 27: Herdrich's calculations: interviews with Don Herdrich, 22 May 1989 and 28 August 1989; confidential financing memo for Houdaille acquisition, prepared by KKR in November 1978.

page 29: Ragged memo: personal observation; phone interview with Herdrich, May 1991.

page 29: Loan offer by Tokarz: interview with Tokarz, 11 August 1989.

page 31: Kravis-Continental exchange: phone interview with Herdrich, May 1991.

page 31: Kravis sounded flustered: *WSJ,* 7 March 1979.

page 33: Hudson's depreciation maneuver: interview with Boyce, 5 June 1989, interview with Hudson, 11 April 1991.

page 34: Kravis and HH Holdings: minutes of HH Holdings board meeting, 5 March 1979.

page 35: Dayan's resistance wore down: interview with Dayan, 2 May 1991.

page 35: SEC's questions: letter from the SEC's V. J. Lavernoich to Howard Altarescu, attorney at Cadwalader, Wickersham & Taft, 14 March 1979.

page 37: Growth of buyout business: *Mergers & Acquisitions* magazine, M&A database, cited in "Volume of Buyouts and the Pot of Gold, 1989 update," a report prepared for the Subcommittee on Oversight and Investigations of the House Committee on Energy and Commerce.

page 37: Goldman, Sachs's Marley fee: disclosed in proxy statement for Marley Co. shareholders' meeting, 30 April 1981.

page 39: "You're the last guy . . .": interview with Herdrich, 28 August 1989.

page 40: Top-paid lawyers: *Forbes,* 16 October 1989.

page 40: KKR's first computer: interview with Herdrich, 28 August 1989.

Chapter 3: In Pursuit of Profits

page 42: "I love Portland": Portland *Oregonian,* 27 July 1989.

page 43: Disputes among Meyer trustees: interview with former trustee Gerry Pratt, 31 July 1989; interview with former trustee Oran Robertson, 2 August 1989.

page 44: ". . . blank check.": interview with Roger Meier, 1 August 1989.

page 45: Failure of first KKR fund-raising: interview with Kravis, 3 May 1989.

page 45: KKR Partners investors: disclosed in limited partnership application filed 1 October 1976 with the New York Secretary of State.

page 45: Ray Kravis's admonitions: interview with Ray Kravis, June 1989.

page 45: Graham's warning: interview with Henry Kravis, 3 May 1989; interview with William Graham, 7 November 1989.

page 47: "We had made money . . .": phone interview with Oran Robertson, March 1989.

page 47: "There is a great deal of clashing . . .": trustees' minutes, 22 December 1980, kept by trustee Gerry Pratt.

page 47: Pratt on Kohlberg: interview, 1 August 1989.

page 48: Meier affinity for Roberts: interview with Meier, 1 August 1989.

page 49: Hanson's memo: disclosed in Portland *Oregonian,* 12 March 1982.

page 50: Hitchman affinity for Roberts: interview with Hitchman, 12 April 1989.

page 50: Kravis in Kuwait: interview with Kravis, 1 December 1989.

page 51: KKR's fees: disclosed in "Kohlberg Kravis Roberts & Co., 1982 Investment Fund," a forty-page private placement memorandum circulated among large investors.

page 52: Bank lenders nearly foreclosed: interview with Continental Illinois banker Michael Murray, 6 November 1989; interview with Kravis, October 1991.

page 53: Goldin's objections to buyouts: quoted in *Time,* 5 December 1988.

page 55: Phone manners at KKR: interview with Canning, 6 June 1989.

page 56: Yale's objections: phone interview with Swenson, March 1989.

page 57: Gains in Oregon portfolio: letter from KKR partner Michael W. Michelson to Oregon treasurer Anthony Meeker, 30 April 1991.

page 58: Cooperman's estimate: "Portfolio Strategy," Goldman, Sachs & Co. report to clients, September 1987.

page 59: Kravis-Raether exchange: phone interview with Raether, June 1990.

page 59: Kehler's proposal: interview with Kehler, 18 October 1989.

Chapter 4: How to Talk to Banks

page 61: Growth in buyout loans: data compiled by Loan Pricing Corporation.

page 61: Bankers Trust's lending to KKR: internal KKR records.

page 63: Tokarz-Raether exchange: phone interview with Tokarz, May 1991.

page 64: Badie-MacDonald exchange: interview with MacDonald, 4 June 1991.

page 64: Roberts approach on Gulf loan: interview with Ron Badie, 11 April 1989.

page 65: Bankers Trust's review of Gulf loan: interview with Ron Badie, 11 April 1989; interview with Joseph Manganello and Terence Mogan, 26 October 1989; phone interview with Roberts, November 1991.

page 67: Tarrytown retreat and aftermath: interview with MacDonald, 4 June 1991.

page 68: Kravis in Africa: interview with Kravis, 18 June 1991; multiple phone interviews with Roberts.

page 70: Bankers' Beatrice tour: interview with Morgan St. John, 3 August 1989.

page 71: Tokarz's pursuit of loans: interviews with Tokarz, 11 August and 9 October 1989.

page 72: "Dialing for dollars": interview with Morgan St. John and George Hartmann, 4 August 1989.

page 72: Kravis-Kominski exchange: phone interview with Kominski, November 1989.

page 73: Beatrice fees: cited in 11 March 1986 proxy statement issued by Beatrice Cos. Increase in Kidder's fee emerged in interview with former Kidder, Peabody investment banker Peter Goodson, 19 July 1989.

page 74: Beatrice closing dinner: reconstruction based on interviews with seven commercial bankers, two KKR executives, two Drexel executives, and incoming Beatrice chief executive Don Kelly.

page 76: Volcker's "Bravo": deposition of Metropolitan Life Insurance Co. chief executive John Creedon, in a 1988 bondholder suit seeking to stop the RJR Nabisco buyout, *Metropolitan Life Insurance Co. et al.* v. *RJR Nabisco Inc.,* filed in federal court for the Southern District of New York.

page 76: Solow's career path: *Institutional Investor,* January 1989.

page 76: Solow approach to Kravis: interview with Solow, 12 June 1989.

page 77: Manganello's views: interview, 26 October 1989.

page 77: Tokarz's Safeway tactics: interview with St. John, Hartmann, and Badie, 11 April 1989; interview with Tokarz, 11 August 1989.

page 79: Roberts-Elorriaga exchange: interview with John Elorriaga, 1 August 1989.

page 80: Roberts-Badie exchange: interview with Badie, 11 April 1989.

page 80: Badie-Greene exchange: interview with Badie, 11 April 1989; phone interview with Greene, January 1990.

page 80: Reed's concern about fees: Reed interview in *Harvard Business Review*, March/April 1990.

page 81: Owens-Illinois bank meeting: interviews with three participants in meeting.

Chapter 5: The Enchanting World of Drexel

page 83: Milken's hours: Connie Bruck, *The Predator's Ball* (New York: Simon & Schuster, 1988), pp. 86–87.

page 83: "They deliver . . .": interview with Kravis, 9 August 1989.

page 85: Charles's ire with KKR: interview with Charles, 16 October 1989.

page 85: Milken and "fallen angels": *Forbes*, 19 November 1984; Bruck, *Predator's Ball*, p. 27.

page 86: Absentminded professor: interview with Lorraine Spurge, 28 June 1991.

page 88: Higgins's remarks: interview with Jay Higgins, 27 April 1989; interview with former Gulf executive vice president Harold Hammer, 8 September 1989.

page 88: Pickens's view of Milken: T. Boone Pickens, *Boone* (New York: Houghton Mifflin, 1987), p. 226.

page 88: Cole National episode: reconstruction based on interview with Kravis and Ammon, 9 August 1989; phone interview with Jeffrey Cole, September 1989; phone interview with Fred Carr, September 1989; and follow-up phone interview with Ammon, July 1991.

page 90: Raether interest in Drexel: interview with Raether, 2 October 1989.

page 90: Herdrich-Kravis exchange: phone interview with Herdrich, February 1990.

page 91: Fox-Roberts exchange: interview with Fox, 24 October 1990.

page 92: Dillon, Read approach to KKR: Storer Communications Inc. proxy statement of 23 October 1985.

page 92: Weigers's opposition: interview with Raether, 2 October 1989; phone interview with Weigers, October 1989.

page 93: Weigers-Raether exchange: interview with Raether, 2 October 1989.

page 93: Jet-to-jet talks: interview with Kravis, 18 June 1991.

page 94: "The conviction . . .": John Kenneth Galbraith, *The Great Crash 1929* (New York: Houghton Mifflin, 1954), p. 169.

page 94: Kehler remarks: cited by KKR executive R. Theodore Ammon in testimony, 19 October 1990, before New York federal court as part of sentencing hearing for Michael Milken. Ammon's account was confirmed in an interview with Dean Kehler, 11 June 1991.

page 96: Overflow crowd in Chicago: interview with Drexel investment bankers Leon Black and Dean Kehler, 5 October 1989.

page 97: Milken-Kravis exchange: interview with Kravis, 9 August 1989.

page 98: "Look at the world . . .": *Forbes,* 19 November 1984.

page 98: Bayse-Storer example: *WSJ,* 24 August 1989.

page 99: Engel on parties: Bruck, *Predator's Ball,* p. 15.

page 100: Dahl's testimony: *Washington Post,* 26 October 1990.

page 100: Joseph's concern: quoted in *Fortune,* 16 March 1987.

page 101: Milken's pay: disclosed in ninety-eight-count federal indictment of Milken, 29 March 1989, on charges of racketeering and securities fraud.

page 101: Kravis's warrant exchange: interview with Kravis, 30 March 1990.

page 101: Cogut warrant query: phone interview with Cogut, January 1991.

page 102: Spiegel's salary, butler, and jet: *Los Angeles Times,* 13 July 1990.

page 103: Fidelity's ads: *Money,* January 1986.

page 103: Small investors' outlays: *WSJ,* 21 March 1990.

page 104: Junk-bond supply and creditworthiness: Barrie Wigmore, "The Decline in Credit Quality of New-Issue Junk Bonds," *Financial Analysts Journal,* September/October 1990.

page 107: Milken's Mexico soliloquy: interview with Scott Stuart, 30 May 1991; phone interview with Roberts, June 1991.

page 108: Ammon-Liman exchange: Milken sentencing hearing, 19 October 1990.

Chapter 6: The Takeover Minstrels

page 109: Duties of "care" and "loyalty": A landmark affirmation of these duties came in a 1986 Delaware state court decision, *MacAndrews & Forbes* v. *Revlon Inc.* In that case, Revlon management had negotiated the sale of the company to a friendly buyer; that agreement was overturned by the Delaware court, which said the terms unfairly denied shareholders the right to benefit from a higher offer by corporate raider Ron Perelman. Subsequently, directors' duties of "care" and "loyalty" were treated with immense gravity in a series of law journal articles, including an article in *The Business Lawyer,* February 1988: "The Emerging Role of the Special Committee: Ensuring Business Judgment Rule Protection in the Context of Management Leveraged Buyouts," by Scott V. Simpson, an attorney at Skadden, Arps, Slate, Meagher & Flom.

page 111: "So you're the guy . . ." and subsequent exchange: phone interview with Roberts, February 1990; phone interview with Katcher, May 1990.

page 112: Total U.S. takeovers in 1981 and 1986: database service of *Mergers & Acquisitions* magazine.

page 112: "It's the leverage": *Institutional Investor,* November 1986.

page 113: Kravis's remarks at Beatrice boardroom and directors' reactions: interviews with Kravis, Paul Raether, and Michael Tokarz, 9 August 1989; phone interviews with four Beatrice directors, William Granger, Alex Brody, Murray Weidenbaum, and Goff Smith, October and November 1989.

page 114: KKR's suspicions: interview with Tokarz, 9 October 1989; interview with KKR associate Kevin Bousquette, 16 November 1990.

page 116: Roberts-Magowan meeting: interview with Magowan, 3 April, 1989; interview with Roberts and MacDonnell, 17 April 1989.

page 117: Katcher-Roberts showdown: interview with Ron Badie, 11 April 1989; interview with Katcher, 13 March 1990; phone interview with Roberts, November 1991.

page 119: "A lot of the art . . .": phone interview with KKR associate Ned Gilhuly, February 1990; phone interview with Roberts, February 1990.

page 120: Oregon's $600 million commitment: board minutes of Oregon Investment Council, 25 June 1987; interview with Oregon Investment Council chairperson Carol Hewitt, 1 August 1989.

page 121: Herrlinger bid for Dayton-Hudson: *WSJ,* 24 June 1987 and 25 June 1987.

page 121: Advisers' doubts about Paine Webber bid: deposition, 4 September 1987, of Shearson Lehman Brothers investment banker Stephen Waters, an adviser to Jim Walter Corporation. Deposition was taken in a shareholder suit filed against Jim Walter Corporation in Florida state court: *Edith Citron et al.* v. *Jim Walter Corp. et al.*

page 121: Paine Webber's inability to win over Walter: interview with Walter, 18 May 1989; Walter deposition of 8 September 1987 in *Citron* suit. Walter in particular took issue with Paine Webber's estimates that overhead could be cut $20 million in the first year of a buyout.

page 122: "I didn't believe anything . . .": Waters deposition in *Citron* suit.

page 122: Beattie-Katcher exchange: interview with Katcher, 21 March 1990; phone interview with Beattie, November 1991.

page 122: Katcher-Roberts exchange: Waters deposition in *Citron* suit; interview with Katcher, 21 March 1990; phone interview with Roberts, June 1991.

page 123: Original price target for Duracell sale: phone interviews with John Richman and John Golden, January 1990.

page 123: Salomon's offer: interview with Robert Kidder, 17 March 1989.

page 124: Forstmann preemptive bid: phone interviews with Golden, Kidder, and Forstmann Little partner Nicholas Forstmann.

page 124: Golden-Bousquette exchange: interview with Bousquette, 16 November 1990.

page 125: Kravis-Richman exchange: phone interviews with Kravis and Richman, January 1990; interview with Bousquette 16 November 1990.

page 126: Duracell finalists' bids: interview with Clayton & Dubilier partner Martin Dubilier, 14 March 1989; interview with Gibbons Green partner Lewis van Amerongen, 9 March 1989; multiple phone interviews with Kravis, Bousquette, Golden, and Kidder. Forstmann Little executives decline to specify their final bid; the $1.7 billion figure is based on four other people's reports.

page 126: Forstmann demanded a chance to bid again: interviews with Kidder and Golden. Forstmann denies that he wanted to rebid.

page 126: Roberts-Kohlberg exchange on RJR: interview with Roberts, 7 September 1989.

page 126: Kravis-Cohen meeting: *WSJ*, 25 October 1988; also described in detail in Bryan Burrough and John Helyar, *Barbarians at the Gate* (New York: HarperCollins, 1990), pp. 201–4.

page 127: Bowman's objections: *WSJ*, 28 October 1988.

page 127: Kravis-Solow exchange: interview with Solow, 12 June 1989; Burrough and Helyar, *Barbarians*, p. 209.

page 127: Fight about Drexel's role: interview with Drexel executive Dean Kehler, 18 October 1989.

page 128: "This is crazy": Burrough and Helyar, *Barbarians*, p. 328.

page 128: Forstmann exchange with Johnson lawyer: described in Hope Lampert, *True Greed* (New York: New American Library, 1990), p. 182; Burrough and Helyar, *Barbarians*, p. 347.

page 128: Johnson's "management agreement": *NYT*, 5 November 1988; *Time*, 5 December 1988.

page 130: Kravis-Atkins exchange: Burrough and Helyar, *Barbarians*, p. 499.

page 130: Kravis attuned to RJR board: *WSJ*, 2 December 1988; *Fortune*, 24 April 1989.

page 130: "We felt used and abused . . .": *WSJ*, 9 November 1988.

page 132: "I had just won a hand . . .": *Fortune*, 2 January 1989.

page 132: "I have two regrets . . .": interview with Roberts, 17 April 1989.

Chapter 7: The Mentor's Fall

page 134: Description of Lehman as "poisoned partnership": Ken Auletta, *Greed and Glory on Wall Street* (New York: Random House, 1986), p. 4.

page 134: Search for Swarthmore president: cited in *Broadcasting*, 4 February 1985.

page 134: Kohlberg's cut in ownership in 1979 and 1981 is cited in *Jerome Kohlberg Jr.* v. *Kohlberg Kravis Roberts & Co.,* filed in New York state court, 21 August 1989.

page 135: Vast amounts of Coca-Cola: interview with KKR partner Paul Raether, 2 October 1989.

page 136: Kravis-Kohlberg exchange about hiring: interview with Kravis, 26 September 1989.

page 136: Jim Kohlberg's résumé: from broker's application filed with the Commodities Futures Trading Commission, 12 April 1984, by James A. Kohlberg.

page 136: Jim Kohlberg's ranking as tennis pro: phone interview with Greg Sharkow, Association of Tennis Professionals, September 1989.

page 136: Kravis opposition to hiring Jim Kohlberg: interview with Kravis, 26 September 1989.

page 136: Kohlberg believed in his son: interview with Kohlberg friend Martin Dubilier, 14 March 1989; interview with Kohlberg friend and publicist Davis Weinstock, 26 September 1989.

page 136: "If you want to hire Jimmy" and subsequent Kohlberg response: interview with Kravis, 26 September 1989.

page 137: Jim Kohlberg's efforts: interviews with Roberts, Bob MacDonnell, and Saul Fox, 6 and 7 September 1989.

page 137: "We've got these other guys" and subsequent response: interview with Roberts, 6 September 1989.

page 138: Building blocks: interview with Carolyne Roehm, 26 July 1989.

page 138: Nancy Kohlberg clipped wool: interview with Dubilier, 14 March 1989.

page 139: Monday-morning meetings and subsequent detail: interview with Kravis, 26 September 1989. Four other KKR executives confirm details.

page 139: March 1985 breakfast clash: This account is based on interviews with Roberts, 6 September 1989, and with Kravis, 26 September 1989, as well as subsequent phone interviews with both men. Kohlberg, through a spokesman, declines to discuss this period in detail. In a written response to questions, 29 April 1991, Kohlberg stated: "I was out for a time due to an operation and recuperation. When I returned, it was clear that my partners and I had grown apart."

page 141: Kohlberg-Aeder discussions: interview with Arthur Aeder, 11 October 1989.

page 142: "We're going to destroy . . .": interview with Kravis, 26 September 1989.

page 143: Red Lion and Jim Kohlberg's stake: interview with Roberts, 6 September 1989.

page 146: Kohlberg's working hours: interviews with Raether, 2 October 1989; with Kravis, 26 September 1989; with KKR associate Kevin Bousquette, 11 October 1989; and with KKR associate Ted Ammon, 5 September 1989.

page 148: Fast-paced ways worried Kohlberg . . . and subsequent detail: interviews with Kohlberg confidants Arthur Aeder, Davis Weinstock, George Peck, Donald Stone, and Martin Dubilier; Kohlberg interview with *Institutional Investor,* November 1986.

page 148: Roberts-Kohlberg clash over Beatrice: interview with Roberts, 6 September 1989; confirmed in letter from Kohlberg dated 29 April 1991.

page 149: Jim Kohlberg's pay for 1986 and subsequent detail: interview with George Roberts, 6 September 1989.

page 150: Early January 1987 meeting: interview with Roberts, 6 September 1989; interview with Kravis, 26 September 1989; phone interview with Lang, October 1989.

page 150: Roberts-Kravis exchange about Kohlberg: interview with Roberts, 6 September 1989; interview with Kravis, 26 September 1989.

page 151: Kohlberg-Raether dialogue: interview with Raether, 2 October 1989.

page 151: Kohlberg-Kravis lunch exchange: This account is based on an interview with Kravis, 26 September 1989, and a follow-up phone interview with Kravis, January 1990. In his written communication of 29 April 1991, Kohlberg says: "After a year of discussion, we reached an agreement that involved a purchase of my interest, a buyout over time. Overall I was delighted with my experience there, delighted to leave and I am very delighted with our new company." Kohlberg, through a spokesman, declines to answer further questions.

page 151: Kohlberg's share of any future buyouts: cited in *Jerome Kohlberg Jr.* v. *Kohlberg Kravis Roberts & Co.,* 21 August 1989.

page 151: Smaller concessions to Kohlberg: interview with Kravis, 26 September 1989; interview with Roberts, 7 September 1989.

page 152: "Overpowering greed . . .": the phrase is recalled by three investors who were present at the meeting.

page 152: Kohlberg remark to Amerman: phone interview with Amerman, September 1989.

page 153: Ambience of Kohlberg & Co.: firsthand observation in January and May 1989.

page 153: Kohlberg's $1 billion goal: *Fortune,* 4 July 1988.

page 155: Flap over Texaco toe-hold profits: multiple phone interviews with Kravis and Roberts.

Chapter 8: Ruling an Industrial Empire

page 156: Comparisons to Chrysler, Texaco, and AT&T: based on sales rankings for 1989, as compiled by *Fortune* magazine. The 500 largest U.S. industrial companies were cited in the 23 April 1990 issue; the largest service companies appeared in the 4 June 1990 issue. American Telephone and Telegraph ranked number one among service companies, with $36.3 billion of sales. Chrysler ranked number eight among industrial companies, with $36.2 billion of sales; Texaco ranked tenth, with $32.4 billion of sales. By comparison, the combined sales of the nine largest KKR-controlled companies—RJR Nabisco, Safeway Stores, Stop & Shop, Beatrice, Owens-Illinois, Fred Meyer, Hillsborough Holdings, Duracell, and Marley—totaled $48.2 billion.

page 156: Total employment at KKR-controlled companies: "Presentation on Leveraged Buyouts by Kohlberg Kravis Roberts & Co.," a January 1989 KKR report that was circulated widely among Washington policy-makers, cited 276,000 employees at KKR-controlled companies other than RJR Nabisco; the 1988 annual report for RJR Nabisco cited a further 116,881 employees.

page 157: KKR's objective in 1978: Quote is from "KKR Investment Fund," a private placement, fund-raising memorandum, January 1978, p. 2.

page 157: KKR's objective in 1987: Quote is from "Kohlberg Kravis Roberts & Co., 1987 Fund, Confidential," a private placement memo, June 1987, p. 4.

page 158: Average stock market gains of 9 percent: Roger G. Ibbotson and Gary P. Brinson, *Investment Markets* (New York: McGraw-Hill, 1987), p. 72. Different long-term studies show average yearly returns of 8.2 to 9.5 percent. All studies count both capital gains and dividend income.

page 159: Kravis sessions with Loomis students: phone interview with James Wilson, January 1989.

page 159: Henry Kravis's view of his father: as quoted in *Manhattan Inc.,* December 1988.

page 159: Lou Roberts's Permian Basin investments: interview with former Bear, Stearns executive Walter Luftman, 16 May 1989.

page 160: Lou and George Roberts's car trips: interview with George Roberts, 17 April 1989.

page 160: Kravis-Roberts exchange over Motel 6 signs: interview with Kravis, 30 March 1990.

page 160: Reluctance to see Fred Meyer stores: interview with Oran Robertson, 2 August 1989.

page 160: Kravis viewing Incom as "boring": phone interviews with Ed Mabbs, 1989–90.

page 161: "When a manager . . .": *NYT,* 19 November 1984.

page 161: KKR's buyout creed: composite, based on interviews with Kravis, Roberts, MacDonnell, Raether, and nine chief executives of KKR-controlled companies. Fullest version is from July 1991 phone interview with MacDonnell, discussing KKR's 1986 buyout of Safeway.

page 163: "Why can't Don be reasonable?": interview with Kravis, 1 December 1989.

page 163: Kelly's ownership stake in Beatrice: bond prospectus, 10 April 1986, for $1.75 billion of debentures issued by BCI Holdings Corporation, p. 51.

page 163: Kelly's profit on Beatrice stake: author's calculation; phone interview with Kelly, October 1991.

page 163: Kravis on Beatrice managers' goals: *BusinessWeek,* 2 December 1985.

page 163: Cutbacks in lavish Beatrice ad budget: phone interview with former Beatrice executive William Reidy, November 1989.

page 163: Kelly eradicating Dutt's style and subsequent detail: interview with Don Kelly, 7 November 1989.

page 164: Kelly's exchange with Tokarz and Bousquette: *Fortune,* 4 July 1988.

page 164: "My job has been . . .": *Institutional Investor,* June 1988.

page 165: Union Texas action plan: interview with Roberts, 16 February 1989; author correspondence with Union Texas executive Carol Cox, August 1991.

page 165: Owens-Illinois cost-cutting and subsequent details: personal observation; interviews with Robert Lanigan, Joseph Lemieux, and O-I chief financial officer Lee Wesselman, 4 January 1990.

page 166: "I knew a lot of people . . .": interview with Magowan, 22 May 1991.

page 166: Roberts's warning to MacDonnell: phone interview with MacDonnell, August 1991.

page 167: "Transitions come with costs . . ." and subsequent details: interviews with Burd, 18 April 1989, 9 February 1990, and subsequent phone interviews.

page 168: Safeway spending and inventory cuts: Safeway annual reports, 1985, 1986, and 1987.

page 168: "I do believe it . . .": interview with Magowan, 3 April 1989.

page 169: Dogs flying on corporate jets: Burrough and Helyar, *Barbarians,* p. 95.

page 169: Kravis on RJR's corporate waste: interview, 3 May 1989.

page 169: Fee of $500,000 for Tom Neff: *BusinessWeek,* 6 February 1989.

page 170: Gerstner telling Neff "Go away": phone interview with Neff, December 1989.

page 170: Kravis-Raether visit to Gerstner's home: interview with Kravis, 14 December 1989; interview with Gerstner, 6 March 1991; phone interview with Raether, October 1991.

page 171: Gerstner's contract to join RJR: bond prospectus for $1.25 billion of debentures offered by RJR Holdings Capital Corporation, 4 April 1989, pp. 76–77.

page 171: New policy on RJR corporate jets: phone interviews with RJR vice president Jason Wright, March 1991.

page 172: Decor of new RJR offices: personal inspection in March 1991; interview with Gene Croisant, 5 March 1991.

page 172: Johnston and Greeniaus ownership stakes: RJR's 10-K filing with the Securities and Exchange Commission for 1989.

page 172: "Having the LBO perform . . .": interview with Greeniaus, March 8, 1991.

page 173: Jones-Kravis exchange: interview with Jones, 10 February 1990.

page 173: Kidder found Kraft stifling and subsequent details: interview with Kidder, 17 March 1989.

page 174: Origin of the "Exorcist Plan" and subsequent details: interviews with Kidder, 17 March 1989 and 5 February 1990; interview with Perrin, 5 February 1990.

page 175: Richman-Kidder dinner: interview with Kidder, 17 March 1989; phone interview with Richman, February 1990.

Chapter 9: The Discipline of Debt

page 176: Kaplan study of buyouts: *Management Buyouts: Efficiency Gains or Value Transfers,* Center for Research in Securities Prices, Graduate School of Business, University of Chicago, 1989. Kaplan surveyed seventy-six buyouts undertaken from 1980 to 1986, including nearly a dozen KKR buyouts.

page 176: "The same managers . . .": Jensen testimony before the House Ways and Means Committee, 1 February 1989.

page 176: Roberts and Kravis on virtues of buyouts: Roberts speech to the Arlington Club, Portland, Oregon, 14 May 1991; *NYT,* 19 November 1984.

page 179: Lanigan on missed targets: interview, 4 January 1990.

page 179: "I don't like O-I . . .": *Toledo Blade,* 21 March 1987.

page 180: Markell's firing at Safeway: Markell deposition, 11 November 1986, in *Robert C. Markell, et al.* v. *Safeway Stores Inc., et al.,* filed in California state court, Alameda County.

page 180: Trujillo's plight: deposition of Raymond Trujillo, 18 November 1986, in *Markell* v. *Safeway.*

page 180: Lorray job hunt: deposition of Mary Ellen Lorray, 12 November 1986, in *Markell* v. *Safeway.*

page 180: Michelson on O-I bureaucracy: interview, 17 April 1989.

page 180: MacDonnell on Safeway cutbacks: interview, 17 April 1989

page 182: Houdaille's stance on wages: quote is from a 14 May 1986 memo jointly prepared by KKR and Houdaille top management, seeking to sell the company.

page 183: Strippit warnings and pay: phone interview with Gregory Stone, August 1991; phone interview with Idex executive Don Boyce, September 1991.

page 183: Slawson's pay: disclosed in Houdaille prospectus for $175 million of debentures, 9 September 1986, p. 32.

page 183: Workers "went crazy . . .": interview with Stone, August 1991.

page 184: Kollig's reaction: phone interviews, December 1989.

page 184: KKR's influence at Safeway: interview with Roberts and MacDonnell, 17 April 1989.

page 184: Safeway's 1.4-percent pay increases: interview with Magowan, 17 April 1989.

page 184: Abeyta reaction: *Seattle Times,* 31 July 1989. Most other major grocery chains in the Seattle area also were struck by workers seeking higher wages; contract terms obtained by Safeway applied to other grocers, too.

page 185: Safeway use of courtesy clerks: interview with Kathy Morris, 1 August 1989; interview with Safeway chief financial officer Michael Pharr, 21 May 1991.

page 185: Owens-Illinois EBIT target: cited in KKR's confidential financing memorandum of February 1987, the "bank book."

page 186: Waller's marching orders: interviews with Waller and Owens-Illinois manager Rob Smith, 9 February 1990.

page 186: Stebbins's work conditions: personal observation; interview with Bob Stebbins, 9 February 1990.

page 187: "We didn't tighten . . .": interview with Saul Fox, 24 October 1990.

page 188: Motel 6 equity ownership: phone interview with Saul Fox, October 1991.

page 188: Motel 6 pay and benefits: deposition of Motel 6 chief executive Joseph McCarthy, 17 May 1991, in *Lisia M. Dykes* v. *Motel 6 G.P. Inc., et al.,* filed in Texas state court, Harris County.

page 188: Kemps' experience at Motel 6: deposition of Samuel and Myrl Kemp, 11 October 1990, in *Dykes* v. *Motel 6.*

page 189: KKR perspective on Motel 6: interview with Fox, 24 October 1990; phone interview with MacDonnell, July 1991.

page 190: "I don't see . . .": phone interview with Roberts, October 1990.

page 190: Extra Safeway jobs: interview with Magowan, 3 April 1989.

page 190: "KKR isn't in the grocery . . .": interview with Morris, 1 August 1989.

page 190: Teninty's view of KKR: interview with Ron Teninty, 7 September 1989.

page 191: Norris tug-of-war: interview with Jack Meany, 26 October 1989.

page 191: KKR office ambience: personal observation.

page 192: Kravis's own airline: An incorporation certificate for East-West Air Inc. was filed with the New York Secretary of State's office by the airline's president, Henry Kravis, on 27 February 1987.

page 193: "And have fun": interview with Owens-Illinois president Joseph Lemieux, 4 January 1990; Roberts confirmed the remark in a phone interview, November 1991.

Chapter 10: Cashing Out

page 194: "The longer you hold . . .": quoted in *Institutional Investor,* November 1986.

page 196: Kohlberg-Mabbs exchange: from minutes of 16 April 1980 board meeting of Incom International Inc., typed up two days later by Prudential Insurance Co. executive Lars Berkman.

page 197: Background of KTLA: Tribune Co. announcement of purchase, 21 May 1985.

page 198: Cook took pride: In a follow-up interview, Cook was quoted in the *WSJ,* 24 May 1985, as saying: "KTLA fills the hole we were missing." An investment banker quoted in *The Washington Post,* 17 May 1985, said: "The Tribune felt they had to have this station for strategic reasons, whatever it cost."

page 198: Banks' insistence on $1.5 billion of Beatrice asset sales: largely disclosed in proxy statement mailed to Beatrice Cos. shareholders, 11 March 1986, p. 31; more fully disclosed in interviews with Bankers Trust Co. executives Ron Badie, Morgan St. John, and George Hartmann, 11 April 1989.

page 200: "Gentlemen, we're fools . . .": interview with Tokarz, 22 February 1990.

page 200: Tokarz's three-month pitch: interview with Tokarz, 22 February 1990.

page 200: Kelly's initial aversion: interview with Kravis, 18 June 1991; interview with Kelly, 7 November 1989.

page 202: Kelly's acquisition plans: *WSJ,* 22 May 1987.

page 202: KKR's claim of a 192-percent return on Beatrice: cited in exhibit 2 of fund-raising memo circulated by KKR to potential limited partner investors, June 1987.

page 202: Kelly support of Tropicana: interview with Kelly, 7 November 1989; phone interview with George Zulanas, November 1989.

page 203: Seagram wanted to diversify: *WSJ,* 11 March 1988,

page 203: Tokarz and Roberts balked: multiple phone interviews with Tokarz and Roberts, 1990 and 1991.

page 204: Kravis called in a mediator: interview with Salomon Brothers Inc. investment banker William Rifkin, 29 November 1990.

page 204: "Henry, you've got to do . . .": interview with Tokarz, 22 February 1990.

page 204: Reconstruction of 5 May 1988 board meeting: interview with

Tokarz, 22 February 1990, and subsequent phone interviews; interview with Salomon investment bankers William Rifkin and Laurel Coben, 13 December 1990; interview with Kravis, 18 June 1991; phone interview with Kelly, October 1991. Kelly and Tokarz each say the other accused them of meddling with Salomon's results; this version combines both accounts.

page 205: "You don't need me . . .": interview with Kelly, 7 November 1989.

page 206: Tokarz and Bousquette reactions: phone interviews, 7 June 1990.

page 206: Carton of Safeway documents: interview with MacDonnell, 17 April 1989.

page 207: Magowan's hopes for turnaround: interview with Magowan, 3 April 1989; and *San Francisco Examiner,* 27 July 1987, in which Magowan said he would have preferred to keep divisions that were later sold, such as Dallas, but added: "There's so much debt in a leveraged buyout that you have to look at your assets in a cold and calculating way. If you don't get returns in a short time, you can't afford to nurse [a division]."

page 207: Magowan's memo to Roberts: interview with Magowan, 3 April 1989; phone interview with Roberts, November 1991.

page 208: Sale of Safeway's U.K. division: *WSJ,* 26 January 1987; interview with MacDonnell, 17 April 1989.

page 208: Safeway wages in Dallas: *Houston Chronicle,* 3 December 1986.

page 209: Safeway closure in Dallas: *Dallas Morning News,* 4 April 1987; *San Francisco Examiner,* 27 July 1987; interview with MacDonnell, 17 April 1989.

page 209: Olwell's assessment: *Daily Oklahoman,* 16 October 1987.

page 210: "Nobody likes the process . . .": *Daily Oklahoman,* 15 October 1987.

page 210: KKR's talks with Vons: proxy statement for meeting of Vons Cos. shareholders, 10 November 1988; phone interviews with MacDonnell, August 1991.

page 211: Burd-Gates exchange: interview with Burd, 9 February 1990; interview with Gates, 22 May 1991.

page 212: Smith study: "Corporate Ownership Structure and Performance," unpublished paper, University of Chicago, 1989.

page 213: Fletcher's assessment of Beatrice: *Advertising Age,* 26 November 1990.

Chapter 11: "We Don't Have Any Friends"

page 214: Roberts scanning *Fortune:* interview, 17 April 1989.

page 215: Kravis-Tufo exchange at Vail: interview with Tufo, 7 February 1991.

page 216: Net worth of Kravis and Roberts: The readiest gauge of the KKR partners' fortunes is the annual ranking of "The Richest People in America," compiled by *Forbes* magazine. The cousins first appeared on the list in October 1986, with fortunes estimated at $180 million each. That amount rose to $330 million apiece two years later, in *Forbes's* 24 October 1988 rankings. Their estimated riches climbed to $400 million apiece in the 23 October 1989 list, and $550 million each in the October 1990 listing. The next year, *Forbes* omitted their stakes in RJR Nabisco and estimated their other holdings at $450 million each. That total would have climbed to about $600 million if RJR had been included.

page 217: Kravis's cashmere cardigans: *Washington Post,* 8 January 1989.

page 217: Farm costing $2.6 million: *Lakeville* (Connecticut) *Journal,* 22 June 1989.

page 217: Six servants: interview with Carolyne Roehm, 28 July 1989.

page 218: Hoisting painting with a crane: interview with Kelly, 7 November 1989.

page 218: Johnson's reluctance to work with Kravis: *Fortune,* 24 April 1989; Lampert, *True Greed,* p. 33.

page 218: "Born into a life of privilege": *USA Today,* 2 February 1989.

page 218: ". . . for what the money can buy": *M,* November 1989.

page 219: Buyout presentation at Chrysler: interviews with Magowan, 3 April 1989, and Lanigan, 4 January 1990.

page 220: Restrictions on mirror subsidiaries: *WSJ,* 18 December 1987.

page 220: Bentsen on recession risk: opening remarks in the Senate Finance Committee's hearings on leveraged buyouts, 25 January 1989.

page 221: Destiny of Beatrice jets: disclosed in the Form 10-K annual report that Beatrice filed with the Securities and Exchange Commission for the year ended 28 February 1989, as part of footnote 20, "Related Party Transactions."

page 221: Kravis-Dorgan exchange: phone interview with Dorgan, January 1990.

page 221: Lipton memo to clients: quoted in *New York Observer,* 14 November 1988.

page 222: "You're already the preeminent . . .": firsthand observation of Beck's call.

page 222: Brennan's wall chart: *Washington Post,* 26 November 1989.

page 223: Roberts's desires for Chevron: interview with former Washington State Investment Board chief John Hitchman, 12 April 1989; repeated phone interviews with Roberts, 1990 and 1991.

page 224: "Our company isn't for sale": *WSJ,* 27 September 1988.

page 225: Hiring a top banker: Adviser's comments were quoted in *WSJ,* 6 June 1989.

page 225: FDIC staff's support for KKR bid: Rep. Charles E. Schumer, "Report on FDIC Bailouts," prepared for the House Budget Committee, January 1991.

page 226: Clarke and Hope responses to KKR: Schumer, "Report on FDIC Bailouts."

page 226: Kohlberg's directorship fees: interview with Richard Beattie, 18 September 1989.

page 226: Kohlberg's suit: *Jerome Kohlberg Jr.* v. *Kohlberg Kravis Roberts & Co.*, filed 21 August 1989 in New York state court.

page 227: "Is hubris . . .": *Economist,* 2 September 1989. The article was drily entitled: "Three Men in a Suit."

page 229: Roberts's incredulity: phone interview with Roberts, May 1990.

page 229: Faludi's incredulity: phone interview with Faludi, May 1990.

page 229: Kravis's glum deal outlook: interview, 30 March 1990.

page 229: "You get paranoid . . .": phone interview with MacDonnell, April 1990.

Chapter 12: Credit Crunch

page 232: "As long as the money doesn't run out . . .": interview with KKR associate Scott Stuart, 30 May 1991.

page 233: Drop in banks' buyout loans: Such loans by all major U.S. banks totaled $80 billion in 1989, according to the Loan Pricing Corporation. Lending volume plunged to $13.3 billion in 1990.

page 233: Roberts called on bank chairmen: phone interview with Roberts, January 1990.

page 233: ". . . hands off": interview with George Gould, 23 March 1990.

page 234: Advent of HLT guidelines: *WSJ,* 23 February 1989.

page 234: Bankers Trust's $60 billion of loans: *WSJ,* October 1988.

page 235: Bank resistance to UAL financing: *WSJ,* 16 October 1989.

page 235: Kravis-Bianco exchange: interview with Bianco, February 1990.

page 236: Carr's optimism: *Forbes,* 17 April 1989.

page 236: Assets of junk-bond mutual funds: Investment Company Institute, as quoted in "High Yield Weekly Market Review" of Donaldson Lufkin Jenrette Securities Corporation, 10 January 1991.

page 236: "You can't be force-fed . . .": *WSJ,* 15 September 1989.

page 237: "I've been away . . .": interview with Milken, 16 March 1989.

page 237: Raether's admission: *WSJ,* 26 September 1989.

page 238: "You reneged . . .": letter from Stanford N. Phelps to George N. Gillett, Jr., 11 December 1989.

page 238: "Don't forget . . .": interview with Stuart, 30 May 1991; multiple phone interviews with Phelps in December 1989 and January 1990.

page 239: Celotex personal injury claims: annual report for Jim Walter Corporation, 1986.

page 239: "substantial negative value": comment by Waters in deposition in *Edith Citron, et al.* v. *Jim Walter Corp., et al.,* previously cited.

page 239: Sale of Celotex: Terms of the sale are spelled out in a prospectus for bonds issued by four subsidiaries of Hillsborough Holdings, 6 October 1988. When Celotex was sold, Hillsborough received $5 million in cash and a non-recourse $95 million note from Jasper Corporation, a business affiliated with Gary Drummond.

page 240: Beaumont trial proceedings: transcript of hearing on special appearances in *Joe Larned Jr.* v. *Kohlberg Kravis Roberts & Co., et al.,* Texas state court, Jefferson County, 12–14 September 1989.

page 242: Mass-Tokarz exchange: phone interview with Tokarz, January 1990; phone interview with Mass, August 1991. Dialogue is Tokarz's version; Mass remembers a "heated" exchange but no specifics.

page 243: "Bondholders should be very firm . . .": interview with Burkhead, 1 February 1990.

page 244: Berman-Tokarz exchanges: phone interviews with Berman and Tokarz in January 1990. Berman's recollection was fuller; Tokarz confirmed general tone and themes.

page 245: 19 December 1989 meeting at Simpson Thacher: reconstruction based on phone interviews in January 1990 with Berman, Tokarz, Kravis, Hillsborough executive Ken Matlock, and Simpson Thacher attorneys Beattie and Garvey.

page 247: Drexel's bonus payments: *WSJ,* 26 February 1990.

page 247: Joseph seeking emergency loans: *WSJ,* 14 February 1990; *Fortune,* 21 May, 1990; interview with Joseph, 27 February 1991.

page 248: Drexel liquidation: *WSJ,* 11 June 1991.

page 248: Grant's notice of KKR bankruptcy: *Los Angeles Times,* 26 August 1990.

page 249: "All of us . . .": interview with Kevin Bousquette, 20 August 1991.

Chapter 13: Fear, Humbling, and Survival

page 250: Meeting at RJR on 26 January: reconstruction based on interview with Ted Ammon, 30 August 1990; interview with Scott Stuart, 7 August 1990; interview with Cliff Robbins, 24 July 1990; interview with RJR general counsel Lawrence Ricciardi, 22 August 1990; phone interview with Karl von der Heyden, October 1991.

page 253: KKR's $3 billion proposal: interview with Ammon, 30 August 1990; phone interview with Kagan, September 1990.

page 254: "Besides, we have a reset . . ." and subsequent detail: interview with Beattie, 21 September 1990; interview with Robbins, 21 September 1990.

page 254: Stern's objection to reset: phone interview with Jonathan Kagan, September 1990.

page 255: "If I were you . . .": interview with Robbins, 21 September 1990; interview with Jeffrey Berenson, 1 August 1990.

page 257: "Don't forget: We made you . . .": interview with Kravis, 30 March 1990.

page 258: Crook-Greene exchange: interview with Crook, 26 July 1990.

page 258: Banks' resistance and eventual yielding: phone interviews with six bank participants in July and August 1990; phone interview with Greene in August 1990.

page 259: Roberts as strategist: interview with Scott Stuart, 7 August 1990; interview with Ammon, 30 August 1990.

page 261: Black's 60-percent profit estimate: interview with Black, 30 April 1990.

page 262: "You need us . . ." and "With all the money . . .": based on interviews with six participants in the meeting. In a phone interview in September 1990, Ferguson did not dispute their account.

page 263: Lipton-Kravis exchange: interview with Kravis, 18 June 1991; phone interview with Lipton, August 1990. Kravis says Lipton presented bankruptcy as the only option; Lipton says he presented it as one of ten.

page 264: "I don't want to be sued . . .": interview with Berenson, 1 August 1990; interview with Rinaldini, 30 August 1990.

page 264: First day of San Francisco conference: interviews with four KKR associates in August and September 1990; phone interviews with seven limited partner attendees in August and September 1990.

page 265: Roberts speech: reconstruction based on phone interviews with Roberts and six limited partner attendees, as well as interview with Tokarz, 28 September 1990. Tokarz's account is the fullest.

page 266: Beechey-Greene exchange: phone interviews with Beechey and two witnesses to conversation, August 1990.

page 267: Calendar for Greene: phone interviews with Greene and Roberts, August 1990.

page 271: Kravis-Roberts exchange: interview with Kravis and Roberts, 17 July 1990.

Chapter 14: Debt Is Out, Equity Is In

page 273: "Enormous power": cited in "The New Morgans," *Fortune,* 29 February 1988. "The Eclipse of the Public Corporation" was the title of a *Harvard Business Review* article by Harvard Business School Professor Michael Jensen, September/October 1989.

page 274: "The cards were dealt . . .": interview with Gerstner, 27 February 1991.

page 275: Gerstner's message to managers: In a 3 October 1991 "Dear Colleagues" letter, Gerstner wrote: "We'll have more latitude to manage our investments in things like new products and marketing programs."

page 276: KKR's investments in publicly traded companies: *NYT,* 9 December 1990.

page 277: Murray's reaction to KKR executives: *WSJ,* 29 April 1991.

page 279: Empty Drexel office building: *Los Angeles Times,* 26 May 1991.

page 279: Berenson and Minella resignations: *WSJ,* 29 August 1990.

page 280: Ackerman's $165 million earnings: *NYT,* 4 October 1991.

page 280: KKR's goals for supplemental fund: *WSJ,* 1 November 1990.

page 280: Resistance from KKR investors: *WSJ,* 11 January 1991; *Business-Week,* 15 April 1991.

page 280: Volume of buyouts in 1980s: statistics cited in "Leveraged Buyouts and the Pot of Gold, 1989 Update," a report prepared for the Subcommittee on Oversight and Investigations of the House Committee on Energy and Commerce, p. 18.

page 283: Estimate of $7 billion in investment gains: author's own, based on rise in value of KKR partnerships' equity in buyout companies. The largest winners as of 1 January 1992 are as follows: RJR Nabisco, in which KKR partnerships paid an average of $5.66 a share for $3.2 billion of stock, which rose in value to $5.8 billion; Duracell, in which KKR partnerships bought $350 million of stock, which rose in value to $1.75 billion; Safeway, in which KKR partnerships bought $150 million of stock, which rose in value to $1.35 billion; and Beatrice, in which KKR partnerships paid $407 million for stock, which rose in value to $1.3 billion. Many of those winnings are paper profits that haven't yet been realized; if they hold up, the KKR executives will be entitled to 20 percent of the gains, or a total of $1.6 billion.

Index